SPACE LAW

SPACE LAW

DEVELOPMENT AND SCOPE

Edited by
NANDASIRI JASENTULIYANA
Foreword by Manfred Lachs

A Publication of the
INTERNATIONAL INSTITUTE OF SPACE LAW

PRAEGER

Westport, Connecticut
London

Copyright Acknowledgments

The author and publisher are grateful for permission to quote from the following sources:

Material in Chapter 18 from *Settlement of Space Law Disputes: The Present State of the Law and Perspectives of Further Development*, from *Enviromental Aspects of Activities in Outer Space: State of the Law and Measures of Protection*, and from *Space Stations: Legal Aspects of Scientific and Commercial Use in a Framework of Transatlantic Cooperation*, all edited by Karl-Heinz Böckstiegel and published in Cologne, Germany, by Carl Heymanns Verlag (in 1980, 1988, and 1984, respectively), is reprinted by permission of the editor and publisher.

Material in Chapter 18 from "Consensus Decisionmaking by the United Nations Committee on the Peaceful Uses of Outer Space" by Eilene M. Galloway, in *Journal of Space Law*, Vol. 7, No. 1 (Spring 1979), pp. 3-13, is reprinted by permission of the publisher. Reprints of volumes of the *Journal of Space Law* are available from William S. Hein & Co., Inc., 1285 Main Street, Buffalo, New York, 14209-1987.

Library of Congress Cataloging-in-Publication Data

Space law : development and scope / edited by Nandasiri Jasentuliyana
; foreword by Manfred Lachs.
p. cm.—(A Publication of the International Institute of
Space Law)
Includes bibliographical references (p.) and index.
ISBN 0-275-94036-5 (alk. paper)
1. Space law. I. Jasentuliyana, Nandasiri, 1938-
II. Series.
JX5810.S6793 1992
341.4'7—dc20 92-10136

British Library Cataloguing in Publication Data is available.

Library of Congress Catalog Card Number: 92-10136
ISBN: 0-275-94036-5

First published in 1992

Praeger Publishers, 88 Post Road West, Westport, CT 06881
An imprint of Greenwood Publishing Group, Inc.

Printed in the United States of America

The paper used in this book complies with the Permanent Paper Standard issued by the National Information Standards Organization (Z39.48-1984).

10 9 8 7 6 5 4 3 2 1

Dedicated to
EILENE MARIE GALLOWAY
For her lifelong contribution
to space law

Contents

Foreword *Manfred Lachs* ix

Dedication *Isabella Diederiks-Verschoor* xiii

Introduction *Nandasiri Jasentuliyana* xvii

Acronyms and Abbreviations xxi

1 The Freedoms of Outer Space and Their Maritime Antecedents
Hamilton DeSaussure 1

2 Evolution of the Doctrine of Space Law
Vladimír Kopal 17

3 The Lawmaking Process in the United Nations
Nandasiri Jasentuliyana 33

4 Sources and Principles of Space Law
Stephen Gorove 45

5 Trends in National Regulation of Space Activities:
The Soviet Union *Vladlen S. Vereshchetin* 59

6 Space Law in the United States
Jonathan F. Galloway 71

7 Space Law and the European Space Agency
Michel Bourély 87

8 Institutional Arrangements for International Space Activities
Nicolas Mateesco Matte 97

9 Law of Satellite Communications
Francis Lyall 113

10 Legal Aspects of Space Commercialization
Stephen Doyle 127

11 Legal Aspects of Military Space Activities
Peter Jankowitsch 143

12 Space Law and the Environment
He Qizhi 159

13 The Scientific and Technological Basis of Space Law
Lubos Perek 175

14 Law Relating to Settlement of Disputes on Space Activities
Aldo Armando Cocca 191

15 Case Law on Space Activities
Karl-Heinz Böckstiegel 205

16 Study and Teaching of Space Law
Gyula Gál 219

17 The Future of Space Law
Carl Q. Christol 227

18 Creating Space Law
Eilene Galloway 239

Publications by Eilene Galloway on Space, 1958-1991 257

Selected Bibliography *Kuo-Lee Li* 263

Index 273

About the Contributors 279

Foreword

Manfred Lachs

The wealth of issues dealt with by the distinguished writers in this volume indicates the far-reaching effects of humanity's venture into outer space. It is a timely work because it reminds us of the many activities which have already been undertaken in outer space, of those which are about to begin, and of the relationships between space activities and our life on this Earth. Yet it is only 35 years ago that the first spacecraft was put into orbit, 31 years since the first human being orbited the Earth, and 23 years since the first astronaut visited the Moon and brought pieces of it back to Earth. There have been many other great achievements since then, reaching beyond the Moon to other planets, and even into interstellar space. Within this short spell of time, much has changed due to technological development and what may be called the "chemistry of time."

The undertaking of this new human venture was welcomed by many, but it was also criticized and condemned by some. Archibald MacLeish, that great poet, welcomed the voyage to the Moon and recalled how humans had thought and dreamed of it "before the first of time, before the first man tasted time." Arthur Koestler, however, had some bitter words on the subject: "Coincident with the cosmic euphoria, the world is in the grip of a cosmic anxiety. Both derive from the same source: the awareness of unprecedented power operating in an unprecedented spiritual vacuum. Prometheus is reaching out for the stars with an empty grin on his face." Such questions about the space venture were certainly in part the result of the political atmosphere in which the journey into space began. It was a time of rivalries between great powers, of armed conflicts breaking out at various points around the world, of dangers of a serious confrontation that could threaten humanity's existence. The possibility inevitably arose of outer space being used as a battleground, as a distant Armageddon. Fortunately those days are past, and we now look upon outer space as an area not of hostile competition but of cooperation and use in the interests of humanity as a whole.

The publication of this volume coincides with an anniversary. Twenty-five years ago the Outer Space Treaty was approved by the General Assembly of the United Nations and then signed in London, Moscow, and Washington on January 27, 1967. Five weeks earlier, in my capacity as Chairman of the Legal Subcommittee of the United Nations Committee on the Peaceful Uses of Outer Space, I had the great privilege to present it to the Political Committee of the General Assembly on December 16, 1966. As I said at the time, the conclusion of the Treaty was "undoubtedly an important step forward in the development of the law of outer space, . . . but we are only at the beginning of the road. Some of the principles laid down will require further clarification. Some specific issues will call for further elaboration." The Treaty constituted a serious commitment, an international commitment of historic dimensions. It was not a repetition of the Treaty of Tordesillas (June 4, 1494) by which Spain and Portugal agreed upon a line separating their areas of exclusive rights to newly discovered areas. Rather, it laid down the principle that is now generally recognized, that outer space and the celestial bodies are "the province of all mankind."

Now, 25 years after the adoption of the Treaty, the chapters in this volume indicate the manifold activities in which humanity is engaged in outer space and relating to space. The chapters reflect the involvement of states, organizations, and individuals not only in government space research and exploration programs but, increasingly, in applied and commercial space activities providing services directly to the public. They also indicate the scope of international cooperation at bilateral, regional, and multilateral levels. All of these activities are intended to serve humanity, hence the principle which I have proposed from the very outset: that the law of outer space should be anthropocentric and human-oriented. Because space activities are having an ever more important influence on events on Earth, space law must solve not only problems relating to human activities in space but also problems relating to Earth-based activities.

Ensuring that outer space is devoted exclusively to peaceful purposes has remained a most important goal, but until now that goal has been achievable only to a limited degree. It has not been politically possible to bar arms from the new dimension. It is only now, with the cessation of the cold war and with new relations developing between all powers, that it may be possible to give full effect to the principle of the use of outer space for exclusively peaceful purposes.

What was recently almost incredible has become so down-to-earth that we now perform many of our daily activities with the assistance of space technology, often unknowingly. Not only do most trans-oceanic telephone calls go via satellite, but airlines and ships can now maintain continual contact with land facilities, so that, for example, fishermen can keep track of fish prices and deliver their catch where the demand is greatest. Space technology means that news and educational information can reach the remotest villages in Asia and Africa by satellite, disseminating knowledge and explaining modern science and technology. The complexity of the technology required for these purposes encourages international cooperation, such as the sharing of satellites and other space equipment. Thus, the distance between countries can be bridged through space as in other dimensions.

This book shows how science and technology have entered into the vast reaches of outer space and are serving humankind constructively through mutual confidence and cooperation. As early as 1905, Paul Curie expressed the fear that science and its great discoveries, instead of bringing blessings, might create dangers if humanity were not mature enough to use them for constructive purposes. This volume shows how law is contributing to cooperation and sharing in the peaceful uses of outer space and to ensuring that the people of all countries can enjoy the social, economic, and cultural benefits of space science and technology. While the relationship between law and technology is complex, it is clear that the two areas are inseparable and must evolve together to ensure that space activities continue to serve the interests of all states and of humanity as a whole.

Dr. Nandasiri Jasentuliyana should be congratulated on the fine work he has done in assembling the work of so distinguished a company of experts writing on so many interesting subjects.

Note by the editor

Judge Manfred Lachs of Poland served as Chairman of the Legal Subcommittee of the United Nations Committee on the Peaceful Uses of Outer Space from its creation in 1962 until he stepped down in 1967 following his election to the International Court of Justice. As Chairman of the Legal Subcommittee, Judge Lachs directed the elaboration and negotiation of the 1967 Outer Space Treaty, leading to its unanimous adoption by the General Assembly in December 1966. Following the adoption of the Treaty, many delegations paid tribute to Judge Lachs's contribution to this historic agreement, which remains today the basis of international space law. Ambassador Goldberg, representing the United States, stressed "the admirable skill and impartiality" of the Chairman and indicated that "much of the credit for the success of our negotiations was due to him." Lord Caradon of the United Kingdom spoke of "the fine lead" given throughout the negotiations, and the Representative of Sweden spoke of "the wisdom, patience, and experience which decisively helped the Subcommittee to advance and to succeed." The Representative of the Philippines spoke of "the Treaty on Outer Space as a fitting capstone to his long and brilliant work in the General Assembly and other organs of the United Nations, coming as it does on the eve of his departure in order to assume functions in the International Court of Justice."

Judge Lachs served for some years as President of the International Court of Justice and continues to sit on the Court. In 1991 he was elected President of the International Institute of Space Law.

Dedication

Isabella Diederiks-Verschoor

The dedication of this book to Dr. Eilene Galloway is an expression of the great esteem in which she is held by the members of the International Institute of Space Law (IISL) and by the space law community for her many contributions to the development of space law. Dr. Galloway has been a pioneer of space law, and for more than 30 years she has contributed to the analysis and solution of international and national legal problems related to the exploration and use of outer space.

When the First IISL Colloquium on the Law of Outer Space was held at The Hague in 1958, Dr. Galloway presented a paper, "The Community of Law and Science," emphasizing the interdependence of space science and space law and the need to consider them together in establishing sound objectives and principles for planning the exploration and use of space for the benefit of society. In her paper, she indicated the principles that would guide her own work: she argued that we must start with an overall understanding of our goals and their interrelationships, for otherwise "our interplanetary thinking will be earthbound by tradition and precedent at a time when creative predictions should enable us to keep international law in pace with scientific achievements."

In October 1957, Eilene Galloway was called upon by the U.S. Congress to assist in policy planning for the U.S. space program and to participate in the first investigative hearings. In 1958, she was appointed Special Consultant to the Senate Committee on Space and Astronautics, followed later by the Committee on Aeronautical and Space Sciences. Her expert counsel was also sought by the House of Representatives Select Committee on Astronautics and Space Exploration. She was thus an active participant in the legislative process which led to the National Aeronautics and Space Act of 1958. Since that law provided the foundation not only for U.S. space activities but also for international cooperation with other nations, her work contributed to the development of international space law and policy as well as to the U.S. program.

In November 1958, Dr. Galloway served as a consultant to Senator Lyndon B. Johnson, when, at the invitation of President Eisenhower, he addressed the United Nations and recommended the creation of an ad hoc Committee on the Peaceful Uses of Outer Space. Later that year, she served as editor of a pioneering volume of space law studies, *Space Law: A Symposium*, published by the U.S. Senate.

During the years when she served as Special Consultant to the Senate, Dr. Galloway was the author of many analytical studies on the outer space treaties, international cooperation in space, satellite remote sensing, space communications, the Moon Agreement, and other space matters that came before the Congress in connection with the authorization of funding for space programs. She was also a consultant to the Congressional Office of Technology Assessment on solar power satellites, international cooperation and competition, and the Space Station.

In addition to her work for Congress, Dr. Galloway has been called upon to advise agencies of the executive branch of the U.S. government: the Department of State, the National Aeronautics and Space Administration, the Federal Communications Commission, and the Civil Service Commission. For many years, Dr. Galloway served as a member of the U.S. delegation to the United Nations Committee on the Peaceful Uses of Outer Space and its Legal Subcommittee, and more recently she has been an official observer for the International Astronautical Federation.

She is a trustee of the International Academy of Astronautics (IAA) and was elected to three terms as Chairman of the IAA Section on the Social Sciences, concerned with examining the effects of space science and technology on society. Dr. Galloway has lectured widely in the United States and Europe, and her contributions to the annual IISL space law colloquia and other meetings constitute an impressive and influential body of work on major legal problems and issues arising from the exploration and use of outer space. A review of this body of work is contained in Chapter 18 of this volume. She is the author of more than 90 scholarly papers and government documents relating to the development of outer space activities, as indicated by the list of her publications following Chapter 18. She serves on the editorial boards of the *Journal of Space Law* and *Acta Astronautica*.

Dr. Galloway has been honored by the International Institute of Space Law, the National Aeronautics and Space Administration, the Library of Congress, the U.S. Air Force Space Command, Women in Aerospace, and other organizations.

A survey of Dr. Galloway's activities in the field of space law would not be complete without some remarks on her more personal contributions to those who have been fortunate to work with her. Dr. Galloway's wise advice, her keen sense of humor and her loyal cooperation with her colleagues have given a special quality to all her work. She has many, many friends throughout the world who respect and love her because of her very special qualities. In addition to her professional dedication, Dr. Galloway is a devoted grandmother to the children of her two sons and is now also a proud great-grandmother. Dr. Eilene Galloway is a great scholar and a very warm, lovely person.

AWARDS TO DR. EILENE GALLOWAY

1967 International Institute of Space Law: elected Vice President; served until 1979, when she was elected Honorary Director.

1968 Andrew G. Haley Gold Medal Award from the International Astronautical Federation, International Institute of Space Law: "In recognition of her outstanding contribution since the beginning of the space age as author, lecturer, editor, and commentator in connection with the creation and development of space law in order to establish and maintain the rule of law in relation to mankind's activities in outer space."

1974 Purdue University: "This testimonial in recognition with appreciation of leadership and meritorious services rendered as Educational Counselor."

1975 Library of Congress, Official Commendation for Distinguished Service: "For your sustained, outstanding performance during 15 years of dedicated government service, and for your exceptional and learned contributions to the Library, to the Congress of the United States, and to the community of nations in the fields of international relations, the peaceful uses of outer space, and especially in the field of international space law."

1984 National Aeronautics and Space Administration, Public Service Award and Gold Medal: "For her outstanding achievements of advising the Congress on legal and technical aspects of outer space, and her further service to the United Nations and other international organizations in helping to develop a rational basis for international space law."

1984 U.S. Air Force Space Command, Award: "Thanks for coming and sharing our vision."

1986 International Academy of Astronautics, Theodore Von Karman Award: "Eilene Galloway, Chairman, Section 4 of the International Academy of Astronautics, Honorary Director of the International Institute of

Space Law, consultant and adviser to government, private enterprise, and academia, is voted the 1986 recipient of the Theodore Von Karman Award of the International Academy of Astronautics for a lifetime of contributions to study of the legal, social, and scientific aspects of astronautics and the advancement of the peaceful uses of outer space."

1986 American Astronautical Society, Award: "In recognition of her significant contributions to astronautics"; elected a Fellow of the Society.

1987 Women in Aerospace, Recognition as "A National Treasure who has pioneered the understanding of the complexities of domestic and international space policy."

1989 International Institute of Space Law, Lifetime Achievement Award: "For unique, untiring, lifetime support, and to commend to all people this outstanding citizen of the world who has contributed so fully to international understanding and cooperation." The Board also approved the book of honor.

1990 Lake Forest College, Lake Forest, Illinois: The degree of Doctor of Laws was conferred on Eilene Galloway "for her significant contributions to national and international law for outer space."

1992 Swarthmore College, Swarthmore, Pennsylvania: Doctor of Laws degree.

Introduction

Nandasiri Jasentuliyana

Space activities have been growing steadily both in quantity and variety since the beginning of the space age more than 30 years ago. More importantly from the point of view of international law, the number of countries involved has been steadily increasing. Almost all countries in the world are dependent on satellites for international communications, and most use satellite data for weather forecasting, resource mapping and environmental monitoring. A large majority own at least a share in a satellite through participation in the International Telecommunications Satellite Organization (INTELSAT), the International Maritime Satellite Organization (INMARSAT), the European Space Agency, or the Arab Satellite Communication Organization (ARABSAT). Over 20 countries now have national satellites in orbit, and the number of countries with a launching capability is slowly but steadily growing. The uses of satellites, in addition to communications and remote sensing, include navigation, astronomy, studies of the upper atmosphere, materials processing under conditions of weightlessness, medical experiments during human space flight, military reconnaissance, and weapons testing. For the future, a large crewed International Space Station complex is being designed by the United States in collaboration with the European Space Agency, Canada, and Japan; a number of countries are developing new technologies for hybrid aerospace planes; studies are being undertaken for crewed missions to the Moon and Mars; and research and development of space weapons are continuing. While the importance of international cooperation in enabling all countries to benefit from space activities is widely appreciated, there is also a need for a generally accepted international political, legal, and regulatory framework to enable countries to use space without conflict, or at least with a minimum of conflict.

As space activities have developed and expanded, so have the scope and substance of space law. National legal regulation of space activities began with the beginning of space activities, and international laws and regulations have expanded steadily since the adoption of the 1967 Outer Space Treaty. In addition to the international space treaties, which establish the general principles of space law and are open to all countries, there are a variety of more specific and detailed intergovernmental agreements that provide the legal basis for the international space activities of such organizations as INTELSAT, INTERSPUTNIK, INMARSAT, the European Space Agency, ARABSAT, EUMETSAT, and others. Other bilateral and multilateral intergovernmental agreements define the mutual responsibilities of countries in bilateral and multilateral space activities, including some constraints on military activities. While space activities are the subject of a growing body of space law, there are many other laws which also have important applications to space activities, such as the Radio Regulations of the International Telecommunication Union.

The large and growing body of space and space-related law described in this volume demonstrates that space law can now be considered a distinct and mature discipline of international law, comparable to maritime law and air law. There are, however, many detailed questions and foreseeable problems that remain unresolved, and new developments in space technology and applications are continually generating new questions and problems that will need to be resolved in the future.

As space activities and space law have expanded, so has the community of lawyers, diplomats, managers of national space programs, officials of international space organizations, scholars, educators, and others concerned with space law. There are also an increasing number of space and other organizations concerned with the field. The growing community has a great need for authoritative and up-to-date information on this rapidly changing field. *Space Law: Development and Scope* is intended to meet the need for a reference book and textbook covering the major issues and indicating the different perspectives on the unresolved issues. The book has been organized, written, and edited for this purpose, with each chapter prepared specifically for this book by an international expert on the subject. The contributing authors represent all political, legal, and cultural regions of the world and provide a range of backgrounds and viewpoints. Their contributions have been edited to ensure an integrated volume with comprehensive coverage of the field, and with a minimum of overlap between the chapters. Each chapter contains numerous references, and the book includes an extensive bibliography of the basic documents of space law and important analytical works in the field, as a guide to original sources and for more detailed research on specific issues.

The International Institute of Space Law, affiliated with the International Astronautical Federation, is an international professional association whose membership includes most of the leading specialists in the field from around the world. The sponsorship of the Institute has made it possible to obtain contributions from the foremost authorities in the field of space law, many of whom have played key roles in the elaboration of the space law that is described herein. As space law evolves and expands, this volume will remain a major reference work on the establishment of the foundations of space law by the pioneers of the field.

The celebration of International Space Year in 1992 provides a fitting occasion to reflect on the past development of space activities and space law and to look forward to future prospects and problems as space activities become steadily more integrated into daily life. It is hoped that this book will contribute to cooperation in the development and application of space technology for the benefit of all humankind.

It has been a rewarding if not always easy task to coordinate the contributions to this work from experts in a variety of specialized disciplines from different cultures and legal systems and with a variety of native languages and writing styles. The contributors have cooperated generously in the process of integrating their writings into a coherent work with a reasonably uniform style.

I would like to acknowledge the able editorial assistance that I have received from Hiroko Miyamura, Cheryl Stoute, Yvonne Lodico, and, above all, Ralph Chipman in revising, editing, and preparing the manuscript as well as for making many useful suggestions on substance. The administrative support provided by Pacita Montanez was also invaluable.

Acronyms and Abbreviations

ABM	anti-ballistic missile
AIAA	American Institute of Aeronautics and Astronautics
APT	automatic picture transmission
ARABSAT	Arab Satellite Communication Organization
ASAT	anti-satellite weapon
ASC	American Satellite Company
ATS	Applications Technology Satellite
BDT	Telecommunications Development Bureau
CCIR	International Radio Consultative Committee
CCITT	International Telegraph and Telephone Consultative Committee
CEPT	Conférence Européene des Postes et Télécommunications
CHM	commmon heritage of mankind
CIDA	Aeronautic and Space Research and Diffusion Center
CNES	Centre National d'Etudes Spatiales
COMSAT	Communications Satellite Corporation
COPUOS	Committee on the Peaceful Uses of Outer Space
CSG	Centre Spatial Guyanais
CTS	Communications Technology Satellite
DARA	German Space Agency
ECS	European Communications Satellite
ECSL	European Centre of Space Law
EEC	European Economic Community
ELA	Ensemble de Lancement Ariane
ELDO	European Space Launcher Development Organisation
ELV	expendable launch vehicle
EOSAT	Earth Observation Satellite Company
ERTS	Earth Resources Technology Satellite

ESA	European Space Agency
ESC	European Space Conference
ESOC	European Space Operations Centre
ESRANGE	European Sounding Rocket Launching Range
ESRIN	European Space Research Institute
ESRO	European Space Research Organization
ESTEC	European Space Technology Research Centre
EUMETSAT	European Organization for the Exploitation of Meteorological Satellites
EUTELSAT	European Telecommunications Satellite Organization
FAO	Food and Agriculture Organisation of the United Nations
GEMS	Global Environment Monitoring System
GIPME	Global Investigation of Pollution in the Marine Environment
GPALS	Global Protection against Limited Strikes
IAA	International Academy of Astronautics
IAEA	International Atomic Energy Agency
IAF	International Astronautical Federation
IASL	Institute of Air and Space Law
IATA	International Air Transport Association
IBS	INTELSAT Business Service
ICAO	International Civil Aviation Organization
ICJ	International Court of Justice
IFRB	International Frequency Registration Board
IGBP	International Geosphere-Biosphere Programme
IGY	International Geophysical Year
IIAL	Institute of International Air Law
IISL	International Institute of Space Law
ILA	International Law Association
IMCO	Inter-Governmental Maritime Consultative Organization
IMO	International Maritime Organization
INMARSAT	International Maritime Satellite Organization
INTELSAT	International Telecommunications Satellite Organization
INTERCOSMOS	Council on International Co-operation in the Study and Utilization of Outer Space
INTERSPUTNIK	International Organization of Space Communicatiosn
IOC	Intergovernmental Oceanographic Commission
ISDN	integrated services digital network
ISRO	Indian Space Research Organization
ISY	International Space Year
ITU	International Telecommunicaton Union
MOU	memorandum of understanding
NASA	National Aeronautics and Space Administration
NASDA	National Space Development Agency

NOAA	National Oceanic and Atmospheric Administration
NPS	nuclear power source
NRCC	National Research Council of Canada
OTRAG	Orbital Transport und Raketen Aktiengesellschaft
PAM	Payload Assist Module
RAI	Radio Audizione Italiana
SALT	Strategic Arms Limitation Talks
SDI	Strategic Defense Initiative
SEI	Space Exploration Initiative
SPOT	Satellite Probatoire pour l'Observation de la Terre
SPS	solar power satellite
START	Strategic Arms Reduction Treaty
UNCITRAL	United Nations Commission on International Trade Law
UNCLOS	United Nations Conference on the Law of the Sea
UNCTAD	United Nations Conference on Trade and Development
UNEP	United Nations Environment Programme
UNESCO	United Nations Educational, Scientific and Cultural Organization
UNIDO	United Nations Industrial Development Organization
UNISPACE 82	Second United Nations Conference on the Exploration and Peaceful Uses of Outer Space
WARC	World Administrative Radio Conference
WARC-ORB	World Administrative Radio Conference on the Use of the Geostationary-Satellite Orbit and the Planning of Space Services Utilizing It
WCP	World Climate Program
WMO	World Meteorological Organization
WWW	World Weather Watch

SPACE LAW

1

The Freedoms of Outer Space and Their Maritime Antecedents

Hamilton DeSaussure

As we celebrate the landing of Christopher Columbus in the new world 500 years ago and compare that age with this age of discoveries in outer space, it is appropriate to reflect upon the impact the law of the sea will have on the maturing law of outer space. Do the oceans and outer space have a commonality that make many maritime principles applicable to outer space? Is there a correlation between the freedom of the seas and the freedoms being established in outer space? Or are the two environments so vastly different in their nature and their utilization as to dismiss ocean law as largely irrelevant to the development of the law of outer space?

To begin, one might consider the status of the two areas and look back in time to see how the customary rules of the freedoms of the seas developed. We can then compare that development with the freedoms present and emerging in outer space.

DIMENSIONS AND STATUS OF OCEAN SPACE AND OUTER SPACE

At one time, not more than five centuries ago, the vastness of the oceans seemed as infinite to the mariners as we know the universe to be today. Although the amazing advances in this century in science and technology bring new knowledge about the universe almost daily, the parallel between sending men to the moon and beyond, and the early explorations of the fifteenth-century navigators is striking.

The oceans have historically been divided into three parts: the territorial sea, the contiguous zone, and the high seas. Only in the high seas have nations enjoyed complete and unqualified freedom of navigation and use. Since the beginning of this century other classifications, to be discussed later, have also become accepted in international law, but they have not altered the three basic components of the oceans. By the twentieth century all the oceans of the world had been charted and the expanse of the high seas was clearly defined, except for inconsistent claims to the breadth of the territorial seas.

The legal status of the public seas was finally codified in the four conventions adopted by the first United Nations Conference on the Law of the Sea at Geneva in 1958 (UNCLOS I).[1]

Above the Earth, the only division has been between airspace and outer space. No zones in outer space have been claimed by states, nor would they be authorized under any treaties regulating the use of outer space. Since airspace and the territorial sea are subject to state sovereignty, while outer space and the high seas are not, controversy in both environments has centered on where sovereignty ends and an open regime begins. In the case of the territorial sea, the dispute is basically political. The great maritime states favor a narrow breadth, while the less developed states, with long coastlines, favor a wide marginal belt. In the case of the airspace border, the dispute is complicated by other factors such as the nature of space flight, the lack of any clear limit to the atmosphere, and the necessity of any border at all.

C. John Colombos defined the high seas as "so much of the ocean as is exterior to a line running parallel with the shore and some distance therefrom."[2] This definition was vague, he wrote, because no consensus existed among maritime states as to the breadth of the territorial waters. Ten coastal states, including the United States and the United Kingdom, claimed three miles; two states claimed four miles; three claimed six; over one hundred claimed twelve; and thirteen claimed two hundred miles.[3] Although Colombos was writing over 60 years ago, well before the process of codification of the law of the sea began, more than a score of coastal states do not adhere to a 12-mile limit. Fortunately, there have been no positive state claims as to the upward reach of territorial airspace. Yet the border between the two regimes of airspace and outer space is just as unsettled as the border between the territorial sea and the high seas has been in the past.

The first of the twentieth-century law of the sea conferences (UNCLOS I) met in 1958 in Geneva. Four separate law of the sea conventions were concluded. They were the Conventions on the High Seas, the Continental Shelf, the Territorial Sea and Contiguous Zone, and Fishing and Conservation of Living Resources of the High Seas. However, no agreement was reached on the breadth of the territorial sea. In 1960, the Second United Nations Conference on the Law of the Sea (UNCLOS II) was held in Geneva to try to establish a territorial sea limit and settle fishing rights on the high seas, but no agreement was reached. In 1973, the third law of the sea conference (UNCLOS III) began at Caracas, Venezuela. Its objective was to completely codify the law of the sea into one composite agreement while at the same time revising and updating it. Among the issues for resolution was the extent of the territorial sea. After many long and often tortuous sessions over nearly a decade, the United Nations Convention on the Law of the Sea was concluded in 1982.[4] As of May 1991, the UNCLOS III Convention had been ratified by only 45 states, and 60 must do so before it to will come into force.[5] Nevertheless, most nations consider the Convention to reflect the current law of the sea, with the exception of those provisions dealing with the international seabed regime. The Convention authorizes a territorial sea up to 12 nautical miles from the coast. The United States has extended its own territorial sea to 12 miles by statute.[6] Other countries, such as Ecuador, Peru, and certain other South American and African nations, have yet to renounce their more expansive claims to a territorial sea extending outward to as much as 200 miles. Such expansive claims are not the only threat to the freedom of the seas. Coastal states have also claimed exclusive economic zones, fishing zones, and health and safety zones which reach well beyond their established territorial sea.

In outer space, a claim of sovereignty has already been made by certain equatorial states over portions of the geostationary orbit, some 22,000 miles above the Earth.[7] While this claim has been rejected outright by all the major spacefaring states, the danger of unilateral claims to protective zones in the near-Earth orbital region, similar to those claimed by coastal states beyond their territorial sea, does exist.

It took centuries for most of the maritime states to reach agreement on the permissible extent of the territorial sea. It is not startling, therefore, that in the short time since the launch of Sputnik I there has been no consensus on the upward limit of airspace. Many nations, among them the United States, do not believe a precise demarcation is necessary at this time. No infringements by the flight of space objects of one state through the airspace of another have ever been cited. Nevertheless, the subject has been on the agenda of the Legal Subcommittee of the Committee on Peaceful Uses of Outer Space (COPUOS) since the creation of that committee. The fact is that after over 35 years of launching satellites, no practical problems have arisen as a result of a lack of a brightline border. The only question of potential significance at this stage of space activity has been whether there will ever be a need for a right of innocent passage similar to that afforded foreign merchant vessels through territorial seas. While some writers contend a right of innocent passage for spacecraft is necessary, neither the United Nations nor any of its members have claimed such a right for its space objects.[8] Even prior to the launch of the first Sputnik in 1957, writers were discussing whether near-Earth space might be subject to a series of zones "subject to differing legal regimes."[9] The adoption of zones in outer space has thus far been rejected, and they are clearly not envisioned by the Outer Space Treaty of 1967.[10]

Prior to the end of the fifteenth century, many nations made claims to sovereignty over vast expanses of the high seas. The Romans claimed the Mediterranean as a *mare nostrum*, and as early as the tenth century, England claimed the North Sea and the English Channel as part of its "Britannic Ocean." Denmark and Sweden at one time claimed the Baltic Sea as part of their territory, and Denmark later extended its claims to all the Atlantic between Norway and Greenland.

Grotius, in his treatise on the freedom of the seas published in 1609, set forth the reasons why the high seas must be open for trade and exploration. All property, he wrote, is grounded upon occupation. This requires that moveables be seized and immovable property enclosed. Whatever cannot be seized or enclosed is not capable of being a subject of property. This means, said Grotius, that "the vagrant waters of the ocean are necessarily free."[11] Grotius wrote that the high seas were to be considered *res communis*, to be shared and used for the benefit of all nations, and not to be viewed as *res nullius*, or areas capable of being appropriated by discovery, occupation, and assertion of title.

While the classic works of Grotius set the legal framework for a freedom of the seas, the practicalities of ocean commerce made maritime states accept the doctrine of the freedom of the seas long before the issuance of the Papal Bulls. These states recognized that they had more to lose by claiming a closed regime on the oceans than they would gain by extending their claims of sovereignty beyond the territorial sea.

Efforts to codify the freedoms which apply to the high seas began early in this century. Most influential were the law of the sea drafts prepared by the Institute of International Law in 1927 and the International Law Association in 1926. The draft of the Institute provided for four distinct freedoms on the high seas: (1) freedom of navigation; (2) freedom of fishing; (3) freedom to lay submarine cables and pipelines; and (4) freedom to fly over the high seas.[12] The work of the Institute in demonstrating that the freedom of the seas was really a composite of specific freedoms had a great impact on the official conventions which followed.

Among the four conventions which were adopted at Geneva in 1958 was the High Seas Convention, which, as of May 1991, had been ratified by 58 states, including the United States. It provides that "the high seas being open to all nations, no State may validly purport to subject any part of them to its sovereignty."[13] The four specified freedoms originally set out in 1927 in the Institute draft were brought into the Geneva High Seas Convention.

As a baseline for classifying freedoms in outer space, we may take these four maritime freedoms, along with two additional high seas freedoms added by UNCLOS III: the freedom to construct artificial islands and other installations thereon, and the freedom of scientific research.[14] The freedom to construct artificial islands on the high seas is comparable to the freedom to erect permanent stations in orbit, as long as they do not impede or interfere with the rights of other states. The freedom of scientific research on the high seas has a precise parallel with the same designated freedom in outer space. This chapter attempts to draw a comparison between the freedoms of the high seas as contained in the UNCLOS I and III Conventions and those which are emerging in the exploration and use of outer space.

In 1958, the same year that the law of the sea was becoming codified by international agreement, the United Nations General Assembly established an ad hoc Committee on the Peaceful Uses of Outer Space, with a membership of 18 countries, including the United States and the Soviet Union.[15] An initial task given the Committee was to study the nature of the legal problems which might arise from outer space activity. In 1959, the Committee began this analysis of potential legal problems in outer space and reported that current activities could not be the basis for claims to sovereignty in outer space.[16] In 1961, the General Assembly, on the basis of the work of the Committee, began to define fundamental principles to be applied in outer space.[17] First, international law, including the United Nations Charter, would apply. Second, outer space and celestial bodies were free for exploration and use, on the basis of equality, by all states. Third, outer space and celestial bodies were not subject to national appropriation by claim of sovereignty, use or occupation, or any other means.[18] In 1963, these principles were embodied in a Declaration of Legal Principles Governing the Activities of States in the Exploration and Use of Outer Space was adopted by the General Assembly.[19] This Declaration was an important milestone in the progressive development of outer space law. Among other things, it set forth the freedoms of outer space, which in some ways were analogous to those exercised on the high seas.

In 1967, the provisions of the 1963 Declaration became a part of the first multinational treaty on outer space, the Outer Space Treaty. This Treaty became the charter for all space flight and the foundation for the four implementing treaties which were to follow: the Rescue Agreement, the Liability Convention, the Registration Convention, and the Moon Treaty. Of the four, only the Moon treaty has not been ratified by the United States, the USSR and the United Kingdom. However, all of the treaties, including the Moon Treaty, have drawn in one way or another on certain principles of maritime law.

While the UNCLOS I Conventions provides for four specific freedoms of the high seas and the UNCLOS III Convention provides for six, the Outer Space Treaty provides for four freedoms of outer space: the freedoms of exploration, use, access, and scientific investigation.[20] The expected rapid expansion in human activity in space over the next century will generate an urgent need to clarify and segregate the particular freedoms of outer space. Opinions may differ as to the exact classification, but the categories in the law of the sea conventions afford a starting point. The freedoms of outer space could thus be separated into the freedom of navigation, freedom of exploration, freedom of trade and commerce, freedom of access, and freedom of domicile. A short analysis of these freedoms follows.

THE FREEDOM OF NAVIGATION

With the launch of Sputnik I into outer space on October 4, 1957, it was obvious that a new legal order for this final frontier would have to be created. The first legal issue created by that flight was whether outer space would be open and free, not subject to appropriation, or whether it would be simply an extension of airspace. Some ranking military officials favored the indivisibility of airspace and outer space. In 1958 General Thomas White, U.S. Air Force Chief of Staff, wrote that for all practical purposes air and space merge, "forming a continuous and indivisible field of operation. . . . It should be recognized that there is no division between the two."[21] While General White was speaking on the operational level and with a view to making certain that outer space came under the national security jurisdiction of the U.S. Air Force rather than the Army or the Navy, his remarks created some confusion as to the legal separation of the two domains. Sputnik I settled the issue, however. No nation protested the orbiting of Sputnik over its territory, and the first freedom, the freedom of overflight, became established with that launch. The absence of any objection from other states meant that the orbiting of satellites around the Earth was not a privilege but a right given to all nations. It was evident from this auspicious beginning that flight through outer space would have more in common with voyages on the high seas than with aircraft flight.

The freedom of navigation is the first ranked of the freedoms of the sea; all other freedoms are rendered meaningless without this elemental one. Lord Stowell observed in the *Le Louis* case that all nations being equal, all have an equal right to the uninterrupted use of the unappropriated parts of the ocean for their navigation. In places where no local authority exists, where the subjects of all states meet upon a footing of entire equality and independence, no one state, or any of its subjects, has a right to assume or exercise authority over the subjects of another.[22] This freedom is not mentioned in any of the outer space treaties, yet it is so basic to the exploration and use of outer space that it must be considered as inherent in the launching and orbiting of all space objects.

However, flight in outer space is three-dimensional and therefore presents more legal issues than does ocean navigation. Ocean travel means travel on a common surface for all ships, while space travel occurs through the atmosphere, in orbit, in deep space, and around and onto celestial bodies. A space launch into orbit has perhaps the most similarity to ocean travel in that it takes place from a fixed point on Earth to a predetermined orbital path. This indeed is like an ocean liner which sails from one port to another along a predetermined ocean path. Once a space object is in orbit, however, its status and function change. No longer is it an instrumentality of transport, but rather a space platform on which other missions can take place. Nonetheless, regardless of the nature and characteristics of space flight, the inherent rights of all states to launch satellites, to place them in orbit, to land them on the Moon or other celestial bodies, and to send them into deep space are all part of the freedom of navigation and resemble the similar freedom of navigation on the high seas. It can be said that both on the high seas and in outer space, this freedom is a settled principle of customary international law.

There remains the question of defining the means of space navigation, the space object. The basic instrumentality for navigation at sea is, of course, the ship; and the ship is the centerpiece for most maritime law. Like aircraft, but unlike cars, trains and buses, ships are endowed with nationality and are carried on national registries. Only the ship, however, has a juridical status and a personal responsibility for its conduct. It has separate liability for contracts made for its benefit and for torts committed through its use. The distinction between the ship and other objects afloat has many ramifications in maritime law. The drydock, for example, is not subject to the law of salvage, and its workers are not given the privileged status of seamen. Unpaid repair bills for work done to the drydock do not create maritime liens, and a drydock cannot be the subject of a libel action.

No particular type of space object has been singled out for the special status accorded to ships and aircraft. All objects launched into outer space are entered on the registry of some nation without regard to navigability or mission. Space objects, which are more likely to be multifunctional than ships or aircraft, are not legally distinguished according to their purpose or their configuration.

To date, only the U.S. Space Shuttle has the capacity to freely navigate in outer space and return for further missions. It is the only reusable and crewed transport vehicle which is fully operational. The European Space Agency spaceplane, Hermes, will not fly crewed space missions until after the year 2000. The Columbus polar platform, to be launched by either Ariane 4 or 5 in 1995, will have a crew-tended free flyer, but the free flyer will not be a fully navigable spacecraft like the Space Shuttle and is not due to be launched by Ariane 5 until 1998.[23] The Soviet space shuttle orbiter Buran, which resembles the U.S. Space Shuttle, was launched into orbit without a crew in 1988 and plans were made for a second automatic flight, followed by a crewed flight.[24] As of early 1992, however, the future of Buran is unclear.

The navigable shuttle is the space object whose functions most closely resemble those of a ship or aircraft, but thus far it has not been the subject of a special regime. As long as objects launched into space are not juridically distinguished, it will be difficult to create a special regime for space transport comparable to that now in place for ships. The multinational conventions themselves use the terms "space object," "space vehicle," and "spacecraft" interchangeably.[25] However, when payloads are regularly lifted into space and transferred between points beyond the Earth, and when space travel becomes frequent, a particular corpus of law centered on the reusable, crewed spacecraft will be needed. This regime will contain rules to regulate orbits and the distance between spacecraft, and to provide for uniform procedures for launching, docking, and orbital flight. Uniform rules for hazard disposal, salvage, signals, and maneuvering will be needed. For these purposes, classification of space objects into those used primarily for transport and navigation and those used for other purposes will advance the safety and efficiency of space flight. It is ludicrous to consider that a crewed space station on the Moon or in permanent planetary orbit needs the same regulation and status as that of a fully maneuverable spacecraft. Crewed space stations such as Skylab, Salyut, Mir, and the planned Space Station Freedom have more in common with artificial islands at sea than with ships. These stations are places for work and living and are not designed or intended for the transfer of payloads from place to place in the skies. Space workers may stay on board for long durations and are not in the transport business. Their status resembles that of the longshoreman and the harbor worker, not that of a ship's crew. The routine carriage of payloads and spacefarers will present opportunities to draw up specialized rules which are predicated on the freedom of navigation in space, and the unique status of a space instrumentality which compares to the ship at sea. Freedom of navigation in space depends upon navigable spacecraft being given the special status accorded the ship at sea and, to a lesser extent, the aircraft in flight. In all three environments, the oceans, airspace, and outer space, the instrumentality of transport needs its own body of law to regulate it.

Some of the maritime conventions which might provide a precedent for navigable spacecraft regulation are the Convention for Preventing Collisions at Sea, the International Convention Relating to the Limitation of Liability of Owners of Seagoing Ships, and the Salvage Convention.[26]

THE FREEDOM OF EXPLORATION

The freedom of exploration is a basic freedom clearly expressed in the Outer Space Treaty. Throughout the ages, one civilization after another enlarged the breadth of the known world through voyages to uncharted regions of our planet. In the sense of traveling into the unknown, the freedom of exploration has been deeply rooted in the customary law of the sea since prehistoric times. The Phoenicians were among the first to extend their knowledge of the world through ocean exploration. In the third millennium B.C., voyages of exploration in the Persian Gulf and in the Arabian sea were promoting trade and settlements in the Tigro-Euphrates river basin, southeastern Arabia, and the Indus River valley.

Space exploration is a logical extension of the ocean voyages of discovery of the Middle Ages and will be as essential to the advancement of knowledge about our universe as the voyages of Columbus were to the Europeans of his time. For example, Mariner 9 made the first successful orbit of Mars in 1971 and captured over 7,000 pictures of its surface and moons. Galileo, the most recent U.S. planetary explorer, has detected "convection cells" similar to Earth's severest thunderstorms near the equator of Venus. Robotic missions that the U.S. National Aeronautics and Space Administration (NASA) is planning in the next five years will add immense knowledge about the nature of the solar system and its planets.

The freedom of scientific investigation provided for in the Outer Space Treaty is really a part of the broader freedom to explore. The UNCLOS III

Convention codified this principle for the first time, although it has long been recognized in customary maritime law. The UNCLOS III Convention provides that all states, wherever located, and competent international organizations have the right to conduct marine scientific research, having due regard to the interests of other states.

A fundamental question connected with the freedom of exploration is whether this freedom is restricted to governments and their agencies or whether it is given to private entities as well. The voyages of Columbus and Magellan, for example, were financed by governments but were not under governmental control. There is a view that exploration should be left to governmental agencies. Article 9 of the Outer Space Treaty requires states to conduct exploration so as to not harm the Earth's environment and with due regard to the interests of other states. Article 8 provides that states shall retain jurisdiction and control over all space objects carried on their registry. Article 6 provides that each state bears international responsibility for its national activities in outer space. It also requires authorization and continuing supervision by each state of the activities of its non-governmental entities in outer space. Do all of these prior restraints on private activity mean that exploration is a limited governmental freedom? The answer appears to be no. In fact, the United States is promoting a vigorous private-industry-oriented space enterprise.

THE FREEDOM OF TRADE AND COMMERCE

The freedom of trade and commerce is not a listed freedom in either the law of the sea conventions or the outer space treaties. It is, however, a well-established maritime freedom in customary international law. Professor Sauser-Hall, arbitrator in *Saudi-Arabia v. Aramco*, wrote that "according to a great principle of public international law, the ports of every State must be open to foreign merchant vessels and can only be closed when the vital interests of the State so require."[27] Professor Hyde explained that since no civilized state has a right to isolate itself, there was an obligation imposed on each maritime power not to deprive foreign vessels of commerce of entry to its ports.[28] This liberty of entry to foreign ports implies the right to load and unload cargoes, and embark and disembark passengers. This general principle of open ports has been expressed in many treaties of friendship, commerce, and navigation.

According to Professor de La Pradelle, the conventions which provide for open ports confirm the concept of free trade and commerce as one of customary law.[29] The open port doctrine has promoted and fostered commerce and given rise to much of the maritime law which exists today. Without free trade, much of the law of the sea would need to be rewritten.

The Outer Space Treaty provides that stations, equipment and space vehicles on the Moon and other celestial bodies shall be open to inspection by a representative of other states parties on the basis of reciprocity.[30] However, this is not a free trade freedom; but rather it is a right deriving from the need for an open visitation and observation regime in order to ensure compliance with international conventions and to preserve international peace and security. As commerce expands into outer space, it will be essential to private enterprise and competition to incorporate into space law the open port and free trade doctrines which are found in law of the sea.

The freedom of use specified in the Outer Space Treaty is too broad to be helpful in shaping the commercial regime in outer space. While the meaning of "exploration" is easily understood and fairly precise, the term "use" is more confusing. As a noun, it has at least eight different meanings.[31] *Webster's* gives a legal definition of "use" as "enjoyment of property" and "advantage, benefit, especially from property." This general definition, when applied in a space context, conveys an impression of employing satellites for private gain as well as for the welfare of the community as a whole. Perhaps it would be helpful to interpret freedom of use narrowly to mean freedom of trade and commerce, and possibly, but not necessarily, freedom of exploitation.

The Report of the U.S. National Commission on Space foresees a greatly expanding private sector as we proceed into the twenty-first century. By the year 2035, the report concludes, there will be three broad categories of space enterprise: supporting industries on Earth, space industries with markets on Earth, and space industries with markets in space.[32] All of these industries will generate trade and commerce in space. Opening outer space to private trade and commerce, combined with an open spaceport entry rule, will facilitate the expansion of trade in, through and from outer space.

Whether a freedom of trade will include the liberty to exploit celestial resources for private gain is put into doubt by the common heritage of mankind (CHM) concept and the Moon Treaty. The early United Nations resolutions referred to freedom of exploitation and use, but this was changed to the freedom of exploration and use in the 1963 Declaration of Legal Principles and subsequently in the Outer Space Treaty. Professor Carl Christol has written that the practices of the spacefaring states since the adoption of the Outer Space Treaty confirm the view that "use" includes the exploitation of the resources in outer space.[33] However, there seems to remain a strong view among the less developed countries that the CHM doctrine, as part of the law of outer space, prohibits unilateral exploitation of the celestial resources either by states or by private entities. The Moon Treaty provides that the Moon's resources "in place" are the "common heritage of mankind."[34] Both the United States and the Soviet Union have interpreted "in place" to mean that once the resources are extracted and thus no longer in place, they can become the property of the mining party.[35] However, it remains an open question as to how states will interpret the CHM concept when extraction of lunar minerals becomes possible.

The CHM formula has been a major reason for the non-acceptance of the UNCLOS III Convention by the United States. The UNCLOS III Convention calls for an International Sea-Bed Authority to organize, carry out, and control, on behalf of mankind, the exploitation of the resources of the international seabed area. The seabed area covers the seabed, ocean floor and subsoil beyond national jurisdiction.[36] It is estimated that 1.5 trillion tons of manganese, nickel, copper, and cobalt in the form of nodules lie on the seabed, mainly in the Pacific Ocean. Most of these minerals are in short supply in many countries, including the United States. The mining of these resources could provide a tremendous profit to those corporations wishing to invest their time and labor in such operations. However, the United States has refused to sign the UNCLOS III Convention because it would deter private mining companies from seeking licenses. The United States believes an international seabed authority would impede the development of seabed mineral resources, deny national access, and create a monopolization by an international authority. A vice president of one of the United States-based consortia created to mine the seabed observed that it would take 10 years and a $1.5 billion to start up the industry. No company would be willing, he said, to participate in an international regime unless it was absolutely sure of a mine site and production quota. The Moon Treaty calls for an international regime which the parties undertake to establish in order to govern the exploitation of its natural resources when this is about to become feasible.[37] Such a regime, sounding to some like the duplicate of an international seabed regime, could chill private incentive to harvest the valuable minerals of the planets and the Moon.

FREEDOM OF ACCESS

This a narrow but important freedom which is expressly referred to in the Outer Space Treaty and the Moon Treaty.[38] The Moon Treaty provides that stations on the Moon cannot be installed in a manner which would impede free access by other states to all areas; the Treaty would guarantee that one spacefaring state could not lock out another by strategic positioning of its facilities. It also reinforces the principle that occupation of any portion of a celestial body does not signify area exclusivity. The Outer Space Treaty expressly prohibits any claim of sovereignty in outer space by means of use or occupation, or by any other means. Denial of access to any portion of a celestial body by one state would amount to the same thing, however. Acknowledgement of this freedom by all spacefaring states is insurance that a state practice of limiting access by strategic positioning of its stations will not be tolerated. It might be tempting for one nation, by enlarging its facilities on the Moon or other celestial body, to claim de facto control over increasing areas to the detriment of access by other states. In the Island of Palmas case, the International Court of Justice observed how the peaceful and continuous display of state authority over an island, or even a small portion thereof, could result in a claim to sovereignty.[39] In celestial regions, area exclusivity would be tantamount to state sovereignty even though not labeled as such. The right to enter, transit, and leave any area is inherent in the freedom of access.

The Outer Space Treaty and the Moon Treaty also provide for an open visitation regime. Both treaties provide that equipment and space vehicles on the Moon and other celestial bodies shall be open to representatives of other states parties upon reasonable advance notice.[40] The practice of states thus far would seem to confirm that orbiting or floating space objects are subject to the exclusive jurisdiction of the launching state. Such objects in orbit cannot be inspected or boarded without prior permission, except possibly in the case of national emergency.[41] This is comparable to the privileges and immunities afforded ships at sea. In the Lotus case, the International Court of Justice held that "vessels on the high seas are subject to no authority except that of the state whose flag they fly."[42] It has also been explained that "to enter into a non-national vessel or to interrupt its course by a foreign power in time of peace . . . is an act of force and is prima facie a wrong, a trespass," which can only be done in exceptional circumstances. This rule of flag state exclusivity is codified in the UNCLOS I and III Conventions,[43] and is a correct rule to apply in outer space as well.

FREEDOM OF DOMICILE OR OCCUPATION

The Moon and (probably) Mars are certain to be inhabited by humans sometime in the twenty-first century. In 1985 the National Commission on Space proposed that settling the solar system be part of the goal of a civilian space agenda. The Commission stated that five centuries after Columbus opened the new frontiers to the west, new worlds can be settled "beyond the planet of our birth." The Commission noted that the broad spectrum of the solar system, not just "the planet of our birth," is the future home of humanity.[44]

The huge expenditures estimated to be necessary for such an effort have prompted new calls for a privatization of space exploration. One writer has proposed a "Space Homesteading Incentive" Act, which would offer $40 million a year to any person who would spend a year in orbit on U.S.-built facilities. As these space homesteaders find profitable occupations, individual payments could be lowered, until at some point the incentives of living beyond the Earth would "spawn a private space habitat industry and invigorate the launcher industry."[45]

Dr. George Robinson of the Smithsonian Institution took the lead decades ago in analyzing the legal and biological problems arising from living in space. He wrote that with the advent of extraterrestrial habitation, a whole new class of people will arise called "spacekind,"[46] who maintain a permanent residence beyond our planet. They are the vanguard of future generations of humans who will be born, marry and die in outer space and on its celestial bodies.

Freedom of domicile is a legal concept meaning that people should be able to choose where they wish to live. This freedom has always been limited on Earth, as between nations, because of restrictive national policies reflected in domestic immigration, citizenship, and expulsion laws. In outer space, an environment without political boundaries, the freedom of domicile and occupation should translate into a freedom of migration and travel for all who venture there. The freedom of domicile is necessary if the high goals and purposes of the Outer Space Treaty are not to be eroded by territorial notions of sovereignty, political borders, and restrictions on the free choice of people to live where they want.

CONCLUSION

The freedoms of the high seas have been essential to the consolidation and harmonization of the law of the sea. Historically, maritime law was thought to be an international law merchant which was impartially administered by the several maritime nations of the world. Judge Addison Brown, an admiralty lawyer, wrote, that "inasmuch as the high seas are the common ground of all nations, and are not governed by the merely municipal laws of either, the quality of acts committed on the high seas, as between persons or ships belonging to different nations whose laws are different, is determined by the maritime law as accepted and administered in the forum where the suit is prosecuted."[47] The U.S. Supreme Court has written that "there can be no doubt that it must be the general maritime law" which applies to cases arising on the high seas involving different nationalities.[48] Identifying the separate freedoms enjoyed in outer space will help create a general law of outer space in a manner similar to the development of the public and private law of the sea.

NOTES

1. Convention on the High Seas, Done at Geneva, Apr. 29, 1958, 13 U.S.T. 2312, T.I.A.S. No. 5200, 450 U.N.T.S. 82 (High Seas Convention of 1958); Convention on the Continental Shelf, Done at Geneva, Apr. 29, 1958, 15 U.S.T. 471, T.I.A.S. No. 5578, 449 U.N.T.S. 311 (Continental Shelf Convention of 1958); Convention on the Territorial Sea and Contiguous Zone, Done at Geneva, Apr. 29, 1958, 15 U.S.T. 1606, T.I.A.S. No. 5639, 516 U.N.T.S. 205 (Territorial Sea Convention of 1958); Convention on Fishing and Conservation of Living Resources of High Seas, Done at Geneva, Apr. 29, 1958, 17 U.S.T. 138, T.I.A.S. No. 5969, 559 U.N.T.S. 285 (Fishing Convention of 1958) (the UNCLOS I Conventions).

2. C. John Colombos, *The International Law of the Sea* (6th ed.), New York, D. Mckay, 1967, p. 47.

3. *Law of the Sea Bulletin*, No. 2, New York, United Nations, March 1985, p. 1.

4. United Nations Convention on the Law of the Sea, Done at Montego Bay, Dec. 10, 1982, Opened for Signature, Dec. 10, 1982, U.N. Doc. A/CONF.62/122,

reprinted in 21 *International Legal Materials* 1261 (1982) (the UNCLOS III Convention).

5. *Id.* at Art. 308.

6. Territorial Sea of the United States of America, Proclamation 5928, December 27, 1988, 54 FR 777, January 9, 1989.

7. Declaration of the First Meeting of Equatorial Countries (Bogota), 1976, by Brazil, Colombia, Congo, Ecuador, Indonesia, Kenya, Uganda, and Zaire; commonly referred to as the Bogota Declaration.

8. Eilene Galloway (ed.), *Legal Problems of Space Exploration: A Symposium*, Washington, Government Printing Office, 1961.

9. C. Wilfred Jenks, "International Law and Activities in Space," *International and Comparative Law Quarterly*, Vol. 99, 1956, p. 101.

10. Treaty on Principles Governing the Activities of States in the Exploration and Use of Outer Space, Including the Moon and Other Celestial Bodies, Done at Washington, London, and Moscow, Jan. 27, 1967, Entered into Force Oct. 10, 1967, 18 U.S.T. 2410, T.I.A.S. No. 6347, 610 U.N.T.S. 205, reprinted in 6 *International Legal Materials* 386 (1967) (the Outer Space Treaty).

11. Colombos, *supra* note 2, p. 62.

12. *Annuaire de l'Institut de Droit International*, vol. 33, part iii, Paris, Pedone, 1927, p. 339; *The International Law Association, 34th Report*, London, Sweet and Maxwell, 1926, p. 101.

13. High Seas Convention of 1958, *supra* note 1, at Art. 2.

14. UNCLOS III Convention, *supra* note 4, at Art. 87.

15. U.N.G.A. Res. 1348 (XIII).

16. S. Houston Lay and Howard J. Taubenfeld, *The Law Relating to the Activities of Man in Space*, Chicago, University of Chicago Press, 1970, p. 77.

17. C. Q. Christol, *The Modern International Law of Outer Space*, New York, Pergamon, 1982, p. 15.

18. U.N.G.A. Res. 1721 (XVI); Lay and Taubenfeld, *supra* note 16, p. 77.

19. U.N.G.A. Res. 1962 (XVIII), of Dec. 13, 1963.

20. The Outer Space Treaty, *supra* note 10, at Art. 1.

21. Kenneth B. Keating, "Space Law and the Fourth Dimension of Our Age," from a Speech of Hon. Kenneth B. Keating of New York, before the Ninth Annual Congress of the International Astronautical Federation, The Hague, Netherlands, August 29, 1958.

22. *The Case of Le Louis*, 2 Dods. 210, 243; 165 Eng. Rep. 1464, 1475 (1817).

23. *Flight International*, February 27, 1991, p. 1.

24. D. I. Fisher, "Soviet Space Program," *Popular Science*, Vol. 328, January 1991, p. 62.

25. See the Outer Space Treaty, *supra* note 10, at Arts. 4, 7, 8, 10; the Rescue Agreement at Arts. 1, 2, 3, 4, 5; the Liability Convention at Arts. 1, 2, 3, 4, 5, 7; the Registration Convention at Arts. 1, 2, 4, 5, 6; and the Moon Treaty at Arts. 3, 8, 11, 12, 13, 15.

26. Convention for Preventing Collisions at Sea; International Convention Relating to the Limitation of Liability of Owners of Seagoing Ships, Brussels, Oct. 10, 1957, U.N.T.S. 429, P. 223, reprinted in *American Journal of International Law*, Vol. 53, New York, Oceana, p. 536.; 1910 Salvage Convention.

27. Professor Sauser-Hall, in the *Saudi Arabia and Arabian-American Oil Co.*

(ARAMCO) arbitration of 1958, in British Yearbook of International Law, London, Oxford University Press, 1959, p.48 and 1967, p.9.

28. I. C. Hyde, *International Law Chiefly as Interpreted and Applied by the United States*, Boston, Little Brown, 1945, p. 581.

29. Paul de La Pradelle, *Annuaire de l'Institut de Droit International*, vol. 2, Paris, Pedone, 1957, p. 209. In contrast to the open port doctrine, landing and overflight rights for foreign aircraft must be expressly conferred.

30. The Outer Space Treaty, *supra* note 10, at Art. 12.

31. *Webster's New World Dictionary* (2d college ed.), Springfield, MA, Merriam, 1982, p. 1,564.

32. *Pioneering the Space Frontier*, Report of the National Commission on Space, New York, Bantam Books, 1986, p. 77.

33. Christol, *supra* note 17, pp. 251-252.

34. The Moon Treaty, at Art. 11.

35. N. C. Goldman, *American Space Law*, Ames, IA, Iowa State University Press, 1988, p. 90.

36. UNCLOS III Convention, *supra* note 4, at Art. 1.

37. The Moon Treaty, at Art. 11.

38. The Moon Treaty at Art. 9 provides that "stations shall be installed in such a manner that they do not impede free access to all areas of the moon."

39. Island of Palmas Case *(United States v. The Netherlands)*, Permanent Court of Arbitration, 2 U.N. Rep. Int'l. Arb. Awards 829 (1928).

40. The Outer Space Treaty, *supra* note 10, at Art. 12; The Moon Treaty, at Art. 15. One important difference in the treaties is that Art. 12 provides open visitation only on the basis of reciprocity.

41. Inspection of a satellite by remote sensors would not appear to violate any treaty or customary rule. What is intended here is inspection by physical entry or by close approach of another satellite.

42. The Case of the S.S. Lotus *(France v. Turkey)*, Permanent Court of International Justice, P.C.I.J. Ser. A. No. 10, 2 Hudson, World Ct. Rep. 20 (1927).

43. High Seas Convention of 1958, *supra* note 1, at Art. 22; UNCLOS III Convention, *supra* note 4, at Art. 110.

44. Report of the National Commission on Space, *supra* note 32, Preface.

45. David P. Gump, "Put Space Programs into Capitalist Orbit," *Spacetravel*, Gannett News Service, August 22, 1990.

46. George D. Robinson, *Living in Space*, Washington, Public Affairs, 1975, p. 96.

47. The Brantford City Case, 29 Fed. 375, 382, 383.

48. The Belgenland Case, 114 U.S. 355, 370-71 (1985).

2

Evolution of the Doctrine of Space Law

Vladimír Kopal

Thousands of articles, studies, and books have been published on the subject of space law, particularly during the second half of this century, and a fair evaluation of this explosion seems almost impossible. More time will certainly be needed in order to see the space law doctrine of our age in a proper light. Any attempt to even recount the main trends in the doctrine will necessarily be rather selective, and some judgements may seem arbitrary. Further efforts of this kind from different authors will therefore be needed before a detailed and reasonably objective picture of this evolution can emerge.

Not all publications relating to space law have been of the same significance, of course. Attractive subjects such as space law inspire works of great creativity and importance, and at the same time give rise to secondary works. Nevertheless, the large volume of legal writing on space problems in general has helped to create a favorable environment in which a new branch of international law—the law of outer space—has emerged and is growing rapidly.

The cornerstones and the first layers of bricks in the structure of space law doctrine were laid down many years before space activities began. In the Preface to the first volume of writings on space law, which was prepared in 1958 for the U.S. Senate, Eilene Galloway, Special Consultant to the Senate Special Committee on Space and Astronautics, noted:

> Long before a satellite was sent into orbit around the earth, many of the legal problems which would be created by this advance in science and technology were anticipated and analyzed. Indeed, the quality and quantity of published articles in this field are a matter of amazement to those who have only recently become aware of the impact of satellite development upon society. It is fortunate that so much fundamental thinking is already in existence at a time when scientific facts are rapidly developing and need to be studied in relation to national and international situations.[1]

Six decades have elapsed since the first study on space law was published, and 35 years have passed since the first artificial object was launched into outer space. This is a long time in the development of any scientific field in the modern world, which is accustomed to rapid scientific and technological progress. An outline of the evolution of thinking on space law must therefore be divided into periods, each of which has its focal points and trends around which the evolution has been centered. This chapter will first examine space-related legal studies undertaken prior to the space era and will consider the emergence of basic space law doctrine in response to the first space flights. The chapter will then briefly assess the establishment of the principles of space law by intergovernmental organizations as well as the contributions of international non-governmental bodies. Finally, some thoughts will be offered on recent trends in space law doctrine as it has developed during the last few years.

SPACE LAW DOCTRINE UP TO THE FIRST SPACE FLIGHTS

Since space science and technology grew out of developments in aviation, it is not surprising that most of the early writers on space law approached the subject with a thorough knowledge of air law; and international law relating to space activities will undoubtedly become an indispensable part of the international law of our times, as was the case with international air law during the first half of this century. However, not all air law specialists were able to properly differentiate the issues arising from the prospective space flights from those relating to aeronautics. What was first considered in many cases were issues of air law raised by the possibility of new forms of flight not covered by the definition of aircraft.

Fortunately, the author of the first monographical study on space law, Dr. Vladimír Mandl, an attorney from Pilsen, Czechoslovakia, who later became Professor of industrial law at the Czech Technical University in Prague, understood well the specific nature of space flight and the prospective legal issues, notwithstanding that he too was a specialist in air law and had published several studies in the field prior to his monograph on space law.[2] His study of space law issues, published in Germany in 1932,[3] was based on the assumption that the prospect of reaching outer space by means of rockets would raise a variety of new questions not settled by air law, which regulated only the legal regime of airspace. Mandl, who also carefully watched the development of rocket technology and published a book on that topic as well,[4] understood correctly that rockets do not require a substantial air density to sustain flight and hence are capable of going far beyond the atmosphere. Mandl's concept of a law for outer space was therefore based on the specificity of space flight, implying a law governed by different principles than those of the law of the air.

Mandl did not neglect the relevance of other branches of law and the usefulness of analogies in special cases. In the first part of his monograph he considered relevant issues of civil law, public law, and international law. The most interesting part of his study, however, is the second part entitled "The Future," in which he made a number of predictions which have since become reality. Mandl held the view that the principle of state territorial supremacy over airspace extended far beyond the then practical limits of aeronautics and established the right of each state to retain sovereign power over any use of its superjacent air zone, whether such use was performed by aeronautics or in any other manner, including flights into outer space. As soon as a spacecraft entered a state's airspace, it was to be subject to its jurisdiction. Mandl made it abundantly clear, however, that the principle of sovereignty applied only to airspace; there was no reason or intention to grant to states any rights reaching farther into space. Where airspace ended, the territorial supremacy, mutually accepted by states both in treaties and in practice, also ended.

> But beyond these Earth coastal spaces is space which does not have any relations whatsoever with our globe, nor with individual parts of the Earth surface either, which no longer has any pertinence to the Earth and is therefore free of any state power, *coelum liberum.* In this area, spaceship traffic is completely free.[5]

World War II interrupted the interest in the legal problems of outer space, but shortly before the war's end, the war machine developed rocket technology capable not only of delivering explosives onto enemy territory but also of reaching into outer space. After the war, the new rocket technology and the preparations for the International Geophysical Year, which included the exploration of outer space, inspired expectations that artificial Earth satellites could soon be successfully launched into outer space. These prospects gave rise to a growing number of studies dealing with questions that seemed to be of imminent practical importance, in particular the questions of the definition of outer space and its legal status.

In a 1951 address, Professor John Cobb Cooper of the United States, founder and first Director of the Institute of International Air Law (IIAL) at McGill University in Montreal, said: "High altitude rocket flights have reopened an old question: How far upward in space does the territory of the state extend?"[6]

Cooper modified his replies to this question several times and even warned against making a premature legal decision without sufficient scientific knowledge, but he indicated a feasible criterion for solving this problem:

> If subsequent calculations based on the observations made during the International Geophysical Year demonstrate that the minimum height of possible satellite orbital flight is in fact at a reasonably exact distance from the earth's surface, an excellent

basis for an upper airspace boundary will be available. Physically it will be quite constant. Legally it will be subject to support on the basis that the column of air appreciably affecting flight ends there, leaving the legal status of true outer space for future international understanding.[7]

A similar position with regard to the need for a definition of outer space and the necessity of establishing special laws governing outer space was taken by Professor Alex Meyer of Germany, Director of the University of Cologne Institute of Air Law, who analyzed these and other legal problems of space flight in his address to the Third International Astronautical Congress in Stuttgart in 1952.[8] Meyer later elaborated his views in his contribution to the First United Nations Conference on the Exploration and Peaceful Uses of Outer Space in Vienna in 1968.[9]

Other authors did not attempt to define outer space, but the need for such a delimitation was nonetheless implicit in their examination of the legal status of space beyond airspace. Professor Oscar Schachter of the United States, Deputy Director of the United Nations Legal Department, in 1952 reached the following conclusion:

Beyond the airspace, as already noted, we would apply a system similar to that followed on the high seas; outer space and the celestial bodies would be the common property of all mankind, over which no nation would be permitted to exercise domination. A legal order would be developed on the principle of free and equal use, with the object of furthering scientific research and investigation. It seems to me that a development of this kind would dramatically emphasize the common heritage of humanity and serve, perhaps significantly, to strengthen the sense of international community which is so vital to the development of a peaceful and secure world order.[10]

However, the need for a definition of outer space in the form of a delimitation of airspace and outer space was not perceived by all. Some scholars in the late 1950s argued that regulation should depend on the nature of the activity rather than on its location with respect to a boundary between air and outer space. The origin of this concept, which became known as the "functional approach," is usually attributed to two Yale University scholars, Professors Myres S. McDougal and Leon Lipson,[11] but a similar approach was suggested almost simultaneously by Professor Eugène Pépin of France, who succeeded J. C. Cooper as Director of the IIAL. Pépin recommended that priority be given to the consideration of practical problems, without concern for abstract principles.[12] This concept was later defended and elaborated by Professors Rolando Quadri of Italy and Charles Chaumont of France,[13] and it also found support in Central and Eastern Europe, particularly from Dr. Gyula Gál of Hungary.[14] Last, but not least, a monograph by Professor Nicolas M. Matte provided a detailed critical analysis of the problem of delimiting airspace and outer space, using a comparison with the law of the sea.[15]

Though the problem of defining outer space and its legal status remained in the foreground of the early doctrine of space law, a number of other questions were also raised. Professor Pépin drew attention to the hazards represented by uncontrolled launchings of spacecraft, which when ascending or descending pass through the atmosphere where aircraft are flying. He warned that there were no international rules on this matter and that aircraft already in flight might not have been informed. Moreover, in cases of collision or damage it would be necessary to identify the responsible spacecraft, and regulation would be indispensable when dozens or hundreds of spacecraft would orbit the Earth. Pépin was also concerned over possible interference to terrestrial radio communications caused by communications with spacecraft.[16]

Other scholars expressed similar concerns in the late 1950s. In 1958, Professor Isabella H. Ph. de Rode-Verschoor of the Netherlands drew the attention of the First Colloquium on the Law of Outer Space, held as part of the International Astronautical Congress, to the question of the responsibility of states for damage caused by space objects and to the need for a new regulation on this subject. Professor de Rode-Verschoor recommended a "compulsory registration of space satellites in order to determine the state to be held responsible." She also proposed an "international guaranty fund" to pay compensation for damage caused by an Earth satellite.[17]

Andrew G. Haley, President of the International Astronautical Federation (IAF) and General Counsel of the American Rocket Society, argued in 1958 that it was absolutely necessary to control the placement of re-entering space vehicles in order to protect human life and property, and to rid outer space of non-functional objects in order to ensure the safety of life and property in future space navigation. He also warned that the radio spectrum was very limited, that the frequencies involved are extremely valuable, and that they might be essential to some other services. Accordingly, he called for a radio command which would silence satellite radio transmitters when necessary. He recommended that the International Radio Consultative Committee of the International Telecommunication Union (ITU) undertake the study of the scientific and technical problems connected with space communications.[18]

While a certain consensus was emerging concerning basic principles of space law, different opinions were advanced concerning the appropriate legal procedures for elaborating international space law. Professor Pépin suggested, immediately after the launching of the first artificial satellite, that a convention be drafted as a step toward agreement on basic space law.

> Its universal acceptance would benefit not only the immediate future of scientific research in space, but also the safety of present circulation within the atmosphere and of the people on the surface; it would also prepare the future of the circulation of man in space.[19]

Professors McDougal and Lipson disagreed:

> A durable agreement by explicit international convention on anything like a code of law for outer space is not, in our opinion, something now to be expected or desired. One may indeed expect with rather more confidence a series of agreements, gradually arrived at, on particular subjects, such as the continuation of the International Geophysical Year; the exchange of certain types of information, such as tracking data and some signaling codes, beyond present levels; the use or abstention from use of certain radio frequencies; and the coordination of launching schedules.[20]

The outline of the first stage in the evolution of space law doctrine would not be complete without mentioning two more works on the newly emerging issues. *Air Law and Space* by Welf Heinrich, Prince of Hanover, was written in 1953, well before the launching of the first satellites, as a doctor of law thesis at the Georg-August University in Göttingen, Germany. It was largely a continuation of the pioneering study of Vladimír Mandl.[21]

The second work is Andrew G. Haley's *Space Law and Government*. It was published in 1963 as a kind of codification of earlier work by the author into book form, covering a 12-year period of his thinking. Together with his young assistants, Andrew G. Haley, an enthusiast for space flights, a promoter of international cooperation in space, and a practicing lawyer with experience in space industry and telecommunications, presented a personal account of all essential problems in the new doctrine of space law. The last chapter was devoted to Haley's favorite subject—metalaw. The concept of metalaw was first elaborated by Haley in 1955 in response to his fears of an indefinite projection of anthropocentric law beyond the Earth, which he saw as "the most calamitous act man could perform in his dealings with the cosmos." As an alternative, Haley offered a precept of metalaw and suggested some preliminary rules derived from it.

> In metalaw we deal with all frames of existence—with sapient beings different in kind. We must do unto others as they would have done unto them. To treat others as we would desire to be treated might well mean their destruction. We must treat them as they desire to be treated. This is a simply expressed but vastly significant premise of metalaw.

One of the rules derived by Haley from the metalaw precept was an absolute prohibition of the use of force, thus implying that the exclusively peaceful use of space should become an essential element of the legal order of space.[22]

Scholars from other parts of the world also contributed actively to the birth and early evolution of space law doctrine. In Argentina, university discussions and publications on space law, many initiated by Professor Aldo Armando Cocca, appeared in the early 1950s, and specialized institutes of air law founded shortly after World War II in Córdoba and Buenos Aires enlarged their scope to include space law. Mexico soon joined these efforts, and by the

1960s space research, including space law issues, was being pursued in several countries of the region.

Studies of space law issues also developed in the then Socialist part of the world, particularly in the Soviet Union.[23] Academician Yevgeniy A. Korovin, whose interest in space problems began in the period between the world wars, wrote the following in a 1959 article:

> It must be concluded that national sovereignty does not extend to cosmic space. However, it does not follow that space is to be considered as some kind of legal "vacuum" where no restrictions on freedom of action prevail. All universally accepted rules of international law (inadmissibility of the use of force in solving international disputes, non-injury of foreign citizens and their property, governmental responsibility for the activities of their representatives, etc.) apply to the Cosmos as well.[24]

THE ROLE OF INTERNATIONAL ORGANIZATIONS

Our survey thus far of views concerning the legal problems relating to space activities leads us to the conclusion that on most issues there was not a great distance between positions held by authors from different parts of the world, and their differences were not insurmountable. This was a good omen for the intergovernmental negotiations on the first space law instruments, which began in the 1960s and continued through the 1970s.

However great the value of the work by the early scholars in the field of space law was, it was evident that, as in other fields of international law, the primary role in the development of legal rules would belong to states. And in a world organized into sovereign states, it was only natural that negotiation of a body of legal rules to govern space activities would take place in the principal intergovernmental organization of our time, the United Nations. The United Nations General Assembly is empowered to encourage the progressive development of international law and its codification (Art. 13, para. 1 of the Charter). Through its Committee on the Peaceful Uses of Outer Space, it has played a major role in the elaboration of international space law.

In promoting international cooperation in space, the United Nations could rely on the cooperation and assistance of various organizations with responsibilities in particular fields, including the International Telecommunication Union (ITU), the Food and Agriculture Organization (FAO), the United Nations Educational, Scientific and Cultural Organization (UNESCO), the World Meteorological Organization (WMO), the International Civil Aviation Organization (ICAO), the United Nations Industrial Development Organization (UNIDO), the International Atomic Energy Agency (IAEA), the United Nations Environment Programme (UNEP), and others. It has thus been the United Nations system as a whole that has stimulated international cooperation relating to space and promoted the progressive development of space law. It was decided at the very beginning of the legislative process in the Committee on the Peaceful Uses of Outer Space that an attempt at drafting a comprehensive code to govern space activities immediately would be premature and that the rule of law in outer space should be elaborated step-by-step, through a number of instruments dealing with the most urgent problems of space activities.

Since the adoption by the General Assembly of Resolution 1721 (XVI) of December 20, 1961, the body of international space law has increased progressively. This is particularly true for the period 1966-1979, which saw the successful elaboration by the Committee and its Legal Subcommittee of the 1967 Outer Space Treaty and four other multilateral treaties which incorporated the initial principles into legally binding instruments and developed them further.

Besides the United Nations and its related international organizations, a number of organizations with special space-related functions were established in the 1960s and 1970s, including the International Telecommunications Satellite Organization (INTELSAT), the European Space Agency (ESA), the European Telecommunications Satellite Organization (EUTELSAT), the International Organization of Space Communications (INTERSPUTNIK), the Council on International Co-operation in the Study and Utilization of Outer Space (INTERCOSMOS), the Arab Satellite Communication Organization (ARABSAT), and the International Maritime Satellite Organization (INMARSAT). These organizations also contributed to the growth of space law, first through the agreements by which they were established, then through the agreements which they concluded with states and other international organizations, and finally through their participation in the work of the United Nations Committee and its two subcommittees, where they have the status of observers. Some of these organizations have made declarations of acceptance of the rights and obligations arising from some of the United Nations space treaties.[25]

A number of international non-governmental organizations have supported the law-making process and have played an important role in the development of space law doctrine. The Institute of International Law (L'Institut de Droit International) and the International Law Association (ILA), both founded in 1873, have for a long time dealt with the development of international law and its codification. The International Institute of Space Law (IISL) of the International Astronautical Federation (IAF) is a relatively new body, established in 1960 in response to the first space flights.

At its 1963 session held in Brussels, the Institute of International Law considered the legal regime of outer space and unanimously adopted a resolution on the subject in a language which deserves admiration for both its substance and clarity of expression.[26] The resolution covered the same issues that were shortly to be covered in the United Nations Declaration of Legal Principles, which was adopted by the Committee on Outer Space and then was approved by General Assembly Resolution 1962 (XVIII) on December 13, 1963.

The International Law Association (ILA) referred to space issues for the first time at its 47th Conference in Dubrovnik in 1956 when it considered a report, "Limitation of Air Sovereignty," by the Chairman of its Air Law Committee, Professor D. Goedhuis of the Netherlands, and decided that the Committee "should continue the study of the nature and contents of air sovereignty, paying special attention to the problems connected with the coming flight in outer space and the legal nature of interplanetary space."[27]

The Congresses of the International Astronautical Federation (IAF) began including reports on legal issues relating to space flight as early as 1952. Reports on legal topics were also presented at the 1954 Congress in Innsbruck (Dr. A. A. Cocca) and at the 1956 Congress in Rome (Dr. A. A. Cocca and Dr. E. Pépin). In 1958, the First Colloquium on the Law of Outer Space was held at The Hague, during the Ninth International Astronautical Congress, at which were assembled 44 participants from 10 countries. A resolution, unanimously approved by the participants, recommended the establishment, within the framework of the IAF, of a Permanent Legal Committee to study all problems concerning space law. In 1959, at the Second Colloquium, held in London, the Permanent Committee became the International Institute of Space Law (IISL). Its basic document, the Statute of IISL, was approved by the IAF Bureau at its 11th Congress held in Stockholm in 1960.

Through its annual colloquia, the IISL has inspired thinking on practically all legal aspects of astronautics and has accumulated a wealth of thoughts on different space law subjects. During the presidencies of Professor Eugène Pépin of France (1963-1973) and Professor Isabella H. Ph. Diederiks-Verschoor of the Netherlands (1973-1990), the Institute became an important center for the development of space law doctrine. The volumes of IISL Proceedings, which include the papers presented in the annual colloquia, "form an irreplaceable collection of studies on the evolution of ideas with respect to space law, the development of new principles and ideas, and even permit the study in depth of various interpretations of international instruments in force." The IISL, in 1969, prepared a "General Table of Teaching and Study on Space Law throughout the World," and it organized further symposia on the subject in Brussels, 1971, and in Baku, 1973. Finally, in 1964 the IISL started publishing a "Worldwide Bibliography for the Year of Space Law and Related Matters," an effort which continued through 1973.[28]

A survey of the contributions of non-governmental organizations to the development of space law doctrine would not be complete without mention of the work of the Hague Academy of International Law. This renowned international institution, dedicated to teaching and research in international law, included in its programs lectures on space law by Professor Rolando Quadri of Italy in 1959, Professor Daniel Goedhuis of the Netherlands in 1963, and Professor Manfred Lachs of Poland in 1964. The Hague Academy continues to discuss the subject of space law in its lectures and publications.[29]

After the adoption of the United Nations space treaties, discussions of space law doctrine began to change. Books and articles began to focus on the legislative process in the United Nations and other international organizations. Scholars interpreted and commented on the instruments that had been adopted, analyzed the problems being encountered in the elaboration of further space law documents, and considered new items suitable for legal regulation.

By the end of the 1960s, the number of space law publications was growing rapidly. Even more significant was the publication of several books by eminent jurists who offered more comprehensive pictures of international space law; their publications are now considered classics of space law.[30] Finally, between 1979 and 1981, the four-volume *Manual on Space Law*, comprehensively reflecting the results of space legislation up to that time, was published by two United Nations officers, Dr. Nandasiri Jasentuliyana and Roy S. K. Lee.[31]

RECENT DEVELOPMENTS IN SPACE LAW DOCTRINE

In the 1970s, the Committee on the Peaceful Uses of Outer Space and its Legal Subcommittee began discussions on some new politically and technically demanding problems, which led in the 1980s to the elaboration of three sets of principles to govern specific types of space activities. The first negotiations were concluded by the adoption of the 1982 Principles Governing Direct Television Broadcasting, which, alas, under deteriorating conditions of international relations, did not command the support of the international community as a whole. Fortunately, the United Nations succeeded in restoring its traditional consensus on space issues in adopting the 1986 Principles Relating to Remote Sensing. The third set of principles, on the Use of Nuclear Power Sources in Outer Space, has not yet been finalized, although substantial progress has been made during the last few years.

Space law developed during this period not only in the United Nations and related organizations but also in other international organizations. Moreover, national space laws and regulations adopted in a growing number of spacefaring nations have further added to the body of space law. These legal norms of individual states regulate the conduct of their nationals in space activities and establish norms governing conflicts arising from such activities.

The broad picture of space law has been reflected in a number of collections of legal and political documents published in recent years. In 1982, Professor Stephen Gorove started a vast documentary collection in three open-ended loose-leaved binders, including national regulations (Binder I), selected cases, reports, and internal agreements (Binder II), and international multilateral and bilateral regulations (Binder III).[32] In 1985, two volumes of an official publication of legal, political and historical documents relating to space activities in which the Soviet Union was involved were printed in Moscow.[33] In Germany, two such collections have appeared in recent years. One was a single volume, prepared by Dr. Stephan von Welck and Dr. Renate

Platzöder under the auspices of two German institutes on foreign relations and including all essential documents of international, regional, and national character, in particular European documents.[34] More recently, Professor Karl-Heinz Böckstiegel and Dr. Marietta Benkö, under the auspices of the Institute of Air and Space Law at Cologne University, published another collection of basic documents on space law in two loose-leaved volumes. This work includes documents of international organizations dealing with outer space and documents relating to international projects, as well as the principal instruments and documents on special subjects such as telecommunications, remote sensing, environmental protection, the geostationary orbit, and disarmament.[35] All these collections of documents have created a solid basis for further exploration of the law of outer space, inviting deeper research into its nature and juridical content.

New substantive works, both collections and monographs, have also appeared during the 1980s, demonstrating the maturity of the doctrine of space law. An outstanding example is the comprehensive treatise published in 1982 on the international law of outer space by Professor Carl Q. Christol.[36] Among other important monographs are the following: E. B. Impallomeni's book on outer space and celestial bodies in international order;[37] G. Zhukov's and Y. Kolosov's *International Space Law*;[38] M. Benkö's, W. de Graaff's, and G. Reijnen's work on space law in the United Nations;[39] E. R. C. van Bogaert's vision of space law in a wider context of international law;[40] V. Vereshchetin's, E. Vasilevskaya's and E. Kamenetskaya's studies on politics and law of outer space;[41] and H. L. van Traa-Engelman's monograph on legal aspects of commercial utilization of outer space.[42] Moreover, the first textbook, officially approved as such for university students specializing in the field of international law, was written at this period by a team headed by Professor A. S. Piradov from the Diplomatic Academy of the Soviet Ministry of Foreign Affairs.[43]

In the 1980s, international non-governmental organizations have continued their efforts to draw the attention of scholars and lawmakers to new topics of space law. The International Institute of Space Law (IISL) at its latest colloquia has considered the following subjects: legal aspects of maintaining outer space for peaceful purposes; space communications, including the geostationary orbit and services utilizing it; commercialization of space activities; space law teaching and the history of space law; legal aspects of outer space environmental problems; legal principles on remote sensing; national space law and bilateral and regional space agreements; the principle of utilization of outer space for the benefit and in the interest of all states; legal status of the geostationary orbit in the light of the recent activities of ITU; recent developments in space law; and others. Moreover, a series of roundtables organized by the Scientific-Legal Liaison Committee, a joint body of the International Academy of Astronautics (IAA) and the IISL, has considered some specific issues that are of common concern to experts in space science, technology, and law, including the following: at the 1985 Roundtable, "Legal and Technical Implications of Space Stations"; at the 1989 Roundtable, "The Impact of Significant Scientific and Technological Changes in the Law of Outer Space"; and at the 1990 Roundtable, "Scientific and Legal Aspects of Management of Space Debris."[44]

The further development of space law and its doctrine is also of interest to the International Law Association (ILA), particularly through its International Space Law Committee. At its 60th Conference, held in Montreal in 1982, the ILA discussed the conflicts in the interpretation of the leading principles of the Moon Treaty of 1979. The ILA also formulated a Draft Convention on the Settlement of Space Law Disputes, which was finalized in 1988,[45] and has discussed legal aspects of the present and projected military uses of outer space[46] and "Environmental Aspects of Activities in Outer Space—State of the Law and Measures of Protection."[47]

The inputs of a number of university institutes and centers specializing in the teaching and research of space law should also not be forgotten. The Institute and Centre of Air and Space Law, McGill University at Montreal, Canada, has long dealt with space law doctrine and has organized a series of meetings to discuss current issues.[48]

In Europe, an important role has been played by the Institute of Air and Space Law of the University of Cologne in Germany. Originally established in 1925 as the Institute of Air Law in Königsberg, it added space law to its program and title in 1959, when it had already relocated to Cologne University. The involvement of the Institute in space matters was the merit of its Director, Professor Alex Meyer, one of the world's senior scholars in this field, who also founded the German *Journal of Air and Space Law (Zeitschrift für Luft- und Weltraumrecht)*.

In the 1980s another European institute, the International Institute of Air and Space Law of Leiden University, was established in the Netherlands. In addition to its teaching and research program, the Institute organizes international conferences. In 1988 a "Latin American Conference on International Air Transport and Activities in Outer Space" was organized in Mexico jointly by the Leiden Institute and the Unversidad Nacional Autonoma de México, México D. F.;[49] and in 1991 a conference was organized in Taipei, Taiwan, jointly with the Graduate Institute of European Studies of Tamkang University.

Last, but not least, the dedicated work of the University of Mississippi Law Center must be recognized for its great contribution to the development of the space law doctrine, particularly through its publication of the only journal devoted exclusively to the legal problems arising out of human activities in outer space—the *Journal of Space Law*. This periodical has for almost two decades published articles, reports on events of international interest, and reviews of books and articles.

CONCLUSION

Judge Manfred Lachs, former President of the International Court of Justice, observes in his introduction to the latest volume of the IISL Proceedings that "the Law of Outer Space has now grown to become a body of substantial principles and rules which are generally accepted. As science and technology are penetrating space at an enormous speed, much more remains to be done. Man's activities in the new dimension are both space- and earth-oriented. In both domains law must keep its eye on future development."[50] These words are equally valid for space law doctrine, which preceded space law and actively contributed to its development.

NOTES

1. *Space Law: A Symposium*, 85th Congress, 2nd Session, December 31, 1958, Washington, Government Printing Office, 1959, p. v.

2. See, for example, Vladimír Mandl, *Letecké právo (Air Law)*, Pilsen, 1928.

3. Vladimír Mandl, *Das Weltraum-Recht: Ein Problem der Raumfahrt*, Mannheim/Berlin/Leipzig, J. Bensheimer, 1932.

4. Vladimír Mandl, *Problém mezihvezdné dopravy (The Problem of Interstellar Transport)*, Prague, 1932.

5. Mandl, *supra* note 3, p. 33. (Translated from German by the author of this chapter.)

6. John Cobb Cooper's address was reprinted in *Space Law: A Symposium, supra* note 1, pp. 1-7.

7. John Cobb Cooper, "The Problem of a Definition of 'Airspace'," in *A Memorandum for the IXth Annual Congress of the International Astronautical Federation*. Reprinted in *Space Law: A Symposium, supra* note 1, pp. 403-409. Cooper's final position can be found in his paper "The Upper Airspace Boundary Question," in *Proceedings of the Sixth Colloquium on the Law of Outer Space*, Vienna, Springer Verlag, 1963, p. 6, and in his article "Backgrounds of International Public Air Law," in *Yearbook of Air and Space Law (Annuaire de Droit Aérien et Spatial*), Montreal, McGill University Press, 1967, p. 26.

8. Alex Meyer, "Legal Problems of Flight in Outer Space," reprinted in *Legal Problems of Space Exploration: A Symposium*, prepared for the Committee on Aeronautical and Space Sciences, U.S. Senate, by the Library of Congress Legislative Reference Service, March 22, 1961, Washington, 1961, pp. 9-19.

9. Alex Meyer, "Legal Problems of Outer Space," in *Space Exploration and Applications*, vol. 2 (Vienna, August 14-27, 1968), New York, United Nations, 1969, p. 1,135.

10. Oscar Schachter, "Who Owns the Universe?" reprinted in *Space Law: A Symposium, supra* note 1, p. 17.

11. Myres S. McDougal and Leon Lipson, "Perspectives for a Law of Outer Space," reprinted in *Space Law: A Symposium, supra* note 1, pp. 381-402.

12. Eugène Pépin, "Space Penetration," address in April 1958 to the Annual Meeting of the American Society of International Law, reprinted in *Space Law: A Symposium, supra* note 1, pp. 284-290.

13. See Rolando Quadri, "Droit international cosmique," *Recueil des Cours*, Vol. 98, The Hague, 1959, pp. 505-598, particularly Chapter 2. See also Charles Chaumont, "Les perspectives que doit adopter le droit de l'espace," *Revue de Droit Contemporain*, Paris, 7e année, No. 2 (December 1960), pp. 5-12.

14. Gyula Gál, *Space Law*, Budapest, Akadémiai Kiadó, 1969, p. 106 (originally published in Hungarian as *Világürjog*, Budapest, 1964).

15. Nicolas Mateesco Matte, *Deux Frontières Invisibles: De la Mer Territoriale à l'Air "Territorial,"* Paris, Editions A. Pédone, 1965; see particularly pp. 157-240.

16. *Supra* note 12, p. 287.

17. I. H. Ph. de Rode-Verschoor, "The Responsibility of the States for the Damage Caused by the Launched Space-Bodies," reprinted in *Space Law: A Symposium, supra* note 1, p. 434.

18. Andrew G. Haley, "Law of Outer Space—Radio Controls Urgently Needed," reprinted in *Space Law: A Symposium, supra* note 1, pp. 458-465.

19. Eugène Pépin, "Legal Problems Created by the Sputnik," lecture given on November 6, 1957, to the Canadian Bar Association, reprinted in *Legal Problems of Space Exploration: A Symposium, supra* note 8, p. 187.

20. McDougal and Lipson, *supra* note 11, p. 400.

21. Welf Heinrich, Prince of Hanover, *Air Law and Space*, reprinted in *Space Law: A Symposium, supra* note 1, pp. 18-76.

22. Andrew G. Haley, *Space Law and Government*, New York, Meredith Publishing Company, 1963, pp. xv, 394, 413.

23. See *Legal Problems of Space Exploration: A Symposium, supra* note 8, pp. 1,037-1,218.

24. Ye. A. Korovin, "International Status of Cosmic Space," reprinted in *Legal Problems of Space Exploration: A Symposium, supra* note 8, pp. 1,062-1,071.

25. ESA has declared its acceptance of three agreements and EUTELSAT of one. "Status of Outer Space Treaties: Informal list prepared by the United Nations Secretariat for the needs of the COPUOS Legal Subcommittee," New York, March 1991, p. 8.

26. *Annuaire de l'Institut de Droit International*, Session de Bruxelles, Septembre 1963, vol. 2, Paris, Pedone, 1963, pp. 36-364.

27. The International Law Association, *Report of the Forty-seventh Conference* (Dubrovnik), Cambridge, Compton, 1956, pp. 1-13 and Annex II, pp. 18-21.

28. Eugène Pépin, *History of the International Institute of Space Law of the International Astronautical Federation (1958-1982)*, New York, American Institute of Aeronautics and Astronautics, 1982.

29. Rolando Quadri, *supra* note 13. Daniel Goedhuis, "Conflicts of Law and Divergencies in the Legal Regimes of Air Space and Outer Space," *Recueil des Cours*, Vol. 109, 1963, pp. 257-346. Manfred Lachs, "The International Law of Outer Space," *Recueil des Cours*, Vol. 113, 1964, pp. 1-115. Guennady P. Zhukov, "Tendences contemporaines du développement du droit spatial international," *Recueil des Cours*, Vol. 161, 1978, pp. 229-328. Nicolas M. Matte, "Aerospace Law: Telecommunications Satellites," *Recueil des Cours*, Vol. 166, 1980, pp. 119-249. Marco G. Marcoff, "Sources du droit international de l'espace," *Recueil des Cours*, Vol. 168, 1980, pp. 9-121. Daniel Goedhuis, "The Problems of the Frontiers of Outer Space and Air Space," *Recueil des Cours*, Vol. 174, 1982, pp. 367-407. Stephen Gorove, "International Space Law in Perspective—Some Major Issues, Trends and Alternatives," *Recueil des Cours*, Vol. 181, 1983, pp. 349-409.

30. Philip C. Jessup and Howard J. Taubenfeld, *Controls for Outer Space and the Antarctic Analogy*, New York, Columbia University Press, 1959. Myres S. McDougal, Harold D. Laswell and Ivan A. Vlasic, *Law and Public Order in Space*, New Haven, Yale University Press, 1963. Nicolas Mateesco Matte, *Traité de Droit Aérien-Aéronautique: Evolution—Problèmes Spatiaux*, Paris, Editions A. Pédone, 1964; published in English as *Aerospace Law*, Sweet and Maxwell, 1969. C. Wilfred Jenks, *Space Law*, London, Stevens and Sons, 1965. Carl Q. Christol, *The International Law of Outer Space*, Newport, RI, Naval War College, International Law Studies 1962, Navpers 15031, vol. 55, Washington, Government Printing Office, 1966. G. P. Zhukov, *Kosmicheskoe Pravo*, Moscow, International Relations, 1966; published in German, H. P. Kehrberger (ed.), *Weltraumrecht*, Berlin, Berlin Verlag, 1968. S. Houston Lay and Howard J. Taubenfeld, *The Law Relating to Activities of Man in Space*, Chicago, University of Chicago Press, 1970. Manfred Lachs, *The Law of Outer Space: An Experience in Contemporary Law-Making*, Leiden, A. W. Sijthoff, 1972. Marco G. Marcoff, *Traité de Droit International Publique de l'Espace*, Fribourg, Switzerland, Editions Universitaires, 1973. Manuel Augusto Ferrer, *Derecho Espacial*, Buenos Aires, 1976. Stephen Gorove, *Space Law: Its Challenges and Prospects*, Leiden, A. W. Sijthoff, 1977. V. S. Vereshchetin, *Mezhdunarodnoe sotrudnichestvo v kosmose (International Cooperation in Outer Space)*, Moscow, Nauka, 1977.

31. *Manual on Space Law*, compiled and edited by N. Jasentuliyana and Roy S. K. Lee, Dobbs Ferry, NY, Sijthoff and Noordhoff, Alphen an den Rijn, Oceana Publications, vols. 1 and 2, 1979, vols. 3 and 4, 1981.

32. Stephen Gorove (ed.), *United States Space Law, National and International Regulation*, New York/London/Rome, Oceana Publications, 1982 and following years.

33. *Bor'ba SSSR za mirnoe ispol'zovanie kosmosa 1957-1985* (*The Struggle of the USSR for the Peaceful Utilization of Space 1957-1985*), documents and materials in two volumes, Moscow, Publishing House of Political Literature, 1985.

34. Stephan Frhr. von Welck and Renate Platzöder, *Weltraumrecht* (*Law of Outer Space*), textsammlung, Baden-Baden, Nomos Verlagsgesellschaft, 1987.

35. Karl-Heinz Böckstiegel and Marietta Benkö (eds.), *Space Law, Basic Legal Documents*, Dordrecht/Boston/London, Martinus Nijhoff Publishers, 1990.

36. Carl Q. Christol, *The Modern International Law of Outer Space*, New York/Oxford/Toronto/Sydney/Paris/Frankfurt, Pergamon Press, 1982.

37. Elisabeth Back Impallomeni, *Spazio cosmico e corpi celesti nell'ordinamento internazionale*, Padua, Cedam, 1983.

38. Guennady Zhukov and Yuri Kolosov, *International Space Law*, New York, Praeger Publishers, 1984.

39. Marietta Benkö, Willem de Graaff, and Gijsbertha C. M. Reijnen, *Space Law in the United Nations*, Dordrecht/Boston/Lancaster, Martinus Nijhoff Publishers, 1985.

40. E. R. C. van Bogaert, *Aspects of Space Law*, Deventer, Kluwer Law and Taxation Publishers, 1986.

41. V. Vereshchetin, E. Vasilevskaya, and E. Kamenetskaya, *Outer Space Politics and Law*, Moscow, Progress Publishing House, 1987.

42. Hanneke Louise van Traa-Engelman, *Commercial Utilization of Outer Space—Legal Aspects*, Rotterdam, 1989.

43. A. S. Piradov (ed.), *Mezhdunarodnoe kosmicheskoe pravo/International Space Law*, Moscow, International Relations Publishing house, 1985.

44. *Proceedings of the 28th Colloquium on the Law of Outer Space* (Stockholm 1985), New York, AIAA, pp. 259-289; *Proceedings of the 32nd Colloquium on the*

Law of Outer Space (Torremolinos-Malaga, Spain, 1989), Washington, AIAA, pp. 461-480; *Proceedings of the 33rd Colloquium on the Law of outer Space* (Dresden 1990), Washington, AIAA, pp. 399-428.

45. ILA, *Report of the 60th Conference* (Montreal 1982), Cambrian News, pp. 12, 479-530. See also Space Law Committee Report containing a Convention on the Settlement of Space Law Disputes (First Draft) prepared by Professor Karl-Heinz Böckstiegel, Rapporteur of the Committee, in ILA, *Report of the 61st Conference* (Paris 1984), Cambrian News, pp. 325-355.

46. ILA, *Report of the 61st Conference, supra* note 45, pp. 356-375; and *Report of the 62nd Conference* (Seoul 1986), Cambrian News, pp. 385-408.

47. ILA, *Report of the 63rd Conference* (Warsaw 1988), Cambrian News, pp. 282-380.

48. *Annals of Air and Space Law*, Nicholas Mateesco Matte (editor-in-chief), Toronto, Carswell; 15 volumes of the Annals have been published from 1976 to 1990.

49. *Conferencia Latinoamericana sobre Transporte Aéreo Internacional y Actividades en el Espacio Ultraterrestre (Latin American Conference on International Air Transport and Activities in Outer Space)*, proceedings published by the International Institute of Air and Space Law, Leiden University Faculty of Law, 1989.

50. *Proceedings of the 33rd Colloquium on the Law of Outer Space* (Dresden 1990), Washington, AIAA, p. v.

3

The Lawmaking Process in the United Nations

Nandasiri Jasentuliyana

Since the beginning of the space age, it has been recognized that this new frontier lies outside the bounds of previous international law. In the past, nations drew up rules and regulations to govern international relations in such areas as shipping and aviation long after national practices had been established. International law therefore generally amounted to a codification of existing practices that had gained international acceptance. International space law, on the other hand, has been quickly elaborated through an imaginative and innovative effort at international legislation within the United Nations.

Since the development of space activities requires international sharing of the orbital domain and at least some global coordination of activities, it is not surprising that from the beginning of the space age the United Nations has been the focal point for the development of space law, in keeping with its general mandate to "maintain international peace and security" and to encourage "progressive development of international law and its codification."

In contrast to many other fields of international law, a well-defined mechanism and procedure has evolved in the United Nations for the elaboration of treaty law dealing with space and space activities. This evolution began in 1958, following the launching of the first Sputnik, when the General Assembly established a Committee on the Peaceful Uses of Outer Space (COPUOS).[1] The original membership of 24 states has over the years increased to 53.[2]

THE LAWMAKING PROCESS

The main steps in the process of elaborating space law in the United Nations are (1) examinations and discussions of proposed texts in the annual meetings of the Legal Subcommittee of the Outer Space Committee;

(2) further consideration and endorsement in the Committee; (3) endorsement by a main committee of the General Assembly, currently the Special Political Committee; and (4) approval by the General Assembly. The Subcommittee has the same membership as the Committee, while the Special Political Committee has the full 166-country membership of the General Assembly. At any given session of the Subcommittee and Committee, a number of treaty instruments on different aspects of space law are generally under consideration, and even each body submits annual reports on its progress—or lack of progress—to the next senior body, offering the senior body the opportunity to give guidance on the preparation of the treaty in question for the next session. This supervisory function is particularly significant when exercised by the General Assembly with its broader and higher-level representation of member states. When appropriate, the Committee may ask the Scientific and Technical Subcommittee to examine technical aspects of a legal issue and to submit its views to the Legal Subcommittee, allowing interaction between scientists, lawyers, and diplomats.

The process of drafting is necessarily detailed, laborious, and time-consuming, involving formal statements of position, general discussions, detailed negotiations, editorial review, and most important, numerous informal consultations which allow delegations to make compromises without having to formally depart from stated positions. The informal negotiations are responsible for much of the progress made, particularly on politically sensitive issues that are often crucial to the treaty negotiation as a whole. These informal negotiations have the disadvantage, of course, that the *travaux préparatoires* of many United Nations treaties do not reflect fully the negotiations involved. Nevertheless, this mechanism has proven successful in the negotiation of the United Nations space treaties and agreements.

The period between the annual sessions is often used not only for national assessment and policy-making with respect to the negotiations but also for consultations among governments to resolve disagreements. United Nations space lawmaking is thus a continuous process punctuated by formal meetings, and the total duration of the process for a particular treaty is indefinite. In part this is a consequence of the informal rule that all decisions in the Outer Space Committee and its subsidiary bodies are made by consensus. After the text of a treaty has been agreed upon by consensus in the Committee, the General Assembly adopts a resolution containing the agreed text and recommends it to states for their approval. Each state can then decide individually whether to sign, ratify, or accede to the treaty, which comes into force among the ratifying and acceding states in accordance with its provisions.

Following this well-established process, the United Nations has produced five international treaties,[3] all of which have entered into force. The Outer Space Treaty of 1967,[4] the first to be completed, now has 91 parties; the Rescue Agreement of 1968[5] has 80 parties; the Liability Convention of 1972[6] has 73 parties; the Registration Convention of 1976[7] has 36 parties; and the Moon Agreement of 1984[8] has eight parties. The first three of these instruments have been signed by 100 or more countries—an impressive achievement, especially when compared with recent efforts in other fields, such as international trade law where three treaties and a protocol have been concluded without any achieving the ratifications necessary to enter into force.

Thus the United Nations, in little more than two decades of space lawmaking, has achieved substantial results compared to many other branches of international law. Without the United Nations, it is unlikely that a legal framework for space activities could have been established in such an expeditious manner, leaving open the possibility of conflict and vested interests which could have hindered the peaceful exploration and use of space.

Nevertheless, this process has been criticized as slow and cumbersome and yielding results that do not effectively control undesirable uses of space. Yet considering the technical complexity and the political importance of the issues, the negotiations must be handled in a manner that allows technical experts, governmental representatives, and lawyers specializing in the field to interact in the treaty-making process. This would not have been possible in strictly legal bodies such as the intergovernmental International Law Commission or the non-governmental International Law Association. It required a body such as the Outer Space Committee, which allowed for technical and political inputs as well as inputs from lawyers with expertise in space activities. The procedure established in the United Nations also enables all countries, including small and developing countries, to participate in the elaboration of space law, thereby promoting the ratification and implementation of treaties by a maximum number of countries.

While these institutional arrangements have certainly had an important effect on the results of the lawmaking process, the quality of the delegates in the Outer Space Committee has also been an important factor in the successes and failures of its work. The participation of such individuals as Ambassador Arthur Goldberg, who later became a U.S. Supreme Court Justice; Ambassador Platon Morozov of the Soviet Union, who later became a Judge of the International Court of Justice (ICJ); Manfred Lachs of Poland, who chaired the Legal Subcommittee before becoming a Judge of the ICJ; and several others of similar standing was in no small measure responsible for the Committee's success during its early years. The fact that in more recent years the quality of representation has been uneven and that some states have sent representatives who lack the necessary expertise and standing and are often lower-ranking diplomats may be related to the slower progress of the current work. This does not imply that generalist government representatives are incompetent, but they do have difficulties in following the subject in depth because they have to cover a variety of other unrelated and simultaneous activities in the United Nations. They must generally operate within the constraints of restricted briefs requiring consultations with their capitals on every detail; and they have little flexibility to negotiate on their own, often slowing down the process, which can in turn lead to further complications. This is particularly true of many developing country representatives, though the problem is not confined to them. When the level of representation falls, the debates have a tendency to degenerate into unproductive and irrelevant polemics. Constructive progress in further space lawmaking would therefore benefit from efforts to keep the quality of participation high, with a balance of generalist diplomats on the one hand and technical and legal experts on the other. In achieving this balance, consideration must certainly be given to the limited capacities of many countries to participate on an expert level in the preparation of such treaties.

THE CONSENSUS PRINCIPLE

The United Nations achievements in space lawmaking have been attributed to the adoption of the principle of "consensus" as the basis of decision-making in the Outer Space Committee, which was the first United Nations standing body—and perhaps still the only one—to use this procedure in its purest form. All of the space treaties elaborated in the United Nations were negotiated and adopted by consensus. It can be argued that the principle can cause and has caused long drawn-out negotiations, that any single state can prevent the adoption of a treaty, and that the principle encourages polarization of positions which are difficult to reconcile without substantial delay.

In practice, however, the consensus rule has actually encouraged compromise. Since differences cannot be resolved by voting, onerous efforts have been made in the negotiations to accommodate a range of positions. Compromises were necessary and trade-offs had to be made on all sides. It seems clear that the consensus decision-making rule accounts for the wide acceptance of the space treaties since they were elaborated to take into account the full range of views and interests, in particular those of the major space powers without whose agreement the legal rules would have little significance. In short, the consensus rule has ensured that the treaties drafted in the United Nations were acceptable not only to the majority of non-space powers but also to all of the space powers. The Outer Space Committee's use of the consensus rule has set a precedent which was later followed, with minor modifications, by other negotiating bodies such as the United Nations Conference on Trade and Development (UNCTAD) and the United Nations Conference on the Law of the Sea (UNCLOS).

Of major consequence to the future of space lawmaking in the United Nations is the continuing challenge, explicit or implicit, to the consensus principle on the grounds that it can block the wishes of a majority of countries, principally of the Third World. The challenge here is that on the one hand, it is obvious that no viable legal regime for space can be established without the agreement of the major space powers; on the other hand, it is equally obvious that a regime imposed by the current space powers which neglected the needs of others would eventually be rejected by subsequent space-active countries, thus jeopardizing the orderly development and use of space activities by all countries.

As the decision-making procedure in international legislation evolves, what may emerge is the use of a qualified consensus rule whereby voting is used as a last resort in cases where a few dissenters from consensus are considered an unreasonable and isolated or unimportant minority. Whether this will be an acceptable and workable modification to the well-established procedure in the Outer Space Committee remains to be seen.

ACCOMMODATING POLITICAL AND LEGAL CONCERNS

With regard to criticisms of the quality of the space treaties, it must be kept in mind that their main objective is the maintenance of international peace and security and the promotion of international cooperation and understanding. The international legal principles in these treaties constitute a contribution to that objective which, though limited in scope, is by no means negligible. Consider for example the space treaty provisions relating to arms control, non-appropriation of space, freedom of exploration, liability for damages, safety and rescue of astronauts and spacecraft, prevention of harmful interference with space activities and the environment, notification and registration of space activities, and the settlement of disputes, to mention only a few of the major issues covered in these treaties.

Although the foundation of space law has thus been solidly laid in the space treaties elaborated in the United Nations, it is certainly imperfect and incomplete as a result of the political compromises required and the limited technological capabilities at the time of adoption of the treaties. The body of space law will therefore need to be regularly reassessed and revised to reflect new political developments and technological progress.

Some scholars have pointed out specific deficiencies in the space treaties, including poorly drafted provisions that are open to varying interpretations.[9] Limitations in scope or clarity, however, are most often rooted in political factors rather than carelessness or incompetence. While it is important to work toward juridical purity, legal perfectionism which ignores political reality would result in the elaboration of magnificent texts which would never come into force. Instead, it is important to continue to find the right balance between political requirements and possibilities and the need for precise legal wording.

The most difficult and complex legal issues that have been brought to the United Nations for negotiation over the years have been those in which space technology impinges directly on national political and economic interests. This has happened particularly in two cases: in the potential use of satellites for broadcasting television programs directly to individual receivers in other countries,[10] and in the use of remote sensing satellites for collecting economically useful information on the natural resources of other countries.

In the case of direct broadcasting satellites, the Committee struggled for many years with the competing principles of free flow of information and the rights of countries to develop and protect their own cultures, without being able to resolve the differences. In 1982, after the debate had apparently reached a total impasse, the question was taken out of the Committee and into the General Assembly, where a resolution was passed by majority vote recognizing the principle of the free flow of information but making the establishment of international television broadcasting by satellite conditional on agreements or arrangements with the receiving country—a modified version of prior consent. This resolution was passed by a large majority of socialist and developing countries over the objections of a number of Western countries. It should be noted that this confrontation occurred at a time when East-West relations and North-South relations were particularly strained. This issue has been the only one on which the Committee's normal consensus procedures have distinctly failed.[11] In 1972, the same debate had taken place in UNESCO with these groups of states taking similarly distinct positions, resulting in the adoption by majority vote of a Declaration of Guiding Principles on the Use of Satellite Broadcasting for the Free Flow of Information, the Spread of Education, and Greater Cultural Exchange.

On the issue of remote sensing, the Committee persisted for 13 years, in spite of periods of apparent impasse, in trying to reach consensus on the conflict between, on the one hand, the freedom of space activities and the general interest in acquiring global environmental and resource data, and on the other hand, the rights of countries to control their natural resources. Finally, in 1986, in the context of generally improving international relations, consensus was reached on a set of principles including a general right to collect data globally, combined with the right of all states to have access to any data collected over their territories by other states.[12]

In the cases of both direct broadcasting and remote sensing, the conflict was intensified in the early stages by fears that these new and somewhat mysterious space technologies would revolutionize television broadcasting in the first case and exploitation of natural resources in the second. As the technologies developed and as the technical and economic limitations of the applications were recognized, it became clear that the potential impact of the technologies had been somewhat exaggerated. The rapid development of cable television distribution has greatly limited the economic attractiveness and commercial viability of satellite direct broadcasting, and many of the plans for such systems have been abandoned. Similarly, satellite remote sensing is still far from commercially viable, and data from the systems are highly subsidized by the operating countries. As countries throughout the world acquired experience with remote sensing and began to understand both its advantages and its limitations, the negotiating positions of the parties gradually became more flexible and agreement was reached. It may be that in the case of direct satellite broadcasting, a few more years of patience would have produced a similar recognition of the complex realities of satellite broadcasting and a generally accepted agreement, as opposed to a disputed majority resolution with no practical effectiveness.

PENDING LEGAL ISSUES

On the more technical issue of international criteria for the safe use of nuclear power sources in outer space,[13] the Committee has made substantial progress in the last few years on a set of legal principles. Negotiations are continuing and further progress appears to be likely, allowing the General Assembly to adopt the full set of principles in the near future.

Another item still under consideration after many years is "Matters relating to the definition and/or delimitation of outer space."[14] When this question was first raised, the debate was confined to the question of where airspace ends and outer space begins, a question for which there is no clear scientific answer and no legal agreement. Nonetheless, space activities have proceeded on the general assumption that anything in orbit or beyond is in outer space. At one time, the wording was revised to refer to "the definition and/or delimitation of outer space and outer space activities," suggesting that space activities might be defined or delimited from non-space activities independent of the definition or delimitation of outer space. This reflected an interest in a "functional" approach to defining the activities covered by space law in addition to the geographic area approach of determining a spatial boundary between airspace and outer space. In 1991, the Soviet Union proposed a study of the practical issues relating to the difference between airspace and outer space, such as the legal status of an aerospace plane capable of both aerodynamic flight in the atmosphere and rocket flight in space, an approach which might help break the long impasse on this issue.

Another pending issue, discussed under the same agenda item as the definition of outer space, is that of the legal status of the geostationary orbit, an issue raised by equatorial countries which claimed sovereignty over the segment of the geostationary orbit above their territories. These sovereignty claims were, in the view of most countries, prohibited by the 1967 Treaty on Outer Space. A more recent concern relating to the geostationary orbit, of particular importance for the developing countries, is that of guaranteed access to the geostationary orbit for future communications satellites. For communications satellites to function effectively, their orbital positions and transmitting frequencies must be coordinated to ensure that the transmissions to not interfere with one another. The coordination procedures established in the International Telecommunication Union (ITU) favored existing satellites, almost all belonging to developed countries, over new satellites, including those of developing countries.[15] The developing countries have called for new procedures that would guarantee them, in practice as well as in theory, access to favorable positions and frequencies in the geostationary orbit, and ideally the right to use relatively simple and inexpensive technology, which may be less efficient in its use of orbital space and the radio-frequency spectrum, in order to give them a maximum of technological and economic self-sufficiency.

Part of the difficulty in dealing with the issue of the geostationary orbit is that it consists of both technical issues, which properly belong in the International Telecommunication Union, and political-legal issues, which belong in the Outer Space Committee. The developed countries, with their technical experts and concerns, tend to prefer the technical orientation of the ITU, while many of the developing countries, lacking technical expertise but having political concerns, tend to prefer the political-legal orientation of the United Nations. The framework for a solution that will guarantee positions for the developing countries is in the process of being worked out through the ITU, based on the results of the World Administrative Radio Conference on the geostationary orbit, which met in two sessions in 1985 and 1988. The Committee on the Peaceful Uses of Outer Space is still working on the question of elaborating general principles of international law relating to the geostationary orbit.

Following the 1986 agreement on remote sensing principles, a new item was added to the agenda of the Legal Subcommittee relating to "the principle that the exploration and utilization of outer space should be carried out for the benefit and in the interest of all states, taking into particular account the needs of developing countries." This item reflects the view of many developing countries that there is insufficient effort or obligation to ensure that space exploration and the applications of space technology benefit all countries. They hope that this agenda item, based on Article 1 of the Outer Space Treaty and on other legal instruments that call for promotion of international development, including the United Nations Charter in Articles 55 and 56, will provide a basis for drafting new legal principles to ensure the widest utilization of space technology. A draft set of principles, including principles on the transfer of technology, has been proposed by the developing countries for discussion next year.

EMERGING LEGAL ISSUES

Among the emerging issues for future discussions and negotiations, concerns over the safety of space activities, including the hazards of space debris and the need to protect the space environment,[16] have already attracted significant attention and preliminary discussions and are likely to be on the agenda in the near future.[17] Here, in view of the complex technical issues and the need to adapt to evolving technological capabilities, as well as the fact that existing space law contains general provisions that could be elaborated to address problems of space debris more specifically,[18] the United Nations might develop broad and general principles, leaving it to an international technical body to establish standards and recommended practices for states to follow.[19]

Finally, in the all-important area of the militarization of outer space,[20] the United Nations has already succeeded in adopting some basic principles of international behavior, and efforts are being made to broaden these principles to further restrain military space activities. Effective limitations on space weapons by the United Nations, however, may only be possible while they are still in a stage of development and susceptible to general prohibitions through multilateral negotiations. Once such systems are tested and deployed, effective control measures may require technically detailed and even quantitative agreements, as in the bilateral Strategic Arms Limitation Talks (SALT) or Strategic Arms Reduction Treaty (START) agreements involving sensitive information on existing weapons systems, carefully balanced limitations on such systems, and difficult questions of verification.

FUTURE DEVELOPMENT OF SPACE LAW: AN APPRAISAL

Since the establishment of the Committee on the Peaceful Uses of Outer Space, the United Nations has been the central body for the development of space law. In the development of laws and principles through its consensus process, it has provided an international forum for technical experts, diplomats, and legal scholars to exchange views and to formulate a generally accepted legal framework for space activities. Since the Committee's inception, its membership has expanded considerably, enabling it to become an essential medium not only for concluding legal agreements but also for introducing new concepts and proposals relating to space activities. The expansion in the Committee's membership and the evolution of space technology, however, also pose new challenges for the Committee.

When the Outer Space Treaty was codified, space activities were still in their very early stages, and general guiding principles were needed for this new endeavor. During the first 20 years of the Outer Space Committee, five treaties were negotiated and adopted, an unprecedented rate for treaty-making in international law. Since the adoption of the Moon Treaty, however, the legislation of space law has slowed substantially. In creating the basic legal framework for space activities, lawmakers were able to borrow from existing principles of international law, including analogies from international maritime law,[21] the Antarctic Treaty, and the Partial Test Ban Treaty. Over the last decade, however, legislating international space law has become more complex and technical. Lawmaking now focuses on specific areas of space technology and space applications rather than on the general principles of public international law.

During the past decade, moreover, an increasing number of countries have become involved in space activities, dedicating extensive economic and political resources to ensure a space capability. The increasing significance of space in terms of economic applications, commercial services, and technological spin-offs has made it more difficult to arrive at compromises and to agree on measures that would impose any restrictions on space activities. The current debates in the Legal Subcommittee on new principles to govern space activities illustrate some of the difficulties. In the discussions on nuclear power sources, for example, the United States has proposed to reopen debate on the previously negotiated and agreed text on guidelines and criteria for safe use because the technical provisions may conflict with the use of Earth swing-by techniques on nuclear-powered planetary missions such as the Galileo and Ulysses missions.

The increasing membership in the Committee and the increasing number of countries with practical interests in space also increase the difficulty in reaching agreement. In the early years of the Committee there were only two space powers, and adoption of a treaty essentially required a compromise between two countries. In the early 1970s, the debate became somewhat more complex as the developing countries became interested, adding North-South issues to the previous East-West issues. However, as the leaders among the developing countries, including Brazil, India, and Mexico, began to develop space capabilities, their interests began to diverge from those of the other developing countries while remaining distinct from the developed country space powers. The recent political break-up of the previously unified Eastern European group has further increased the number of independent views, and the decline in group solidarity among the Eastern European and developing countries has encouraged the development of more specific and divergent national positions among the Western countries. Negotiating international space law in the 1990s on the basis of consensus will require reconciliation of a wide diversity of specific national interests.

Further space legislation that goes beyond the general principles will need to be more precise and technically detailed in order to effectively regulate a sophisticated and diverse space industry. In a global forum, elaborating such laws will be difficult and time-consuming. In addition to the need to reconcile more national interests, each nation will need more time to reconcile different domestic interests. Nonetheless, there is a clear interest and desire on the part of many states to negotiate further international space law, both to promote international cooperation in space and to limit hazardous and undesirable space activities. For this purpose, the United Nations and the Committee on the Peaceful Uses of Outer Space will remain an essential forum.

The United Nations can continue to play an effective role in the development of space law as it has done in the past as long as certain requirements are accepted: states must be willing to work slowly and gradually to build a body of space law in a manner that allows effective participation by all countries; the procedures must allow for the interdisciplinary nature of space activities; the desire for juridical perfection must be reconciled with the need for politically meaningful and technically feasible principles; and there must be a willingness to balance the conflicting interests of the spacefaring nations and countries without space capabilities.

NOTES

1. The Committee on the Peaceful Uses of Outer Space was initially established as an ad hoc committee in 1958 by U.N.G.A. Res. 1348 (XIII) of December 13, 1958. It became a permanent body the following year by U.N.G.A. Res. 1472 A (XIV) of December 12, 1959. The mandate of the Committee was to review the area of international cooperation and to study practical and feasible means for giving effect to programs in the peaceful uses of outer space which could be undertaken under United Nations auspices. It was also requested to organize the exchange and dissemination of information on outer space research and the encouragement of national research programs. The Committee was also mandated to study legal problems which might arise from exploration of outer space.

2. Member states are Albania, Argentina, Australia, Austria, Belgium, Benin, Brazil, Bulgaria, Burkina Faso, Cameroon, Canada, Chad, Chile, China, Colombia, Czechoslovakia, Ecuador, Egypt, France, Germany, Hungary, India, Indonesia, Iran, Iraq, Italy, Japan, Kenya, Lebanon, Mexico, Mongolia, Morocco, Netherlands, Niger, Nigeria, Pakistan, Philippines, Poland, Portugal, Romania, Russian Federation, Sierra Leone, Sudan, Sweden, Syria, Turkey, Ukraine, United Kingdom, United States, Uruguay, Venezuela, Viet Nam and Yugoslavia.

3. See Chapter 4 of this volume by Stephen Gorove for a discussion of the provisions of these treaties.

4. Treaty on Principles Governing the Activities of States in the Exploration and Use of Outer Space, Including the Moon and Other Celestial Bodies (hereinafter Outer Space Treaty), Entered into Force Oct. 10, 1967, 18 U.S.T. 2410, T.I.A.S. No. 6347, 610 U.N.T.S. 205.

5. Agreement on the Rescue of Astronauts, the Return of Astronauts, and the Return of Objects Launched into Outer Space (hereinafter Rescue Agreement), Entered into Force Dec. 3, 1968, 19 U.S.T. 7570, T.I.A.S. No. 6599, 672 U.N.T.S. 45.

6. Convention on International Liability for Damage Caused by Space Objects (hereinafter Liability Convention), Entered into Force Sept. 1, 1972, 24 U.S.T. 2391, T.I.A.S. No. 7762, 961 U.N.T.S. 187.

7. Convention on Registration of Objects Launched into Outer Space (hereinafter Registration Convention), Entered into Force Sept. 15, 1976, 28 U.S.T. 695, T.I.A.S. No. 8480.

8. Agreement Governing the Activities of States on the Moon and Other Celestial Bodies (hereinafter Moon Treaty), Entered into Force July 11, 1984, 18 *International Legal Materials* 1434.

9. See, for example, B. Cheng, "The 1968 Astronauts Agreement or How to Make a Treaty," *Yearbook of World Affairs,* London, Stevens, 1969, p. 185.

10. See Chapter 9 of this volume by Francis Lyall.

11. V. Kopal, "Evolution of the Main Principles of Space Law in the Institutional Framework of the United Nations," *Journal of Space Law*, Vol. 12, 1984, p. 25.

12. See U.N.G.A. Res. 41/65, Jan. 22, 1987, Principles 10, 11, 12.

13. See Chapter 13 of this volume by Lubos Perek.

14. See Chapter 2 of this volume by Vladimir Kopal.

15. See Chapter 13 of this volume by Lubos Perek.

16. See Chapter 12 of this volume by He Qizhi.

17. See U.N.G.A. Res. 45/72, paragraphs 22 and 23.

18. See I. H. Ph. Diederiks-Verschoor, "The Increasing Problems of Space Debris and the Legal Solution," in *Proceedings of the 32nd Colloquium on the Law of Outer Space*, Washington, American Institute of Aeronautics and Astronautics (AIAA), 1990, pp. 77-79.

19. N. Jasentuliyana, "Space Activities and International Environmental Protection: Perspectives on the United Nations Role," in *Proceedings of the 33rd Colloquium on the Law of Outer Space*, New York, AIAA, 1991, pp. 152-154.

20. See Chapter 11 of this volume by Peter Jankowitsch.

21. See Chapter 1 of this volume by Hamilton DeSaussure.

4

Sources and Principles of Space Law

Stephen Gorove

The second half of the twentieth century witnessed the emergence of two revolutionary advances in human history. The first has been called the atomic age, and the second, which followed closely on its heels, is known as the space age. Both of these developments were brought about by major scientific and technological breakthroughs and innovations creating not only countless benefits to society but also many challenges, particularly for lawyers and policymakers who are responsible for ensuring that the events in these fields take place within the framework of law and order.

The beginnings of the space age were outward-looking, which was quite understandable because it was the first time that mankind was given an opportunity to leave the planet Earth and reach out into the unknown. Nonetheless, it was soon realized that the new technology not only provided a springboard for the exploration of outer space but also offered unique inward-looking opportunities for the improvement of the quality of life here on Earth.

The purpose of this chapter is to provide a brief overview of the emergence of space law as a new legal discipline in the wake of the spectacular achievements ushering in the space age. It will be a brief bird's eye view of both international and domestic aspects of space law in a historical, institutional, and substantive context. For the international aspects, this chapter will pinpoint the role played by the United Nations; review the provisions of the main space treaties; and provide examples of international multilateral, regional, and bilateral agreements as well as other international instruments which, together with international customary law, constitute the main sources of international space law. With respect to national law, consideration will be given to examples of U.S. space law developments, followed by examples from the gradually growing body of national space laws in other countries, mostly dealing with the establishment and operation of foreign governmental institutions dealing with space matters. In conclusion, the chapter will touch upon ongoing institutional and scholarly efforts to further the development of space law, emphasizing the importance of a multidisciplinary approach for a better understanding of the legal framework and for a successful effort to shape future policies in this increasingly vital area.

INTERNATIONAL SPACE LAW

Establishment of the United Nations Committee on Outer Space

The worldwide interest and the concern of all nations with emerging space activities manifested itself in the United Nations at an early stage. Shortly after the launch of the first artificial satellite in 1957, on the basis of a proposal by the United States and 19 other states, the United Nations General Assembly established a committee which became known as the Committee on the Peaceful Uses of Outer Space (COPUOS), consisting initially of 24 and now of 53 members.[1] The Committee's early purpose was to determine the practical and feasible ways in which space-related programs could be appropriately undertaken under United Nations auspices and to study the legal problems that might arise from the exploration and use of outer space.

Because of the close interrelationship between scientific and legal developments, the Committee created two standing subcommittees of the whole, the Scientific and Technical Subcommittee and the Legal Subcommittee, for the drafting of legal regulations. Guided by the principle of consensus in its decisions, the Committee has succeeded in drafting five international agreements, all of which are currently in force, although their significance and the number of states adhering to each agreement differ markedly. The greatest support has been given to the 1967 Outer Space Treaty,[2] and the least adherence to the 1979 Moon Agreement,[3] which lacks, in particular, the support of the spacefaring nations. The other treaties elaborated by the United Nations include the 1968 Rescue Agreement,[4] the 1972 Liability Convention,[5] and the 1975 Registration Convention.[6]

The Outer Space Treaty

Undoubtedly the most important international space convention, or what may be termed the Magna Carta of international space law, is the Outer Space Treaty of 1967, which built on several principles already enunciated in 1963 in the Declaration of Legal Principles Governing the Activities of States in the Exploration and Use of Outer Space. While the Treaty is predicated on the cardinal principle of freedom of exploration and use of outer space, encompassing the freedom of scientific investigation and free access to all areas of celestial bodies, a closer glance at its provisions reveals that this broad freedom is carefully limited by a number of both general and specific provisions. For instance, the freedom of exploration and use entails the requirement that the exploration and use must be carried out for the benefit and in the interests of all countries, without discrimination of any kind, on a basis of equality, in accordance with international law, including the Charter of the United Nations, and in the interest of maintaining international peace and security and promoting international cooperation and understanding. The freedom of access to celestial bodies is subject to a ban on national appropriation, certain arms control provisions, the obligation to use the Moon and other celestial bodies exclusively for peaceful purposes, the duty to avoid harmful contamination and adverse changes in the environment of the Earth resulting from the introduction of extraterrestrial matter, and the requirement of reciprocal access to installations on the Moon and other celestial bodies with reasonable advance notice.

In some of its other highlights, the Outer Space Treaty declares astronauts to be the envoys of mankind who are to be assisted in case of emergency or distress. It also ties jurisdiction and control of space objects to the state of registry, establishes international responsibility for national activities in outer space, and makes the launching state internationally liable for damage caused by space objects.

The Rescue Agreement

The Outer Space Treaty was not expected to remain the sole instrument governing human activities in the exploration and use of outer space. It was envisaged that the basic principles set forth in the Treaty would be further elaborated and specifics provided for their implementation. As human space flight developed, the increasing concern, particularly by the spacefaring nations, about assistance to astronauts in distress and the return of space objects led to the drafting of the Rescue Agreement. Some of the Agreement's key provisions require cooperation between the launching authority and another state to effect a prompt rescue of the personnel of a spacecraft which, owing to accident, distress, emergency, or unintended landing, lands in territory under the jurisdiction of the latter state. Other stipulations provide for assistance in search and rescue operations to personnel who have come down on the high seas or in any other place not under the jurisdiction of any state and call for their safe and prompt return to the launching authority. In addition, the agreement imposes the obligation on a state where a space object has been discovered to take practicable steps, upon request of the launching authority, to recover and return such object to that authority.

The Liability Convention

The third major international treaty, the Liability Convention, provides for rules governing international liability for damage caused by space objects and for a procedure for the presentation and settlement of claims. One of the valuable contributions of the Convention to the development of space law has been to provide for two sets of complete definitions of vital terms. The concept of damage, which assumes central significance in cases of liability, is defined to mean loss of life, personal injury, or other impairment of health, or loss of or damage to property of states or of persons, natural or juridical, or property of international intergovernmental organizations. Another crucial definition identifies the launching state as a state which launches or procures the launching of a space object, as well as a state from whose territory or facility a space object is launched. In addition, two partial definitions make it clear that the term "launching" includes attempted launching, and that a "space object" includes component parts of a space object as well as its launch vehicle and parts thereof.

As to degrees of liability, the Convention distinguishes absolute liability for damage caused on the surface of the Earth or to an aircraft in flight, from liability based upon fault when the damage occurs in space. The Convention provides for joint and several liability in case of a joint launching and stipulates a recommendatory award unless the parties agree otherwise. The amount of compensation must be determined in accordance with international law and the principles of justice and equity, so as to restore the aggrieved party to the condition which would have existed if the damage had not occurred.

The Registration Convention

The fourth major space treaty, the Registration Convention, requires launching states to register their launched objects in an appropriate national register and also requires them to furnish certain data on such launchings to the United Nations Secretary-General, who is to maintain a central register of such objects and related information on a mandatory basis. The Convention also calls upon states possessing space monitoring and tracking facilities to provide assistance in the identification of space objects which cause damage.

The Moon Agreement

It took the Committee on the Peaceful Uses of Outer Space approximately 10 years to draft the provisions of the Moon Agreement, which, in addition to restating some of the provisions of the Outer Space Treaty, has several novel stipulations, including those on arms control, environmental protection, and natural resources. The Moon Agreement declares the Moon and its natural resources to be the common heritage of mankind and requires states to establish an international regime to govern the exploitation of the Moon's natural resources as such exploitation is about to become feasible. Concerns mostly with respect to the common heritage provision have prevented U.S. adherence to the Moon Agreement, which has also failed to receive endorsement from the other spacefaring nations.

Other United Nations Legal Principles and Resolutions

Apart from the five major international agreements, the United Nations Committee has also succeeded in elaborating a set of principles to guide states in civilian remote sensing of the Earth from space.[7] While the principles on remote sensing were unanimously approved by the General Assembly, another set of principles, on direct television broadcasting by satellites and predicated on prior consent, failed to obtain unanimous support, due largely to lack of U.S. support, though it was approved by a wide margin.[8] In addition to these two sets of principles, there were a number of other space-related resolutions and other international instruments, including those of the Second United Nations Conference on the Exploration and Peaceful Uses of Outer Space (UNISPACE 82), which must be kept in mind when tracing the broad development of space law.

The Specialized Agencies

If one turns from the United Nations and looks at the panorama of the specialized agencies within the United Nations system, practically all of them have been interested in applications of space technology within their fields of competence.[9] The International Civil Aviation Organization, for instance, has been interested in the use of space technology for air navigation. The World Bank is concerned with the contribution of space technology to the development process that the Bank is promoting in member countries. The World Meteorological Organization supports and coordinates the use of satellites for weather forecasting. UNESCO has promoted the use of satellites for education, telecommunications, remote sensing, and environmental monitoring. Normally, these activities of the specialized agencies have little bearing on the development of space law, though an occasional resolution or activity by these agencies may entail legal ramifications and result indirectly in lawmaking. For instance, the World Intellectual Property Organization, together with UNESCO, was instrumental in organizing a conference in 1974 which adopted the Convention Relating to the Distribution of Programme-Carrying Signals Transmitted by Satellite.

However, there is one specialized agency, the International Telecommunication Union (ITU), which has played and continues to play an important role affecting not only terrestrial but also space communications. In 1971, a resolution was passed by the World Administrative Radio Conference (WARC) for Space Telecommunications, which convened under the auspices of the ITU, declaring that all countries were to have "equal rights" in the use of both the radio frequencies allocated to various space communication services and the geostationary satellite orbit for these services.[10] The same resolution also declared that the radio-frequency spectrum and the geostationary satellite orbit were "limited natural resources," which were to be "most effectively and economically used." While WARC resolutions were recommendatory in nature, the principle of "equitable access" found its way into the legally binding 1973 ITU Convention[11] and its 1982 revision.[12] At the same time, subsequent WARCs held in 1977, 1979, 1985, and 1988 witnessed a continuing and fairly successful effort on the part of developing nations to replace the "first-come-first-served" principle, in use since the beginning of the space age, with a priori planning and thereby guarantee equitable access by all countries to the geostationary orbit and the space services utilizing it.[13]

International Organizational and Other Legal Agreements

In addition to the United Nations and its specialized agencies, there are a growing number of major intergovernmental space organizations whose organizational instruments constitute significant additions to the expanding scope of international space law. Among such entities are the European Space Agency (ESA),[14] the International Telecommunications Satellite Organization (INTELSAT),[15] the International Organization of Space Communications (INTERSPUTNIK),[16] the Council on International Co-operation in the Study and Utilization of Outer Space (INTERCOSMOS),[17] the International Maritime Satellite Organization (INMARSAT),[18] the Arab Satellite Communication Organization (ARABSAT),[19] the European Telecommunications Satellite Organization (EUTELSAT),[20] and the European Organization for the Exploitation of Meteorological Satellites (EUMETSAT).[21]

In addition to the multilateral agreements establishing these major international space organizations, there are other significant multilateral agreements which relate to outer space. Examples include the Limited Test Ban Treaty,[22] the Convention on the Prohibition of Military or Any Other Hostile Use of Environmental Modification Techniques,[23] the Convention Relating to the Distribution of Programme-Carrying Signals Transmitted by Satellite,[24] and the recent United States/International Space Station Agreement.[25]

By far the greatest number of agreements dealing with outer space fall within the bilateral domain. For instance, apart from the well known Anti-Ballistic Missile (ABM) Treaty with the Soviet Union,[26] the United States is a party to over a thousand bilateral international agreements, memoranda of understanding, and exchanges of notes dealing with cooperative projects, reimbursable launchings, tracking and data acquisition facilities, personnel exchanges, defense, and other matters.[27] In addition to the United States, the Soviet Union, France, Great Britain, China, Japan, and other countries have also concluded scores of bilateral space agreements. For instance, Germany cooperates bilaterally with a number of developing countries including China, Argentina, Brazil, India, and Indonesia. Some of these agreements concern cooperation in scientific research and technological development relating to space, while others deal with satellite communication, remote sensing, environmental cooperation, and other applications.

International Customary Space Law

Rounding out the ever-growing body of international space law is international customary space law, an early manifestation of which has been acceptance by the international community of the practice to regard the area where artificial satellites orbit the earth and the region beyond it as outer space.

DOMESTIC SPACE LAW

United States Space Law

While the United States lent its full support to the worldwide effort for the establishment of international organizations and the drafting of a set of new international rules to govern the emerging human activities in outer space, it also took a bold step by enacting the first national legislation concerning outer space. The National Aeronautics and Space Act (NASA Act) of 1958,[28] passed by the U.S. Congress a year after the launch of Sputnik, was a landmark law in which the United States pledged that its activities in space would be devoted to peaceful purposes and for the benefit for all mankind.[29] The Act established the National Aeronautics and Space Administration (NASA) to plan, direct, and conduct space activities.[30]

The NASA Act addressed many legal issues, and additional enactments dealt with liability insurance and indemnification, administrative claims and litigation, NASA's relationships with other federal agencies, and scores of other issues. In addition, existing laws were amended and applied to space activities.[31]

The highlights of U.S. domestic legislation over the years include the Communications Satellite Act of 1962,[32] which recognized the increasing importance and vital role of space telecommunications and ensured subsequent U.S. participation in both the INTELSAT and INMARSAT systems through the Communications Satellite Corporation, a private corporation subject to governmental regulation. Congress also took action by amending extant patent and trademark laws[33] and passed an "inventions in outer space" act to deal with issues associated with the United States/International Space Station project.[34] The purpose of another major law, the Land Remote-Sensing Commercialization Act of 1984,[35] was to create a framework for phased commercialization of remote sensing, while assuring continuous data availability to the federal government and providing for a transition from government operation to private, commercial operation. Also in 1984, in order to regulate private satellite launching and associated services, Congress enacted the 1984 Commercial Space Launch Act,[36] and several years later, for the purpose of facilitating the private acquisition of government launching equipment and services, the Commercial Space Launch Act Amendments of 1988 was passed.[37]

The development of domestic space law and policy has not been the sole prerogative of the legislative branch of the government; an increasingly large share has been relegated to the executive branch. There are more than 18 federal governmental entities participating in or concerned with space activities, with different roles in space law and policy-making. For instance, delegates from some agencies may represent the United States in international negotiations with other governments on space issues and may participate in the work of international organizations involved in space. They may represent the administration in congressional hearings or advise the President and coordinate executive branch policies in space matters. Other departments may be concerned not with law but with the application and development of space technology for the management of natural resources, environmental monitoring, satellite communications, the Strategic Defense Initiative, or the National Aerospace Plane Program. Yet other agencies may engage solely in scientific research or disseminate information on space achievements.

From the viewpoint of actual lawmaking, in particular the drafting of rules and regulations, the lion's share of the work appears to fall to NASA, though other agencies also play an important role. The Federal Communications Commission, for instance, authorizes the construction and launch of telecommunications satellites and was represented in the U.S. delegation to the World Administrative Radio Conference on the Use of the Geostationary Orbit and the Planning of the Space Services Utilizing It (WARC-ORB). The Department of Commerce's National Oceanic and Atmospheric Administration provides satellite data services, while its National Telecommunications and Information Administration is the principal telecommunications adviser to the President. The Department of Transportation, through its Office of Commercial Space Transportation, regulates private commercial launches and establishes insurance as well as third-party liability requirements. These rules, as well as those issued by other departments and agencies, appear in the Code of Federal Regulations.

The interdisciplinary nature of the use of space-based technology is reflected not only in the relevance of space activities to the work of various federal agencies but also in the multiple facets of NASA's activities. These activities include, for instance, the study of the universe, the use of space technology for solving practical problems on Earth, and the research and development needed to expand the human presence beyond the Earth into the solar system.

Adding to the framework of national laws and regulations, including many presidential executive orders, pronouncements, policy statements, directives, and determinations, are occasional state laws concerning space-related activities. Finally, there is a growing body of domestic case law which has increasing importance for the development of space law. While a large number of these cases deal with telecommunications and relate to proceedings before administrative bodies such as the Federal Communications Commission, there have also been a handful of cases, both federal and state, touching on other issues.[38]

Complementing this expanding field of domestic space laws and regulations are a series of joint-endeavor agreements and agreements for launch services and spacecraft retrieval between the United States and other parties, including private companies. In addition, model agreements such as those prepared by the Air Force for commercial utilization of expendable launch vehicles, as well as by NASA, are significant in indicating the development of space laws.[39]

National Space Laws in Other Countries

While the United States has certainly led the nations of the world in the establishment of national laws, regulations, and decisions governing space activities, it is by no means the only country that has enacted domestic space legislation. Even a glance at foreign institutional structures reveals a growing panorama of maturing organizations in different countries. Most of these entities have their origins in space research committees, councils, or commissions established within a governmental body or intergovernmentally. In Japan, however, a university institute has become one of the pillars of Japanese space activity.[40]

As scientific and technological advances open new opportunities, policy and law follow suit in creating new institutions or upgrading and streamlining existing capabilities so that they can better respond to new demands and expectations. For example, France, the third nation to orbit a satellite, recognized early that there was a need to provide an administrative framework for the development of space activities. Already in 1959, a Space Research Committee (Comité des Recherches Spatiales) was established to provide an inventory of the means available for space research in France. In 1961, a National Center for Space Studies (Centre national d'études spatiales—CNES) was created, as a scientific and technical organization with an industrial and commercial character, to continue and enlarge the work undertaken by the Space Research Committee and to be responsible for France's civil space program and its execution.[41]

In some countries, more formal institutional structures emerged in response to national interest and a willingness to allocate resources to space activities. For example, in 1970, shortly after the establishment of its National Space Development Agency (NASDA), Japan became the fourth nation to place a satellite in orbit. In India, the Indian Space Research Organization (ISRO) was established in 1969, and its budget and activities have been steadily increasing ever since.

More recently, Great Britain, Italy, Germany, and Canada have been added to the list of countries with civilian space agencies. While these agencies are usually responsible for the country's civilian space programs, policies and political supervision often remain in the hands of one of the ministries of the government. The British National Space Centre, for instance, was created in 1985 and placed under the Department of Trade and Industry.

In Italy in 1988, after many years of debate and parliamentary procedure, the Italian legislative bodies established the Italian Space Agency. The Agency took the place of the former National Space Plan (Piano Nazionale Spaziale) of the National Council for Research (Consiglio Nazionale delle Ricerche), which up to then had been in charge of determining Italy's space policy in cooperation with concerned ministries. The new Italian Space Agency is in charge of arranging and managing national scientific research, technological development, and application programs in the space field as well as international programs, including ESA activities and bilateral projects.[42]

In Germany, where space activities have remained mainly governmental activities, space management was fundamentally restructured in 1989 with the establishment of the German Space Agency (DARA) as the central space management agency.

The basic purpose of the Canadian Space Agency, established in 1990, is to promote the peaceful use and development of space, to advance the knowledge of space through science, and to ensure that space science and technology provide social and economic benefits for Canadians. Generally, the Agency can take action on matters concerning space over which Parliament has jurisdiction and which are not by law assigned to any other department, board, or agency of the government.[43]

While the Soviet Union, unlike the United States, did not establish a separate civilian space administration or a set of national space laws, it did create the Glavcosmos agency in 1985 to offer space services and facilities on a commercial basis to other countries. Russia, in early 1992, established the Russian Space Agency, but its organization and function are not yet clear. China is also offering commercial launch services to foreign countries.

In addition to laws establishing national space agencies, there are a few examples of legislation dealing with state authorizations and licenses required for non-governmental launches. For instance, the Swedish Space Activities Act governs space activities conducted from Swedish territory, including the launching of objects into outer space. All such activities, if conducted by a body other than the Swedish state, require a special license.[44] In the United Kingdom, the Outer Space Act of 1986 confers licensing and other powers on the Foreign Secretary to secure compliance with international obligations of the United Kingdom with respect to the launching of space objects and the carrying on of other activities in outer space by persons belonging to that country.

CONCLUSION

It is a difficult, if not insurmountable, task to do full justice in a brief chapter to all aspects of the development of space law during its more than three decades of history. Nonetheless, the preceding highly condensed review has been intended to reveal the rapid growth of the law, as reflected not only in the organizational framework of a multitude of space agencies created by international or domestic law but also in the many legal provisions affecting rights and obligations which are gradually filling in areas of substantive and procedural space law.

As a manifestation of the continuing international lawmaking process, the United Nations Committee on the Peaceful Uses of Outer Space, for instance, has been considering draft principles relevant to the use of nuclear power sources in outer space as well as matters relating to the definition and delimitation of outer space and to the character and utilization of the geostationary orbit. Under a new agenda item, the Committee is also considering legal aspects related to the application of the principle of carrying out the exploration and utilization of outer space for the benefit and in the interests of all states, particularly taking into account the needs of developing countries. While the consensus decision-making process in the Committee will, in most instances, continue to be slow, the resulting decisions are likely to be enduring.[45]

Even without the anticipated further accomplishments of the Committee, there is little doubt that the already voluminous body of space laws, regulations, and cases will expand in the future with the expected increase of human presence and activities in space. The issues likely to arise during the operation of the United States/International Space Station and the planned Moon and Mars missions will provide further fertile ground for new legal regulations.

In general, laws do not stand alone; they respond to human needs and exigencies. Seen in such a light, the institutional and substantive developments in space law reviewed in this chapter are essentially a response to the various challenges arising from the application of space technology in the fields of space exploration, remote sensing, and telecommunications.

Currently, about a dozen countries have launch capabilities and many more have their own satellites in orbit. As newcomers enter the growing club of spacefaring nations, it may be safe to assume that many new institutions will spring up to direct space projects and draft laws and regulations as the need arises. In addition to new organizations and regulations called for by space developments, the existing framework of space laws, as well as the possible extension of the applicability (with or without modification) of other laws to activities in outer space, will have to be reviewed. Also, attention will have to be directed toward harmonizing efforts within the domestic and international fields and toward clarifying uncertainties, especially of undefined or insufficiently defined terms such as "outer space" and "space object," which may give rise to divergent interpretations and thereby undermine legal stability.

Fortunately, apart from the work of public entities, many private international and national organizations—including the International Institute of Space Law of the International Astronautical Federation, the International Law Association; the American Society of International Law, a number of space law institutes, and research and teaching centers—as well as individual scholars in the United States, Russia, Canada, Germany, France, Holland, Indonesia, and other countries continue to work on the development, critique, and refinement of space law and address many unresolved issues and foreseeable problems. A recent example of such work was the Draft for a Convention on Manned Space Flight, which was presented to the recent session of the Legal Subcommittee of the Committee on the Peaceful Uses of Outer Space as a result of a common research project undertaken by three scholarly institutions in Germany, the United States, and the Soviet Union.[46]

In their efforts to shape future rules and policies affecting the further development and growth of space law, and in recognition of what Congress has aptly called the profound impact of science and technology on society and the importance of recognizing the interrelations of scientific, technological, economic, social, political, and institutional factors,[47] both policymakers and legal technicians will need a multidisciplinary understanding of a wide range of issues relating to advances in the various applications of space technology. Only then can it be hoped that the events accompanying these advances will take place with a minimum of friction both internationally and nationally.

NOTES

1. U.N.G.A. Res. 1472 (XIV), 1959.

2. Treaty on Principles Governing the Activities of States in the Exploration and Use of Outer Space, Including the Moon and Other Celestial Bodies, Done Jan. 27, 1967, Entered into Force Oct. 10, 1967, 18 U.S.T. 2410, T.I.A.S. No. 6347; 610 U.N.T.S. 205 (hereinafter Outer Space Treaty).

3. Agreement Governing the Activities of States on the Moon and Other Celestial Bodies, adopted by the United Nations General Assembly Dec. 5, 1979, Opened for Signature Dec. 18, 1979, Entered into Force July 11, 1984, U.N.G.A Res. 34/68 (1979) (hereinafter Moon Agreement).

4. Agreement on the Rescue of Astronauts, the Return of Astronauts, and the Return of Objects Launched into Outer Space, Done Apr. 22, 1968, Entered into Force Dec. 3, 1968, 19 U.S.T. 7570, T.I.A.S. No. 6599, 672 U.N.T.S. 119 (hereinafter Rescue Agreement).

5. Convention on International Liability for Damage Caused by Space Objects, Done Mar. 29, 1972, Entered into Force Sept. 1, 1972, 24 U.S.T. 2389, T.I.A.S. No. 7762, 961 U.N.T.S. 187 (hereinafter Liability Convention).

6. Convention on the Registration of Objects Launched into Outer Space, Opened for Signature Jan. 14, 1975, Entered into Force Sept. 15, 1979, 28 U.S.T. 695, T.I.A.S. No. 8480, 1023 U.N.T.S. 15 (hereinafter Registration Convention).

7. Principles Relating to Remote Sensing of the Earth from Outer Space, U.N.G.A. Res. 41/65 (1985).

8. Principles Governing the Use by States of Artificial Earth Satellites for International Direct Television Broadcasting, adopted by the United Nations General Assembly Dec. 10, 1982. U.N.G.A. Res. 37/92, annex (1982).

9. For details on the activities of the United Nations, the specialized agencies and other international space organizations, see *Space Activities of the United Nations and International Organizations*, U.N. Doc. A/AC.105/358 (1986).

10. Final Acts of the World Administrative Radio Conference for Space Telecommunications, Res. Spa 2-1 (Geneva 1971).

11. International Telecommunication Convention, Oct. 25, 1973 (Malaga-Torremolinos), 28 U.S.T. 2495, T.I.A.S. No. 8572, Art. 33.

12. International Telecommunication Convention (Nairobi), Nov. 6, 1982, (entered into force for the United States Jan. 10, 1986).

13. The 1985 and 1988 sessions of the World Administrative Radio Conference (WARC-ORB '85 and '88) resulted in the revision of the Radio Regulations, giving more concrete expression to the guarantee in practice of equitable access to the geostationary satellite orbit. As a result, one orbital location, within a predetermined arc and within the frequency band identified for "allotment planning," has been designated for each country.

14. See Convention for the Establishment of a European Space Agency, Done May 30, 1975, Entered into Force Oct. 30, 1980. The text of the Final Act of the Conference of Plenipotentiaries for the Establishment of a European Space Agency and the text of the Convention appear at 14 *International Legal Materials* 855, 864 (1975).

15. See International Telecommunications Satellite Organization (INTELSAT) Agreement, Aug. 20, 1971, 23 U.S.T. 3813, T.I.A.S. No. 7532; (entered into force for the United States Feb. 12, 1973). Operating Agreement relating to the International Telecommunications Satellite Organization (INTELSAT), Aug. 20, 1971, 23 U.S.T. 4091, T.I.A.S. No. 7532, (entered into force for the United States Feb. 12, 1973).

16. The INTERSPUTNIK Foundation Agreement was signed in November 1971 and came into force upon ratification in July 1972.

17. INTERCOSMOS is not an international organization; it is a program of cooperation among the Soviet Union and other socialist countries for the peaceful exploration and use of outer space. *Id.* at 150.

18. See Convention on the International Maritime Satellite Organization (INMARSAT), Sept. 3, 1976, 51 U.S.T. 135, T.I.A.S. No. 9605 (entered into force for the United States July 16, 1979); Operating Agreement on the International Maritime Satellite Organization (INMARSAT), Sept. 3, 1976, 31 U.S.T. 135, T.I.A.S. No. 9605, (entered into force for the United States July 16, 1979).

19. Members of the Arab League founded the Arab Satellite Communication Organization (ARABSAT) by means of an ARABSAT charter signed in April 1976.

20. EUTELSAT was created in 1977 on a provisional basis and attained its definitive form on September 1, 1985, upon entry into force of an Intergovernmental Convention and an Operating Agreement, signed by 26 European states.

21. EUMETSAT was provisionally set up in 1983 by 12 European nations which signed the EUMETSAT Convention. It became fully operational upon entry into force of the Convention on June 19, 1986.

22. Treaty Banning Nuclear Weapon Tests in the Atmosphere, in Outer Space, and Under Water, done at Moscow Aug. 5, 1963 (entered into force Oct. 10, 1963, 13 U.S.T. 1313, T.I.A.S. No. 5433, 480 U.N.T.S. 43).

23. Convention on the Prohibition of Military or Any Other Hostile Use of Environmental Modification Techniques, May 18, 1977, 31 U.S.T. 333, T.I.A.S. No. 9614, 1108 U.N.T.S. 1541 (entered into force for the United States Jan. 17, 1980).

24. Convention Relating to the Distribution of Programme-Carrying Signals Transmitted by Satellite, Done at Brussels May 21, 1974, T.I.A.S. No. 11078, I 144 U.N.T.S. 3, reprinited in 13 *International Legal Materials* 1,444 (entered into force for the United States Mar. 7, 1985).

25. Agreement among the Government of the United States of America, Governments of Member States of the European Space Agency, the Government of Japan, and the Government of Canada on Cooperation in the Detailed Design, Development, Operation, and Utilization of the Permanently Manned Civil Space Station, signed Sept. 29, 1988.

26. Treaty Between the United States of America and the Union of Soviet Socialist Republics on the Limitation of Anti-Ballistic Missile Systems, May 26, 1972, 23 U.S.T. 3435, T.I.A.S. No. 7503 (hereinafter ABM Treaty).

27. A number of U.S. bilateral space agreements may be found in S. Gorove (ed.), *United States Space Law—National and International Regulations* vol. 3., New York, Oceana, 1991.

28. Pub. L. No. 85-568, 72 Stat. 426, U.S.C. sec. 2451 et seq. (1988) (hereinafter NASA Act).

29. *Id.* at sec. 102(a).

30. *Id.* at sec. 203(a).

31. For details, see S. Gorove, "The Growth of Domestic Space Law: A U.S. Example," *Journal of Space Law*, Vol. 18, 1990, p. 99.

32. Pub. L. No. 87-624, 76 Stat. 419, 47 U.S.C. sec. 701 (1982).

33. An Act to Amend the Patent and Trademark Laws of 1980, Pub. L. No. 96-517, 94 Stat. 3024, 35 U.S.C. sec. 200 (1982).

34. Pub. L. No. 101-580, 104 Stat. 2863 (1990).

35. Pub. L. No. 98-365, 98 Stat. 451, 15 U.S.C. sec. 4201; amended in 1988 by Pub. L. No. 100-147, 101 Stat. 876, 15 U.S.C. sec. 4201 (1988).

36. Pub. L. No. 98-575, 98 Stat. 3055, 49 U.S.C. app. sec. 2601 (1982).

37. Pub. L. No. 100-657, 102 Stat. 3900, 49 U.S.C. app. sec 2601 (1982).

38. For a selective compilation of these materials, see S. Gorove (ed.), *supra* note 27, vol. 3.

39. For a text of the Department of the Air Force, Expendable Launch Vehicle Commercialization, Model Agreement, see Senate Committee on Commerce, Science and Transportation, *Space Law and Related Documents*, 101st Cong., 2d Sess. 547-563, Washington, Government Printing Office, 1990.

40. Ojalehto et al, "A Look at the Growing Civil Space Club," *Aerospace America*, Vol. 29, No. 2, p. 12.

41. For historical details, see "France: Législation et participation aux accords internationaux dans le domaine spatial," *Yearbook of Air and Space Law*, Montreal, Institute of Air and Space Law, 1965, p. 407.

42. For details, see Catalano Sgrosso, "Establishment of the Italian Space Agency," in *Proceedings oof the 31st Colloquium on the Law of Outer Space*, Washington, AIAA, 1989, p. 162.

43. See Canadian Space Agency Act, secs. 4 and 5, 13 Canada Gazette Part III 223, at 224 (No. 2, 1990).

44. Law No. 963 of 1982 and Decree No. 1069 of 1982.

45. On consensus decision-making, see Eilene Galloway, "Consensus Decision-making by the Committee on the Peaceful Uses of Outer Space," *Journal of Space Law*, Vol. 7, 1979, p. 3.

46. For a text of the Draft for a Convention on Manned Space Flight, see *Journal of Space Law*, Vol. 18, 1990, p. 209.

47. See National Science and Technology Policy Organization Act of 1976, Pub. L. No. 94-282, 90 Stat. 459, 42 U.S.C. 6601 et seq. (1982).

5

Trends in National Regulation of Space Activities: The Soviet Union

Vladlen S. Vereshchetin

THE NOTION AND SCOPE OF NATIONAL SPACE LAW

Space and space-related activities are to a great extent governed not by national laws and regulations specifically tailored to space issues but by general national legislation and implementing acts.[1] This has been true for all spacefaring nations including the Soviet Union.[2] In this sense, many of the rules in different areas of Soviet national law were applicable to space-related activities within Soviet territory, and some even applied to activities in outer space, providing that the latter were permitted by international space law.

For example, with respect to labor relations pertaining to space activities, the relevant rules of Soviet federal law and republic codes applied. Tort liability problems, contract matters, and property rights also fell within the domain of the laws and civil codes of individual Soviet republics and of the Soviet Union.[3] The legal position of a space industry facility, for instance, was determined by the law on enterprises in the Soviet Union and corresponding republic laws.[4] Space insurance problems were generally solved in accordance with national insurance regulations. There are many other examples of how space-related matters were governed by general national laws and regulations.

Some authors have suggested that the applicability of a given rule of domestic law to some space-related activity can serve as a basis for including it in a body of national space law.[5] If we adopt this line of reasoning, we would be compelled to include in national space law most areas of domestic law, or at least substantial parts of it. We need to realize that in general,

Editor's note:

This chapter was submitted for publication in July 1991 and reflects the situation at that time.

space-related activities on Earth, like other activities, are regulated by legal rules of general application, which do not become component parts of national space law as a result of their applicability to terrestrial activities related to the study and use of outer space. What is really needed is timely enactment of new specific legislation to regulate space activities when and where it becomes necessary. In my view, only this specific legislation, which may include comprehensive laws as well as separate legal rules relating expressly to space activities, should be considered part of national space law. These specific space-related rules may also belong to other branches of domestic law.

The enactment of specific legislation for space-related activities depends on legal requirements which may differ from country to country irrespective of the scope of their space programs. The need for such legislation depends to a large extent on the degree of participation by the private sector in national space activities, since, pursuant to the rules of international space law, "the activities of non-governmental entities in outer space, including the moon and other celestial bodies, shall require authorization and continuing supervision by the appropriate State."[6] It is difficult to regulate and supervise private sector space activities without appropriate national space legislation. In market economy countries, national space legislation is largely devoted to rules specifying the requirements which must be met by private sector entities conducting activities in outer space.

Every spacefaring nation, whether or not it has a private space sector, requires a governmental structure responsible for national space activities. The designation of such a governmental body and the determination of its terms of reference require a special legislative act. Some examples of this are the U.S. National Aeronautics and Space Act of 1958, the Japanese National Space Development Agency Law of 1969, the Swedish Space Activities Act of 1982, the U. K. Outer Space Act of 1986, and the Law on the Establishment of the Italian Space Agency of 1988.[7]

Depending on the specific structure of domestic law, the implementation of international obligations under the existing space treaties may also require the adoption of national legislative acts on space-related activities, or the introduction of special implementing provisions into existing regulations. In addition to the obligation of "authorization and continuing supervision" over the activities of non-governmental entities in outer space, states also have an international obligation to maintain a national registry of space objects under Article 2 of the Convention on Registration of Objects Launched into Outer Space of 1976. Furthermore, Article 8 of the Outer Space Treaty implicitly requires the determination of the property rights of a particular state or international organization over a space object.[8] The peculiarities of different space activities, such as space communications, remote sensing, or the issues connected with space commercialization and intellectual property rights related to inventions made in outer space, may also require special national regulations and the introduction of space-related norms into existing domestic law such as commercial law, administrative law, labor law, and criminal law. As Dr. Phillip Dann has correctly noted, "it is likely that several states will enact legislation in order to extend the application of their domestic laws to space, or perhaps to declare that such laws already apply."[9] Some states have already taken such measures.

GLASNOST AND SPACE ACTIVITIES IN THE SOVIET UNION

Coming back to the situation in the Soviet Union, national space regulations existed in the Soviet Union from the very outset of the space era. But they were all, or almost all, classified, making them virtually non-existent to the outside world and to the majority of Soviet citizens.

The Soviet Council of Ministers, individual ministries and agencies, and several agencies jointly, have over the years enacted a great number of regulations which determined, among other things, the distribution of responsibilities between civilian and military ministries and agencies in executing Soviet space programs, appropriation of funds for space and space-related activities, establishment of space programs as a whole or in part according to specific missions, the provisions of launch services, space control centers, yearly launching plans, and the selection and training of cosmonauts.

According to these regulations, for example, the Soviet Academy of Sciences was authorized to conduct scientific research in outer space; the Ministry of Communications was designated as the body responsible for satellite communication systems; the Meteorological Service was put in charge of space meteorology; and the Ministry of Health was responsible for biomedical investigations in space and health protection of cosmonauts. The development of space technology was the responsibility of several industrial ministries, primarily of the Ministry of General Machine Building.

As further examples of Soviet space regulations, the Ministry of Communications was authorized to control the allocation of radio frequencies and regulate the assignment and allocation of orbital slots in the geostationary orbit for all users. The Intercosmos Council of the Soviet Academy of Sciences, established in 1965, had the authority to conclude, on behalf of the Academy of Sciences and other interested agencies, agreements on international cooperative space projects and missions. Glavcosmos, established in 1985, is entitled to enter into space-related commercial transactions with foreign agencies and private organizations.

A major drawback of the legal framework of space-related activities in the Soviet Union was the seal of secrecy which was applied to most of these regulations. This secrecy was detrimental both internally and internationally. It hampered the progress of international cooperation in space and the application of the results of space research to different areas of the national economy. The classifying of information concealed a very important field of modern science and technology from the scrutiny of public institutions. Certain programs and budgets of space research and application remained "grey zones" not only to the public at large but to the national parliament as well.

The situation began to change radically with the advent of *glasnost* and *perestroika*. In 1989, for the first time, the space budget was made public. Premier Nikolai Ryzhkov in his speech to the Supreme Soviet disclosed that spending on military and civilian space programs in 1989 amounted to 6.9 billion rubles, including 1.7 billion rubles for space research and civilian applications, 3.9 billion rubles for the military program and 1.3 billion rubles specifically for the Soviet reusable spaceship, Buran.[10]

Space launches and the planned duration of all crewed space flights are now announced in advance, and major space projects—for example the planned Mars missions—are debated in the mass media. Formerly classified information on space centers, space enterprises, launching sites, and high-ranking persons engaged in space activities have gradually appeared in the press.[11] Moreover, these centers, enterprises, and launching-sites have been opened to foreigners. Failures of space missions are no longer hidden from the public at large, and criticism of many aspects of space activities, including organizational questions, are becoming commonplace.[12]

Unfortunately, *glasnost* came to space activities at a time when their romantic flavor had practically evaporated, and accordingly, public interest has faded and become highly critical. Moreover, against the backdrop of economic difficulties, the space budget has been shrinking. The new critical attitude toward space research and applications has given rise to demands for more openness and more public knowledge of all space developments. This has stimulated the introduction of new legal regulations to make information accessible to all those interested.

Additionally, the transition to a market economy, the diffusion of forms of property rights, and the commercialization of space activities pose a number of new legal questions, including the licensing of certain kinds of space activities and modifications of industrial and intellectual property laws, insurance regulations, and others.

CONSTITUTIONAL NOVELTY

It is significant that among the constitutional amendments passed by the Congress of People's Deputies in 1990, one dealt directly with the governing of space activities in the Soviet Union. The newly formulated Article 132 of the Soviet Constitution, which determined the powers of the Cabinet of Ministers, provided, inter alia, that the Cabinet would govern space research jointly with the constituent republics.[13]

Some explanation is necessary for understanding the significance of this amendment. For the first time, space activities were mentioned in the Constitution. This became necessary in light of the so-called "parade of sovereignties" of the Soviet republics and the debate over the division of competence between the central government and the republics in the various fields of the national economy. Unfortunately, the adoption of the formula "governing jointly," which was supposed to reflect the idea of shared competence, did not clarify the situation very much. Given the cost factor and the huge infrastructure needed, space-related activities will long be out of reach for most of the republics of the Soviet Union. In this sense, the governing could only be nominally joint.

The largest republic, the Russian Republic, established a Ministry of Communications, Informatics, and Outer Space, and a draft text for the future constitution of the Russian Republic mentions "activities in space" as a part of the competence of the Republic.[14] On the other hand, the draft text of the Union Treaty, which was to determine the basic principles of relations between the Union and the constituent republics, treated "space research" as within the competence of the Union.[15]

It should also be pointed out that "space research" in Article 132 of the Soviet Constitution was interpreted broadly to include not only scientific research in space but all space applications as well, so as to cover all space and space-related activities. A narrower interpretation would have been too restrictive and would not have corresponded to the intentions of the legislators. The draft constitution of the Russian Republic uses a broader but still inadequate term, "activities in space."

Finally, it is worth noting that the powers of the Soviet Cabinet of Ministers were of executive character. The Cabinet reported to the President and Supreme Soviet of the Soviet Union (Article 130 of the Constitution), which meant that, according to Article 132, space activities were dealt with by the highest level of the executive branch. But this did not preclude a role for the Congress of People's Deputies of the Soviet Union or the Supreme Soviets of the constituent republics in enacting corresponding space legislation.

THE CONCEPT OF A MAJOR SPACE LAW

These and other developments and exigencies made necessary the enactment of new space legislation and, in particular, the introduction of a major law governing space activities in the Soviet Union to lay the groundwork for future domestic space law.

The idea for such a major legal act was first voiced by Soviet space lawyers many years ago, in the late 1970s.[16] But only recently did the prospects for this idea become more realistic, with the Soviet legislature actively involved in enacting a multitude of new laws dealing with the different areas of political and economic life of the country.

One of the conceptual problems of drafting such a law has already been discussed: the distribution of competence in governing space-related activities between the central bodies and the constituent republics. In general, it appeared that national space activities would need to be dealt with primarily by central organizations. On this assumption, a future law on space activities should define the respective roles of different organs of the state in governing space and space-related activities, bearing in mind that in the process of reorganization taking place in the Soviet Union, new structures relating to space activities are likely to emerge. For example, the establishment of a civilian space agency has been proposed on several occasions.[17]

Procedures for establishing space programs, both civilian and military, and space budgets should be more clearly defined in a new law, and responsibilities for the execution of civilian and military space programs should also be made clear-cut. The programs, or at least their civilian parts, should be developed with consideration of possible alternatives and should be publicly discussed before their adoption.

The overall picture of the future governance of space and space-related activities on a national scale, from my perspective, could be presented as follows. The Supreme Soviet and the President of the Soviet Union would exercise general regulation and control over these activities in the Soviet Union, the former as the main legislative body, with a special presidential council or committee responsible for working out Soviet space policy. The direction of Soviet space activities, in accordance with applicable legislation and established space policy, would be entrusted to the highest executive body of the Soviet Union, jointly with the appropriate bodies of the constituent republics. The development and implementation of the national program for space research and applications would be exercised by the National Space Agency (civilian part of the program) and the Ministry of Defence (military part of the program). The contents and funding of the national space program would be examined and approved by the Supreme Soviet. Certainly, it is hard to say at the present stage whether this ideal scheme will be realized in law and practice, and if so, when.

Another concern for Soviet space law was the advisability of introducing a system of licensing space activities in the Soviet Union. Such a system has never existed in the Soviet Union in the past due to the purely state-centered nature of these activities. Now, as space commercialization increases and new areas of space activity arise, the issue of licensing acquires a new significance. Until recently, practically all space activities were carried out by the state and in accordance with state plans. One rare exception to this rule was the All-Union Maritime Satellite Communications Association, which is financially independent and acts on its own behalf.[18]

Today, we witness the growth of legal and economic independence in industrial enterprises, including those acting in the field of outer space. This trend embraces state-owned enterprises, including space industries. Space industrial enterprises and other entities, acting as independent juridical persons, are authorized to conclude contracts with other Soviet and foreign juridical persons. In this situation, the licensing of space activities may be regarded as highly advisable even for state-owned enterprises. Otherwise, the state may lose its power to provide authorization and continuing supervision over its national activities in space, as required by Article 6 of the Outer Space Treaty. The state organ or organs authorized to grant licenses and to establish the appropriate procedures for granting them must be defined in the law on space activities. On the national level such an organ could be the highest executive body or, by its designation, the National Space Agency.

Among the issues that will need to be dealt with in future national space law will be the question of property rights over space objects and space systems. We can presume that the majority of space objects will continue to be owned by the state as a whole, that is, they will be state property. This rule should be stipulated in the law, however, with a reservation that other forms of property may be authorized by legislation. Such a reservation is necessary because while the recent Soviet law, "On Property of the USSR," listed "space systems" among the items of state (all-Union) property,[19] a law of the Russian Republic, enacted later, has ruled that the provisions of the law "On Property of the USSR" would not apply on the territory of the Russian Republic.[20] Bearing in mind that the draft text of the constitution of the Russian Republic refers to "activities in space" as within the competence of the republic, "space systems," or at least some of them, might well be declared republic or other type of property. Space objects, being part of space systems, are covered by the provisions just discussed.[21]

Environmental risks connected with space activities pose another problem for national space legislators. Environmental aspects of space activities have already become a major concern of national and international communities. The issue of space debris and pollution resulting from activities in outer space has been taken up at a number of different international conferences and colloquia and at the United Nations.[22] The accident of the Soviet satellite Cosmos-954 with a nuclear power source on board in 1978, and the uncontrolled re-entry to Earth of the Salyut-7 space station in 1991, are two major reminders of the necessity to tighten the responsibility and liability of designers and operators of space technology.

The problem of the pollution of vast areas around launching sites with spent rocket stages, toxic fuel residues, and debris has also been brought to the attention of the public in the Soviet Union in recent years. As a result, in 1990 the Regional Committee on the Protection of Environment in the Dzhezkazgan region (Kazakhstan) brought a suit against Glavcosmos claiming 1.7 million rubles for the pollution of a great area around the Baikonour Cosmodrome.[23] In my opinion, future space law must include a special article or articles aimed at preventing and mitigating pollution on Earth and in outer space. Non-compliance with the demands of ecological safety on the part of the designers and operators of space technology should lead to administrative, civil, and criminal responsibility.

A special commitment should be made concerning cooperation with other countries in drawing up international guidelines and standards for protecting the space environment. One good example of such a measure is the U.S.

National Space Policy, first put forth in 1988. The policy requires all U.S. space programs to try to minimize the creation of space debris. Unfortunately, the mandatory character of this policy was weakened by making it conditional on mission requirements and cost effectiveness.[24]

In discussing the contents of future space law, it is also necessary to stress the importance of including provisions relating to such matters as measures for the safety of space flights, persons involved, and the general public; the question of transit flights of foreign space objects through national airspace; the rights and duties of the commander and crew of a spaceship; and insurance policies. Implementing provisions of international obligations (such as the registration of space objects, assistance and rescue of astronauts, responsibility, and liability) should also be given due consideration.[25]

INTEGRATING INTERNATIONAL AND NATIONAL SPACE LAW

Practical work on the elaboration and drafting of domestic space law requires good knowledge of the interrelation between international law and national law in the legal system of a particular state. Space and space-related activities are regulated both by international law and domestic law. The degree of influence of one or the other upon space activities depends on the place, nature and time of the activities. If they take place within the boundaries of a state territory, they are mainly governed by the rules of national law. Upon entering outer space, these activities primarily come under the rules of international space law. This "geographical" delimitation of the spheres of operation of national law and international law, however, is valid only to the extent that there is dominance of one or the other type of law.[26]

This gives rise to the important question of the mechanism of application of international law within a given state and the binding force of its rules over the organs of a state and juridical and natural persons. It is not by chance that in the course of the debates over this issue in the European Space Agency, some states, in particular Sweden and Austria, have argued that drawing up national space legislation was useless for states which do not launch space objects, providing that the rules of international conventions are applied in the internal legal system of these states. Yet, as is known, the legal doctrine and practice with regard to the direct applicability of the rules of international conventions in a national legal system vary from state to state.[27]

Let us now turn to the relevant rules of Soviet legislation. Like the constitutions of most other countries, the Soviet Constitution did not contain a general provision regarding the procedures for implementing international legal rules in the territory of the Soviet Union or regarding the procedures for settling conflicts between national and international legal rules. According to the Soviet Law on the Order of Conclusion, Execution and Denunciation of International Treaties (1978), the need for appropriate implementing acts was determined by the Cabinet of Ministers of the Soviet Union.[28]

Recommendations on the adoption of domestic laws necessary for the implementation of an international treaty obligation were submitted by ministries, state committees, and agencies concerned, upon agreement with the Soviet Ministry of Justice.[29] These state organs could also issue their own rules and regulations if necessary and assure the observance of international obligations.

Of fundamental importance to the national implementation of international legal obligations was the provision of the Law of 1978, in which "ministries, state committees, agencies of the USSR, Councils of Ministers of Union Republics and other state organs whose sphere of competence covers questions regulated by international treaties of the Soviet Union, assure the fulfillment of treaty obligations undertaken by the Soviet side."[30] This clearly extended the binding character of provisions of international treaties to which the Soviet Union was a party to state organs and agencies, irrespective of whether or not these provisions are incorporated in domestic law. This implies that according to Soviet legislation, provisions of international treaties concluded by the Soviet Union were binding, not only for the state as a whole but also for state organs and organizations, which, within their competence, were to apply the provisions of these treaties in their space and space-related activities, even when no national implementing act had been issued.

This does not rule out, however, the desirability of implementing some of these clauses in future national legislation and including in the text of a future constitution a general provision on the legally binding character of duly ratified and officially promulgated treaties signed by the Soviet Union for all state organs, organizations, legal persons, and individuals. In any case, such a constitutional provision would fully comply with the concept of the primacy of international law upheld by the Soviet Union.[31]

SUMMARY AND CONCLUSIONS

Generally, space-related activities in the Soviet Union, as in other spacefaring nations, were regulated by legal rules belonging to different areas of domestic law. However, there was also a need for specific space legislation arising from various factors, including the need to determine the terms of reference of a national space agency, to implement international obligations, and to grant licenses for space activities by nationals and other entities.

National space regulations existed in the Soviet Union from the very outset of the space era, but most of these regulations were classified. With the advent of *glasnost* and *perestroika* and the transition in the Soviet Union to a market economy, the need to enact new legislation and set up a regulatory framework for space activities is increasingly evident.

In 1990, for the first time, space activities were mentioned in the text of the Soviet Constitution. The newly formulated Article 132 of the Constitution stipulated that the Cabinet of Ministers of the Soviet Union, inter alia, would "govern space research jointly with the republics." Similar provisions are also stated in the draft text of the Constitution of the Russian Republic, and a somewhat different provision was in the draft text of the Union Treaty. The recent Soviet law, "On Property of the USSR," listed "space systems" among the items of all-Union state property, but this law was questioned by some of the republics.

The idea of having a major new law to govern space activities in the Soviet Union has been discussed by Soviet legislators and in legal literature. This law would define the role of different state organs in governing space and space-related activities and the procedures for adopting space programs and for granting licenses for space activities. The law would also deal with the issues of property rights to space objects, environmental risks connected with space activities, liability, and other matters.

The adoption of such a law would be a major breakthrough in the development of national regulation of space activities in the Soviet Union.

NOTES

1. See E. Galloway, "The United States Congress and Space Law," *Annals of Air and Space Law*, Vol. 3, 1978, pp. 395-407; "The Definition of Space Law," *Proceedings of the 32nd Colloquium on the Law of Outer Space*, Washington, AIAA, 1990, pp. 331-335; Phillip Dann, "The Future Role of Municipal Law in Regulating Space-Related Activities," *Space Law: Views of the Future*, Deventer/Antwerp, Kluwer Law and Taxation Publishers, 1988, pp. 126-128.

2. See G. Silvestrov, "Special and General Regulations of the National Space Activities in USSR," *Proceedings of the 32nd Colloquium on the Law of Outer Space*, New York, AIAA, 1990, pp. 402-403.

3. See, for instance, the Soviet Law, On Property in the USSR, of March 6, 1990; the Law of the Russian Republic, On Property in the Russian Soviet Federated Socialist Republic, of December 24, 1990; Civil Code of the Russian Republic of 1964.

4. The Soviet Law on Enterprises in the USSR, of June 4, 1990. *Vedomosty Syezda Narodnych Deputatov SSSR i Verhovnogo Soveta SSSR*, No. 25 (June 20, 1990); The Law of the Russian Republic, On Enterprises and Entrepreneurial Activities, of December 15, 1990; *Sovetskaya Rossiya*, January 12, 1991.

5. Dann, *supra* note 1, p. 125.

6. Article 6 of the Treaty on Principles Governing the Activities of States in the Exploration and Use of Outer Space, Including the Moon and Other Celestial Bodies.

7. For general issues on national space law, see E. Galloway and J. Galloway, "United States National Space Legislation on the Exploration and Use of Outer Space for Peaceful Purposes," *Proceedings of the 30th Colloquium on the Law of Outer Space*, Washington, AIAA, 1988, pp. 32-41; M. Bourely, "National Space Legislation in Europe," *id.*, pp. 197-202; G. Sgrosso, "Establishment of the Italian Space Agency," *Proceedings of the 31st Colloquium on the Law of Outer Space*, Washington, AIAA, 1989, pp. 162-164; E. Zhukova and E. Kamenetskaya, "Osvoeniye kosmosa:

nazionalnoye regulirovaniye," in *Novoe V kosmicheskom prave* (New Developments in Space Law), Moscow, 1990, pp. 117-138; Dann, *supra* note 1; D. de la Rochere, "Les sources du droit de l'espace," *Droit de l'Espace*, Paris, Editions Pedone, 1988, pp. 11-29.

8. The Article provides in part that "ownership of objects launched into outer space, including objects landed or constructed on a celestial body, and of their component parts, is not affected by their presence in outer space or on a celestial body or by their return to Earth."

9. Dann, *supra* note 1, p. 19.

10. See *Izvestia*, June 8, 1989. An amount of 6.9 billion rubles constituted 1.5 percent of the state budget in 1989.

11. See, for instance, A. Tarassov, "Orbital Plant," *Pravda*, May 17, 1990; V. Litovkin, "Without Stamp 'Classified'" (an interview with the heads of space units of the Ministry of Defence), *Izvestia*, December 11, 1990.

12. See B. Konovalov, "Astronautics Came to the Crossroads" (an interview with the head of the Space Training Center, General V. Shatalov), *Izvestia*, May 17, 1989; S. Leskov, "Monopoly on Astronautics in the Epoch of *Glasnost*," *Izvestia*, January 10, 1991; S. Leskov, "Salyut-7 Is Falling," *Izvestia*, January 17, 1991.

13. Unofficial translation, made by the author. The text of the Soviet Law on Amendments to the USSR Constitution (Basic Law) concerning the improvement of the system of state government, in *Pravda*, December 27, 1990.

14. See Draft Constitution of the Russian Republic, Art. 4.2.2.(9), *Rossiyskaya Gazeta*, No.4, November 22, 1990.

15. See the Draft Union Treaty, Art. 5, *Izvestia*, March 9, 1991. The Law on the Delimitation of Competence between the USSR and Subjects of the Federation of April 26, 1990 refers to the governing of space research as within the exclusive competence of the Soviet Union (Article 6.9), *Izvestia*, May 3, 1990.

16. See V. S. Vereshchetin, "Outer Space and Law," *Pravda*, August 20, 1977. Also see E. Zhukova and E. Kamenetskaya, *supra* note 7, p. 19.

17. For example, see interview with General V. A. Shatalov, *supra* note 12; S. Leskov, "Salyut-7 Is Falling," *supra* note note 12; "Space Agency Is Needed," *Izvestia*, January 31, 1991.

18. For the statute of this association, see *International Legal Materials*, p. 1365 (1981).

19. Art. 21 of the Soviet Law, On the Property of the USSR, of March 6, 1990, *Vestnik Verhovnogo Soveta*, No. 11 (March 14, 1990).

20. Art 3. of the decision of the Supreme Soviet of the Russian Republic on enactment of the law, On Property in the Russian Soviet Federated Socialist Republic, of December 24, 1990. *Sovetskaya Rossiya*, January 10, 1991.

21. The term "space system" is not defined in the law.

22. See, for instance, "Environmental Aspects of Activities in Outer Space," K.-H. Böckstiegel (ed.), *State of the Law and Measures of Protection*, Cologne, Carl Heymanns Verlag, 1990.

23. *Izvestia*, December 8, 1990.

24. See *Presidential Directive on National Space Policy*, Washington, The White House, Office of Press Secretary, February 11, 1988.

25. Most of the ideas put forth here are reflected in the draft Law on Space

Activities in the Soviet Union, elaborated at the Institute of State and Law (USSR Academy of Sciences), *Sovetskoye Gosudarstvo i Pravo*, No.7, 1991 (published in Russian).

26. For more details, see V. S. Vereshchetin, "International Space Law and Domestic Law: problems of interrelations," *Journal of Space Law*, Vol. 9, Nos. 1 and 2, 1981, pp. 31-40.

27. See D. de la Rochere, *supra* note 7, p. 19.

28. Article 20 of the Law of 1978. The text of the Law can be found in *Vedomosty Verhevnogo Soveta SSSR* No.29, 1978.

29. Article 24 of the Law of 1978.

30. Article 21 of the Law of 1978.

31. For more details, see V. S. Vereshchetin, G. M. Danilenko, and R. A. Mullerson, "Constitutional Reform in the USSR and International Law" (in Russian), *Sovetskoye Gosudarstvo i Pravo*, No. 5, 1990, pp. 13-22.

6

Space Law in the United States

Jonathan F. Galloway

In the United States, the most important national law governing the development and scope of space law is the National Aeronautics and Space Act (NASA Act) of 1958.[1] This national legislation was developed in the context of the International Geophysical Year (IGY), which symbolized and epitomized international scientific cooperation, and in the aftermath of the October 1957 launching of Sputnik, which pointed toward competition and possible conflict between the superpowers. Space law, both national and international, attempts to promote cooperation, peaceful purposes, and the prevention of international conflict. Competition is beneficial between private firms in a competitive market, but not between superpowers. These three Cs—cooperation, conflict, and competition—were all part of the environment in 1957--58, and they are found in varying proportions in different treaties and national laws and at different times since the beginning of the space age. Fortunately, since 1989, with the end of the cold war, encounters between the world's semi-sovereign states have been marked by an emphasis on cooperation and peaceful competition.

THE BEGINNINGS OF SPACE LAW IN THE UNITED STATES

On November 21, 1957, shortly after Sputnik was launched, the U.S. Rocket and Satellite Research Panel made a proposal which was quite prescient, calling for a National Space Establishment not dependent upon direct military appropriations. The proposed establishment would engage in space research and manned expeditions. Research areas could include materials, electronics and communications, propulsion, meteorology, the life sciences, psychology, physics, chemistry, geophysics, astronomy, astrophysics, astronautics and cosmology. For space exploration, planning and preparation were to be initiated with regard to vehicles and other problems of human space flight as a first step toward crewed satellite stations, as well as studies relating to lunar flight. In short, "the National Space Establishment will unify the efforts and contributions of science, industry and the military to space research, and will draw the youth of our country into science."[2] This agenda is basically that of the NASA Act and is continuing today. The United States remains committed to both crewed and uncrewed missions, the separation but not isolation of a civilian program from a military program and an emphasis on interdisciplinary programs. The program has been based on proposals by scientists and engineers, proposals which have been far-reaching and idealistic but also—in most cases—realistic, as we can see in retrospect.

These space activities proposed by scientists and engineers have, of course, required congressional authorization and financial appropriations in order to be realized. Initial authorization of the new U.S. space program began with the hearings on satellite and missile programs by the Senate Preparedness Investigating Subcommittee of the Armed Services Committee on November 25, 1957. Bipartisan unanimity was expressed by Senator Lyndon B. Johnson, the chairman of the Subcommittee, and Senator Styles Bridges, ranking minority member, in their statement that "the same forces, the same knowledge, and the same technology which are producing ballistic missiles can also produce instruments of peace and universal cooperation, . . . the truly worthwhile goal is a world of peace."[3] In considering the suggestions of the Rocket and Satellite Research Panel and those of the American Rocket Society, the Subcommittee recognized that many of the goals, such as satellite communications and a crewed expedition to the Moon by 1968, did not fall within the jurisdiction of the Department of Defense, nor could they be attained by ad hoc arrangements nationally or internationally. The stage was therefore set for the passage of the far-reaching NASA Act of 1958. The Declaration of Policy and Purpose in this law, as later amended, is as follows:

Sec. 102. (a) The Congress hereby declares that it is the policy of the United States that activities in space should be devoted to peaceful purposes for the benefit of all mankind.

(b) The Congress declares that the general welfare and security of the United States require that adequate provision be made for aeronautical and space activities. The Congress further declares that such activities shall be the responsibility of, and shall be directed by, a civilian agency exercising control over aeronautical and space activities sponsored by the United States, except that activities peculiar to or primarily associated with the development of weapons systems, military operations, or the defense of the United States (including the research and development necessary to make effective provision for the defense of the United States) shall be the responsibility of, and shall be directed by, the Department of Defense; and that determination as to which such agency has responsibility for and direction of any such activity shall be made by the President in conformity with section 201(e).

(c) The Congress declares that the general welfare of the United States requires that the National Aeronautics and Space Administration (as established by Title II of this Act) seek and encourage to the maximum extent possible the fullest commercial use of space.

(d) The aeronautical and space activities of the United States shall be conducted so as to contribute materially to one or more of the following objectives:

(1) The expansion of human knowledge of the Earth and of phenomena in the atmosphere and space;

(2) The improvement of the usefulness, performance, speed, safety, and efficiency of aeronautical and space vehicles;

(3) The development and operation of vehicles capable of carrying instruments, equipment, supplies, and living organisms through space;

(4) The establishment of long-range studies of the potential benefits to be gained from, the opportunities for, and the problems involved in the utilization of aeronautical and space activities for peaceful and scientific purposes;

(5) The preservation of the role of the United States as a leader in aeronautical and space science and technology and in the application thereof to the conduct of peaceful activities within and outside the atmosphere;

(6) The making available to agencies directly concerned with national defense of discoveries that have military value or significance, and the furnishing by such agencies, to the civilian agency established to direct and control nonmilitary aeronautical and space activities, of information as to discoveries which have value or significance to that agency;

(7) Cooperation by the United States with other nations and groups of nations in work done pursuant to this Act and in the peaceful application of the results thereof;

(8) The most effective utilization of the scientific and engineering resources of the United States, with close cooperation among all interested agencies of the United States in order to avoid unnecessary duplication of effort, facilities, and equipment; and

(9) The preservation of the United States preeminent position in aeronautics and space through research and technology development related to associated manufacturing processes.

In 1975, Title IV on Upper Atmosphere Research was added:

Sec. 404. In carrying out the provisions of this title, the Administration, subject to the direction of the President and after consultation with the Secretary of State, shall make every effort to enlist the support and cooperation of appropriate scientists and engineers of other countries and international organizations.

It is appropriate to highlight these objectives of U.S. space policy because, astonishingly, many books on space policy omit any reference to the official legal policy of the United States, apparently on the assumption that law is not policy. Clearly, any analysis of U.S. space policy must be based on knowledge of the legislative specification of the policy and purpose of the U.S. space program.

Let us examine the provisions of the Act with respect to cooperation with other nations as a goal of U.S. policy. Further to the general mandate provided in Sec. 102 (d) (7), Section 205 of the Act provides that:

The Administration, under the foreign policy guidance of the President, may engage in a program of international cooperation in work done pursuant to this Act, and in the peaceful application of the results thereof, pursuant to agreements made by the President with the advice and consent of the Senate.

In signing the bill, President Eisenhower stated that he regarded this section "as recognizing that international treaties may be made in this field, and as not precluding, in appropriate cases, less formal arrangements for cooperation."

Over the past 33 years, NASA has carried out an outstanding program of international cooperation; indeed, there are many countries and organizations whose contributions to various forms of space activity were made possible only through bilateral arrangements with NASA. Since the beginning of the space age, NASA's international cooperation has been based on the recognition that most other nations would not develop launching facilities; a variety of opportunities have therefore been made available to other nations for scientific research and development, applications of engineering skills, construction and operation of tracking stations, and planning future space exploration missions.

The policy guidelines adopted by NASA for cooperation with other nations and groups of nations provide for:

1. Designation by each participating government of a government agency for the negotiation and supervision of joint efforts;
2. Conduct of projects and activities having scientific validity and mutual interest;
3. Agreement upon specific projects rather than generalized programs;
4. Acceptance of financial responsibility by each participating agency for its own contributions to joint projects;
5. Provision for the widest and most practicable dissemination of the results of cooperative activities.[4]

In accordance with these guidelines, cooperation agreements used by NASA, in cooperation with the Department of State, include letter agreements, agency-to-agency memoranda of understanding (MOUs), executive agreements, and treaties, which are negotiated at the presidential level but may involve NASA and other agencies. Agreements may be entitled "conventions" or "agreements" but have treaty status and are submitted by the President to the Senate for advice and consent.[5] In general, the less formal arrangements apply to cooperative spacecraft projects, experiments on NASA missions, U.S. experiments on foreign spacecraft, cooperative sounding rocket projects, and cooperation on ground activities, in such areas as remote sensing, communications, meteorology, geodynamics, studies of the atmosphere and space environment, human spaceflight, and solar-terrestrial studies. Other categories of cooperation are reimbursable launchings, tracking and data acquisition, and personnel exchanges. The cooperative program involving the greatest number of countries has been the automatic picture transmissions (APT) from meteorological satellites, while over 50 countries have participated in communications satellite and remote sensing experiments, and over 40 in geodynamics and space environment studies. All types of countries have participated in these space cooperative ventures: developed and less-developed, capitalist, socialist, and communist, including the Soviet Union and China. In addition, NASA has had programs with international organizations, including the International Telecommunications Satellite Organization (INTELSAT), the European Space Agency (ESA), and the United Nations Food and Agriculture Organization (FAO). This record of international space cooperation during the past 33 years reveals that the U.S. policy of cooperation for peaceful purposes has been strongly implemented in practice.

Besides NASA, there are 13 other parts of the executive branch of government which are involved in national and international space programs. Each year the President submits to Congress, via NASA, an "Aeronautics and Space Report," with a wealth of information on the activities of the 14 governmental departments and agencies engaged in space endeavors.[6] Besides NASA, these are the Departments of Defense, Commerce, Energy, Interior, Agriculture, Transportation and State; the Federal Communications Commission; the Environmental Protection Agency; the National Science Foundation; the Smithsonian Institution; the Arms Control and Disarmament Agency; and the U.S. Information Agency.

To fulfill the mandate of coordinating these departments and agencies "in order to avoid unnecessary duplication of effort, facilities and equipment," the 1958 NASA Act established a National Aeronautics and Space Council as an executive coordinating body. The Council was given a mandate to (1) survey all significant aeronautics and space activities, including the policies, plans, programs, and accomplishments of all U.S. agencies engaged in such activities, and (2) develop a comprehensive program of aeronautical and space activities to be conducted by agencies of the United States. It was further mandated to provide for effective cooperation between NASA and the Department of Defense, and to specify which of such activities could be carried out by both agencies, notwithstanding the assignment of primary responsibility to one or the other. It was also to resolve differences arising among the agencies with respect to such activities.

At first the President, and subsequently the Vice President, was in charge of the Council, but in a decentralizing reorganization in 1973, President Nixon abolished the Council, leaving coordination to inter-agency committees. This mechanism, however, proved ineffective, and in 1988 Congress re-established the Council, now called the National Space Council and not having responsibility for aeronautics. The Council, chaired by the Vice President, includes the Secretaries of State, Defense, Commerce, Transportation, and Treasury; the Director of the Office of Management and Budget; the Chief of Staff to the President; the Assistant to the President for National Security Affairs; the Director of Central Intelligence; the Assistant to the President for Science and Technology; and the NASA Administrator.

The recent U.S. launches, including satellites for meteorology, navigation, defense, communications and planetary research, demonstrate the variety of missions that need coordination. It should be noted that these missions include not only a variety of U.S. government missions but private and international spacecraft as well, reflecting the wide range of space responsibilities of the government, the diverse space interests within the U.S. economy, and the increasingly integrated global society and market, in which borders are more and more porous. Military experiments undertaken as part of the Strategic Defense Initiative (SDI) may run counter to this observation, but SDI may in time give way to SEI—the Space Exploration Initiative—as a result of the end of the cold war and the increasing extent of international cooperation.

By 1984, NASA alone had engaged in 2,318 cooperative international projects, in collaboration with both large spacefaring states and small states and international organizations.[7] Worldwide users of the most highly commercialized space service—communications—have particularly benefited from early U.S. space leadership, and international organizations have made extensive use of data from U.S. satellites for remote sensing, weather forecasting, and other developmental purposes.

EXAMPLES OF INTERNATIONAL AGREEMENTS

An example of an agency-to-agency agreement is one concluded on October 1, 1986 between NASA and the French Centre National d'Etudes Spatiales on the use of SPOT (*Satellite Probatoire pour l'Observation de la Terre*) data and U.S. experimental sensor data for research purposes. The objective of the cooperation is to advance the state of the art in the processing, scientific analysis and use of experimental remote sensing data. The agreement provides for the establishment of a joint steering committee to oversee cooperation, approve investigators, promote cooperative studies, and determine the benefits from the joint use of spacecraft and aircraft data. Such agency-to-agency agreements seek to anticipate problems so that any difficulties can be avoided. Provision is made for the publication of research results, and each agency bears the costs of discharging its responsibilities under the agreement.

An example of an executive agreement is one on Space Station Freedom signed on September 29, 1988, between the Government of the United States, the governments of the member states of the European Space Agency, the government of Japan, and the government of Canada.[8] Article 1 of the agreement states, in part, that:

> The object of this Agreement is to establish a long-term international cooperative framework among the Partners, on the basis of genuine partnership, for the detailed design, development, operation and utilization of a permanently manned civil space station for peaceful purposes, in accordance with international law. This permanently

manned civil Space Station will enhance the scientific, technological and commercial use of outer space.

U.S. responsibility for funding this agreement's purposes is not primarily the responsibility of the executive branch, but of the Congress. Consequently, as the democratic process unfolds, one would expect to see, and one does see, the waxing and waning of commitment to Space Station Freedom.

Another example of an executive agreement is the Agreement between the United States of America and the USSR Concerning Cooperation in the Exploration and Use of Outer Space for Peaceful Purposes, signed on April 15, 1987.[9] The agreement comprises seven articles and an annex listing 16 cooperative projects. The preamble calls attention to the role of the two countries in exploring and using outer space for peaceful purposes, and the desire to make the results available not only to themselves but to all peoples of the world. The areement recalls both the 1967 Outer Space Treaty and the previous U.S.-Soviet agreement of November 21, 1985, on "contacts, exchanges, and cooperation in scientific, technical, educational, cultural, and other fields."[10] Article 6 of the executive agreement states that "the Parties shall encourage international cooperation in the study of legal questions of mutual interest which may arise in the exploration and use of outer space for peaceful purposes."

THE SPACE COMMERCIALIZATION LAWS

Communications Satellite Act of 1962, As Amended

Communications satellites were developed in the United States with government assistance and subsidies, and it is this space technology which has had the greatest commercial success and the greatest degree of international cooperation. In 1962, only four years after the NASA Act, the Communications Satellite Act was passed to provide for the establishment of an operational communication satellite system. That the United States took a global view of this use of outer space is evident from the declaration of policy and purpose in Section 102:

(a) The Congress hereby declares that it is the policy of the United States to establish, in conjunction and in cooperation with other countries, as expeditiously as practicable, a commercial communications satellite system, as part of an improved global communications network, which will be responsive to public needs and national objectives, which will serve the communication needs of the United States and other countries, and which will contribute to world peace and understanding.
(b) The new and expanded telecommunication services are to be made available as promptly as possible and are to be extended to provide global coverage at the earliest practicable date. In effectuating this program, care and attention will be directed toward providing such services to economically less developed countries and areas as

well as those more highly developed, toward efficient and economical use of the electromagnetic frequency spectrum, and toward the reflection of the benefits of this new technology in both quality of services and charges for such services.[11]

After the establishment of the Communications Satellite Corporation, COMSAT, the U.S. government worked toward the establishment of the International Telecommunications Satellite Consortium (INTELSAT), which was established in 1964 through the Interim Arrangements for a Global Commercial Satellite System.[12] In the initial system, the United States held 60 percent of the votes because it handled over half of the international point-to-point traffic through the system. Under the Definitive Arrangements of 1973, by which INTELSAT became the International Telecommunications Satellite Organization,[13] the United States gave up its majority position in order to encourage a more broadly based international organization. The success of this approach is evident from the fact that by 1992 there were 122 member countries in INTELSAT and the U.S. voting share had declined to 24 percent.

While the legal and organizational basis of INTELSAT was being developed, space communications technology was rapidly advancing. The first INTELSAT satellite, Early Bird, had a capacity of 240 telephone circuits or one television channel, while each of the latest INTELSAT VI satellites has a capacity of 24,000 telephone circuits as well as three television channels. While 119 countries are members of INTELSAT, the system in 1989 was used by more than 150 countries with over 640 earth stations connected by 2,259 transmission paths. While the Soviet Union and other socialist countries did not join INTELSAT but set up the international INTERSPUTNIK system, cooperation between the two systems gradually developed. By the August 27, 1985, Memorandum of Understanding between INTELSAT and the Ministry of Posts and Telecommunications of the Soviet Union, Soviet Earth stations were granted the same legal treatment in using INTELSAT satellites as the Earth stations of INTELSAT member states, formalizing years of less formal cooperation. Space technology and the global need for international communications have brought about the highest degree of international cooperation in space for peaceful purposes.

International Maritime Satellite Telecommunications Act of 1978

In 1978, the United States passed the International Maritime Satellite Telecommunications Act[14] to promote maritime satellite communications through INMARSAT, the International Maritime Satellite Organization, which was established in 1976 in London. As with INTELSAT, the COMSAT Corporation was assigned the role of "designated entity" to represent the United States on the INMARSAT Council.

Land Remote-Sensing Commercialization Act of 1984

The Land Remote-Sensing Commercialization Act of 1984 (Landsat Act)[15] promotes the commercial distribution and use of data from the civilian Landsat remote sensing satellites, which Congress recognized as being of major benefit in managing the Earth's natural resources and in many other economic activities. Remote sensing of other countries from space by the government or by private parties has been an issue of some sensitivity, and the Act recognizes that U.S. remote sensing activities must conform to international treaty obligations.

The primary purpose of the Act was to transfer remote sensing activities from the public to the private sector. This process, often called privatization, is intended to make the acquisition and use of the data more economically efficient and less costly to the government by phasing out government funding for operational satellite remote sensing.

The commercialization of remote sensing is quite different from the situation in satellite communications. The Secretary of Commerce is made responsible for the Landsat system and for contracting with a private company, currently the Earth Observation Satellite Company (EOSAT), for marketing the data received from the satellite. U.S. policy affirms the right to acquire and disseminate such data and the obligation to make it available to all potential users on a nondiscriminatory basis consistent with antitrust laws. Congressional findings recognize that "certain Government oversight must be maintained to assure that private sector activities are in the national interest and that the international commitments and policies of the United States are honored."[16] This oversight in part reflects the government's international responsibility for space activities carried out by non-governmental entities and for authorizing and supervising those activities, in accordance with Article 6 of the 1967 Outer Space Treaty.

During the consideration of the Landsat Act, the issue arose of whether to also commercialize meteorological satellites, a government function carried out by the National Oceanic and Atmospheric Administration in the Department of Commerce. Following a heated debate, Congress found no compelling reason to commercialize meteorological satellites at that time. Congress considered that while it was appropriate to privatize commercial goods where the market can set prices based on scarcity, it would not be appropriate where there is no market and where public or collective goods are concerned.

Commercial Space Launch Act of 1984

The purpose of the Commercial Space Launch Act of 1984,[17] like that of the Landsat Act, was to commercialize or privatize launching services, which were previously in the public sphere. The objective in this case, however, is not complete privatization but a combination of government and private sector responsibilities, with the government maintaining its own launching capabilities. Noting that the private sector is capable of launching satellites and providing associated services, and that these private capabilities complement those of the government, Congress decided to encourage private enterprise while requiring government regulation of launchings and services. According to Section 2 (7), this was done "in order to ensure compliance with international obligations of the United States and to protect the public health and safety, safety of property, and national security interests and foreign policy interests of the United States."

To achieve these purposes, the Act designates the Department of Transportation to promote commercial launches by the private sector. Section 6 (a) (1) of the Act provides that "No person shall launch a launch vehicle or operate a launch site within the United States, unless authorized by a license issued or transferred under this Act" and makes the Department of Transportation responsible for establishing consistent licensing requirements. Furthermore, Section 11 (a) states that "The Secretary may terminate, prohibit, or suspend immediately the launch of a launch vehicle or the operation of a launch site which is licensed under this Act if the Secretary determines that such launch or operation is detrimental to the public health and safety, safety of property, or any national security interest or foreign policy interest of the United States." The licenses must permit the government to monitor sites, production facilities, or assembly sites when the Secretary decides it is necessary to determine compliance with the license.

Such government regulation and monitoring are essential to control potential hazards to health and safety and damage to property, to coordinate private and government launches, and to fulfill the requirement for registering space objects in accordance with the 1976 Convention on the Registration of Objects Launched into Outer Space. The procedures for regulating private launching activities are thus quite distinct from those adopted for satellite communications and satellite remote sensing, with the procedures adapted to the specific technical requirements in each case.

EXAMPLES OF OTHER SPACE-RELATED LAWS

It is not feasible to describe all U.S. laws that affect space policies, programs, and budgets. NASA's annual authorization and appropriation laws since 1958 would by themselves require several volumes. There are two laws, however, that are worth considering because of their special significance for U.S. policy.

Implantation of the Flag on the Moon or Planets

The U.S. law of 1969 on the Implantation of the United States Flag on the Moon or Planets illustrates the elaboration of national legislation in accordance with international commitments, in this case with respect to the 1967 Outer Space Treaty. The 1969 law provides as follows:

Sec. 8. The flag of the United States, and no other flag, shall be implanted or otherwise placed on the surface of the moon, or on the surface of any planet, by the members of the crew of any spacecraft making a lunar or planetary landing as a part of a mission under the Apollo program or as a part of a mission under any subsequent program, the funds for which are provided entirely by the Government of the United States. This act is intended as a symbolic gesture of national pride in achievement and is not to be construed as a declaration of national appropriation by claim of sovereignty.[18]

The last sentence is a reference to international commitments under the 1967 Outer Space Treaty, which was ratified by the United States in 1967 and which provides, in Article 2, that:

Outer space, including the moon and other celestial bodies is not subject to national appropriation by claim of sovereignty, by means of use or occupation, or by any other means.

National Science and Technology Policy, Organization and Priorities Act of 1976

The purpose of the National Science and Technology Policy, Organization and Priorities Act of 1976 is to establish a science and technology policy for the United States. By this Act, Congress recognized the impact of science and technology on society, and the interrelations of scientific, technological, economic, social, political and institutional factors. Among the 13 priority goals are two of special significance for international space cooperation:

1. Fostering leadership in the quest for international peace and progress toward human freedom, dignity, and well-being by enlarging the contributions of American scientists and engineers to the knowledge of man and his universe, by making discoveries of basic science widely available at home and abroad, and by utilizing technology in support of United States national and foreign policy goals.

13. Advancing the exploration and peaceful uses of outer space.[19]

It should be noted that many of the other goals listed in the Act require the application of space science and technology for their attainment, or can be more effectively achieved through space-related technology. Space activities can contribute to economic opportunity, assuring adequate supplies of food and energy, improving health and the natural environment, preserving national security, increasing educational opportunities, and improving transportation and communications.

INTERNATIONAL LAW AND U.S. SPACE LAW

U.S. national space law has undergone substantial historical development in the years since 1957. Under Article 6 of the U.S. Constitution, international treaties to which the United States is a party are the "supreme law of the land," and the four United Nations space treaties that have been ratified by the United States have become part of U.S. space law. The provisions of these treaties, the 1967 Outer Space Treaty, the 1968 Rescue Agreement, the 1973 Liability Convention, and the 1976 Registration Convention are considered elsewhere in this volume. The fifth space treaty elaborated and recommended by the United Nations, the Moon Agreement, entered into force in 1984 after ratification by five nations and has now been ratified by seven countries. The United States is among the nations that have not ratified this treaty.

In addition to the United Nations-sponsored space treaties, the United States is a party to a number of other international conventions and agreements which relate to space law. Among these are the 1972 Anti-Ballistic Missile Treaty; the 1963 Treaty Banning Nuclear Weapons Tests in the Atmosphere, in Outer Space and Under Water; the 1977 Convention on the Prohibition of Military or Any Other Hostile Use of Environmental Modification Techniques; and the Final Acts of the Conferences of the International Telecommunication Union.[20]

RECENT POLICY INITIATIVES

On July 29, 1989, on the 30th anniversary of the first human landing on the Moon, President Bush announced the U.S. commitment to returning humans to the Moon and then proceeding on to Mars, a program he called the Space Exploration Initiative (SEI). For such a proposal to become law in the United States, however, it must be approved not only by the President but also by the Senate and House of Representatives. In the Senate, it will have to be authorized by the Committee on Commerce, Science and Transportation; and in the House by the Committee on Science, Space and Technology. When authorized, it will need to be funded by the Appropriations Committees in both chambers. President Bush may say, "Why the Moon? Why Mars? Because it is humanity's destiny to strive, to seek, to find. And because it is America's destiny to lead," but we must remember that the legal implementation of programs requires concerted action from both the executive and legislative branches of the government.

CONCLUSION

As the space age enters its 35th year, a year which has been proclaimed as International Space Year and which marks the 500th anniversary of

Columbus's "discovery" of America, an assessment of the scope and development of U.S. space law indicates considerable progress toward realization of the basic objectives of U.S. space policy as set out in the 1958 NASA Act. The subsequent national laws and the U.S. ratification of international treaties have fulfilled the promise of peaceful cooperation and the peaceful use of space. There has been a growing pattern of peaceful competition among nations engaged in certain space applications, such as remote sensing, while the mechanisms of international cooperation have been strengthened in other space activities, such as communications, meteorology, and maritime services. Potential for conflict still exists, but it seems less threatening given the end of the cold war. The role of the government in space in relation to the private sector is still being defined at a time when there is strong movement toward the privatization of certain space activities. There are debates within the United States about specific projects, such as the Shuttle, the Space Station, the Aerospace Plane, Mission to Planet Earth and the Moon/Mars Proposal, but agreement on overall policy goals has gradually pushed the United States toward a new vision of spaceship Earth, a fragile blue oasis in the universe. Problems loom on the horizon with respect to the role of the military in space programs and to limits on funding for new programs, but it is myopic to divide space policy implementation into an expansive "Apollo Paradigm" and a narrower "Post-Challenger Paradigm."[21] The reality is more complicated, and the lessons learned from successes and failures have accumulated over the years, resulting in a complex mixture of policies and programs.

The continuing challenges indicate that politics itself may be the endless frontier, nonetheless, with a view to building a new consensus on the national space program, the problems and opportunities have been examined in a number of recent policy studies including the *Report of the National Commission on Space* (1986),[22] the Ride report on *Leadership and America's Future in Space* (1987),[23] the *Report of the Advisory Committee on the Future of the United States Space Program* (1990),[24] the Stafford report on *America at the Threshold: America's Space Exploration Initiative* (1991),[25] and the Office of Technology Assessment study on *Exploring the Moon and Mars: Choices for the Nation.*[26] There was such strong leadership in the United States at the beginning of the space age that the legacy of that time allows the country some leeway to muddle through times of questioning and reappraisal.

The good, strong, and energetic beginnings have left lasting benefits for the development of U.S. space law and policy. As Eilene Galloway writes of the 1957-1958 foundations, "At this crucial juncture in our history, all the elements essential for swift foresighted decision and action were present: spearheading leadership, knowledgeable scientists and engineers, an industrial base, resources, harmony between the Executive and Legislative Branches of the government on objectives, and an institutional structure on which to build."[27] The legacy of this fortunate and happy confluence is still with us and has had a lasting influence on law, policy, and programs. It should be recalled in these sometimes agonizing times of reappraisal that the 1958 NASA Act commits the United States to being "a" leader—not "the" leader—in space, and this objective can be and is being fulfilled in our increasingly interdependent and integrated world.

NOTES

1. Pub. L. No. 85-568, 72 Stat. 426, 42 U.S.C. sec. 2451, 2484.
2. "A National Mission to Explore Outer Space: A Proposal of the Rocket and Satellite Research Panel," November 21, 1957, U.S. Senate, Special Committee on Space and Astronautics, Committee Print, *Compilation of Materials on Space and Astronautics*, No. 1, 85th Cong., 2d Sess., Government Printing Office, March 27, 1958, pp. 14-16.
3. "Inquiry into Satellite and Missile Programs," Hearings before the Preparedness Investigating Subcommittee, Committee on Armed Services, U.S. Senate, 85th Cong., 1st and 2d Sess., Part 3, Washington, Government Printing Office, p. 2,429.
4. *Twenty-six Years of NASA International Programs*, NASA International Affairs Division, Washington, Government Printing Office, 1984, p. 2.
5. *United States International Space Program: Texts of Executive Agreements, Memoranda of Understanding, and Other International Arrangements, 1959-1965*, U.S. Senate, Document No. 44, 89th Cong., 1st Sess., Committee on Aeronautical and Space Sciences, July 30, 1965, pp. 1-8.
6. *Aeronautics and Space Report of the President 1989-1990*, Washington, NASA, 1991.
7. *International Cooperation and Competition in Civilian Space Activities*, U.S. Congress, Office of Technology Assessment, Washington, Government Printing Office, 1985, p. 37.
8. For the text of this and other important laws and agreements, see U.S. Senate, Committee on Commerce, Science, and Transportation, *Space Law and Related Documents: International Space Law Documents and United States Space Law Documents*, Committee Print, 101st Cong., 2d Sess., June 1990. Hereinafter cited as *Space Law and Related Documents*.
9. 26 *International Legal Materials* 622.
10. 25 *International Legal Materials* 105.
11. Pub. L. No. 87-624, 76 Stat. 419, 47 U.S.C. Sec. 701, Aug. 31, 1962.
12. For the early history of communications satellites, see Jonathan F. Galloway, *The Politics and Technology of Satellite Communications*, Lexington MA, Lexington Books, 1972.
13. 18 U.S.T. 2410; T.I.A.S. No. 6347.
14. 92 Stat. 2392.
15. Pub. L. No. 98-365, 98 Stat. 451, 15 U.S.C. Sec. 4201, July 17, 1984; amended in 1988 by Pub. L. No. 100-147, 101 Stat. 876, 15 U.S.C. Sec. 4201 (1988).
16. *Id.*, Sect. 101 (13).
17. Pub. L. No. 98-575, 98 Stat. 3055, 49 U.S.C. app. sec. 2601, Oct. 30, 1984.
18. 83 Stat. 202, Sect. 8, November 18, 1969.

19. 42 U.S.C. 6601, May 11, 1976.

20. For these and other agreements, see *Space Law and Related Documents*, *supra* note 7. See also Stephen Gorove (ed.), *United States Space Law—National and International Regulations (1982-1990)*, Dordrecht, Martinus Nijhoff, and K.-H. Böckstiegel and M. Benkö (eds.), *Space Law: Basic Legal Documents*, Martinus Nijhoff, 1990.

21. Byerly Radford (ed.), *Space Policy Reconsidered*, Boulder CO, Westview, 1989, pp. 1-9, 175-190.

22. *Pioneering the Space Frontier: Report of the National Commission on Space*, Thomas Paine, Chairman, New York, Bantam Books, 1986.

23. *Leadership and America's Future in Space*, Report to the Administrator by Sally K. Ride, Washington, NASA, August 1987.

24. *Report of the Advisory Committee on the Future of the United States Space Program*, Norman R. Augustine, Chairman, Washington, Government Printing Office, December 1990.

25. *America at the Threshold: America's Space Exploration Initiative*, Thomas F. Stafford, Chairman, Washington, Government Printing Office, May 1991.

26. *Exploring the Moon and Mars: Choices for the Nation*, U.S. Congress, Office of Technology Assessment (OTA-ISC-502), Washington, Government Printing Office, July 1991.

27. Eilene Galloway, "U.S. Congress and Outer Space," Chapter 3 in Frederick C. Durant III (ed.), *New Perspectives on American Astronautics*, San Diego, American Astronautical Society, 1981, pp. 139-160.

7

Space Law and the European Space Agency

Michel Bourély

The 1967 Outer Space Treaty, unlike most other international agreements, expressly states that it is not solely applicable to governments.[1] Article 6 of the Treaty, which forms the basis of space law, stipulates that its provisions must be respected by governmental agencies, by international organizations, and by non-governmental entities, thus allowing private enterprises to engage in space activities.

The negotiating history of the Treaty shows that this provision was not accepted without difficulty by all signatories. In particular the Soviet Union was opposed at first, arguing that a treaty, by its nature, only binds the governments of its member states and not intergovernmental organizations or non-governmental entities. The Soviet Union finally agreed to withdraw its objections in exchange for a confirmation of the principle that governments would bear final responsibility for all space activities. Article 3 of the Treaty stipulates that all space activities of states (including those of public and private entities for which the states are responsible) must be carried out in accordance with international law.

As described in other chapters, there are many intergovernmental organizations which are very active in space activities, and these organizations are expected to comply with international law, including space law. The European Space Agency (ESA), an intergovernmental organization, is an interesting example to study because ESA is at this time, the only real "space" organization, that is an organization whose objective is to carry out space activities in all areas, whatever their nature. The purpose of this chapter is to analyze the position of the European Space Agency in relation to public international law, and space law in particular. To that end, I will consider the legal regime governing this organization from various points of view, first examining ESA as an actor, then as a subject, and finally as a source both of public international law and of space law.

ESA AS AN ACTOR IN PUBLIC INTERNATIONAL LAW

As an institution, the organization of ESA is not unusual. However, there are certain particularities in the structure and operating rules. An institutional analysis of ESA will be useful in order to understand the place it occupies and the role it plays among other intergovernmental space organizations. To do so, we must briefly consider the circumstances of its creation, before analyzing its legal status.

The Creation of the European Space Agency

High technology is one of the fields in which Western European states have best proven their ability to contribute to technical progress in the interest of their respective populations and for the benefit of all humankind. In the company of the United States, the Russian Federation, and Japan, and in such fields as aviation, nuclear power, and computers, Western Europe is certainly capable of maintaining a stature commensurate with its history, intellectual heritage and capabilities, economic importance, industrial level, and prospects for the future. Unfortunately, for a long period during the early years of space activities, the European states divided their efforts in the space field, unaware of the serious disadvantages of doing so. The various states acted on their own, rather than uniting their intellectual, industrial, and financial resources to create a group of sufficient size to play a significant role.

At the beginning of the space age, some Western European countries attempted to develop national programs of modest size. It was not until 1962 that 10 states agreed to cooperate in a multinational space effort in a regional framework. In that year, two Conventions were signed, coming into force two years later in 1964. The first created the European Space Research Organization (ESRO), and the second established the European Space Vehicle Launcher Development Organization (ELDO).

However, it very soon became clear that these measures did not suffice to enable Western Europe to play the role it should play in the worldwide space race. Therefore, in 1967, a meeting of ministers responsible for space affairs—the European Space Conference (ESC)—was convened to give serious consideration to this problem.

After a long series of hard discussions, the ESC reached agreement on two elements which allowed Europe to establish a basis for a true European space program. First, in 1972, two satellite applications programs were adopted, the Spacelab program and the Ariane launcher program; second, on May 30, 1975, a Convention was signed providing for the creation of a unique organization with general competence, the European Space Agency (ESA).

The Convention came into force five years later, on October 30, 1980, but the European Space Agency actually became operational on May 31, 1975. It took over all the activities and programs of the two previous space organizations, as well as the coordination function which the ESC has informally undertaken. Thereafter, periodic meetings of the responsible ministers of ESA's member states have been held for the purpose of adopting new Agency programs to fulfill the needs of Western Europe.

The Legal Status of ESA

ESA is a regional intergovernmental organization. Its purpose is to carry out various activities in the space field. Its legal status derives from the Convention of May 30, 1975,[2] and its major provisions can be summarized as follows:

Purpose. According to Article 2 of the Convention, the purpose of ESA is to provide for and to promote cooperation among European states in space research and technology; the Agency's activities should serve scientific purposes and be applied to operational space applications systems. In the spirit of the 1967 Outer Space Treaty, to which all signatories of the Convention are parties, Article 2 provides that the activities of the Agency should be carried out for exclusively peaceful purposes.

In practice, the Agency's objectives relate to two different levels of activities. One level is that of the Agency itself, which must elaborate a long-term European space policy and define and carry out space programs and activities (Art. 2.b). As part of that effort, the Agency must develop an appropriate industrial policy (Art. 2.a and 2.d). The other level is that of the member states. The Agency must recommend objectives for national space policies and coordinate these policies with respect to other national and international organizations and institutions (Art. 2.a). ESA must also coordinate the European space program with the national programs, with the ultimate purpose of integrating the national programs into the regional program (Art. 2.c).

Composition. The founders of ESA established an intergovernmental organization with a legal personality. The Agency is one of a number of European organizations engaged in space activities, but it differs from such organizations as EUTELSAT and EUMETSAT in that its field of action is not limited to a particular application; rather it covers all aspects of space activities.

The Agency presently has 13 member states: Austria, Belgium, Denmark, France, Germany, Ireland, Italy, the Netherlands, Norway, Spain, Sweden, Switzerland,and the United Kingdom. Finland is an associate member, and Canada has a special position within ESA, participating in certain activities and special programs based on a general agreement of cooperation.

Structure. Like most other international operational organizations, ESA is divided into a decision-making organ and an executive organ. Decision-making is the responsibility of the Council, which is composed of representatives of all member states (who may be the responsible ministers themselves) and is assisted by various committees specializing in scientific, administrative, or financial matters, external relations, and so forth. (Art. 11). The executive power is vested in the Director General, who is assisted by an international staff of some 2,000 persons (Art. 12).

The Agency has its headquarters in Paris and has a number of major establishments in other places: the European Space Research and Technology Centre (ESTEC) with laboratories and test facilities, in the Netherlands; the European Space Operations Centre (ESOC) in Germany; and the European Space Research Institute (ESRIN) for documentation and space data distribution, in Italy. In addition, there are ESA installations, such as ground stations, in several countries and a center for training astronauts in Germany. Finally, the Agency has the Ariane launcher facilities at the Guiana Space Centre in French Guiana.[3]

Programs. The Council considers the proposals submitted by member states or by the Director General in the framework of the long-term plans which have been approved by the ministries. The Council decides which programs ESA shall carry out in the various fields of space activities such as science, space communications, Earth observation (remote sensing and meteorology), micro-gravity processing, space transportation systems, or participation in the United States/International Space Station program.

In each of these fields, the approved programs are divided into projects, which are sometimes further divided into phases, and a global budget and provisional schedule is determined for each program. The execution of programs is monitored by program boards, which function as delegates of the Council for that purpose.[4] The Convention provides that, in general, the participation of member states in programs is optional, but that participation in the scientific program is mandatory, representing a minimum commitment and involvement of member states in Agency programs (Art. 5). The optional programs include the building of satellites and launch facilities, while the mandatory activities include space scientific research, studies for future programs, technological research, distribution of documentation, a fellowship program, and so forth (Art. 5.1). Finally, ESA can carry out "operational activities" for other national or international bodies, on the basis of reimbursement of costs (Art. 5.2)

Budget. The main source of finance for ESA activities is the contributions by its member states, which are calculated differently for mandatory and optional programs. All member states must contribute to the mandatory program according to a scale determined by the Council, based on the member states' national incomes (Art. 13.1). The contribution of a member state to the various optional programs in which it has decided to participate is determined freely by the state concerned. This may result in one member state providing the major share of the budget of a particular program in which it has a particular interest (Art. 13.2). This was the case for France in the Ariane launcher program, for Germany in the Spacelab program, and for the United

Kingdom in the Marecs maritime communication satellite program.

Relationship with Member States. The legal personality of the Agency as an institution is conferred upon it by the Convention (Art. 15.1), and is therefore recognized by the states party to that Convention. On behalf of the Agency, the Director General is authorized to carry out various activities to which member states shall be committed.

The relationship of the Agency with its member states concerns, first, the adoption and realization of programs and activities. Decisions are taken by the Council or its subordinate bodies, in conformity with the procedures (notably the voting rule) prescribed by the Convention (Art. 11). This is particularly the case for decisions concerning the approval of new programs, the adoption of budgets, and the like. The Council must also approve agreements between the Agency and member states concerning, for example, the creation and functioning of its headquarters and other facilities.

The most difficult aspect of the Agency's relationship with its member states concerns the national programs. According to the Convention, one of the purposes of the Agency is to coordinate the various national space programs with a view to integrating them progressively into the European space program (Art. 2.c). This goal is far from being realized because the majority of member states are not prepared to give up their independent national activities. Nonetheless, currently none of the national space programs is greater than that country's share in the ESA programs. At the same time, the existence of national capacities undeniably plays a positive role in the realization of collective space programs.

International Relations. In addition to its relations with member states and other states participating in its programs, the Agency maintains relations on a worldwide basis with states and national and international organizations involved in space activities. By establishing legal ties with the Agency, these states and organizations recognize—explicitly or implicitly—its legal personality.

In the framework of its systematic policy of international cooperation, ESA may either establish informal relations or conclude formal agreements with other states or organizations. With the major space powers (United States, Soviet Union, Japan, India), coordination agreements have been concluded in exchange for information. The legal form of such relations may vary from a simple exchange of letters between space agencies to a formal, intergovernmental agreement.

Other relationships on a smaller scale are established when ESA and a government or government agency decide to participate in the realization of a common program or project. This was the case with the agreements with the United States for Spacelab, the European contribution to the U.S. Space Shuttle program. Similarly, agreements were concluded on September 29, 1988, for the participation of ESA (on behalf of Europe) in the United States/International Space Station program. ESA may also sign agreements with non-member countries which decide to participate in one of ESA's programs or projects. Canada, for example, in addition to its general cooperation agreement with ESA, participates in a number of specific ESA programs.

ESA AS A SUBJECT OF SPACE LAW

As an international intergovernmental organization engaged in space activities, the European Space Agency is bound, in the same way as states, to observe both the general provisions of international law and the specific principles elaborated in international space treaties and agreements. It must be noted, however, that treaty obligations bind the Agency directly only if the Agency has made a declaration as provided for in the implementation provisions of the treaty. Indirectly, the Agency is also bound to observe the provisions of space law which are binding on its member states, including both the general principles of the 1967 Outer Space Treaty and the specific rules of other international legal agreements and instruments. Article 6 of the Outer Space Treaty obliges international organizations, as well as states parties to the Treaty, to respect its provisions.

Declaration of Acceptance

The international agreements which elaborate the general principles of the Outer Space Treaty each contain a provision inviting international organizations engaged in space activities to declare their acceptance of the rights and obligations of those agreements. In addition to this Declaration of Acceptance, a second condition is also specified: that the majority of the member states of the organization must also be parties to both the Outer Space Treaty and the agreement. Under these provisions, the ESA Council has issued Declarations of Acceptance for three of the four international agreements implementing the general provisions of the Outer Space Treaty:[5]

Rescue Agreement: Declaration of December 31, 1975;
Liability Convention: Declaration of September 23, 1976;
Registration Agreement: Declaration of January 2, 1979.

Through its own declarations and through its member states, ESA is therefore obliged to observe international law, including space law. This has important implications for the activities of the Agency, both practically and legally.

International Liability. ESA can be treated as a "launching state" in the terms of Article 1.c of the Liability Convention. ESA launches objects into outer space and thus is internationally liable for damage caused by these objects as provided in the Liability Convention; it is thus exposed to claims for reparation of damage caused by any such space object. It must be noted that the term "space object" includes the launching vehicle and parts thereof, as well as satellites and all other objects launched into outer space. The nature of the Agency's liability depends on whether the Agency is a partner in a cooperation program, is a launch procurer, or is a launch services provider. It also depends on whether the activity involves only the Agency and its member states or whether other countries are involved.

The various aspects of international liability are very complex since private agreements, national laws, and general international law may also have to be taken into consideration. After an in-depth examination of the matter, the ESA Council adopted a resolution on December 13, 1977, which sets out procedures for resolving problems that might arise if the Agency is charged with international liability as a result of its space activities.

Space Rescue. The Agency has sent several European astronauts into outer space and will continue to do so in the future. The Agency expects to have its satellites returned to it should they reach the ground, and it will be prepared to take part, if need be, in operations for the rescue of astronauts or the return of space objects. Therefore, the Agency explicitly stipulated in its Declaration of Acceptance of the Agreement on the Rescue of Astronauts, the Return of Astronauts and the Return of Objects Launched into Outer Space, that it considered itself a "launching authority" in terms of Article 5 of the Agreement.

Registration of Space Objects. On the basis of various agreements with its member states, the Agency owns, on their behalf, space objects to which member states have contributed financially. In accordance with its acceptance of the Registration Agreement, the Agency has adopted certain practical measures. ESA keeps a registry of the launches of satellites it owns and informs the Secretary-General of the United Nations about these launches; the matter of jurisdiction and control, which remains the competence of states, is settled on a case-by-case basis between the Agency and the member states.

Direct Satellite Broadcasting. The Agency developed and built a pre-operational direct broadcast satellite called Olympus, which was launched by Ariane for ESA in 1989. ESA, however, was not the direct operator of the satellite, except for some experiments which the Agency conducted. On the basis of agreements with ESA, the European broadcasting entities using the satellite were responsible for observing the principles of Resolution 37/92 on international satellite television broadcasting, adopted on December 10, 1982, by the United Nations General Assembly.

Remote Sensing. The Agency also has a remote sensing satellite program including the ERS-1 remote sensing satellite, which was launched by Ariane in July 1991 and is being operated by ESA. The agreements between the Agency and the various user organizations concerning use of ERS-1 data oblige the latter to observe the principles of Resolution 41/65 on satellite remote sensing, adopted on December 4, 1986, by the United Nations General Assembly.

ESA AS A SOURCE OF SPACE LAW

As we have seen, the elaboration of specific rules of space law, by the United Nations or other bodies such as the International Telecommunication Union, is of direct and essential importance for the present and future activities of the European Space Agency. It is therefore particularly desirable that the Agency be involved in the work of various international organizations which elaborate international space laws for adoption by states. In turn, the Agency can provide those who are engaged in the elaboration of such texts with the experience it has gained and with its know-how in dealing with practical problems. In practice, ESA's participation in the elaboration of new texts takes place at two levels, as a participant in the work of other organizations such as the United Nations and as a creator of law.

Participation in the Work of the United Nations

The Agency takes part in the work of other organizations which formulate space law, including the United Nations. To deal with the United Nations, the Council has created a Committee on International Relations within the Agency, whose responsibilities include coordinating the relations of member states with the international bodies dealing with space matters. ESA's coordination of international relations involves both coordination between its member states and coordination of ESA's position with those of its member states, ensuring a full flow of information between all parties.

Of particular importance for ESA is the work of the United Nations Committee on the Peaceful Uses of Outer Space and its Scientific and Technical, and Legal Subcommittees. ESA has observer status with these bodies and is represented at their meetings. ESA can therefore voice its concerns directly to the Committee. In addition, ESA maintains working relations with the Secretariat of the United Nations and in particular with its Outer Space Affairs Division. ESA has been invited several times by the United Nations to provide information documents not only about ESA activities but also about such technical matters as observation of Earth resources, the delimitation of outer space, and space debris. The Agency is also closely involved with the International Telecommunication Union (ITU), which actively contributes to the elaboration of space law. The Agency's status in the ITU is similar to its status in the United Nations.

ESA as a Creator of Space Law

The European Space Agency, like all international intergovernmental organizations, is itself a creator of law, in particular in the form of the Convention and its Annexes of May 30, 1975, which established the European Space Agency. In addition, in order to implement international laws, the Council has adopted a number of internal laws, generally called "Rules," which regulate the relations of the Agency with its member states or with the outside world. The Council has also sometimes adopted "Resolutions" for the same purpose.

The legal personality which the member states conferred upon the Agency enables it to conclude numerous international agreements. However, these fall within the scope of institutional law rather than that of space law. In particular, ESA has concluded many cooperation agreements with its member states or with other states, including, for example, agreements for the participation of the Agency in certain national programs and for the participation of non-member states in programs of the Agency. These agreements may complement or enhance the general rules of space law.

Most recently, a series of agreements were concluded for the participation of Europe in the United States/International Space Station program. These texts contained rules which were adopted by common agreement to solve issues such as the ownership of different parts of the international station; their registration, jurisdiction, and control; the intellectual property regime; and so on. Although these texts are only binding upon those who signed them, they provide a precedent, or at least a model, for future legal agreements.

CONCLUSION

Thanks to the will of the majority of its states, Western Europe is actively participating in the space race which started more than 30 years ago. This participation is naturally of interest to the countries of the Old Continent, which have at their disposal substantial economic, technological, and human resources. These are crucial factors in pursuing space activities. In the spirit of the appeal for international cooperation made by the Outer Space Treaty, the European Space Agency has enabled other countries with limited means to be part of this major undertaking. For more than 25 years, ESA, as an instrument of space cooperation among European states, has been contributing substantially to the development of this branch of public international law, as an actor, as a subject, and as a source of space law.

NOTES

1. Treaty on Principles Governing the Activities of States in the Exploration and Use of Outer Space, including the Moon and Other Celestial Bodies; Adopted on December 19, 1966, Opened for Signature on January 27, 1967, and Entered into Force on October 10, 1967. As of December 1991, 91 states were parties to the Treaty.

2. Convention for the Establishment of a European Space Agency; signed in Paris on May 30, 1975, Entered into Force on October 30, 1980, with five Annexes which form an integral part of it and which deal with privileges and immunities, financial provisions, optional programs, internationalization of national programs, and industrial policy.

3. The Guiana Space Centre (CSG), established in Kourou, French Guiana, belongs to the Centre National d'Etudes Spatiales (CNES), a body of the French government. On the basis of an agreement with CNES, ESA has the right to use the

CSG installations and to build other installations required for the Ariane launcher. These installations are called the Ensemble de Lancement Ariane (ELA) and are the property of ESA. ESA makes them available to the enterprise Arianespace, a French commercial enterprise which produces and markets the Ariane launches.

4. For each of the Agency's optional programs, a programme board is created, whose composition, competence, and rules of procedure are determined on a case-by-case basis. One programme board may be charged with the monitoring of various programs.

5. The four international agreements following the Outer Space Treaty deal with, respectively: the rescue of astronauts and the return of objects launched into outer space (Agreement of December 19, 1967); international liability for damage caused by space objects (Convention of November 29, 1971); the registration of objects launched into outer space (Convention of November 12, 1974); and the activities of states on the Moon and other celestial bodies (Agreement of December 5, 1979). The provision for a Declaration of Acceptance is provided in Article 6 of the Rescue Agreement, Article 22 of the Liability Convention, Article 7 of the Registration Convention, and Article 16 of the Moon Agreement. ESA has made a Declaration of Acceptance concerning the first three agreements, but not for the Moon Agreement.

8

Institutional Arrangements for International Space Activities

Nicolas Mateesco Matte

There was no substantive law dealing with outer space when mankind first ventured into space. Space technologies, however, especially those relating to communications satellites, developed so rapidly that the international community was constantly pushed to make decisions and to create or update rules, regulations, and arrangements dealing with space.

This chapter describes the evolution of certain international institutions established by states in order to solve practical problems arising from the rapidly advancing space technology, particularly in the fields of communications and meteorology. Although the fundamental legal principles for space conduct have been, and will continue to be, formulated in "traditional" institutions such as the United Nations and its specialized agencies, new organizations have had to be created to deal with some specific issues which could not be dealt with by the United Nations or its agencies because these organizations were created before the start of the space age and hence are constitutionally limited in certain aspects.

Both international and regional organizations have been formed to ensure the efficient and cooperative use of space technology. This chapter concentrates on some of the most important of these organizations, an examination of all existing international and domestic space institutions being outside its scope. The discussion is preceded by a short description of the historical and political background that set the stage for the formation of the organizations that are discussed.

HISTORICAL BACKGROUND

At the dawn of the space age, following the launch of Sputnik I, the United Nations General Assembly made known its interest in outer space through the adoption of a series of resolutions. On the one hand, concerned that earthly conflicts would be carried into space, the General Assembly quickly declared "that outer space should be used for peaceful purposes only."[1] At the same time, it expressed the belief that space could be used to better the lot of mankind, a view which was reiterated in many subsequent resolutions. More significant, the General Assembly, recognizing the "common interest of mankind" in outer space, called upon the international community to establish international cooperative space programs.[2]

The practical utility of space for commercial purposes became evident with the launch of the early experimental communications satellites, which indicated the potential global impact of this technology. President Kennedy, in 1961, laid the basis for a communications satellite policy when he declared his intention to accelerate the "use of space satellites for worldwide communications" and to have communications satellites serving the United States and other nations, especially developing nations, on a global basis.[3] On June 24, 1961, he formally called for a single global communications satellite system and invited all nations to participate in the proposed system.[4] On August 31, 1962, President Kennedy signed the Communications Satellite Act, which established the Communications Satellite Corporation (COMSAT) with a mandate to cooperate with other countries, to expeditiously develop an operational system, and to provide services to other countries on a global scale.[5]

The idea of an international communication satellite system controlled by the United States raised concerns in other countries.[6] These concerns led to the convening, in October 1962, of intergovernmental discussions between the United States and a number of European countries on the creation of a world communications network,[7] and in July 1963, an intra-European conference on satellite communications. By this time it had become evident that an international organization was required in order to establish a global satellite network and satisfy international and national political demands and needs. Formal negotiations to create a global network began in Rome in February 1964, and on August 20, 1964, interim arrangements were adopted for the establishment and operation of a "global" commercial communications satellite system, INTELSAT. These arrangements were the result of two interrelated agreements: the Interim Agreement signed by governments, and a Special Agreement signed either by governments or by their designated public or private telecommunications entities.[8]

The main objective of the interim arrangements was to establish a single operational, commercial, global satellite telecommunications system which would develop and apply the most advanced satellite technology. This joint venture was initially established for a limited period because of the uncertainties and the immaturity of satellite technology during the early 1960s. It was clear from the interim agreements, however, that if the technology proved successful and beneficial, the agreements could be renegotiated and be made definitive. In 1971, definitive arrangements were made after prolonged negotiations resulting in two texts: the INTELSAT Agreement, with four annexes, open for signature by states; and the Operating Agreement, with one annex, open for signature by governments or their public or private telecommunications entities.[9]

Although both the interim and definitive INTELSAT agreements were intended to create one global system for satellite communications, that goal was not fully realized. The Soviet bloc soon formed its own INTERSPUTNIK system, and satellite systems with more specific functions (e.g., INMARSAT) or providing regional services came into being. A discussion of these developments will follow that of INTELSAT, the first international satellite organization.

INTELSAT

The purpose of INTELSAT is set out in the Agreement: "to achieve a global commercial telecommunications satellite system to provide, for the benefit of mankind, the most efficient and economical facilities possible, consistent with the best and most equitable use of the radio-frequency spectrum and orbital space."[10] Participation is open to any member state of the International Telecommunication Union (ITU). As of April 1992, there are 122 state members of INTELSAT. Since non-member countries can also use the INTELSAT space segment, there are a total of some 180 countries, territories, and possessions being served by INTELSAT. About 40 of those countries also use INTELSAT satellites for domestic telecommunications services.

A country contributes financially to the organization in proportion to its use of the system, and the "investment shares" of the member governments or their designated entities are recalculated periodically. The user members profit in proportion to their investment. Service charges are the same for all users.[11]

INTELSAT has a four-tiered organizational structure: the Assembly of Parties, the Meeting of Signatories, the Board of Governors, and an Executive Organ.

The Assembly of Parties is composed of all governments which are parties to the INTELSAT Agreement and is the principal organ of INTELSAT. Each party has one vote. The Assembly considers "those aspects of INTELSAT which are primarily of interest to the Parties as sovereign States" and has the power "to give consideration to general policy and long-term objectives of INTELSAT" (Art. 7.b). Ordinarily, the Assembly meets every two years, although extraordinary meetings may be convened. Decisions on substantive matters require a two-thirds majority of members present and voting, while procedural matters require only a simple majority. The Assembly embodies the basic principle of international organizations: the participation by all member states based on the principle of sovereign equality. However, the

Assembly, as an essentially political body, was given only limited powers in commercial operational matters (Art. 7.c).

The Meeting of Signatories was created to enable all of the investors, whether governments or telecommunications entities, to participate equally in the making of INTELSAT's general policies. The functions and powers of the Meeting of Signatories concern mainly the financial, technical, and operational interests of the signatories in their capacity as investors (Art. 8.b). The voting and decision-making arrangements are as in the Assembly.

The Board of Governors is the principal managing organ of the organization and has the real decision-making powers with respect to commercial questions. The Board is responsible for the design, development, construction, establishment, operation, and maintenance of the INTELSAT space segment (Art. 10.a).

Numerous efforts were made during the negotiation of the final arrangements to provide low-investment signatories with equitable representation on the Board. The result was a Board with three categories of governors and a weighted voting system.[12] Each governor controls a number of votes equal to the investment share of the signatory or group of signatories represented. Since investment shares are determined by use of the system, the largest users have the greatest influence on the Board. The governors may meet as often as necessary, but at least four times a year.

The Executive Organ is headed by a Director General, who is the chief executive and legal representative of INTELSAT. He acts in accordance with the policies and directives of the Board of Governors, to whom he is directly answerable (Art. 11.a, 11.b). Initially, COMSAT performed the executive and management function, but INTELSAT took over in 1979.

In general, INTELSAT has been fairly successful in establishing a global telecommunications satellite system. Eilene Galloway has succinctly summarized the reasons for INTELSAT's success:

> Demand for global communications, the solution of problems of equitable access, voting according to the type of decision to be made, efficient technical and economic operations, adoption of relevant United Nations principles, clear definitions, a realistic combination of governmental and non-governmental entities, and cooperation with other relevant institutions, particularly the International Telecommunication Union.[13]

INTELSAT is unique because it is an international organization and an international enterprise, operating on a commercial basis and as a public utility service. INTELSAT's global network carries roughly two-thirds of the world's overseas telecommunications traffic, including telephone, telegraph, telex, television, data, and facsimile services. At present, the organization has 15 satellites in orbit.

The fact that INTELSAT has provided such great practical benefits from the use of space technology to so many countries and territories makes the organization very important in the development of space law and in the implementation of the fundamental principle enshrined in the 1967 Outer Space Treaty: "The . . . use of outer space . . . shall be carried out for the benefit and in the interests of all countries, irrespective of their degree of economic or scientific development, and shall be the province of all mankind."[14]

INTERSPUTNIK

While INTELSAT was intended as a single global system, this goal was not accomplished because of Soviet bloc non-participation. In the view of the Soviet Union, the United States had a dominant position in INTELSAT since the organization was managed by COMSAT, a private U.S. corporation, and operated as a commercial entity. In addition, it did not have a distinct legal personality; decision-making was based on weighted voting thereby negating the principle of the equality of all states; and it was open only to ITU members, thereby violating the principle of universality.[15] In addition, the Soviets "shrank from a global (communications satellite) system because it might break their monopoly of information in the East bloc."[16]

The Soviet Union and several other Socialist countries instead signed the Agreement on the Establishment of the International System and Organization of Space Communications (INTERSPUTNIK Agreement) of November 15, 1971.[17] Although the purpose of the INTERSPUTNIK Agreement was to establish "an international system of communications via satellite," there is no indication that it aimed to be a single global system. The basic purpose of INTERSPUTNIK was to ensure "cooperation and coordination of efforts in the design, establishment, operation and development of the satellite communications system" (Art. 1.2), a purpose not too dissimilar to that of INTELSAT. The organization is intergovernmental, with its own distinct legal personality, and is open to any state (Art. 2.2).

The Board of INTERSPUTNIK is the governing body, composed of one representative of each member state (Art. 11). There is no weighted voting; each representative has one vote. Decisions are to be reached by unanimity or, failing that, by a two-thirds majority. However, the decisions of the Board are not binding on those members who do not approve their adoption. The main functions of the Board are to consider and determine the general policy of the organization; approve measures for the establishment, acquisition, or leasing and operation of the space segment; and determine the specification of Earth stations (Art. 12).

The Directorate is the permanent executive and administrative body of INTERSPUTNIK. It is headed by a Director General, who is accountable to the Board and executes its decisions. His functions include negotiations for designs and specifications of satellites and other equipment, and the launchings of communications satellites (Art. 13).

The organization leases two Soviet geostationary satellites, which are used primarily for exchange of television programs between Eastern European and other Socialist countries. The satellites, supported by twenty-one earth stations, are also used for telephone and telegraph links and for distribution of radio programs. INTERSPUTNIK satellite channels are made available to both member and non-member countries on the basis of uniform tariffs fixed by the Board.[18]

The one major drawback of INTERSPUTNIK is that it does not allow the participation of private telecommunications enterprises, and the organization therefore has been unattractive to countries where telecommunications systems are operated by private or semi-private commercial entities. It is clear that the INTERSPUTNIK model of an international organization for satellite communications has been much less successful than the INTELSAT model for the vast majority of states.

INMARSAT

It would seem that cooperation between the two major space powers in a single global satellite system would have a unifying effect on all the states of the world. When INTELSAT was formed, major ideological and other difficulties kept the United States and the Soviet Union from cooperating. Fortunately, they later found enough common ground to cooperate in establishing INMARSAT, the International Maritime Satellite Organization.

INMARSAT, which was established in 1976, aims "to make provision for the space segment necessary for improving maritime communications and, as practicable, aeronautical communications, thereby assisting in improving communications for distress and safety of life, communications for air traffic services, the efficiency and management of ships and aircraft, maritime and aeronautical public correspondence services and radio-determination capabilities."[19]

INMARSAT is open to use by all states, unlike INTELSAT, which is open only to ITU members. Thus, the principle of universality as contained in the Outer Space Treaty of 1967 is reinforced by the INMARSAT Convention. As of May 1, 1992, the organization has 64 members. The principle of weighted voting exists in INMARSAT, as in INTELSAT. Acceptance of this principle by the Soviet Union signaled its acknowledgement of the general practice that "one shares as one consumes." The changing Soviet attitude was also reflected in its acceptance of the participation of private companies in the organization.

INMARSAT is a combination of a public service organization and a commercial enterprise. This was the result of a controversy over the proposed nature of the organization during the conference that drafted the INMARSAT Convention. Western European countries, along with other major maritime powers, wanted INMARSAT to be a public service organization, while the United States insisted that it be operated on a profit-making basis. In the end, a provision was adopted requiring the organization to operate "on a sound economic and financial basis having regard to accepted commercial principles," thus making INMARSAT a "hybrid" organization (Art. 5.3). INMARSAT has three governing organs: the Assembly, the Council and the Directorate.

The Assembly is composed of all member states, each having one vote, with decisions taken by a two-thirds majority on substantive matters and by a simple majority on procedural matters. The Assembly's principal functions are to consider and review the organization's activities, purposes, general policy, and long-term objectives, as well as to ensure that the activities of INMARSAT are consistent with its Convention and with the purposes and principles of the United Nations Charter (Art. 10-12).

The Council, the managing body of INMARSAT, consists of 22 representatives of the signatories to the Operating Agreement and is required to meet at least three times a year. Decision-making procedures are similar to those in the INTELSAT Board of Governors. The Council's functions include the responsibility for making provision for the space segment necessary for carrying out the purposes of INMARSAT in the "most economic, effective and efficient manner consistent with (the) Convention and the Operating Agreement" (Art. 13-15).

The Directorate is headed by a Director General who is the chief executive officer and the legal representative of the organization. He is responsible to the Council (Art. 16).

The operations of INMARSAT are now being extended beyond the original purpose of providing satellite communications for maritime uses. In the 1985 amendments to the INMARSAT Convention, the organization was given the mandate to provide global aeronautical communication services as well as maritime service, and its space segment is available to aircraft as well as ships of all nations, on a non-discriminatory basis (Art. 3.2 and 7.1 as amended).[20] Commercial aeronautical services for airlines and corporate aircraft, introduced during the second half of 1990, currently include telephone, facsimile, telex, mail, data, position reporting, and fleet management, as well as distress and safety communications. Services are also being provided for land mobile communications.[21]

INMARSAT is a good example of international cooperation. The United States and the Soviet Union succeeded in putting aside their differences to work together in this major space telecommunications organization. The objections that the Soviet Union had with regard to INTELSAT either did not arise or seemed unimportant; the benefits promised by INMARSAT outweighed all of the Soviet reservations concerning cooperating with the United States.

REGIONAL SYSTEMS

Just as INTELSAT, INMARSAT, and INTERSPUTNIK are global organizations providing cooperative space services, there are regional institutions that serve similar purposes. Three regional communication satellite organizations will be considered here: ARABSAT, EUTELSAT, and EUMETSAT.

The issue of regional satellite systems was raised when the formation of INTELSAT was being discussed. The Western Europeans, concerned about the development of their own satellite capabilities, felt that though regional or domestic satellite systems should "not be approved if they would jeopardize INTELSAT, the right of establishment of such systems (ought to) be recognized" if they were to be used for specific telecommunication demands in particular areas.[22]

In addition, the U.S. position with regard to a single global satellite system also started to change when, in 1965, proposals were made to establish domestic telecommunications satellite systems in the United States. Yet the United States, while supporting establishment of its own domestic systems, opposed other international or regional systems that would compete with INTELSAT and economically harm the organization. For this reason, the interim agreements had not recognized regional systems.[23] Ultimately, however, the European view prevailed and the Definitive INTELSAT Agreement, in Article 14, acknowledged the rights of its members to set up separate domestic or regional systems, subject to several conditions, including that these systems should not cause INTELSAT "significant economic harm."[24]

ARABSAT

One such regional system that has been approved under Article 14 of the INTELSAT Agreement is ARABSAT, the satellite system formed by the member states of the Arab League on April 14, 1976.[25] ARABSAT is expressly a regional system, since only Arab states who are members of the Arab League may become parties (Art. 4.1). The objective of this regional satellite system is "to provide and set up an Arab Space Sector for general and specialized services in the field of telecommunications for all member states of the Arab League in accordance with technical and economic criteria accepted in the Arab and international quarters." In addition, the organization may undertake other specified activities, including laying down regulations and organizing the use of television and radio channels in such a manner as to satisfy the local and collective needs of the Arab states (Art. 3). The organizational structure of ARABSAT consists of the General Body, the Board of Directors, and the Executive Body.

The General Body consists of the telecommunications ministers of the member states, each member having one vote. This body is the supreme authority of the corporation and is entitled to undertake any action necessary to attain the objectives of the organization (Art. 10, 11).

The Board of Directors is comprised of nine members, five of which are elected according to the proportion of their shareholding in the corporation's capital, and four from the other members on an alternating basis for a non-renewable period of two years. The Board's main duties are to monitor and maintain the ARABSAT space segment and to execute the policies adopted by the General Body (Art. 12, 13).

The Executive Body, which comprises a number of sectors and administrative units, is headed by a General Manager who is the legal representative of ARABSAT. The General Manager is appointed by, and is accountable to, the Board of Directors (Art. 14).

EUTELSAT

The European Space Agency (ESA) was created in 1975 in order "to increase the efficiency of the total of European space efforts by making better use of the resources at present devoted to space and to define a European space program."[26] Although the ESA Convention authorized the organization to operate satellites for various applications (Art. 5.1.b), it chose to remain basically a space research organization and let other European institutions take over the operational activities.

In 1977, the ESA Council decided that a separate organization should be established to commercially operate the European Communications Satellites (ECS) developed by ESA.[27]

Consequently, on May 13, 1977, member states of the Conférence Européenne des Postes et Télécommunications (CEPT) established the Interim EUTELSAT, a provisional European telecommunications satellite organization. Definitive arrangements for EUTELSAT were signed on July 15, 1982, and came into force on September 1, 1985.[28] The Convention was open for signature and ratification by European states, and as of March 31, 1991, 27 countries were members of EUTELSAT. The Operating Agreement must be signed by an appropriate public or private telecommunications entity designated by a member state. The prime objective of the organization is the "provision of the space segment required for international public telecommunications services in Europe" (Art. 3.a).

The financial basis of EUTELSAT is very similar to that of INMARSAT. The organization is "to operate on a sound economic and financial basis having regard to accepted commercial principles" (Art. 5.b). Thus, it can be said that EUTELSAT, like INMARSAT, is a hybrid mixture of public service organization and commercial enterprise. The organizational structure of EUTELSAT consists of three organs: the Assembly of Parties, the Board of Signatories, and the Executive Organ.

The Assembly of Parties is composed of all the parties to the organization, with each party having one vote. Decisions on matters of substance require a two-thirds majority of the parties present and voting, whereas decisions on procedural matters may be by simple majority. One of the Assembly's principal functions is to consider general policy and long-term objectives of the organization (Art. 7-9).

The Board of Signatories is composed of the representatives of all Signatories to the Operating Agreement. It is the principal decision-making body and has been entrusted with extensive functions and responsibilities. Each signatory has a voting weighted according to its investment share, which is equal to its share of the use of the EUTELSAT space segment for international and domestic public telecommunications, on the condition that no signatory is to have more than 20 percent of the total vote in the organization. Decisions by the Board on matters of substance are generally required to be taken unanimously (Art. 11, 12).

The Executive Organ is headed by a Director General appointed by the Board, subject to confirmation by the parties. He is the chief executive and legal representative of the organization.

EUTELSAT, with six satellites in orbit and 16 Earth stations, is the largest provider of satellite capacity for telecommunications within Europe. The satellites are being used for a variety of communications services including telephony, distribution of television and radio programs, data transmissions, "real-time news gathering" via transportable Earth stations, and business communications.[29] Since January 1991, land mobile message and localization services have been made commercially available.

EUMETSAT

The European Organization for Meteorological Satellites (EUMETSAT), which came into being on June 19, 1986,[30] was established in order to ensure the operational continuation of Meteosat, the first European meteorological satellite. Plans for the establishment of a European meteorological satellite system had begun soon after the launch of the first U.S. weather satellite in 1960. In 1972, the Meteosat Programme was initiated by eight European states and entrusted to the European Space Research Organization (ESRO), the forerunner of ESA. The first Meteosat satellite was launched by ESA in 1977 as the European contribution to the global meteorological satellite observing system, which forms part of the World Weather Watch (WWW) of the World Meteorological Organization (WMO).

The primary objective of EUMETSAT, which has 16 member states as of 1989, is to establish, exploit, and maintain European operational meteorological satellites. The organizational structure of EUMETSAT consists of just two organs: the Council and the Secretariat.

The Council is the supreme body of the organization, with each member state having one seat and one vote. The Convention sets out the various powers of the Council and the different voting procedures associated with each class of powers (Art. 5).

The Secretariat, responsible for the day-to-day management of the organization, is headed by a Director, who is the legal representative of the organization and who is responsible for the implementation of the decisions taken by the Council and the execution of the tasks assigned to the organization.

At present, there are two functioning Meteosat satellites in orbit. In addition to providing data for use in operational meteorology, Meteosat has contributed to programs relating to the study of the climate and the environment.

IMPLICATIONS FOR SPACE LAW

The objectives common to these communications and meteorological satellite systems is clear: to make practical arrangements for international cooperation in the peaceful uses of outer space for the benefit of humankind.

INTELSAT has proven to be a great success. Founded on the principles of international cooperation and the common heritage of mankind, as well as on sound commercial principles, it has become a dynamic international organization. INMARSAT's achievements similarly serve to indicate that an international "give-and-take" attitude can exist, together with diverse political ideologies, to unite the world.

Institutional space arrangements, both global and regional, have gone a long way toward accomplishing the ideal set out in the Outer Space Treaty: cooperation in the peaceful uses of outer space for the benefit and in the interests of all countries. They have also served to alter some traditional and outdated concepts of international law: the absolute sovereignty, de facto equality, and independence of states have been modified by limiting functional sovereignty and accepting the de jure equality and interdependence of states in order to better serve humanity. All indications point to a continuation of this trend in the continuing evolution of space law.

The question still remains whether or not the original ideal, dating to the pre-INTELSAT days, of having a single global communications satellite organization can, and should, be sought. Considering the current political situation, the possibilities of closer links between INTELSAT and INTERSPUTNIK have been greatly enhanced. Very recently, an INTELSAT Business Service (IBS) link was inaugurated between the United States and the Soviet Union to enable geophysicists to analyze and share earthquake and other seismic data. Indeed, it is possible and advisable for the two organizations to merge, to form one single communications satellite network, so as to conserve resources and encourage better international cooperation and understanding.[31]

Regional satellite systems, less overwhelming than global arrangements, work better to serve nations which may share similar regional interests and needs. If need be, as in the case of meteorological satellites, inter-regional cooperation can create instant global networks.

CONCLUSION: HOPES FOR THE FUTURE

Human beings went into outer space and exploited it to bring benefits to Earth, benefits that could, in many cases, only be realized through international cooperation. Organizations were therefore established to ensure effective international cooperation. These organizations have proved their worth and have had a great effect on most aspects of human life. Moreover, they have contributed to a dramatic shift in international law by promoting the accommodation of interests and leading to the development of cooperative space law. States are gradually moving away from the concept of a self-centered absolute sovereignty and toward an outward-looking concept of international cooperation.

It is hoped that this trend will continue well into the future. International cooperation, through the establishment of institutions for using outer space, provides continuous opportunities for states to develop a sense of community in a more solid way, enabling them to jointly formulate policies to protect general interests.

These institutions have created links between developed and developing states in the economic and technological fields. In the field of space activities, such links are essential; they represent examples for a new system of survival, cooperation/collaboration for world organization. Even if the benefits derived do not meet all expectations, the common effort made toward the distribution of the benefits on an equitable basis can be a big step in establishing a new order of international cooperation.

NOTES

1. U.N.G.A. Res. 1348 (XIII), Dec. 13, 1958.

2. U.N.G.A. Res. 1472 (XIV), Dec. 12, 1959; and U.N.G.A. Res. 1721 (XVI), December 20, 1961.

3. "Special Message to the Congress on Urgent National Needs," May 25, 1961, *Public Papers of the Presidents: John F. Kennedy*, 1961, pp. 396-404. "Letter to the Vice-President on the Need for Developing Operational Communications Satellites," June 15, 1961, in *id.*, p. 472

4. "Statement by the President on Communication Satellite Policy," June 24, 1961, in *id.*, p. 529-530.

5. For the history of COMSAT, see, for example, A. M. Tedeschi, *Live Via Satellite: The Story of COMSAT and the Technology that Changed World Communication*, 1989; L. D. Musolf (ed.), *Communication satellites in Political Orbit*, San Francisco, Chandler, 1968; J. T. Kildow, *Intelsat: Policy-Makers' Dilemma*, 1973; Chapter 4 of J. F. Galloway, *The Politics and Technology of Satellite Communications*, 1972; and N. M. Matte, *Aerospace Law*, 1969, pp. 185ff.

6. W. A. McDougall, *The Heavens and the Earth: A Political History of the Space Age*, New York, Basic Books, 1985, pp. 349-352.

7. N. M. Matte, "Global Satellite Telecommunications: The End of a Dream?" in M. Bos and I. Brownlie (eds.), *Liber Amicorum for the Rt. Hon. Lord Wilberforce*, Oxford, Clarendon Press, 1987, p. 62.

8. Agreement Establishing Interim Arrangements for a Global Commercial Communications Satellite System and "Special Agreement," August 20, 1964, 15:2 U.S.T. 1705 (1964), T.I.A.S. No. 5646. For a detailed discussion of the Interim Agreements, see Matte, *supra* note 5, p. 195.

9. Agreement Relating to the International Telecommunications Satellite Organization (INTELSAT Agreement) and the Operating Agreement Relating to the International Telecommunications Satellite Organization (Operating Agreement), Opened for Signature August 20, 1971, Entered into Force February 12, 1973, 10 *International Legal Materials* 909 (1971), T.I.A.S. No. 7532.

10. Preamble to the INTELSAT Agreement.

11. As of March 31, 1991, the investment share held by COMSAT (United States) was 26.9 percent (down from over 60 percent when the organization was formed). At the other end, Zimbabwe, the Vatican, Viet Nam, and others held a 0.05 percent investment share, the minimum allowable. For more details on the financial arrangements see J. N. Pelton and J. Howkins (eds.), *Satellites International*, New York, Stockton, 1987, p. 119; and R. Colino, "INTELSAT: Facing the Challenge of Tomorrow," *Journal of International Affairs*, Vol. 39, 1985, pp. 129-130.

12. INTELSAT Agreement, Art. 9 (a) and (f). One category includes signatories whose investment share is not less than a minimum determined under the provisions of Art. 9 (b). A second category includes groups of signatories, not included in the first category, whose combined investment share is not less than the minimum. A third category includes groups of at least five signatories, not represented otherwise, from any one of the five ITU regions, regardless of the total investment shares held by the signatories constituting the group; the number of such governors, however, must not exceed a total of two from any one region and five from all regions.

13. E. Galloway, "International Institutions to Ensure the Peaceful Uses of Outer Space," *Annals of Air and Space Law*, Vol. 9, 1984, pp. 303, 314.

14. Treaty on Principles Governing the Activities of States in the Exploration and Use of Outer Space, Including the Moon and Other Celestial Bodies, U.N.G.A. Res. 2222 (XXI), December 19, 1966; 610 U.N.T.S. 205, 1967 Can. T.S. No. 19, 18 U.S.T. 2410, T.I.A.S. No. 6347, 1968 Gr. Brit. T.S. No. 10 (Cmnd. 3519) (Opened for Signature Jan. 27, 1967, Entered into Force Oct. 10, 1967).

15. N. M. Matte, *Aerospace Law: Telecommunications Satellites*, London, Butterworths, 1982, p. 141. See also Galloway, *supra* note 5, p. 121.

16. McDougall, *supra* note 6, p. 351.

17. The Agreement came into force on July 12, 1972. See 862 U.N.T.S. 3 (1973). The INTERSPUTNIK Agreement has been reproduced in Matte, *supra* note 5, p. 236, and in Matte, *supra* note 15, p. 277. Also see K-H. Böckstiegel and M. Benkö (eds.), *Space Law: Basic Legal Documents*, vol. 2, Dordrecht, Martinus Nijhoff, 1990, in which other agreements discussed in this chapter can be found.

18. N. M. Matte, "Outer Space and International Organizations," in R.-J. Dupuy (ed.), *A Handbook of International Organizations*, The Hague, Hague Academy of International Law, 1988, pp. 558-574. The information on ground stations is as of January 1, 1989, from an INTERSPUTNIK information brochure.

19. Convention on the International Maritime Satellite Organization (INMARSAT Convention) and the Operating Agreement on the International Maritime Satellite Organization (INMARSAT Operating Agreement), Opened for Signature at London Sept. 3, 1976, Entered into Force in July 1979, 15 *International Legal Materials* 1051 (1976). The agreements are also contained in Matte, *supra* note 5, p. 285. The

Convention and the Operating Agreement were amended on October 16, 1985. These amendments are reproduced in S. von Welck and R. Platzöder (eds.), *Law of Outer Space*, Baden-Baden, Nomos, 1987, p. 491. The purpose of the organization is defined in Article 3 (1), as amended.

20. Providing aeronautical as well as maritime services was initially considered, but the Panel of Experts appointed by the Inter-Governmental Maritime Consultative Organization (IMCO) to study the establishment of the system decided that the "first phase of a maritime system should be confined to meeting maritime needs and that consideration should be given to the possibility of suitable form of sharing as the system developed": N. Jasentuliyana, "The Establishment of an International Maritime Satellite System," *Annals of Air and Space Law*, Vol. 2, 1977, p. 323.

21. For further details on INMARSAT and its new activities, see D. Sagar, "International Maritime Satellite Organization (INMARSAT)," *Annals of Air and Space Law*, Vol. 15, 1990, p. 461; J. L. Magdelenat, "INMARSAT and the Satellite for Air Navigation Services," *Air Law*, Vol. 12, 1987, p. 266; and W. D. von Noorden, "Space Communications to Aircraft: A New Development in International Space Law" (parts 1 and 2), *Journal of Space Law*, Vol. 15, 1987, pp. 25, 147; INMARSAT News Bulletin, December 10, 1990. W. D. von Noorden and P. Dann, "Land Mobile Satellite Communications: A Further Development in International Space Law" (in 2 parts), *Journal of Space Law*, Vol. 17, 1989, pp. 1, 103.

22. S. Kageyama, "International Cooperation and National Sovereignty —Unchanged Role of National Sovereignty in the Provision of International Telecommunications Services," *Case Western Reserve Journal of International Law*, Vol. 16, 1984, p. 265.

23. *Id.*, p. 270.

24. For further discussion of competition between INTELSAT and regional and national systems, see N. M. Matte, *supra* note 15, p. 125; R. Colino, *supra* note 11; S. Schwartz, "Pirates or Pioneers in Orbit? Private International Communications Satellite Systems and Article XIV (d) of the INTELSAT Agreements," *Boston College International and Comparative Law Review*, Vol. 9, 1986, p. 199; R. Rodriguez, "International Telecommunications and Satellite Systems—Intelsat and Separate Systems: Cold War Revisited," *International Business Lawyer*, Vol. 15, 1987, p. 321; and D. Burch, "The Evaluation of Article XIV (d)," *Intelsat News*, February 1991.

25. The Agreement of the Arab Corporation for Space Communications (ARABSAT), Signed on Apr. 14, 1976, Entered into Force July 15, 1976. The text has been reproduced in Matte, *supra* note 15, p. 302. See also von Kries, "The ARABSAT Agreement—Text and Comments," *Zeitschrift für Luftrecht und Weltraumrechtsfragen*, Vol. 27, 1978, p. 179; and Ziadat, "Arabsat: Regional Development in Satellite Communications—Lessons from the Arabsat Venture," *Zeitschrift für Luftrecht und Weltraumrechtsfragen*, Vol. 37, 1988, p. 35.

26. Convention for the Establishment of a European Space Agency, Opened for Signature on May 30, 1975, Entered into Force on October 30, 1980, 1981 Gr. Brit. T.S. No. 30 (Cmnd. 6272; Cmnd. 8200), from the Preamble. The text of the Convention is reproduced in Matte, *supra* note 5, p. 211.

27. "The main objective of the ECS program is the development and establishment of a regional operational telecommunications satellite system which would make Western Europe self-sufficient in its intra-European, long-distance, public communications traffic and television broadcasts": Matte, *supra* note 15, p. 154.

28. Convention Establishing the European Telecommunications Satellite Organization (EUTELSAT) and the Operating Agreement Relating to the European Telecommunications Satellite Organization, 1990 Gr. Brit. T.S. No. 15 (Cmnd. 956). The text has been reproduced in *Annals of Air and Space Law*, Vol. 11, 1986, p. 416.

29. *EUTELSAT Annual Report 1989*, Paris, p. 3.

30. Convention for the Establishment of a European Organization for the Exploitation of Meteorological Satellites (EUMETSAT), Signed on May 24, 1983, Entered into Force June 19, 1986. The text of the Convention is in Welck and Platzöder, *supra* note 19, p. 583.

31. Considering that the Soviet Union and a few other INTERSPUTNIK members already use INTELSAT, this merger should not be very difficult. In the INTERSPUTNIK Agreement, there are no restrictions similar to Art. 14 of the INTELSAT Agreement, so it would be easier for members of INTERSPUTNIK to join INTELSAT; since all members of INTERSPUTNIK are members of the ITU, they can adhere to the INTELSAT Agreement. For a discussion of these and other factors that support an INTELSAT - INTERSPUTNIK rapprochement, see N. M. Matte, *supra* note 15, p. 144.

9

Law of Satellite Communications

Francis Lyall

Satellite communications are the most important product of space development and have affected almost all of us. They provide the best example of the benefits which Eilene Galloway foresaw coming from space.

The laws that regulate satellite communications have two main arms: one deals with technical matters relating to radio communications to and from satellites and their orbital positioning, while the other is directed to the particular application of satellites for telecommunications. As to the first, there is a body of law dealing with the technicalities of radio-frequency use and with the assignment of positions in the geostationary orbit. This area is largely the province of one international body, the International Telecommunication Union (ITU), through which such matters are negotiated, agreed to, and (within limits) policed. The second, laws governing the use of satellites for telecommunications, covers a wide range of issues, from the constitution of the several organizations that provide satellite telecommunications to the conditions on which their services are provided, and the rules which protect the organizations in their business.

Both arms of this subject operate within the general context of space law. Through a series of resolutions early in the space age, the United Nations sought to have accepted worldwide the principle that the benefits of space exploration and use should be extended to all mankind.[1] This aspiration was converted into law by the provision of Article 1 of the Outer Space Treaty:[2] the 1 "use of outer space . . . shall be carried out for the benefit and in the interests of all countries, irrespective of their degree of economic or scientific development." Although this Article has general validity, it also forms the particular context within which satellite communications systems are established and operated. The Article's principle is reflected in both areas of my topic: in the use of the radio spectrum and orbital positions, and in the constitution and operation of the international telecommunications satellite organizations. It even affects how states organize their own municipal systems and telecommunications laws.

In this chapter I deal first with the International Telecommunication Union, the body which has most to do with the technicalities of space communications. I then briefly review the providers and provision of satellite telecommunications facilities before outlining some current problems in the field of satellite communications.

TECHNICAL MATTERS: THE INTERNATIONAL TELECOMMUNICATION UNION

Without a clear radio link between a satellite and the ground, a satellite is useless: there can be no command, control, or telemetry; virtually no recovery of scientific data from, and no telecommunications traffic through, a satellite. To prevent these problems, an international system tries to guarantee that space radio links are free of man-made radio interference. The system to allocate frequencies to be used for satellite communications and the method of supervision of actual radio-frequency assignment and use operates on the basis of agreement.

When the need for such a system for space emerged, the ITU had already been dealing with similar requirements for terrestrial radio services for half a century and was able to expand its activities to encompass the new requirements without great difficulty. In addition, it was also able to extend its activities to take on responsibilities in respect of orbital allocations.

The history of the ITU is fascinating but will not be discussed here.[3] Suffice it to say that the ITU is little noticed among the United Nations family and does its work quietly. The purposes of the ITU include fostering international cooperation in the improvement and rational use of telecommunications, promoting their efficiency, and increasing their usefulness.[4] More contentiously, in recent years the purposes of the ITU have been extended to facilitating "economic and social development among peoples by means of efficient telecommunication services."[5]

Membership of the ITU is open only to states, although private operating agencies and similar bodies take part in the discussions of its Consultative Committees, and international organizations attend its conferences as observers. The constitution of the ITU is periodically revised and adopted in the Final Acts of the ITU Plenipotentiary Conference, which is the supreme organ of the Union and is convened approximately every five years.[6] The Plenipotentiary Conference sets policy, revises the constitution and other documents, and elects the officials of the Union.[7] Two other organs meet on a non-permanent basis. A 41-member Administrative Council, which is elected by the Plenipotentiary Conference with due regard to geographic distribution, meets yearly and plays a supervisory and governing role between Plenipotentiary Conferences. Administrative Conferences convened for particular purposes constitute the other non-permanent organ of the Union, with the World Administrative Radio Conferences being of particular importance for space communications.

The ITU Administrative Conferences are very important. They may be of regional or of global scope and may deal with a particular matter (e.g., one communication service) or with a broader range of subjects. The result of these conferences, the Regulations, are detailed provisions complementing the International Telecommunication Convention and deal with all matters affecting telecommunications. The Regulations of the ITU have the same legal status as the Convention itself.[8] The Radio Regulations are important in the functioning of telecommunications, while other Regulations deal with tariffs and the settlement of accounts.

The General Secretariat of the ITU, one of its permanent organs, is based at the ITU headquarters in Geneva and services the Union as a whole. The other permanent organs are the International Telegraph and Telephone Consultative Committee (CCITT), the International Radio Consultative Committee (CCIR), and the International Frequency Registration Board (IFRB). The Plenipotentiary Conference of Nice in 1989 added the Telecommunications Development Bureau (BDT) to the organs of the Union, but at the time of this writing (1991), this body has not been set up.

Both Consultative Committees work by way of Study Groups, with a limited number of permanent staff. Apart from member states of the ITU, recognized private operating agencies and other organizations can take part in the work of Study Groups. Both bodies make recommendations, some directly to other organs of the Union, and some codified through their respective Plenary Assemblies, which meet every four years. The recommendations of the Consultative Committees are influential and frequently reappear with greater legal effect in ITU Regulations.

The CCITT sets tariffs for international communications generally. It also adopts international standards and procedures for telephone and telegraph services as well as specifications for terminals for data links, integrated services digital networks (ISDN), and the like.[9]

The CCIR, as its name implies, deals with radio matters. The recommendations of the CCIR have great influence in the development of the efficient use of radio in all forms of telecommunications, including space communications.

The five members of the IFRB are elected by the Plenipotentiary Conference as "custodians of an international public trust."[10] They also conduct studies on radio matters and advise at Administrative Radio Conferences. However, their main importance for my topic is as the body which, with its Specialised Secretariat, supervises compliance with the Radio Regulations.

The ITU Radio Regulations are of the highest importance for my topic. World Administrative Radio Conferences, and similar conferences organized on a regional basis, have adopted regulations allocating all parts of the usable radio spectrum to particular uses on a universal or limited basis.[11] It is each state's right, as a matter of sovereign authority, to oversee the use of the radio-frequency spectrum by transmitters within its jurisdiction through appropriate frequency assignment procedures. But it is also the responsibility of the members of the ITU to assign frequencies to transmitters with due respect to the internationally agreed allocations, thereby reducing the potential for interference between radio transmissions in different countries.[12] A continuing series of administrative radio conferences, organized as required, reviews the Radio Regulations by functional service or frequency band. The most recent edition of the Radio Regulations was published in 1982, but they have been subject to considerable amendment by later administrative radio conferences.[13]

But merely using a frequency in the correct frequency band will not necessarily prevent transmissions in one state from interfering with communications in another which is lawfully using that same frequency. Apart from deliberate jamming,[14] a badly tuned or unduly powerful transmitter may well affect reception of signals from another transmitter. An international system of priority of frequency use is therefore superimposed on the general rules of use. A state assigning a frequency to a transmitter has to notify the new assignment to the IFRB. The Board oversees the registration of a frequency assignment, checking its conformity with the Radio Regulations; assessing its propensity to cause interference with other registered assignments, existing or planned; and facilitating any necessary coordination with registered assignments. The IFRB maintains the Master International Frequency Register, which constitutes the official record of all frequency assignments. An assignment duly and properly recorded in the Master Register is entitled to protection from interference caused by later assignments. These procedures were worked out for terrestrial radio, and have been refined and improved to cope with the requirements of satellite communications. They afford good prospects for the "clear radio links" which are essential to radio communications. As satellite systems are expensive, difficult to design, and not easily modified once in orbit, it is not surprising to find that the lead time for assignments for satellite services is lengthy.[15] The ITU procedures are reasonable and justifiable for civilian satellites. It may come as a surprise, however, to find that many states also notify frequencies to be used by military satellites that are otherwise secret, even during times of international tension and despite the fact that military transmitters are exempt from the ITU requirements.[16] But states have an interest in ensuring that their satellites, irrespective of their function, can operate through clear radio communications. The ITU procedures are also sanctioned by the laws of physics, a unique and highly effective mode by which compliance with international law is secured. An unregistered satellite frequency assignment could well be inadvertently interfered with.

A separate technical matter which has also become an ITU responsibility is the positioning of satellites in the geostationary orbit. Since the ITU does not usually deal with the positioning of terrestrial transmitters, this responsibility appears odd. However, the efficient use of the limited resources of the geostationary orbit is necessary, and since the ITU already had responsibilities in respect of frequencies, it was sensible to use the ITU as the forum in which to deal with the geostationary orbit.

The geostationary orbit, at 36,000 km above the equator, is the most useful place to locate most communication satellites as well as direct broadcasting satellites and many Earth observation and other satellites. As its name implies, a satellite revolving from west to east in the geostationary orbit remains "stationary" with respect to positions on Earth. Satellites in lower orbits move across the sky and have to be tracked by ground stations, which can be difficult—an important operational factor. A geostationary satellite is also simultaneously visible to a larger area of the surface of the Earth than a satellite in lower orbit. Arthur C. Clarke pointed out in his seminal article of 1945 that three geostationary satellites placed 120° apart could serve all the main populated areas of the globe.[17]

Because land masses and centers of population are not spread equally around the globe, geostationary orbital positions nearer to centers of population, or visible to several such centers are more useful than positions not so placed. The geostationary orbit therefore poses two problems which the law can solve. First, in the absence of appropriate mechanisms, there is a slight chance that two satellites might be sent to the same orbital position and physically collide, and a much higher chance that satellites placed close to each other would mutually interfere with their radio transmissions.[18] Second, in the absence of agreed measures, the developed nations might simply occupy all the most useful positions on a first-come-first-served basis.

The ITU procedures, and in particular those of the IFRB, were readily adaptable to cope with the problem of collision, and interference was already handled through existing IFRB procedures for satellite frequencies. Now, as part of the notification procedures for frequency assignments already outlined, a state planning a geostationary satellite service must also notify the orbital positions to be used, must coordinate the new satellites with existing and previously notified systems, and must respect certain existing, agreed, and reserved assignments of orbital positions.

The last few words indicate the partial solution to the second problem, the potential occupation of the best positions on the geostationary orbit by those who got there first. At administrative radio conferences in 1977 and 1983, the ITU allotted particular orbital positions and frequencies to all states in order to meet their potential needs for direct broadcasting services.[19] In 1988 these decisions were subsumed into the Radio Regulations. Another administrative radio conference met in 1985 and 1988 and took similar steps for conventional communication satellite services in the geostationary orbit.[20] Every state (including those not represented at the conference) was guaranteed a position (the specific position was not specified) within a particular arc of the geostationary orbit, and frequency bands were reserved for this use. As these allotments do not exhaust the potential of the geostationary orbit within these frequency bands, useful positions and frequencies which remain unallotted may be used by international satellite organizations and by states in addition to the positions allotted to them.

As indicated, the question of frequencies was dealt with concurrently with that of geostationary positions in the 1985/1988 conference. Long-standing arguments within the ITU underlay much of the debate. Should states be able to occupy frequencies by being first to make use of them, or should the radio-frequency spectrum be "engineered" by dividing it by agreement both as to the services and as to the users of the frequencies available? Should spectrum matters be dealt with a posteriori or a priori? Putting it another way, should the technically advanced states be able to help themselves to the best frequencies, leaving the less developed to meet their eventual needs from what is left over; or should all states be guaranteed frequency space in advance of their actual need? The questions raised by geostationary satellite communications dramatized an old problem. Should those presently capable of launching satellites be able to take the best positions at the expense of latecomers?

Put like that, the answer may seem clear, particularly if one remembers the principle of Article 1 of the Outer Space Treaty: the use of space should be for the benefit of all states irrespective of their degree of economic or scientific development. But there is a very strong counter-argument: space frequencies and orbital positions should be used as efficiently as possible. This means that states having the technical capability should not be prohibited from using desirable frequencies and orbital positions just because some other state may at some point in the (perhaps remote) future wish to use them.

The result of the debate has been a compromise. As indicated, there is now a measure of planned development, with the reservation of geostationary positions and frequencies for every state.[21] The orbit and the radio spectrum has to that extent been engineered through planning and allotment ahead of state requirements.[22] On the other hand, the remaining positions and frequencies (and indeed the allotted positions and frequencies until they are taken up by those for whom they are reserved) remain available for use and protection through the traditional mechanisms of assignment, notification, coordination and entry on the Master Register.

The Future of the ITU

As far as the future of the ITU and its responsibilities are concerned, there will always be a need for such a body, but some change is in the wind. Three matters may be noted. First, in 1989, the Nice Plenipotentiary Conference provided for the structure and functioning of the Union to be considered by a High Level Committee. This is likely to result in organizational change and a re-grouping of the present activities of the ITU. The functions presently divided between the IFRB, the CCIR and the CCITT will be re-allocated into three areas: telecommunications development, the standardization of network systems, and radio-communication matters. The CCIR and the IFRB would be thus brought together into a single organ to deal with radio communications, the IFRB perhaps being reduced to a part-time body with narrowed responsibilities. Such institutional alterations need not result in a marked change in procedures regarding satellite communications. One technically feasible procedural change would be for states to have access to the IFRB computer, thus making the coordination of new proposals easier and perhaps swifter and more satisfactory.

However, while the High Level Committee goes about its business, a Voluntary Group of Experts is examining the simplification of the Radio Regulations and their amendment procedures. Certainly it would be useful if the procedural, administrative, and substantive provisions of the Radio Regulations (and of the Constitution and Convention) were codified as separate documents. That could also help streamline and simplify the methods by which the substantive provisions of the ITU regime are determined.

Second, irrespective of these organizational questions, the doctrinal debate between those who wish to see the radio spectrum and the geostationary orbit divided and allocated between states in advance, and those who advocate a first-come-first-served regime, will continue. The best result will be a compromise, modeled on that already reached for geostationary questions, a partly allotted radio spectrum and geostationary orbit with the non-alloted elements remaining available to those who can bring together enterprise, finance, and technological competence.

Third, over the last three Plenipotentiary Conferences, the purposes of the ITU have been altered to embrace more specifically than before technical assistance and technology transfer from the developed to the less developed countries. At the same time the financing of the Union has come under strain, with the less developed countries, which contribute proportionately extremely small sums, exercising pressure for aid and assistance. Some in the developed countries may come to consider that the basic function of the ITU in telecommunications is being unduly overshadowed by matters more properly dealt with by other organizations. If the support of the ITU by the developed countries were to diminish, that would be a tragedy.

SATELLITE TELECOMMUNICATIONS

Of all the uses of space, satellite telecommunications has had the most impact on modern life. Satellite links are now an essential part of the global telecommunications network, and a mature industry offers attractive services, mostly to the traditional providers of telecommunications but also directly to end-users.

The potential of satellite telecommunications was early recognized. Indeed, the exploration of space first found economic justification for its vast expenditures in the tangible benefits afforded by even the relatively unsophisticated first generation of telecommunication satellites. Good telecommunications are essential in all countries, developed and underdeveloped. The United Nations was therefore adamant that the benefits of the new technology should be shared by all. Early in the space age, the General Assembly believed that satellite telecommunications "should be available to the nations of the world as soon as practicable on a global and nondiscriminatory basis."[23] That has in large measure been achieved.

International telecommunications by satellite are provided by a variety of organizations, three global and others regional. In the global sphere the International Telecommunications Satellite Organization (INTELSAT) dominates.[24] It has 122 members, and a further 25 or so non-members use its system. The International Maritime Satellite Organization (INMARSAT) (about half the membership of INTELSAT, and in monetary terms one-tenth of its size) originally provided only maritime services but is now expanding to all mobile services. INTERSPUTNIK draws its members mostly from the former Communist bloc, and it also provides global services. Regional services are offered by the European Telecommunications Satellite Organization (EUTELSAT) and by ARABSAT (the Arab Satellite Communication Organization).[25]

In the sphere of international public telecommunications services, INTELSAT and INMARSAT are the main organizations. The Preambles of the Agreements setting up both organizations refer to the "benefit of all," using terms drawn from United Nations Resolutions. Both systems may be used by non-members, and both charge uniform rates worldwide for a given service. Interestingly, within each organization, ownership, return on investment, and voting weights are linked to utilization of the system—a welcome reflection of relativities in an international organization.

Naturally some countries, although members of one or more of these international organizations, have also developed domestic satellite systems. Large countries, and those where the terrain makes telecommunication by other means difficult, find satellite links ideal and cost-effective. Conflicts with membership in international telecommunication satellite organizations can emerge, however, when a domestic system finds potential users outside its home state. For example, the Indonesian system, Palapa,[26] began as a domestic satellite telecommunication system for Indonesia, where jungles and the degradation of microwave signals by heavy rainfall make telecommunications between islands of the archipelago by traditional methods difficult. But soon other countries in the area saw that they too could use the Palapa system for domestic and international purposes, so what amounts to a regional system has developed.[27] In the United States, distance, the variety of markets, the fact that telecommunications was already a private business, and sheer entrepreneurial skill led to the establishment of several domestic systems, a development accelerated by the break-up of the Bell System in 1984. Although limited approval has been given nationally and internationally for U.S. domestic systems to be used within their "spill-over" range in Canada, Mexico, and some Caribbean and other islands near the U.S. mainland, the general question of domestic systems providing international services is not something that has been fully treated.[28]

Specific Problems

While the general position as to satellite communications is satisfactory, some matters deserve comment.

What about the "global" telecommunications system referred to in the 1961 United Nations Resolution 1721 D? A global system established and run by a United Nations agency is not feasible. The United Nations itself has not that expertise, and other international systems have since been developed.[29] Ideally, one would like to see a single agency providing a nondiscriminatory global public telecommunications satellite service. The unwillingness of the Communist bloc to enter the INTELSAT organization frustrated that. The development of the INMARSAT organization to provide a specialized maritime communication service and now air and land mobile services, and the creation of regional organizations such as EUTELSAT and ARABSAT with their separate raisons d'être, ensures that the ideal of a single global agency will not materialize. However, the difficulties which the former Communist bloc is experiencing place great strains on the viability of the INTERSPUTNIK system, and it may be that a way will be found to integrate INTELSAT and INTERSPUTNIK. The prospects for public telecommunications services on a global scale would thereby be enhanced.

The international telecommunications satellite organizations were created at a time when notions of public service were dominant. Now, privatization and competition are the watchwords of many, and systems "separate" from the global system are extolled as offering better and less expensive services on certain telecommunication routes. Competition is here to stay. But competition was taken account of when the present international organizations were set up. For example, it was recognized that members of INTELSAT were likely to participate in other satellite networks, in part to protect national space industries, in part to secure a service more tailored to specific national needs. Since such developments could not be prohibited, what was needed in the INTELSAT Agreements was some procedure to ensure that members' participation in other systems would not injure INTELSAT, either technically or economically.

The solution adopted by INTELSAT and followed elsewhere is a consultation procedure in which members who wish to join (or to allow persons under their jurisdiction to join) an international satellite system separate from that of INTELSAT are required to consult with INTELSAT. INTELSAT then expresses its view on the matter. INTELSAT's opinion is, however, only the expression of a view, and does not by itself bar a member from joining another system. However, there must be a point at which INTELSAT would consider the activities of a member incompatible with its obligations under the INTELSAT Agreements and deem the member to have withdrawn from the organization.

Technical questions, such as compatibility between INTELSAT and other systems, are dealt with by negotiation.[30] That is unexceptionable. The more difficult issues arise when a new system might cause economic harm to INTELSAT. This is dealt with by the consultation requirements of Article 14.d of the INTELSAT Agreement, versions of which appear in the constituent agreements of the other global satellite telecommunications organizations.

Article 14.d deals with public international telecommunication services, including fixed and mobile services available for public use.[31] "Public use," INTELSAT has determined, includes so-called private facilities established or used by any members of the public (e.g., linking the offices of a company internationally).[32] Consultation between INTELSAT and a member proposing to license a separate international system takes into consideration (1) technical compatibility, (2) whether the services planned are ones which INTELSAT does or intends to provide, (3) whether the new system will carry traffic that otherwise would have gone through the INTELSAT system, and (4) whether the new system would prejudice direct links between INTELSAT and the new system's participant countries.[33] Finally, the consultation considers (5) whether the new development will cause "significant economic harm" to the INTELSAT global system. This last is crucial.

Over the life of INTELSAT, the concept of significant economic harm has undergone clarification and change. Clearly it does not prohibit members from involving themselves with other organizations which minimally affect INTELSAT. The language makes room for INTELSAT to determine whether any harm caused is significant. The term "significant" is not defined in the INTELSAT Agreements, which is useful, leaving INTELSAT as judge of what economic harm it can tolerate. There has been discussion whether the significance of a development means the harm caused only by the particular instance, or whether INTELSAT should consider the total cumulative effect caused by all separate systems. This has not been finally settled. In the meantime INTELSAT has accepted INMARSAT, EUTELSAT, ARABSAT, Palapa, members using INTERSPUTNIK services, and some transborder services provided peripherally to a national service as not causing significant economic harm.[34] However, moves by U.S. companies to provide international services to South America and, later, across the Atlantic have caused more discussion.[35] At present the U.S. companies provide only "private facilities" that are not available for general public use.

But while some have worried that as traffic was creamed off from high-density routes, the service provided on low-density routes would become more expensive, INTELSAT is actually becoming more relaxed about such matters. The fact is that the perception of what harms INTELSAT's interests has changed. When INTELSAT was set up, the organization was seen as a public service requiring protection lest it be made unable to provide global services. But we are now a quarter of a century from its first incarnation as Interim INTELSAT, and two decades from the definitive arrangements. While it is true that any traffic carried by other systems "harms" the INTELSAT system economically, INTELSAT can afford to consider much of this as not significant since INTELSAT is now a very large organization. The system is not yet in jeopardy even though appreciable harm is caused by the new private facilities operators. A full-scale, competitive, unrestricted satellite service, not restricted to private facilities, on the Atlantic or Pacific routes would be a different story. That might attract a significant proportion of business which INTELSAT depends on.

This raises the correlative question of cable. New long-distance fiber optic cables provide competition to satellites. Many telecommunications entities which are also members of the satellite organizations offer cable services. Nonetheless, the two types of system are separate and coordination between the two modalities is not formalized. It is ironic that satellite systems provide "restoration" services in case of disruption of cable traffic, but not the other way around. Perhaps the two should formally coordinate to help attain the United Nations ideal for global telecommunications services.

CONCLUSIONS

Satellite communications is the single area in which the coming of the space age has provided immense economic benefit and in which legal development has been swift and skillful. The ITU has adapted to meet the new challenges posed by satellites, but the massive use of radio for space communications has revealed weaknesses in the ITU organization which may require some structural change. The ITU is mainly a service organization, and whatever improves the service is to be welcomed. As for satellite telecommunications, much has been achieved. It is to be hoped that the attempts of some U.S. companies to provide separate systems does not cause INTELSAT significant economic harm through short-sighted decisions by the U.S. government. As Article 1 of the Outer Space Treaty requires, the benefits of space should be for all mankind.

NOTES

1. "International Cooperation in the Peaceful Uses of Outer Space," U.N.G.A. Res. 1721 (XVI), Dec. 20, 1961, and U.N.G.A. Res. 1802 (XVII), Dec. 19, 1962.

2. Treaty on Principles Governing the Activities of States in the Exploration and Use of Outer Space, Including the Moon and Other Celestial Bodies, Oct. 10, 1967, 610 U.N.T.S. 205; (1968) Cmnd. 3519 (United Kingdom); 18 U.S.T. 2410, T.I.A.S. No. 6347 (United States); 6 *International Legal Materials* 386 (1968); 61 American Journal of International Law 644 (1968).

3. G. A. Codding, Jr., *The International Telecommunication Union: An Experiment in International Cooperation*, Leiden, E. J. Brill, 1952, reprinted in New York, Arno Press, 1972, passim; D. M. Leive, *International Telecommunications and International Law: The Regulation of the Radio Spectrum*, Leiden, A. W. Sijthoff, and Dobbs Ferry, NY, Oceana Publications Inc., 1970, pp. 29-80; F. Lyall, *Law and Space Telecommunications*, Aldershot, England, Dartmouth, 1989, and Brookfield, VT, Gower Publishing, 1989, pp. 311-409.

4. ITU Convention, Article 4 (see note 6 below).

5. ITU Convention, Preamble. See also Article 4.

6. At the time of writing (1991), the current constitutional document is the International Telecommunications Convention of Nairobi, 1982. Final Acts containing a new Constitution and Convention, adopted at Nice in 1989, are not likely to enter into force. Instead, an Extraordinary Plenipotentiary Conference has been called for December 1992 to consider proposals to restructure the Union made by a High Level Committee set up by the Nice Conference. The proposals would group standardization, radiocommunication, and development elements from the existing organs into three separate sectors.

7. The Nice Conference separated the Constitution (containing Basic Provisions) from the Convention (institutional matters subject to change). The 1992 Conference (*supra* note 6) is likely to follow that model.

8. Nairobi Convention, Article 42.

9. Telephone and computer terminals are the means through which most people interface with telecommunication networks, whether the signal traffic goes by cable or satellite.

10. Nairobi Convention, Article 10.3. The High Level Committee has proposed that a part-time nine member Board be part of the new Radiocommunication Sector.

11. Many of the frequencies used by radio astronomy are kept free from artificial interference by not being allocated to any communication service.

12. A state has the right to disagree with an otherwise agreed allocation, and a note is entered in the Regulations indicating the reservation, thus protecting the state's right to go its own way. The procedure is not practical in areas where there are many assigning authorities.

13. The Radio Regulations are published by the ITU, Geneva.

14. Deliberate jamming is not something the ITU has coped with well. See J. G. Savage, *The Politics of International Telecommunications Regulation*, San Francisco and London, Westview Press, 1989, index, "Jamming."

15. For details, see Lyall, *supra* note 3, pp. 372-380.

16. Nairobi Convention, Article 38.

17. A. C. Clarke, "Extra-terrestrial Relays: Can Rocket Stations Give World-Wide Radio Coverage." *Wireless World*, October 1945, pp. 303-308. Because of atmospheric attenuation of the signal, at least four equally spaced geostationary satellites are needed for a global telecommunications system. Remote sensing satellites in geostationary orbit, such as weather satellites, concentrate on the central 60° circle they "see".

18. R. L. White and H. M. White, *The Law and Regulation of International Space Communication*, Boston and London, Artech House, 1988, pp. 9-15.

19. Region 2, the Americas, was dealt with in 1983, while the rest of the world settled these matters (perhaps before technology was adequately developed) in 1977; see Lyall, *supra* note 3, pp. 381-387. Their needs were reconsidered in 1988.

20. The World Administrative Radio Conference on the Use of the Geostationary Satellite Orbit and the Planning of the Space Services Utilizing It (WARC-ORB-1985/1988) met in two sessions in 1985 and 1988 and eventually added significantly to the Radio Regulations both in terms of procedures and in terms of allotments.

21. At the end of 1991, the new states emerging from the Soviet Union had not yet been provided for.

22. See Appendix 30 of the Radio Regulations.

23. U.N.G.A. Res. 1721 (XVI) (A/5026) of December 20, 1961, "International Cooperation in the Peaceful Uses of Outer Space," Section D.

24. The INTELSAT Agreement and Operating Agreement are 23 U.S.T. 3813, T.I.A.S. No. 7532, 10 *International Legal Materials* 909 (1971), and 23 U.S.T. 4091, T.I.A.S. No. 7532, 10 *International Legal Materials* 946 (1971), respectively.

25. The detail of these organizations (and citation for their basic texts) is dealt with in Chapter 8 of this volume by N.M. Matte. See also N. M. Matte, *Aerospace Law: Telecommunications Satellites*, Toronto and London, Butterworths, 1982; M. S. Snow, *International Telecommunications Satellite Organization (INTELSAT): Economic and Institutional Challenges Facing an International Organisation*, Baden-Baden, Nomos Verlagsgesellschaft, 1987; and *supra* note 3, pp. 74-310.

26. An Indonesian word referring to unity: see Lyall, *supra* note 3, p. 200, nn. 98 and 99.

27. *Id.*, pp. 172-173.

28. *Id.*, pp. 173-174.

29. G. Clarke and L. B. Sohn, "A United Nations Space Agency" in *World Peace through World Law: Two Alternative Plans*, 3d ed., Cambridge, MA, Harvard University Press, 1966, pp. 296-302.

30. INTELSAT Agreement, Article 14.

31. INTELSAT Agreement, Article 1(k).

32. See INTELSAT Doc. BG-60-48, August 10, 1984, with Annex, "Scope of INTELSAT's Public Telecommunication Services," and related Board of Governors discussion and decision in BG-60-3.

33. For detail see Lyall, *supra* note 3, pp. 162-166.

34. U.S. systems provide limited transborder services to Canada, Mexico, the Caribbean, Bermuda and the British Virgin Islands.

35. See Lyall, *supra* note 3, pp. 177-178, 182-194, 412-415.

10

Legal Aspects of Space Commercialization

Stephen Doyle

PRIVATE VENTURES IN SPACE

The current commercial uses of outer space involve many nations, some acting alone, some in regional cooperative organizations, others in large international cooperative ventures. These activities extend from design, development and manufacturing of satellites, launch vehicles, Earth stations, and other ground support equipment, components of these products, and consulting and engineering services to support them, to the operation of launch systems and spacecraft, to provide products and services for governments, businesses, or the using public. This chapter deals primarily with the owners and operators of launch services and operational satellite systems. These "flying components" in space (which have generated most of the new law I discuss) depend upon the ground-based elements of the industry.[1]

Roy Gibson, a distinguished leader of European space programs and organizations, addressed the question "What Is Space Business?" and stated: "I believe any operation qualifies as space business where somebody makes, or tries to make, a profit from a series of operations which at some stage use satellites, launchers or the associated ground segment."[2] Gibson refers to the portion of the industry dealing with non-flight systems as "the enabling operations."[3] He sees the industry as being dependent on governmental services in many areas where, because of the early stage of industrial development, government investments are critical to the development and growth of commercial space activities. Although satellite communication began early and soon proved to be financially self-sustaining, there are few space ventures that can succeed on a go-it-alone commercial basis at the current stage of their development.[4] I revisit this point later in this chapter.

Commercial spaceflight activities include, inter alia, the operation of (1) launch services; (2) communication satellite services; (3) earth observation satellite systems; (4) meteorological services; and (5) navigation and position determination services. We must also consider some of the changing roles of satellite manufacturers. Under current conditions, a satellite manufacturer, in order to sell satellites commercially, must sometimes procure the launch, place the satellite in its operational orbit, and test it on orbit for performance of critical on-board systems, before transferring ownership to the buyer. This recent practice places most of the risk of space vehicle loss, which is higher during the initial stages, on those who are in the best position to prevent loss. This development also relates to the insurance of spacecraft, which will be discussed later in this chapter.

Competition in commercial space ventures has been slowly emerging. The technological challenges are formidable; the start-up investments are tens to hundreds of millions of dollars; the risks are high; and several to many years of operations are required to recover the original investment and start earning profits. Although the risks and costs are daunting when compared to other commercial ventures, there always seem to be dauntless investors and operators willing to take risks to reap the high anticipated benefits. Still, much of the perceived "high value" remains to be demonstrated.

The earliest of the commercial space systems were communication satellites. Although meteorological services were also among the early services provided, they are primarily government-sponsored and -funded services. Although navigation services appeared in the 1960s, their general commercialization did not occur until the 1980s. Remote sensing for Earth observation was initiated by NASA in a civilian program called the Earth Resources Technology Satellite (ERTS) in 1972, which evolved into the Landsat system, operated by NASA through the 1970s and into the mid-1980s. In the 1980s, Congress transferred the Landsat program to the National Oceanic and Atmospheric Administration (NOAA) and then to private industry. China, Europe (ESA), France, India, Japan, and Russia also have earth observation satellite systems, but the United States and France were the only countries offering commercial services until the 1990s, when the Soviet Union started marketing its remote sensing data, including radar images. Several countries have experimented with materials processing in space, but space processing and manufacturing are speculative activities which have yet to prove viable for our markets. The costs of getting to orbit and returning to Earth are so high that space manufacturing appears to be of little value for commercial commodity sales, with very few possible exceptions.[5] In due course, however, such activities will likely be useful to and necessary for space settlements.

Markets select out weak and poorly managed ventures through competition and reward the efficient competitors with profit. The function of governments is to protect the public interest by licensing or otherwise regulating the use of resources and ensuring that commercial operations are safe and environmentally acceptable. Effective government regulation of new commercial space ventures is facilitated by the fact that commercial space activities are often government subsidized.

THE GENERAL LEGAL FRAMEWORK

Since the 1960s, the United Nations has developed a framework of basic law regulating the expansion of human activity in outer space, beginning with the 1967 Outer Space Treaty.[6] For the purposes of this chapter, the most relevant provision of the Treaty is Article 6:

> States parties to the Treaty shall bear international responsibility for national activities in outer space, including the Moon and other celestial bodies, whether such activities are carried on by governmental agencies or non-governmental entities, and for assuring that national activities are carried out in conformity with the provisions set forth in the present Treaty. The activities of nongovernmental entities in outer space, including the Moon and other celestial bodies, shall require authorization and continuing supervision by the appropriate State Party to the Treaty. When activities are carried on in outer space, including the Moon and other celestial bodies, by an international organization, responsibility for compliance with this Treaty shall be borne both by the international organization and by the States Parties to the Treaty participating in such organization.

Pursuant to the provisions of Article 6, non-governmental entities, including private companies, can be active in the use of outer space, but only with the authorization and under the continuing supervision of the appropriate state party.

COMMERCIAL LAUNCHING SERVICES

NASA began offering reimbursable launch services in the early 1960s, but it was only in the 1980s that competition for commercial launch services began. In 1980, the European Ariane launch vehicle entered service, and by 1986, the Soviet Union and China were advertising the availability of commercially reimbursable launches. In the 1990s, there will be a robust launch service competition among the United States, Arianespace, China, and perhaps Russia, depending on the fate of its space program. Before the end of the 1990s, there could be additional competition from Japan, India, and perhaps other countries such as Australia or Brazil.

The relationships among countries competing in the launch services market are politically complex because the governments of all major space launching states consult frequently about the terms, conditions, and prices relating to uses of their respective launch services. There are frequent debates over whether or not there is "fair" competition. The idea of competition is to promote differentiation of products and services, usually accompanied by pricing differences. In the absence of clear predatory pricing or product dumping, which is prohibited by the General Agreement on Tariffs and Trade, there appears to be little to argue about fairness in competition.

SATELLITE COMMUNICATION SERVICES

Among the earliest entities established exclusively for commercial space activities was the U.S. Communications Satellite Corporation (COMSAT),[7] which was set up as a special, mixed entity with predominantly private enterprise characteristics, but with a clear governmental presence in the authorization and continuing supervision of activities.[8] COMSAT was incorporated under the laws of the District of Columbia by a group of incorporators appointed by the President of the United States with the advice and consent of the Senate.[9] COMSAT played a major role in the early and mid-1960s, assisting in the creation of the global commercial International Telecommunications Satellite Organization (INTELSAT), now owned and operated by 122 nations. INTELSAT was established as an interim organization in 1964, came under definitive arrangements in 1971,[10] and was the first international organization to own and operate space resources for revenue-earning purposes. INTELSAT was also first to bring private businesses and governments into direct collaborative ownership of an operational space system, a model later used by the International Maritime Satellite Organization (INMARSAT). Some of INTELSAT's administrative and organizational features found their way into other organizations for the exploitation of space applications systems.

Today, there are several international organizations operating space systems for commercial purposes. National and international commercial communication satellite systems are now offering competing services such as fixed, broadcasting, and mobile communication services. There is also competition in space launch services and different, technically incompatible, Earth observation services using a variety of sensors including optical, infrared, and radar systems. There are also national and international meteorological systems, loosely coordinated through the World Meteorological Organization in Geneva; navigation and position determination systems; search and rescue services on a government funded and internationally cooperative basis; and a massive, expanding, competitive, international industrial structure to support all of these services. An increasing number of international regulatory activities are undertaken as the industry grows, and there is more and more national legislation to provide the necessary authorization and supervision of activities in outer space.[11]

PRACTICAL ISSUES FOR COMMERCIAL SPACE SYSTEMS

The practicalities of entering commercial operations in outer space involve many hurdles. Initial financing is always a problem due to the enormous investments required and the great risks associated with a technological environment of expansion, change and frequent failures. If the financing hurdle can be cleared, there are several regulatory hurdles for U.S.

organizations: construction permits to build spacecraft that will include any radio operations (just about every conceivable useful spacecraft);[12] a radio license for spacecraft transmissions;[13] radio licenses for any ground facilities transmitting to a spacecraft;[14] and a launching license from the Department of Transportation.[15] Before these hurdles are cleared, there are complex and expensive contracts to negotiate for spacecraft construction, ground facility construction, launch services, radio-frequency environment and compatibility analyses, and institutional arrangements (possibly including incorporation of the operational entity).[16] Finally, for any commercial service to be offered, there must be an organization established or designated for system operation, maintenance (including spacecraft health monitoring), and marketing.

Such an undertaking is not for the weak or faint-hearted. The time required for an idea to materialize as an operational spacecraft is generally from 10 to 14 years or longer. A pre-designed satellite usually takes from three to five years to build, depending on its size and complexity. A launch generally requires a contract 30 to 36 months prior to the launch. Extended construction periods add considerably to system cost. Huge sums of money must be committed and spent at the rate of tens of millions of dollars per year for years before the system is operational and can start paying back investors and eventually earn a profit, if any profit is to be earned.

These are only some of the initial practical problems facing an entrepreneur in commercial space applications. Even if we assume that financing is arranged, contracts are let, licenses are obtained, the launch is arranged and successfully conducted, and the spacecraft is in orbit ready for commercial operation, we still have other practical issues to consider. If the spacecraft develops operational problems, it probably cannot be repaired. If the satellite's reaction control systems should fail (and for various reasons, they frequently do), control of the spacecraft is lost and it becomes a wandering source of liability to the owner(s), meandering in space at speeds of thousands of meters per second, such that, were it to collide with another object moving across its path, there would be an instantaneous fragmentation of both objects, resulting in a ball of debris that would slowly expand as it aged, constantly broadening its path of potential destruction of other space objects.[17]

SPACE SYSTEM INSURANCE

The potential for damage caused by space activities led to the early elaboration of an international convention dealing with liability for damages to third parties arising out of spaceflight operations.[18] The Liability Convention, drafted by and promulgated through the United Nations, elaborated on Article 7 of the 1967 Outer Space Treaty. The Convention stipulates that "A launching State shall be absolutely liable to pay compensation for damage caused by its space object on the surface of the

Earth or to aircraft in flight" (Art. 2).[19] If damage occurs to the space object of one state by the space object of a second state, "the latter shall be liable only if the damage is due to its fault or the fault of persons for whom it is responsible" (Art. 3). It is also provided that whenever two or more states jointly launch a space object, they shall be jointly and severally liable for any damage caused (Art. 5).

There is a one-year limitation on the submission of claims for damage, the one year extending from the time of the occurrence, or from the time of identification of the launching state which is liable, or from the time when the injured party learns of—or reasonably should have learned of—the damage, in the reasonable exercise of due diligence (Art. 10). There is no time limit on the duration of responsibility of the launching state; consequently, once an object is launched,[20] and for as long as it remains in space and is identifiable, the launching state bears absolute liability for any damage the space object may do on the surface of the Earth or in airspace, and may be liable for damage to other space objects if the damage is due to its fault.

A commercial entity entering into spaceflight operations must consider the nature and duration of the liability issue in order to adequately self-insure or commercially insure itself against losses or liability claims. Although launching states bear primary responsibility, any state that pays damages pursuant to the terms of the Convention "shall have the right to present a claim for indemnification to other participants in the joint launching" (Art. 5.2.) and may look to the spacecraft owner for indemnification pursuant to national law or prior contract arrangements.

The technological risks and liability risks inherent in space operations generate the need for insurance. Since many aspects of the industry are still technologically new, premiums for insurance are substantial, ranging from 10 to 20 percent of the amount of coverage desired. Thus, insuring a $50 million satellite on an $80 million launch vehicle would cost between $13 million and $26 million in today's insurance market; liability insurance and revenue loss insurance would add to that cost.[21] When investors other than the system operators are involved, they want to see all of the identifiable risks insured. One knowledgeable pundit recently noted:

> There are several types of insurance that are specific to commercial space ventures. These include launch insurance, space flight insurance, credit enhancement insurance, and flight delay insurance. Commercial space ventures will also require standard types of insurance including property and casualty insurance, commercial general liability, employers' liability, directors' and officers' liability, fidelity bonds, loans liability and finally an umbrella policy.[22]

More and more attention is being paid to the problems of insuring space systems. Sharing the costs of risks over the broadest available base of interested parties permits commercial space enterprises to exist, with the costs and risks of their existence passed on to the users who derive the benefits. The immediate consequence of the high costs of insurance during the early years of space commercial operations is the maintenance of somewhat higher prices for services than might otherwise prevail. As commercial space systems mature, the technology becomes better understood, more durable, and more reliable, and the costs of insurance and the costs of services are reduced. But there is very little in the space industry that is sufficiently developed to obtain low rates. Years, if not decades, of experience are still needed. Consequently, the necessary qualities of an early space entrepreneur are patience, persistence, and vision.

SECURING INTERESTS AND MANAGING RISKS

When money is invested in assets to produce revenue, the owners or financiers who provide the invested capital have a legitimate interest in the security of the investment. But investing in facilities to be launched into outer space to generate revenue is a high risk business because of the novelty of technologies, the non-accessibility of the property once it is launched, and the hostility of the environment into which the property is placed. Investing in a communication satellite is not like investing in an apartment building. In the space business, so many more things can go wrong (and frequently do) that insurers avoid carrying large amounts of coverage on space programs.[23]

There are definable, quantifiable risks associated with spaceflight ventures, but there are also the unquantifiable and uninsurable risks that are not unique to space. There are risks that apply in any industrial setting where (1) investments are high; (2) years are needed to amortize investments; and (3) a stable market is needed for technological continuity and orderly investment recovery. In what is referred to as market risk, a rapid evolution of technology can render a system non-competitive compared with new technology. Economists favoring competition dismiss the desire for stability in the marketplace as technology-stifling and anti-competitive. They argue that the costs of a system should be recovered within the technological lifetime of the system. Taking into account only the "economic" argument, however, they miss many other benefits accruing from the development of new service technologies.

One of the classic cases of such an economic argument pushed to its absurd conclusion is seen in the U.S. approach to the Earth observation services provided by the Landsat satellite system. Economists explain that the system should be operated on a strictly commercial basis. They contend that the government should not support such systems because there are commercial activities that use the services provided, and the users should pay the costs; if the users are not prepared to support the system, then the service should not be provided. This theoretical approach was not applied when the railroad and telegraph industries emerged in the mid-nineteenth century, nor when the merchant marine fleets expanded in the late nineteenth and early twentieth centuries. The theory did not apply to the new air mail service in the second quarter of this century, nor to development of the nation's highways and airports, all of which needed federal government subsidies for decades in order to become established. Such ventures were supported because they were beneficial public services important to national economic growth, to national security, or to public convenience and necessity.

Bringing new space services through their infancies and childhoods to maturity before demanding that they support and sustain themselves offers countless benefits to the nation and to society as a whole. These economic theories stifle investment; countries that follow them will be left behind by competitive nations whose governments support new space technology.

It is extremely difficult to secure the interests of owners and financiers in assets that are circling hundreds of kilometers above the Earth at speeds of many kilometers per second. Independent of the availability of insurance, owners can obtain some security, at very high cost, by providing redundant on-board systems or even spare satellites in orbit. Because of the time and costs of development and launching, it seems likely that the risks of space business will remain very high for the foreseeable future, even into the early decades of the twenty-first century. Recognizing the enormous strides humanity has taken in the development and use of space technology in the twentieth century, however, we should not assume that risk problems are insoluble, even if we cannot now see their solutions. Given the value and utility of some of the emerging space services, I am bound to agree with Roy Gibson's observation that, for a time at least, governments must remain in partnership with the emerging space industries to bring them into a period of relative stability and maturity.[24]

INTELLECTUAL PROPERTIES IN OUTER SPACE

In addition to capital assets, there are intellectual properties such as patents that are crucial to space business. New laws are emerging that address space-related patent issues in some detail. Simply stated, a patent is a registered, legally protected claim, held by an inventor, to an exclusive right to hold, produce, use, sell, license, or otherwise profit from a product or a process defined in the patent for a period of years (in current U.S. law, 17 years).[25] In many cases, inventors do not commercialize patents themselves but license the patent to companies in return for a financial share in the commercial exploitation of the patent. As one writer recently opined,

> The U. S. Government has [encouraged] and will continue to encourage international space cooperation, private investment, and commercialization of space. Once the present [1986] reexamination of the nation's space objectives is completed, investigation of the boundless potential of space will commence. Space ventures and

entrepreneurs brave enough to seek the secrets of microgravity will help unleash new technology for future generations. Protection of the products of that research provides an incentive to those industronauts who are intent on developing space factories for manufacture of space products yet to be conceived.[26]

The same writer cautions, however, that:

Scientific and commercial applications of space technology could improve ground based production techniques and lead to new processes. However, the commercialization of space is only in the exploratory stage. Years of basic research and experimentation must be completed before industry can establish a foothold in a space factory.[27]

There has been debate in recent years about the extent of jurisdiction of U.S. patent law with regard to activities undertaken in outer space, with some writers arguing that the law is not sufficiently specific about patent protection of inventions made in outer space.[28] In 1990, Congress passed a law which amended the U.S. Code, Title 35, by adding a new section:

Sec. 105. Inventions in outer space
(a) Any invention made, used or sold in outer space on a space object or component thereof under the jurisdiction or control of the United States shall be considered to be made, used or sold within the United States for the purposes of this title, except with respect to any space object or component thereof that is specifically identified and otherwise provided for by an international agreement to which the United States is a party, or with respect to any space object or component thereof that is carried on the registry of a foreign state in accordance with the Convention on Registration of Objects Launched into Outer Space.
(b) Any invention made, used or sold in outer space on a space object or component thereof that is carried on the registry of a foreign state in accordance with the Convention on Registration of Objects Launched into Outer Space, shall be considered to be made, used or sold within the United States for the purposes of this title if specifically so agreed in an international agreement between the United States and the state of registry.[29]

Other than matters of patent rights and protection, there are a number of legally recognized intellectual property rights under the laws of many industrially developed countries, including the United States. Protection is provided in many jurisdictions for trade secrets, copyrights, and trademarks, and international agreements provide reciprocal international recognition of such protection under specified circumstances.[30] During the first three decades of space operations, with the exceptions of commercial communication satellite services and later remote sensing services, governments have been the main users of space for technology development, national defense, science, and exploration purposes. There are emerging national policies in the United States and other countries urging greater investment and involvement of private enterprise in space activities. As the base of private investment and involvement expands, the issues and implications of intellectual properties will become more clear and more important.

COMMERCIALIZATION OF REMOTE SENSING

During the 1970s and 1980s, the number of states participating in remote sensing programs, through either national or multilateral systems, grew considerably. As explained in a recent United Nations report, several states now have abilities to operate civilian satellites generating high-resolution remote sensing data.[31] Using satellite remote sensing techniques, it is possible for one state to collect data concerning another state's agricultural production, natural resources, fresh water, patterns of land use, environmental change, conditions of forestation, and a host of other land and water information. The particular utility of a given remote sensing system will always be related to the characteristics of the sensors, the frequency of viewing and other technical factors.

Despite the increasing number of remote sensing satellites, however, most states cannot take full advantage of the technology. There is no international standardization of data; varying methods of data analysis are used; most countries have few trained experts in data interpretation; different systems use different sensors operating in different spectral regions; and operating parameters differ from one satellite to another. Thus, imagery is often incompatible for inter-system comparative uses. Consequently, different ground receiving and recording equipment, different data processing equipment, and different analytical software are needed for different data systems operated by different countries.

Smaller developing countries, which have neither the experts nor the equipment to use remote sensing data, are increasingly concerned that data about their economic or other resources and information affecting their military or economic security will become available to anyone who can pay for it, without the knowledge or consent of the sensed state. In response to such concerns, the United Nations Committee on the Peaceful Uses of Outer Space formulated a set of principles relating to remote sensing from space, which were adopted by the General Assembly in Resolution 41/65 of December 3, 1986.

REQUIREMENTS FOR INTERNATIONAL COORDINATION

Constantly expanding technology requires ever greater cooperation among states. During the twentieth century, terrestrial technologies have facilitated rapidly expanding travel and transport of goods, and space technologies have expanded communications, improved meteorology, refined navigation and position determination (including global search and rescue capabilities), and provided the first comprehensive surveys of the Earth's resources. All these technologies require constant political interaction, negotiation, compromise, and, in many cases, cooperative creation of international institutions to manage the new technology-driven relationships. I have previously characterized this phenomenon as technopolity: the politics of technology manifest in modern cooperative organizations.[32]

Many organizations and agreements exist today only because technological innovations require them. If we had no aircraft capable of traveling through the atmosphere, we would not need the International Civil Aviation Organization (ICAO), or the International Air Transport Association (IATA), or the Warsaw Convention.[33] If there were no telegraphs, telephones, or radios, we would not need an International Telecommunication Union (ITU). If there were no ocean-worthy trading vessels, we would not need an International Maritime Organization (IMO) or the recently established International Maritime Satellite Organization. The list could be expanded, but the point is clear: there are numerous international organizations, created through political processes and required as a result of technological innovation and international expansion in the use of technology. Most of the legal, political, institutional, and regulatory agreements that relate to the uses of outer space are products of modern space technopolity.

A purely twentieth century technology complex, space is a tool and a catalyst for expansion and strengthening of global cooperation among nations. Mankind's progress in space, whether through national, regional, or global programs, depends heavily on the quality and continuity of the organizations involved. Adequate financial resources, physical facilities, cadres of qualified experts, and the capacity and willingness to sustain work over years of endeavor are essential elements of any successful program in space. Coordination of the diverse institutions and programs in space is an increasing necessity for the realization of the full potential of space technologies, but there is no central coordinator. The cooperation required must be structured, coordinated, and administered through an international organization that is set up for that purpose. The number of public international organizations created during the last 35 years to manage specific uses of space technology already exceeds 25, and that number is growing, demonstrating that few new industry segments stimulate as much technopolity as space systems do. The importance of space technopolity will become even more evident with time, as the numbers of states and organizations active in space increase.

Inevitably, our world is becoming a globally integrated community, managed by institutions reflecting and responding to technology-driven politics. Our technologies and politics increasingly intermix and re-enforce one another. Modern communication and transportation technologies are essential and pervasive in our social, political, and economic lives, and they draw nations into interdependent global management and regulatory systems. Institutional responses to the needs for technological cooperation have been generally timely up to the present, but the pace of change is quickening. Now, space activities need a new response, a central coordinating mechanism to collect and disseminate information, to monitor basic rules for the use of the space environment, and to prevent confusion, miscalculation, duplication of effort, and wasteful or uneconomic uses of resources.

The existing complex of national, regional, and international organizations active in space is extensive. Space activities today are registered, regulated, reported, and constrained in accordance with various treaties, conventions, rules and national laws. The pace of expansion of spaceflight activity is accelerating, and new launching nations are emerging. As we move outward from the Earth, first to low Earth orbit, then to higher orbits, to the Moon, to the planets, to their moons and beyond, more and more functions will require globally centralized and standardized monitoring, coordination, reporting, and regulation. Eventually, there will have to be a central intergovernmental regulatory organization for space, as there are for aviation, communication, postal affairs, maritime affairs, and meteorology.

The United Nations is the logical starting point for establishment of a world space organization. I recently addressed this need for a new organization, noting reasons why early action should be taken and how that action could be organized and phased.[34] The problem arising from the lack of such an organization will only intensify and become more complex with time. The longer the problem is put off, the more difficult its solution will become. But this need is being increasingly recognized.

PROSPECTS FOR COMMERCIAL SPACE ACTIVITIES

We see that there are a number of organizations active in space or using space facilities for commercial purposes. Because of the novelty of the technologies involved, it is essential that governments continue their support and cooperation in the development of space commerce. Several of the major spacefaring nations are encouraging greater commercial involvement in space services and systems and greater investment in space systems by private enterprises. A variety of systems operate commercially and competitively today in satellite communications, launch services, and remote sensing. Although experimentation continues in space processing of materials and in new manufacturing techniques, it does not seem likely that large-scale space manufacturing will occur in this century. We can expect space technology to advance, the costs of access to space and insurance to decline, and more efficient systems for generating power in space to emerge. Creative entrepreneurs will turn their attention to space as its exploitation becomes more practical and affordable. Consequently, there is a bright future for space commerce.

If governments continue to support the development of useful technology, if they continue to assist in taking the risks inherent in the start-up of new space businesses, and if the appropriate coordinating and regulatory organizations are put in place on a timely basis, it is likely that there will be continued expansion of the commercial uses of outer space.

NOTES

1. For an interesting discussion of the environment in the United States with respect to space commercialization, see George Robinson and Pamela Meredith, "Domestic Commercialization of Space: The Current Political Atmosphere," in *American Enterprise, the Law, and the Commercial Use of Space*, vol. 1, Washington, DC, National Legal Center for the Public Interest, 1986, pp. 1-29.

2. Roy Gibson, "What Is Space Business?" in *Space Commerce*, John Egan (ed.), *Proceedings of the Third International Conference on the Commercial and Industrial Uses of Outer Space*, New York and Montreux, Gordon & Breach, 1990, p. 3. The biennial space commerce meetings held in even numbered years in Montreux, Switzerland, are becoming a major meeting place for commercial space system operators.

3. *Id.*, p. 4.

4. *Id.*, pp. 2-4. Concerning issues of financing space ventures, see Neil Hosenball, "Financing Space Ventures," *Journal of Law and Technology*, Vol. 4, No. 1, 1989, pp. 15-19; and N. Senghas, "Private Debt Financing for Space Projects," in *Space Commerce*, Egan (ed.), *supra* note 2, pp. 417-422.

5. For current activities in the materials processing and pharmaceutical developments in space, see papers collected in *Space Commerce*, Egan (ed.), *supra* note 2, pp. 61-109 and 147-172.

6. Treaty on Principles Governing the Activities of States in the Exploration and Use of Outer Space, Including the Moon and Other Celestial Bodies, in 18 U.S.T. 2410, T.I.A.S. No. 6347, 610 U.N.T.S. 205.

7. See the Communications Satellite Act of 1962, as amended, Pub. L. No. 624, 87th Cong., 2d Sess., 76 Stat. 419, approved August 31, 1962.

8. In addition to provision for U.S. presidential appointment of the initial Incorporators and 20 percent of the Board of Directors, there are provisions throughout the law for supervisory, advisory, and regulatory roles for agencies of the U.S. government.

9. *Hearings before the Senate Committee on Aeronautical and Space Sciences: Nomination of Incorporators*, 88th Cong., 1st Sess., March 19, 1963, Washington, DC, Government Printing Office, 1963; see also the annual reports on the progress of the Corporation, beginning with "Communications Satellite Act of 1962—The First Year," Report of the House Committee on Interstate and Foreign Commerce, H.R. No. 809, 88th Cong., 1st Sess., October 3, 1963, Washington, DC, Government Printing Office, 1963.

10. Agreement Relating to the International Telecommunications Satellite Organization (INTELSAT) with annexes, and Operating Agreement Relating to the International Telecommunications Satellite Organization with annex; Done at Washington, DC, Aug. 20, 1971; Entered into Force Feb. 12, 1973, 23 U.S.T. 3813, T.I.A.S. No. 7532.

11. See Karl-Heinz Böckstiegel and Marietta Benkö (eds.), *Space Law: Basic Legal*

Documents, Dordrecht, Martinus Nijhoff, 1990; also Edward Finch and Amanda Moore, *Astrobusiness: A Guide to the Commerce and Law of Outer Space*, New York, Praeger Publishers, 1985.

12. Licensing procedures are described by Bernard Strassburg, Chief, Common Carrier Bureau, Federal Communications Commission, in U.S. Congress, *Hearings before a Subcommittee of the House Committee on Government Operations, Satellite Communications—1964 (Part 1)*, 88th Cong., 2d Sess., Washington, DC, Government Printing Office, 1964, pp. 309-342.

13. Testimony by Bernard Strassburg, *supra* note 12; see also William Coulter, "Regulatory Changes and Trends," *Journal of Law and Technology*, Vol. 5, No. 1, 1990, pp. 39-43.

14. The current regulatory environment in the United States is described in Coulter, *supra* note 13, pp. 39-43.

15. Gerald Mussara, "Commercial Space Transportation: Regulatory Activities of the U.S. Department of Transportation," *Proceedings of the 30th Colloquium on the Law of Outer Space*, Washington, DC, AIAA, 1988, pp. 224-227.

16. See proceedings of the panel on contract issues, including papers by Paul Dembling, panel moderator, "Introduction to Contract Issues," and Ralph Kissick, "Commercial Space Launch Contracts: Disputes and Remedies," *Journal of Law and Technology*, Vol. 4, No. 1, 1989, pp. 29-42.

17. Nicholas Johnson and Darren McKnight, *Artificial Space Debris*, Orbit Books, 1987; Howard Baker, *Space Debris: Legal and Policy Implications*, Dordrecht, Martinus Nijhoff, 1989; see also a recent study by the U.S. Congress, Office of Technology Assessment, "Orbiting Debris: A Space Environmental Problem—Background Paper," OTA-BP-ISC-72, Washington, DC, Government Printing Office, 1990.

18. Convention on International Liability for Damage Caused by Space Objects, Opened for Signature at Washington, London, and Moscow, Mar. 29, 1972; Entered into Force Sept. 1, 1972; 24 U.S.T. 2389, 961 U.N.T.S. 187.

19. Article 1 provides that "(c) The term 'launching State' means: (i) A State which launches or procures the launching of a space object; (ii) A State from whose territory or facility a space object is launched; (d) The term 'space object' includes component parts of a space object as well as its launch vehicle and parts thereof."

20. Article 1 provides that "(b) The term 'launching' includes attempted launching."

21. William Thiele, "Assessing the Role of Insurance in the Commercialization of Space," in *American Enterprise, the Law, and the Commercial Use of Space*, vol. 3, Washington, DC, National Legal Center for the Public Interest, 1987, pp. 137-164; Giovanni Gobbo, "Space Insurance: An Exciting Perspective for New Losers," in Egan (ed.), *supra* note 2, pp. 405-415.

22. Neil Hosenball, "Financing Space Ventures," *Journal of Law and Technology*, Vol. 4, No. 1, 1989, pp. 15-18; see also, in the same volume, John O'Brien, "Liability and Insurance," pp. 19-20, and Peter Nesgos, "The Challenges Facing the Private Practitioner: Liability and Insurance Issues in Commercial Space Transportation," pp. 21-27.

23. Because of the very high amounts of insurance coverage required, insurance policies on space systems are written by a broker who distributes the actual risks over many underwriters, each receiving a portion of the premium corresponding to the share

of the coverage. This avoids an unacceptably large potential liability for one or a few underwriters.

24. Gibson, *supra* note 2.

25. Relevant current U.S. patent laws are collected in Title 35 of the United States Code.

26. Dennis Helfman, "Patents in Space, Encouraging and Protecting Out-of-This-World Investments," in *American Enterprise, the Law, and the Commercial Use of Space*, *supra* note 21, vol. 3, p. 135.

27. *Id.*, p. 122.

28. Richard Dalbello, "Jurisdiction, Intellectual Property, and Tort Law Aboard the Space Station," in *American Enterprise, the Law, and the Commercial Use of Space*, *supra* note 21, vol. 3, pp. 39-66, particularly pp. 53-59; for a more detailed discussion, see Helfman, *supra* note 26.

29. Pub. L. 101-580, Section 1(a), 104 Stat. 2863, Nov. 15, 1990.

30. Raymond Vickery, "The Laws and Outer Space: Intellectual Property," *Journal of Law and Technology*, Vol. 4, No. 1, 1990, pp. 9-14.

31. United Nations Institute for Disarmament Research, *Disarmament: Problems Related to Outer Space*, Geneva, UNIDIR Doc. No. 87/35; UN publication Sales No. GV.E.87.0.7, 1987, pp. 11-13.

32. Stephen Doyle, "Technopolity in Astronautics: Past, Present, and Future," *Proceedings of the 33rd Colloquium on the Law of Outer Space*, Washington, DC, AIAA, 1991, pp. 293-296.

33. See United States Congress, *Air Laws and Treaties of the World*, House Committee on Science and Astronautics, 87th Cong., 1st Sess., Committee Print, Washington, DC, Government Printing Office, 1961; or A. Keenan, A. Lester, P. Martin, and J. P. McMahon (eds.), *Shawcross and Beaumont on Air Law*, 2 vols., London, Butterworths; or Isabella Diederiks-Verschoor, *An Introduction to Air Law* (2nd edition), Deventer, Antwerp, Kluwer, 1985.

34. Stephen Doyle, "International Space Plans and Policies: Future Roles of International Organizations," paper presented at the 39th International Astronautical Congress, Bangalore, India, Oct. 1988, AIAA Preprint No. IAA 88-622; *Journal of Space Law*, Vol. 18, No. 2, 1990, pp. 123-137.

11

Legal Aspects of Military Space Activities

Peter Jankowitsch

Within a year of the launching of the first Sputnik in 1957, the United Nations General Assembly adopted a resolution recognizing that "outer space should be used for peaceful purposes only" and expressing the wish "to avoid the extension of national rivalries into this new field."[1] The international community was thus aware almost immediately of the possible uses, both civilian and military, to which this sphere could be put. Nevertheless, during the first years, the issues addressed by the United Nations Committee on the Peaceful Uses of Outer Space were mainly civilian, focusing primarily on the peaceful potential of outer space and on ensuring the freedom of exploration and use of outer space by all states for the benefit and in the interest of all mankind.[2]

In 1962, the international community was jolted and the situation changed dramatically when the first nuclear weapon was tested in outer space. Suddenly, the extension of the arms race into outer space posed a real and present threat to international peace and security, and the question of the prevention of the militarization of outer space gained importance. International concern became even more intense when, in March 1983, the President of the United States, Ronald Reagan, announced a new U.S. program called the Strategic Defense Initiative, commonly called "Star Wars," and called on U.S. scientists to find means to render nuclear weapons "impotent and obsolete." That year, deep dismay was expressed in various bodies of the United Nations by delegations who felt that the major powers were extending their arms race into the outer space environment, making "space war" no longer a figment of science fiction but a growing component of their global military strategies.[3]

Over the past three and a half decades, the United Nations has generally considered the civilian and military uses of space separately. The civilian or peaceful uses and the "ways and means of maintaining outer space for peaceful purposes"[4] have been discussed primarily in the Outer Space Committee and its two subsidiary bodies, while the question of space weapons has been discussed mainly in the Conference on Disarmament and its Ad Hoc Committee on the Prevention of an Arms Race in Outer Space. As a result of the discussions held in these bodies, as well as in bilateral meetings between the United States and the Soviet Union, several important international legal instruments dealing with both military and peaceful aspects of outer space have been formulated and adopted.[4] While recognizing that most of the general provisions of the space treaties are applicable to military as well as civilian space activities, this chapter will examine only those legal agreements that specifically relate to the military uses of outer space and will evaluate their success in maintaining outer space exclusively for peaceful purposes.[5]

THE MILITARY USES OF SPACE

The military services of the major space powers have been among the leading users of space technology. Although space has not yet become a venue for weapons deployment, military support missions have been routinely conducted from outer space, including communications, reconnaissance and surveillance, navigation, meteorology, and geodesy. The facility with which global command and control can be exercised through satellite communications makes military commanders ever more dependent on space systems. Reconnaissance and surveillance techniques are used for locating targets, tracking fleet movements, identifying supply and transport facilities, monitoring air activities, intercepting communications, warning of enemy preparation or attack, and so on. Satellite navigation systems provide precise worldwide three-dimensional position-fixing services and information for updating inertial navigation systems such as those on strategic missiles. Meteorological satellites provide information for planning military operations and reconnaissance gathering. Geodetic satellites provide information on the Earth's gravitational field, allowing precision targeting of ballistic missiles. This military support technology is continuing to develop, particularly in the areas of satellite sensors, spacecraft survivability, and improved communications and information capabilities for field commanders.

Prospective or potential military space technologies that have been the subject of research or development include anti-satellite weapons, anti-ballistic missile weapons and space-based nuclear weapons.[6] However, as was pointed out in the United Nations Secretary-General's 1990 report, "Scientific and Technological Developments and Their Impact on International Security," some of these technological possibilities are widely considered to be either technically fanciful, of peripheral military interest, or prohibitively expensive. In order to be effective as ballistic missile defense systems, for example, kinetic-energy and directed-energy space weapons would need effective target surveillance and acquisition systems, decoy discrimination capability, pointing and tracking systems, kill assessment capability, and infallible command and control arrangements. All these require substantial technological development and may offer only a limited defense against nuclear weapons. The costs of these hypothetical military missions remain incalculable.[7]

There are at any one time about 175 operational military satellites in orbit.[8] Since these satellites perform many crucial military support functions, it is obviously in the interest of an adversary to try to render them ineffective. Substantial efforts have therefore been devoted to the development of anti-satellite weapons, and these efforts have, in turn, given rise to efforts to protect satellites from attack. This situation could, of course, easily develop into a competition to produce ever more destructive anti-satellite weapons and ever more complex and expensive technology for protection against those weapons.

MULTILATERAL AGREEMENTS RELATING TO MILITARY SPACE ACTIVITIES

The United Nations Charter

The United Nations Charter, in Article 2.4, states that all members shall refrain from the "threat or use of force." This general provision presumably applies to outer space as to any other area, and therefore any aggressive action by one state against the satellites or space objects of another is prohibited. The applicability of the Charter to outer space is affirmed by Article 3 of the 1967 Treaty on Principles Governing the Activities of States in the Exploration and Use of Outer Space, including the Moon and Other Celestial Bodies (the Outer Space Treaty), which calls on states parties to carry out activities in the exploration and use of outer space "in accordance with international law, including the Charter of the United Nations." Similarly, Article 2 of the 1979 Agreement Governing the Activities of States on the Moon and Other Celestial Bodies (the Moon Treaty) declares that all "activities on the Moon, including its exploration and use, shall be carried out in accordance with international law, in particular the Charter of the United Nations."

Although these provisions would seem to be fairly straightforward in their intent, the notion that the Charter should be included in the body of international law governing outer space continues to raise questions. One such question, for example, arises with regard to Article 51 of the Charter, which reaffirms the inherent right of states to protect themselves, individually or collectively, in case of an armed attack. One review of interpretations of Article 51 with respect to space has noted that:

Some United States writers have argued that the right of self-defence referred to in the Charter in case of an "armed attack" must be interpreted in the light of subsequent technical advances and that even the presumed threat of an attack would justify preemptive action in self-defence. Other writers, including those of the socialist countries, maintain that the right of self-defence under the Charter can be used only in the "context of an armed attack" and not as a pre-emptive action.[9]

Another view of Article 51 warns that even though the article allows a response to an armed attack, it does not allow attacks against spacecraft of states that are not part of the armed conflict. Further, that author argues that the article does not permit an attack on a satellite when that attack coincides with the beginning of the hostilities.[10]

Pragmatically, while the Charter's ban on the use of force can be cited as one of the existing measures for the protection of spacecraft, the Charter is usually considered to be a statement of general principles rather than a set of specific, binding rules of international behavior. Its frequent violation by various countries, large and small, further undermines its application to specific situations. Compliance with the Charter is therefore not a significant issue in current disarmament discussions.

The 1967 Outer Space Treaty

In 1963, the United Nations General Assembly adopted the Declaration of Legal Principles Governing the Activities of States in the Exploration and Use of Outer Space as one of the first efforts by the international community to set up a legal regime for outer space. This Declaration did not specifically recognize the military possibilities of outer space. That same year, the Treaty Banning Nuclear Weapon Tests in the Atmosphere, in Outer Space and under Water (the Partial Test Ban Treaty) was adopted, becoming the first legally binding document containing a specific prohibition of a military use of outer space.

Subsequently, the 1963 Declaration was further developed to become what is considered as the Magna Carta of outer space, the Outer Space Treaty, which was adopted by the General Assembly in 1966 and entered into force in 1967. Incorporating the language of the Declaration, this treaty is one of the most important measures legally restricting military activities in outer space as well as establishing the fundamental principles of international law governing space activities.

It is Article 4 of the Outer Space Treaty which deals directly with military activities in space. The first paragraph of Article 4 calls on states parties to the Treaty not to place in orbit around the Earth any objects carrying nuclear weapons or any other kinds of weapons of mass destruction, install such weapons on celestial bodies, or station such weapons in outer space in any other manner. The second paragraph proclaims that the Moon and other celestial bodies shall be used by all states parties exclusively for peaceful purposes; forbids the establishment of military bases, installations and fortifications, the testing of any type of weapons, and the conduct of military maneuvers on celestial bodies; but allows the use of military personnel for scientific research or for any other peaceful purposes, as well as the use of any equipment or facility necessary for peaceful exploration of the Moon and other celestial bodies.

The specific banning from Earth orbit of "nuclear weapons or any other kinds of weapons of mass destruction," generally assumed to include chemical and biological weapons which cause severe and extensive damage, implies that conventional weapons and military support systems are not prohibited from Earth orbit. While some commentators have argued that the spirit of the Outer Space Treaty is incompatible with any military uses of outer space, the narrowly specific scope of the prohibition was clearly intentional, and the existing military uses of space, in particular the military support systems, are generally accepted as compatible with the Treaty.

Similarly, the obligation "not to place in orbit around the earth" nuclear weapons is generally taken to apply only to objects which complete at least one full orbit of the Earth, thus not prohibiting ballistic missiles, which may reach an altitude well above that of many orbiting satellites but fall back to Earth before completing a full circuit.

The implicit acceptance of conventional weapons in Earth orbit has, until recently, been of purely theoretical interest. With the development of non-nuclear anti-satellite (ASAT) weapons and research into space-based directed-energy weapons such as laser and particle beam weapons, the exclusion of such systems from the scope of the Treaty has become of practical military importance. One proposed system, an X-ray laser powered by a nuclear explosion, raises the question of what precisely constitutes a nuclear weapon. It has been argued by some proponents of "star wars" systems that a nuclear-powered laser is not a nuclear weapon.

In addition to these deliberate exclusions, there are also some ambiguities that raise questions. The first paragraph, for example, bans the installation of nuclear weapons "on celestial bodies" rather than using the usual phrase, "the moon and other celestial bodies," raising the question as to whether the lack of specific reference to the Moon indicates a deliberate ambiguity as to its status.

Developments in military technology, such as the nuclear-powered X-ray laser, can raise new questions of interpretation of the Treaty and the legal classification of the new systems. In some cases, whether or not a system is deemed to be a weapon prohibited by the Treaty will depend on the point of view of the state making the interpretation. Would any of the laser or directed-energy weapons, for instance, be considered as "weapons of mass destruction"?

Although the second paragraph of Article 4 would appear to be more comprehensive in its prohibition on military activities on the Moon and other celestial bodies, it has its share of possible interpretation problems. Does the prohibition apply only to the surface and body of the Moon, or also to orbits around it? In explicitly allowing the use of military personnel and implicitly the use of military support equipment, the Treaty raises but does not answer the question of precisely what sort of non-peaceful activities are prohibited.

There have been various attempts to define the terms "peaceful" and "military" without much agreement. As one author has concluded after discussing the differing points of view,

> It would appear much more productive to abandon reference in arms control agreements to the terms "peaceful" or "military" unless there is a clear indication of their more precise meanings in the given context. For instance, it might have been stipulated that the phrase "exclusively peaceful" means "complete deweaponization," that is, the absence of any weapon. Such provision would still leave open the meaning of a "weapon" but the area of potential disagreement regarding the interpretation of "peaceful" would be considerably reduced.[11]

The Outer Space Treaty, in providing a beginning and a foundation for space law, also provides a substantial first step in limiting the military uses of outer space. However, there is also a substantial range of military activities that are not covered by the Treaty, and some of its provisions need to be made more precise, either due to lack of clarity in the original wording or due to technological advances since the drafting of the Treaty.

The 1979 Moon Treaty

In 1979, the United Nations General Assembly adopted the Agreement Governing the Activities of States on the Moon and Other Celestial Bodies (the Moon Treaty), which filled some of the gaps and ambiguities in Article 4 of the Outer Space Treaty. Article 1 of the Moon Treaty, in defining the areas covered by its provisions, states that the provisions relating to the Moon "shall also apply to other celestial bodies within the solar system, other than the earth," and that "reference to the moon shall include orbits around or other trajectories to or around it."

Article 3 of the Moon Treaty, which deals specifically with military matters, reaffirms the principle that the Moon shall be used by all states parties exclusively for peaceful purposes; prohibits any threat or use of force or any other hostile act or threat of hostile act on the Moon, or the use of the Moon to commit any such act; and forbids the placing in orbit around or other trajectory to or around the Moon of objects carrying nuclear weapons or any other kinds of weapons of mass destruction or the placing or use of such weapons on or in the Moon, as well as the establishment of military bases, installations, and fortifications, the testing of any type of weapons, and the conduct of military maneuvers on the Moon.

The Moon Treaty, in these two articles, reaffirms the Outer Space Treaty's demilitarization of the Moon and the prohibition on the placing of nuclear weapons and other weapons of mass destruction on the Moon, and clearly extends those provisions to lunar and planetary orbits and trajectories. Thus, all of outer space beyond Earth orbit is to be used for exclusively peaceful purposes. The ambiguity left by the omission of explicit reference to the Moon in the nuclear weapons ban in the Outer Space Treaty is resolved in the Moon Treaty. Similarly, under paragraph 4 of Article 3 of the Moon Treaty, the Outer Space Treaty's prohibition on the establishment of military bases, installations, and fortifications, the testing of any type of weapons, and the conduct of military maneuvers on the Moon and other celestial bodies is extended to other lunar and planetary orbits and trajectories.

The Moon Treaty, however, leaves most of the conceptual problems of the Outer Space Treaty unresolved. For instance, paragraph 4 of Article 3, like Article 4 of the Outer Space Treaty, allows the use of military personnel for scientific research or for any other peaceful purposes. The term "peaceful purposes," however, remains subject to different interpretations. According to legal scholars from the former Soviet Union and some other countries, and in the tradition of socialist jurisprudence,[12] the provision for exclusively peaceful purposes implies a prohibition of all military activities except those specifically permitted by the Treaty. Scholars from the United States and some other Western countries, on the other hand, interpret "peaceful" to exclude only aggressive or offensive activities, allowing defensive military activities.[13] It has been argued, for example, that the verification function of military reconnaissance satellites facilitates agreement on arms control measures and should therefore be considered a peaceful space activity. The Moon Treaty does not provide any more precise distinction between peaceful and non-peaceful space activities.

In addition to its failure to provide solutions to some of the existing disagreements on definitions and interpretations, the Moon Treaty has added a new element in paragraph 2 of Article 3. That paragraph prohibits, among other things, any threat or use of force or any other hostile act on the Moon or the use of the Moon to commit any such act. It does not, however, define the prohibited acts any more precisely, leaving a good deal of room for interpretation. The question has arisen, for example, as to whether non-aggressive military action could or should be perceived as a threat of force.

The Moon Treaty thus significantly clarifies and extends the demilitarization of deep space, reinforcing the framework of space law established in the Outer Space Treaty. Unlike the Outer Space Treaty, however, the Moon Treaty has not been ratified by the space powers. The Treaty was elaborated in the Outer Space Committee through its usual consensus procedures and was unanimously endorsed by the General

Assembly, including all the space powers, in 1979. When it was opened for signature in 1980, however, the United States had reservations over some non-military provisions and did not sign or ratify, and other space powers also withheld ratification. The Treaty entered into force in July 1984 and now has eight states parties, but without the space powers its effectiveness is limited.

International space law has provided a basic framework for regulating the uses of outer space and has prohibited or limited certain military uses. As has often been pointed out, however, the activities that have been prohibited, such as installing nuclear weapons on the Moon, are of little practical interest. The important practical military uses, including military support functions and non-nuclear anti-satellite weapons, are left open by international space law. In the case of military support systems, there is a widespread, though hardly unanimous, view that these command, control, and intelligence-gathering functions contribute to global stability and should not be limited. In the case of weapons systems, there is a much broader feeling that they are destabilizing and should be banned. While this issue has been raised many times in United Nations bodies, there has been no significant movement toward an agreement to limit them. The only agreements that have been reached relating to conventional military activities in Earth orbit have been bilateral agreements.

BILATERAL TREATIES

During the early years of the space age, outer space was the domain of the United States and the Soviet Union. A major fear of the international community was that the United States-Soviet military strategic rivalry of the cold war would inevitably extend the arms race into outer space. Decisions on the development and deployment of space-based weapons or ground-based weapons for use in space were being taken in Washington and Moscow, with no opportunity for other countries to influence the outcome. Since the end of the 1960s, the United States and the Soviet Union have held a series of arms control discussions known as the Strategic Arms Limitation Talks (SALT I and SALT II) and the Strategic Arms Reduction Treaty (START). While most of these discussions focused on ballistic missiles, which are not regarded as coming within the scope of space law, they had some provisions relating to military space activities in the accepted sense.

With respect to military space activities, the most important of the four agreements concluded as part of SALT I was the 1972 Anti-Ballistic Missile (ABM) Treaty.[14] The ABM Treaty was based on the "doctrine of deterrence," which assumed that a state would hesitate to launch a nuclear attack if it knew that its opponent was capable of responding in kind. The central provision relating to space activities is Article 5, in which the parties agree "not to develop, test or deploy ABM systems or components which are sea-based, air-based, space-based or mobile land-based." Article 2 defines an ABM system as a system to counter strategic ballistic missiles or their elements in flight trajectory and lists the components of an ABM missile system. The parties also agreed, in Agreed Statement D, that for any future ABM systems based on physical principles other than missiles, "specific limitations on such systems and their components would be subject to discussion."

Verification of compliance with the ABM Treaty is by "national technical means," with "deliberate concealment measures which impede verification by national technical means" prohibited. Such means include satellites, aircraft, and ground systems; they use high-resolution cameras for observing ground facilities, radar for tracking missiles tests, and sensitive radio receivers for intercepting communications. Article 12 provides that the parties will not interfere with each others' "national technical means of verification." Some of the military support functions which are not mentioned in the United Nations space law treaties are thus specifically protected by this bilateral legal agreement.

Despite the detailed technical specifications of the space weapons to be prohibited by this treaty, its principles, like those of its multilateral cousins, have been the subject of intense debate and varied interpretation, particularly since the announcement of the U.S. Strategic Defense Initiative in 1983. Even the nature of its obligations has been a source of disagreement and debate, with some political analysts in the United States arguing that the Treaty ought not to be treated as though written in stone, but should evolve with the changing technical and political environment. Others, however, argue that it would be dangerous to assume that the Treaty's integrity could be maintained if either country begins tampering with it or introducing amendments, even so-called modest ones. This debate is still of a somewhat hypothetical nature since no irrevocable decisions have yet been taken by either party with regard to how, when and in what way the existing treaty should be amended.

The agreement that new ABM technologies, presumably including laser or directed-energy systems, should be the subject of future discussions on specific limitations has raised questions concerning the legality of such systems under the original Treaty. To some, the new technologies are covered by the general definition in Article 2 and are subject to the general prohibition of Article 5, with only specific details to be worked out in further negotiations. The fact that Article 2 lists only the components of missile systems simply represented the state of the technology at the time as indicated by the phrase, "currently consisting of," clearly foreseeing the possibility of future technologies that would fall within the general definition. Others argue that their exclusion from the list of ABM system components in Article 2 and the provisions of Agreed Statement D indicate that the original Treaty does not impose any specific limitations on such systems.

Another topic of debate is the question of research on ABM systems, which is not clearly prohibited in the Treaty as are deployment, development, and testing of ABM systems. Therefore, it has been argued, research is permitted. This interpretation is supported by the argument that many research activities are not subject to verification by the other side, hence a prohibition would be ineffective and a likely source of disputes. The Soviet position has been that the Treaty does ban most research, although it has acknowledged that some "fundamental" research at the laboratory stage may not be a violation of the Treaty. The United States has argued that research is acceptable, with some writers noting that the word used for "development" in the Russian text is "create" and that, therefore, it is not research that is prohibited but only creation, following study and research. The United States has insisted that its SDI project, being a research program, is therefore in compliance.

If it is accepted that some research is allowed but that development is prohibited, the question of the precise delimitation of the two activities arises. The most popular interpretation has been that research takes place in the laboratory, while development includes field testing stages, an interpretation which takes into account the need for verification of the prohibited activities. The prohibition on the development of ABM "components," as well as systems, also raises the question of the definition of a component; at what point would a high-power laser with a steerable beam be considered a component of a prohibited ABM system? Agreed Statement D, which foresaw the need for discussions on "specific limitations" on new technologies, seems intended as a mechanism for dealing with just such questions.

These and the other unresolved questions may become irrelevant if one of the parties withdraws from the Treaty, as provided for in Article 15 if "extraordinary events . . . have jeopardized its supreme interests." Some of the proponents of the U.S. SDI program have suggested just such a move.

The 1979 SALT II Treaty on the Limitation of Strategic Offensive Arms prohibits, among other things, the development, testing, or deployment of nuclear weapon systems or other weapons of mass destruction in orbit around the Earth, including fractional orbital missiles (Article 9). It also reaffirms the principle of non-interference with "national technical means of verification" (Article 15), which remain unspecified but are understood to include a variety of satellite intelligence-gathering techniques.

The Strategic Arms Reduction Treaty, signed in July 1991 by Presidents George Bush and Mikhail Gorbachev, provides for reductions in ballistic missiles. While it does not extend the limitations on military space activities, it reinforces the framework of bilateral arms control measures, thus reaffirming the provisions of the ABM and SALT II treaties.

Nonetheless, support for these agreements is still a matter for debate within the United States. According to Paul C. Warnke, chief U.S. arms negotiator during the Carter administration, START is "the latest triumph" for the ABM Treaty. But, he notes, "in a sadly ironic twist, the completion of START coincides with a major and misguided effort to scuttle the treaty that made it possible."[15] This view was shared by Gerard C. Smith, chief U.S. negotiator of the ABM Treaty and the SALT I agreement, who states that, "With weighty irony, on the very day that Presidents Bush and Gorbachev signed history's most sweeping nuclear arms reduction pact, the Senate approved a measure that places the ABM Treaty and the entire process of strategic arms control in serious danger."[16]

The measure to which they refer was the proposed Missile Defense Act of 1991, an amendment to the defense authorization bill that was adopted by the Senate. The Missile Defense Act envisages a near-term deployment of an anti-ballistic missile system at Grand Forks, North Dakota, and describes this system as the initial step in deploying a nationwide defense against limited attacks by ballistic missiles. The act recognizes that subsequent steps will require amendment of the ABM treaty. "Even this first step would shift the Star Wars program from research to deployment—a fundamental change," Smith argues. Another writer notes that the legislation was a compromise between the administration's proposed Global Protection against Limited Strikes (GPALS) system, which calls for an extensive deployment of space-based "brilliant pebbles" interceptors and ground-based components, and the House of Representatives' rejection of the GPALS and brilliant pebbles concepts. "If any of these developments lead to abrogation or fundamental revision of the ABM Treaty, the current opportunity for major progress in achieving substantial reductions in strategic offensive arms will be jeopardized if not lost," the writer argues.[17]

These most recent developments in the United States have therefore focused increased attention on the ABM Treaty, on its link to other bilateral United States/Soviet arms agreements, as well as to multilateral arms control agreements governing the military uses of outer space.

CURRENT AND FUTURE WORK

In the United Nations Conference on Disarmament, the main multilateral forum for negotiations on disarmament, including space disarmament, various delegations have stated repeatedly that the present legal regime governing military activities in outer space is no longer adequate. There has been general recognition of the importance of bilateral negotiations between the United States and the Soviet Union, although many delegations have emphasized that those negotiations do not diminish the urgency and importance of multilateral efforts. It is generally accepted that bilateral and multilateral efforts are complementary.

Recent initiatives in the Conference on Disarmament on controlling the militarization of space have proposed a variety of approaches: additional protocols to existing agreements; universal adherence to existing agreements; new treaties to ban the development and deployment of specific weapons in space; a comprehensive international regime outlawing any military use of outer space; a strengthening of technical verification to ensure compliance with agreements; and a growing emphasis on confidence-building as an important means for ensuring the peaceful uses of outer space.[18] Most of the recent proposals continue to run into the now familiar objections that they are either too limited or too broad in their scope, and that they do not provide for effective measures to ensure compliance.

In spite of such objections, the last few years have seen a perceptible improvement in the political climate for compromise, in particular because of the easing of hostility between the United States and the Soviet Union. At its 1991 sessions, the Conference on Disarmament once again held discussions on the prevention of an arms race in outer space, dividing the topic into three sub-topics: examination and identification of issues; reviewing existing agreements; and consideration of existing proposals and new initiatives.

The proposals in the Conference include efforts toward a variety of goals: improved definitions and classifications of different types of space activities; a definition of "aggressive" uses of space that need to be controlled; improved means for verification; more precise agreed interpretations of existing agreements such as the Outer Space Treaty; and the establishment of information systems for the purpose of confidence-building. There were calls for a comprehensive ban on anti-satellite weapons, in part to ensure that countries could safely rely on satellite technology for economic and social development and international cooperation.

The most ambitious proposals have generally come from developing and socialist countries. Some Western countries, while agreeing to discuss these proposals, have argued that political conditions were not ripe for in-depth negotiations. In general, the debates at the 1991 session of the Conference on Disarmament continued to reflect the many and varied views of states concerning the potential dangers of the use of outer space for military purposes, although in a less confrontational manner than in previous years.

While the prospects for space weapons seem quite undecided, the use of satellites for military command, control, communications, and intelligence-gathering is developing. The Gulf War was a powerful demonstration of the advantages that space technology offers both for strategic military planning and for tactical operations. It also demonstrated the disadvantages for a combatant that does not have access to such technology. That demonstration will certainly promote more widespread use of military support satellites. The increasing dependence of military forces on satellite support also increases the potential impact of anti-satellite weapons. In a conflict between two space powers, the destruction of an opponent's eyes and ears in space could have an important effect on the outcome. One effect would be a reduction or loss of central control of forces, possibly leading to greater destruction than would otherwise occur. The development and deployment of such space weapons might therefore have an important destabilizing effect on balances of power. For the moment, however, while there is no agreement to ban such weapons, there is also less development activity, allowing more time for the diplomats to negotiate.

The recent decentralization of power in the former Soviet Union, including apparently the decentralization of the space program, introduces new uncertainties into the situation. It seems likely that the former Soviet space program will be significantly reduced, diminishing the threat of an arms race in space and perhaps reducing the importance of bilateral arms negotiations. The role of multilateral negotiations, in the United Nations Conference on Disarmament and perhaps in the Outer Space Committee, would thus be enhanced, allowing broader participation in the important discussions. From the U.S. point of view, however, the lack of an equal negotiating partner could reduce the inclination to make concessions to the concerns of other countries which are not in a position to make reciprocal concessions.

CONCLUSION

The future will undoubtedly see an increasing number of countries active in space, further advances in space technology, and an increasing dependence on satellite services. As it was noted during a recent conference on "Space Strategy: Three Dimensions,"

> For the high-tech industry, space is a ticket to survival and a good cash flow. For the military, it's a threat environment to be overcome as well as an opportunity for enhanced surveillance, an answer to problems such as the need for warning time. For arms controllers, it is either the nightmare of the weaponization of a pristine arena, or the solution to verification problems which would obviate the need for on-site inspection and allow independent objective verification by the international community. For lawyers, it's another place to restrict and regulate.[19]

Evidently, no single forum and no single treaty could effectively address all of the issues that have been raised concerning the military uses of space. A constructive approach to these issues will require a pragmatic balance between national interests and international cooperation, between considerations of national security and concerns over militarization.

NOTES

1. U.N.G.A. Res. 1348 (XIII) of Dec. 13, 1958, preambular paragraphs 1 and 3.
2. U.N.G.A. Res. 1472 (XIV) of Dec. 12, 1959, preambular paragraph 1; and Res. 1721 (XVI) of Dec. 20, 1961, preambular paragraph 1.
3. *The United Nations Disarmament Yearbook*, vol. 8 (1983), New York, United Nations, 1984, p. 324.
4. For the texts of space treaties and agreements cited throughout this chapter, see *Status of Multilateral Arms Regulation and Disarmament Agreements*, 3d ed., New York, United Nations, 1987; *Arms Control and Disarmament Agreements*, Washington, U.S. Arms Control and Disarmament Agency, 1990; see also Jozef Goldblat, *Agreements for Arms Control: A Critical Survey*, Stockholm International Peace Research Institute (SIPRI), London, Taylor and Francis Ltd., 1982.

5. In addition to the treaties and bilateral agreements which contain provisions relating specifically to space military activities (the Outer Space Treaty, the Moon Treaty, and the ABM Treaty), there are a number of other military agreements which contain principles applicable to space activities: the Treaty Banning Nuclear Weapon Tests in the Atmosphere, in Outer Space and under Water (PTBT), signed on Aug. 5, 1963; the Agreement on Measures to Reduce the Risk of Outbreak of Nuclear War between the United States and the Soviet Union, signed on Sept. 30, 1971; the Agreement between the United States and the Soviet Union on Measures to Improve the USA-USSR Direct Communications Link (Hot Line Modernization Agreement), signed on Sept. 30, 1971; the Interim Agreement between the United States and the Soviet Union with Respect to the Limitation of Strategic Offensive Arms (SALT I), signed on May 26, 1972; the Convention on the Prohibition of Military or any Hostile Use of Environmental Modification Techniques, signed on May 18, 1977; the Treaty between the United States and the Soviet Union on the Limitation of Strategic Offensive Arms (SALT II), signed on June 18, 1979; and the Strategic Arms Reduction Treaty (START) between the United States and the Soviet Union, signed in July 1991.

6. Ashton B. Carter, Joseph S. Nye, and James A. Schear (eds.), *Seeking Stability in Space: Anti-Satellite Weapons and the Evolving Space Regime*, Lanham, MD, University Press of America, 1987, pp. 29-71.

7. Secretary-General's Report, *Scientific and Technological Developments and Their Impact on International Security*, U.N. Doc. A/45/568, New York, United Nations, Dec. 17, 1990, paragraphs 34-47.

8. John Pike and Mark O'Gorman, *What's Up in Space: Operational Satellites on the Anniversary of Sputnik 1*, Washington, Federation of American Scientists, 1987.

9. Nandasiri Jasentuliyana, "Space Weapons and International Law: A Critique of Existing Treaties," in *An Arms Race in Outer Space: Could Treaties Prevent It?* Proceedings of the Symposium held on October 30 and November 1, 1985, Montreal, McGill University, pp. 71-103.

10. Sune Danielsson, "International Security and Outer Space," *Disarmament: A Periodical Review by the United Nations*, Vol. 10, No. 2, Summer 1987, pp. 1-9.

11. Stephen Gorove, "Article IV of the 1967 Outer Space Treaty and Some Alternatives for Further Arms Control," in N. Jasentuliyana (ed.), *Maintaining Outer Space for Peaceful Uses*, Tokyo, United Nations University, 1984, p. 82.

12. See G. Gál, *Space Law*, Leiden, Sijthoff, 1969, pp. 164-180; M. Lachs, *The Law of Outer Space: An Experience in Contemporary Law Making*, Leiden, Sijthoff, 1972, pp. 106-108; A. S. Piradov (ed.), *International Space Law*, Moscow, Progress Publishers, 1976, pp. 91-94.

13. D. Goedhuis, "The Changing Legal Regime of Air and Outer Space," *International and Comparative Law Quarterly*, Vol. 27, 1978, pp. 576, 584-585; S. Gorove, *Studies in Space Law: Its Challenges and Prospects*, Leiden, Sijthoff, 1977, pp. 85-94; N. Matte, *Space Policy and Programmes Today and Tomorrow*, Montreal, McGill University Press, 1980, p. 68. See also O. Ogunbanwo, *International Law and Outer Space Activities*, The Hague, Nijhoff, 1975, p. 101; and S. Bhatt, *Legal Controls of Outer Space*, London, Books from India, 1973, pp. 175-176.

14. The other three treaties adopted during the SALT I process are: the Accidents Measures Agreement of 1971 and the Prevention of Nuclear War Agreement of 1973,

which prohibit the Soviet Union and the United States from interfering with or attacking each other's missile early warning systems, and the so-called Hot Line Modernization Agreement of 1971, by which the Soviet Union and the United States agreed to maintain two full-time direct communication lines, using communication satellites.

15. Paul C. Warnke, "Success Linked to ABM Treaty," *Bulletin of the Atomic Scientists*, Vol. 47, No. 9, November 1991.

16. Gerard C. Smith, "A Dangerous Plan for Missile Defense," *Arms Control Today*, September 1991.

17. Spurgeon M. Keeny, Jr., "Limited ABM Defense: Dangerous and Unnecessary," *Arms Control Today*, October 1991.

18. For information on the debates of the Conference on Disarmament, see its annual reports to the General Assembly, the latest of which is document A/46/27, New York, United Nations, 1991.

19. Canadian Institute of Strategic Studies, *Space Strategy: Three Dimensions*, Toronto, CISS, 1989, p. 117.

12

Space Law and the Environment

He Qizhi

Since the beginning of the space era, scientists and engineers have tried to identify the environmental risks associated with space activities. In recent years, with the rapid development of space activities and increasing concern over their effects on the environment, efforts in this direction have been strengthened, advancing from scientific and technical studies to the development of legal measures to protect the environment.[1]

Space law has long recognized the rights of states to explore and use outer space, including the Moon and other celestial bodies.[2] However, the environmental impact of the exploration and use of outer space, and the potential hazards of space activities, have increasingly become a major concern of the space community. It is the purpose of this chapter to examine the issue in a comprehensive way. After an overview of the general effects of space activities on the environment, a number of specific environmental threats due to space activities will be examined, and the potential of space technology to monitor the Earth's environment will be reviewed. Finally, the existing laws relating to the environmental effects of space activities will be analyzed, their inadequacies will be identified, and recommendations will be made for future work in space law.

In dealing with the environmental problems of space activities, airspace and outer space need to be treated together, because there is no recognized boundary between the two[3], and because space activities are carried out from the Earth's surface to outer space through airspace. Space activities may therefore be a source of risk to the terrestrial environment, to the atmosphere, and to outer space.

POSSIBLE ENVIRONMENTAL EFFECTS

Because space activities use materials from the environment and release undesirable materials to the environment, they generate pollution and contamination in various degrees to different parts of the space-Earth environment. Here, pollution and contamination denote an excessive presence of substances or human activities that upsets the balance of the environment or interferes with space activities.[4] With increasing space flight activity, the likelihood of harming the environment becomes greater. Because the natural composition and state of the environment at various altitudes and places is different, the effects of pollution and contamination from space activities may be significantly harmful in certain parts of space but harmless in other areas. Damage may be physical and tangible or non-physical and intangible. Space pollution and contamination may take a variety of forms, including chemical pollution, biological pollution, or electromagnetic interference.

Chemical Pollution

Chemical pollution is caused by the release of chemicals into the Earth or space environment. The launching of a rocket produces a so-called ground cloud consisting of exhaust gases, cooling water, sand and dust, and other substances. Air and ground pollution from launches at the present rate poses no grave danger, but if launching activities increase—particularly if very large scale space systems, such as solar power satellites with huge solar panels, are deployed—the air and water around the launching site may be polluted significantly.[5]

After launching, space vehicles first traverse the lower atmosphere, but it is perhaps the least affected part of space because of the relatively dense atmosphere, which has a tendency to quickly return to a normal state after a disturbance. The large volume of gases and particles discharged by a launch vehicle is usually quickly dispersed with the wind, hence the comparatively limited effect.

The greatest effect on the space environment occurs in the upper atmosphere where the atmospheric density decreases rapidly with height. Due to the very thin atmosphere, there is little mixing and dilution of even a small amount of released exhaust gases and substances, which could drift and persist for a long time over a large area.

Chemical releases from spacecraft are composed mainly of nitrogen oxide, carbon dioxide, chlorine, and hydrogen chloride. The latter two deplete the ozone layer, between about 16 km and 50 km in altitude, which protects life on Earth by absorbing the Sun's harmful ultraviolet radiation. In an effort to protect the ozone layer from depletion by chlorine from industrial sources, the Vienna Convention for Protection of the Ozone Layer of March 22, 1985,[6] was signed by 29 states and came into force on September 22, 1988; the Montreal Protocol on Substances That Deplete the Ozone Layer of September 16, 1987,[7] was signed by 24 states and came into force on January 1, 1989. There are a number of natural and human processes affecting the ozone layer, and the issue requires more study to determine the importance of space flights.

Another important part of the high atmosphere is the ionosphere, consisting of several layers at altitudes from about 50 km to 200 km and higher. Chemical releases and operational water releases, by reducing the density of electrons, may change the radio reflection properties of the ionosphere, disturbing radio communications. Even a small amount of water vapor may remove free electrons. In addition, satellites in low Earth orbit lose energy and altitude due to atmospheric drag, and below about 100 km they fall quickly into the upper atmosphere and disintegrate and vaporize owing to the high temperatures generated from air friction. The resulting production of metal vapors can also influence ionospheric conditions affecting radio communication. The present level of satellite re-entry appears to be less than that of meteorites,[8] and is not now of critical concern. But if large numbers of satellites were vaporized on re-entry, the contamination of the upper atmosphere could become a serious concern. In this case, the introduction of reusable vehicles like the Space Shuttle, which returns to the ground intact, would avoid the problem.

Biological Pollution

Biological contamination due to space activities has been divided into two categories: (1) contamination of outer space by terrestrial micro-organisms carried by spacecraft, called "forward contamination"; and (2) contamination of the Earth by extraterrestrial micro-organisms carried by spacecraft, called "backward contamination." In addition, terrestrial micro-organisms exposed to the space environment might acquire mutations that could be dangerous to human beings.[9]

During the early phase of the space age, fears of biological contamination were matters of serious concern. However, it appears that conditions on other planets of the solar system do not permit the existence of terrestrial-type micro-organisms, so the dangers of backward contamination are of little immediate concern. NASA, analyzing the results of the Apollo Program, concluded that there are no infectious substances on samples brought back from the Moon and decided to stop further disinfection and quarantine of crews, spacecraft, and materials. Soviet space lawyers, however, protested that such a decision should be made only after international consultation with others possessing appropriate experience and adequate information on space exploration.[10]

It seems likely that terrestrial micro-organisms isolated for long periods of time in high mountains, caves, or polar regions, and sharing a common evolutionary process with other inhabitants of the Earth, would present a danger greater than samples brought back from other planets. But biological research over many years has not revealed a mutant capable of infecting or destroying terrestrial organisms, and there is no evidence that any real danger exists.[11] Although there is still fear that biological research in infectious diseases on spacecraft could result in forward contamination,[12] it is believed that since the environments of other planets in the solar system are so hostile to life, the risk of such contamination is negligible.

Biological contamination therefore seems to be of no grave concern at present, but the possibility of forward or backward contamination in the course of increasing space activities cannot be entirely ruled out.

Electromagnetic Interference

Electromagnetic waves produced by high-powered radio transmitters on Earth or on satellites generate electric and magnetic fields over large areas, potentially disturbing the communications of other satellites and radio astronomy. The most powerful transmissions are from ground-based transmitters, including radars. The problem of interference by such transmitters has been clearly demonstrated, but the magnitude of its effects is not clear.

Satellite transmissions of radio waves also generate electric and magnetic fields at large distances. In the extreme case of solar power satellites, which may be developed in the future, the huge energy flux could greatly disturb the ionosphere and, at the Earth's surface, even be harmful to the biosphere.

Disturbances to radio communications and to astronomical observations, particularly in the infrared spectral region, can also be caused by rocket exhaust gases, water vapor, and chemical releases. All of these issues relating to electromagnetic interference are being dealt with by the International Telecommunication Union.

Laser beams generated in space or directed from the ground into space could also have a great impact on space environment and activities. The development of high energy lasers and particle beams for military use will constitute a threat to the peaceful uses of outer space.

PRACTICAL DANGERS OF SPACE ACTIVITIES

Currently, there are two major concerns over environmental threats arising from space activities: the use of nuclear power sources (NPS) in outer space, and debris generated by space activities. The use of nuclear power sources is one of the most active items on the agenda of the United Nations Committee on the Peaceful Uses of Outer Space and its two subcommittees,[13] while space debris is the subject of discussions in various forums.[14]

Nuclear Power Sources

Nuclear explosions in the upper atmosphere or outer space wreak havoc in the space environment. The radioactive fallout will travel long distances, not only changing the space environment but also destroying electronic devices on satellites. The ban on nuclear explosions in space in the Partial Test Ban Treaty was intended to prevent such events.

Worldwide concern has emerged over the use of nuclear power sources (NPS) in outer space, particularly following the malfunctioning and disintegration of two Soviet nuclear-powered satellites, Cosmos-954 in 1978 and Cosmos-1402 in 1984. The use of NPS in outer space is based on sophisticated technology that offers great advantages in providing electric power when sunlight is inadequate. There is, therefore, general acceptance of the use of NPS in space, particularly on long-duration missions.

It must be recognized, however, that the use of NPS in space involves an inherent risk, which cannot be completely eliminated, due to the large amount of radioactive materials used. Nuclear-powered satellites on missions to deep space and those re-boosted to higher orbits after the completion of missions in low orbit will not damage the terrestrial environment. In the case of malfunctioning nuclear-powered satellites that re-enter the atmosphere, however, it will be impossible to exclude radiological hazards resulting from the dispersal of their radioactive materials in the environment. The hazards to humans will primarily be radiological, arising from radiation exposure through both direct external radiation and internal radiation from inhalation or ingestion.[15] The potential environmental damage is considerable. In view of such possible dangers, the elaboration of legal principles relating to NPS in outer space for protecting human life and environment from harmful effects caused by radiological material released by malfunctioning nuclear-powered satellites has become an important issue facing the space community.

Space Debris

The greatest practical threat to space activities has been recognized to be the hazards due to artificial debris from space activities. The potential danger of collisions between spacecraft and the debris accumulated in Earth orbit have greatly increased.

The term "space debris" covers spent objects,[16] used rocket stages, separation devices, shrouds, clamps, and all large and small fragments, including the particles remaining after the disintegration of a space object. These are products of space activities which, in certain Earth orbits, already exceed the flux of natural meteoroids, which is relatively constant.[17] As a result, a satellite now has a greater probability of colliding with orbital debris than with natural meteoroids.[18]

According to a status report on space debris published by the United Nations,[19] there are about 7,000 objects larger than 20 cm in size in near-Earth orbit, of which about 23 percent are inactive satellites, 10 percent are burned out rocket stages, 62 percent are fragments, and only 5 percent are active space objects. It is expected that by the year 2000 this number will increase to 10,000.[20] In addition, at least 2,000 pieces of debris from 10 to 20 cm in size and about 50,000 from 1 to 10 cm are scattered throughout near-Earth space. Moreover, there are millions to billions of chips in the millimeter and submillimeter size range. Such an enormous and uncertain amount of debris represents a serious picture of pollution in the near-Earth space environment.[21]

The main sources of space debris are explosions and collisions of space objects,[22] both of which can occur accidentally or intentionally. Most debris is created by accidental explosions of propulsion systems. Some explosions, regarded as the most serious, occur shortly after launch, while others occur years after launch due to residual propellants self-igniting. Intentional explosions and collisions of satellites have occurred through military space activities, particularly the testing of anti-satellite weapons (ASATS). The Soviet ASAT program is reported to have conducted more than 20 tests of an ASAT system, while the United States has conducted tests of airborne ASAT systems.[23]

Collisions and explosions are closely related, as debris ejected from explosion can collide with other objects, thus creating additional debris. A collision between two space objects can generate hundreds of trackable pieces of debris and probably millions of untrackable particles.

The existence of space debris in Earth orbit poses grave dangers to operating satellites and space transportation systems. According to one estimate, assuming 10,000 trackable objects in space, a large satellite at an altitude where debris is concentrated may have a probability of collision of 10 percent over its lifetime. With a predicted increase of traceable objects to 20,000 by 1995, the probability of collision could increase to 20 percent.[24] While no satellites are known to have been destroyed by accidental collisions, there are examples of satellites which have suddenly stopped functioning for no apparent reasons, possibly due to collisions with untrackable debris. A notable example of such a collision is the 1983 chipping of the Space Shuttle Challenger's window by a tiny paint chip, necessitating the replacement of the window at considerable cost.[25] Such accidents have probably repeatedly occurred. Unless proper measures are taken in time, it may be too late to alleviate the situation in the future.

MONITORING AND PROTECTING THE EARTH'S ENVIRONMENT

After 35 years of space activities, the space community is celebrating International Space Year (ISY) in 1992, with emphasis on monitoring and improving the Earth's environment. With satellite meteorology and remote sensing technology rapidly developing, the Earth's environment has never before been so closely observed. Various space programs, particularly the International Geosphere-Biosphere Programme (IGBP), clearly demonstrate the benefits that can be derived through the use of space technology. Humanity's understanding of the global environment is recognized as being of the highest importance. Despite deficiencies and impediments existing in these undertakings, the achievements of and benefits from space activities will be addressed below.

Land

Land and water resources are being monitored from outer space regularly on a national, regional, and global basis. The inherent capabilities of space observation make it ideally suited to the study of land masses and activities such as resources management, agricultural production, forestation, hydrology, flood prevention, drought, desertification, soil erosion, and other natural disasters.

Sea

Marine remote sensing observations are extremely helpful for predicting and analyzing periodic and cyclical phenomena of the ocean, thus making climate forecasts more reliable and valuable. They can also be used in marine hydrology, for monitoring sea ice areas, floating vegetation, fish habitat, shoreline, estuary and channel position, and water turbidity. Satellite surveillance is also the best way to monitor ocean pollution by detection of chemical pollution, oil slicks, sewage, solid wastes and other matter in the sea. The Global Investigation of Pollution in the Marine Environment (GIPME) project, established by UNESCO's Intergovernmental Oceanographic Commission (IOC), continuously assesses the health of the sea through various techniques and projects. The primary objective of this project is to determine the relationship between marine pollution and its effects on ocean organisms and people. It constitutes an important contribution to the study of global habitability.

During the recent Gulf War, satellite surveys showed that millions of gallons of oil pouring from Kuwaiti terminals formed a slick about 56 km long by 16 km wide in the Gulf, causing severe damage to the environment, marine life, and birds.[26] These examples indicate the enormous potential of satellite remote sensing in the study of marine pollution and other oceanographic questions.

Air

The study of the Earth's atmosphere is coordinated through numerous international programs such as the World Climate Program (WCP) and the World Weather Watch (WWW) established by the World Meteorological Organization (WMO), and the Earth Watch or Global Environment Monitoring System (GEMS) organized in the early 1970s by the United Nations Environment Programme (UNEP). The WWW includes a global observing system that gathers and disseminates atmospheric data generated by the weather satellites operated by various countries. These data serve as the basis for weather forecasts, storm warnings and other environment assessment worldwide.

Satellites are also used to monitor the deterioration of the ozone layer, including the ozone hole over Antarctica, due to chlorine compounds, and to study global warming due to the greenhouse effect caused by emissions of carbon dioxide and other gases. These are grave issues confronting humankind, and space technology has an important role to play in dealing with them. But if the problems due to space activities and those that are revealed by satellite observations are to be solved, environmental protection laws need to be examined and improved.

LAWS TO PROTECT THE ENVIRONMENT

In examining existing laws relating to space activities and the environment, a number of space treaties providing piecemeal measures must be considered, since there is no general convention codifying universal principles relating to environmental protection.

The earliest treaty dealing with the space environment is the 1963 Partial Test Ban Treaty, which prohibits nuclear explosion in the atmosphere and beyond, including outer space.[27] More extensive environmental protection is provided by the 1967 Outer Space Treaty and the 1979 Moon Agreement, which essentially demilitarize the Moon and other celestial bodies, thus protecting them from the environmental impact of military activities.[28] But these treaties only partially demilitarize outer space, since in Earth orbit only the placement of nuclear weapons and "any other kinds of weapons of mass destruction" are banned.[29] Thus, they leave the following loopholes: (1) no ban on testing and deploying other space weapons, including ASAT weapons; (2) no ban on warheads carried by strategic missiles on trajectories traveling through outer space; (3) no definition of "weapons of mass destruction." In short, these treaties leave open the possibility of testing, deploying, and utilizing space weapons other than nuclear weapons, thus leaving the possibility of a further worsening of the debris situation.

The 1976 Convention on the Prohibition of Military and Other Hostile Use of Environmental Modification Techniques also contributes to the protection of the environment, since such techniques include any means of modification of the dynamics, composition, and structure of the Earth or space environment, through intentional control of natural processes.[30]

For protecting the environment from potentially dangerous non-military activities, Article 9 of the Outer Space Treaty is the most important legal provision. Article 9 obliges states parties to (1) avoid harmful contamination of outer space or introduction of extraterrestrial matter that could result in adverse changes in the environment of the Earth, and (2) enter into international consultation if their space activities would cause potential harmful interference with space activities of other parties.[31] Since "harmful contamination" has to be related to outer space, whereas "adverse changes" cover only those effects on the Earth's environment that are due to the introduction of extraterrestrial matter, these two provisions are rather limited in providing protection of the Earth environment. The consultation envisaged in the article, although very important, is not mandatory, nor is any procedure established or recommended. If the party concerned does not initiate consultation or refuses consultation demanded by another party, it does not constitute violation of the Treaty.

Article 7 of the Moon Agreement makes an improvement on the general obligations contained in the Outer Space Treaty. It obliges states parties to the Treaty to (1) take measures to prevent disruption to the existing balance of the environment of the Moon and other celestial bodies, whether caused by introduction of adverse changes, by harmful contamination, or otherwise; (2) avoid harmful effects to the Earth environment through the introduction of extraterrestrial matter or otherwise; (3) inform the United Nations of the measures being adopted to prevent the disruption of the existing balance of the environment of the Moon and any plans to place any radioactive material on it. In this article, the prevention of disruption of the existing balance of the environment of the Moon is the key obligation of all states parties. This provision of the Moon Agreement on environmental protection makes up for some of the inadequacy of the corresponding provision of the Outer Space Treaty.

The 1976 Registration Convention requires the registering of launchings with the United Nations, but it does not require notification of explosions or malfunctioning space objects, nor registration of the type or amount of fuels or exhaust, chemical or radioactive substances, or other contaminants which might affect the space environment.

The ITU Convention and Radio Regulations prohibit harmful interference with space communications and provide two procedures to prevent interference. The first is notification and registration of frequency assignments in the Master Register maintained by the International Frequency Registration Board (IFRB). The other is through coordination by various conferences.[32]

The question of liability for environmental damage has been partially dealt with by the 1972 Liability Convention, which establishes a launching state's absolute liability for all damage caused by its space object on Earth or to aircraft in flight. It also covers damage caused by one object in space to another on condition that such damage is caused by the fault or negligence of the launching state. According to the definition given in Article 1 of the Convention, "damage" could cover damage to the Earth's environment as long as this means the surface of the Earth under the jurisdiction of a state. Following the Cosmos-954 incident, Canada based its claim for compensation for damage from the Soviet Union mainly on the provisions of the Liability Convention, and the claims were settled by diplomatic negotiation between the two countries.[33] Damage to the atmospheric or space environment, or to areas outside national jurisdiction, such as the high seas and Antarctica, does not seem to be covered by the Convention. This appears to be one of the lacunas which needs to be filled by further elaboration of space law.

Customary International Law

As space law is a branch of international law, it would be useful to identify customary principles of international law applicable to environmental problems generated by space activities. In the international community, customary law has been developed on the basis of the general practices of states, with "general practices" referring to actions habitually carried out, and thus acquiring the status of legal right.[34]

The general rule of customary international law regarding environmental protection has developed based on the often-cited 1941 Trail Smelter case.[35] The United States and Canada Arbitration Tribunal, in dealing with such a case for the first time, formulated the legal principle that no state has the right to use or permit the use of its territory in a manner to cause damage in or to the territory of another state. This principle was recognized by the 1979 Convention on Long-Range Transboundary Air Pollution[36] and the 1982 Law of the Sea Convention.[37] It was further embodied in the ILA Montreal Rules on International Law Applicable to Transboundary Pollution, which reads: "States are in their activities under an obligation to prevent, abate and control transfrontier pollution to such an extent that no substantial injury is caused in the territory of another state."[38]

Principle 21 of the Stockholm Declaration on the Human Environment[39] covers environmental dangers in areas beyond national jurisdiction, and stipulates that states have "the responsibility to ensure that activities within their jurisdiction or control do not harm the environment of other states or of areas beyond the limits of national jurisdiction." Though the legal significance of this principle is not undisputed, it is generally regarded as a reflection of existing customary law by many respected international lawyers,[40] and some states expressed the view at the Stockholm Conference that this principle is an expression of existing international law.[41] This general rule prohibiting environmental pollution of the environment of other states or areas beyond national jurisdiction has been elaborated in Article 9 of the Outer Space Treaty.

More specific issues relating to space activities, such as eliminating or minimizing space debris, are not covered by customary international space law. However, some of the principles contained in Article 9, such as the principles of cooperation and paying due regard to the corresponding interests of other states, as well as the process of consultation, may lead to international agreements dealing with specific questions of environmental protection relating to space activities.

FUTURE PERSPECTIVES

As the foregoing discussion shows, environmental issues posed by space activities have become a matter of concern for humankind as a whole. It is now generally accepted that protective measures should be taken on the basis of a comprehensive and in-depth understanding of the situation. In recent years, discussions on these issues have been active.[42] Space law specialists have demanded that before it is too late, legislative bodies dealing with space and states concerned should direct their attention to the elaboration of a legal framework for environmental protection.

The examination of existing law shows that effective protection of the environment requires not only general principles but also more detailed specific legal rules. This indicates the need for further progressive development of space law relating to the environment mainly on a treaty basis, since existing treaty law regarding environmental protection is very inadequate and customary law "can of its nature provide only a few basic legal principles which lay down guidelines to be followed."[43]

In such circumstances, and bearing in mind the political and legal realities of the international system, the development of a comprehensive system of space environmental law has to take a piecemeal approach, dealing with issues separately and step by step. The following section will consider a number of issues which now seem appropriate for action.

The Need to Incorporate Principles on NPS into a Convention

The use of nuclear power sources in outer space is one of the two major environmental hazards to be confronted, as it involves risks inherent in the possibility of malfunctioning of satellites with radioactive materials on board. The United Nations Legal Subcommittee, after long years of deliberations, began making significant progress in 1988, and in 1990 it achieved consensus on a key principle: guidelines and criteria for the safe use of NPS in outer space. These principles are expected to be completed in the near future, in spite of some difficulties in reaching agreement on a few remaining draft principles. Most probably these principles will be adopted in the form of a United Nations General Assembly resolution, which is only recommendatory in nature, without any legal, binding force.

These principles have been drawn up on a solid scientific and technical basis by agreement in the Scientific and Technical Subcommittee. The question is whether further steps should be taken to convert these principles into a formal treaty.

Strong demands were made for the establishment of specific legal rules after the disintegration of Cosmos-954 over Canada, and particularly after the explosion of the Chernobyl nuclear power station on April 26, 1986,[44] leading to the conclusion of two treaties, the Convention on Early Notification of

Nuclear Accident[45] and the Convention on Assistance in the Case of a Nuclear Accident or Radiological Emergency.[46] The NPS principles can be considered as a supplement to these two treaties and should be transformed into formal legal instruments with full, binding force to provide a complete set of legal rules to prevent radiological pollution.

International Expert Group on Space Debris

The issue of minimizing and eliminating space debris is becoming an international technical-legal question of growing importance, and it might be useful to establish a group of well-qualified space scientists and technicians of various space states and other interested states to address the question. The group could be asked to review and assess space debris and the environmental effects of space activities and to establish standards in these areas. The group would be provided with information, before and after each launch, concerning the type and amount of fuels, radioactive payloads, exhaust gases, and other chemicals released in all stages of flights of spacecraft, as well as information on explosions, collisions, and other events producing debris, so that after full examination, international standards and recommended practices could be established. The standards thus elaborated could be adopted by COPUOS and the General Assembly as recommended practices, which states would be expected to make best efforts to follow in the interest of reducing debris and preventing environmental pollution. Such standards and practices would be subject to reviewing, amending, and updating. In the absence of an international space agency, such an Expert Group could be set up within the framework of COPUOS, which is the only competent body to deal with such space issues. Given the difficult and protracted treaty-making process, this might be an initial step toward further practical measures in establishing a code of conduct.

Legal Aspects of Monitoring the Global Environment

The application of space technology for monitoring the terrestrial and space environment is an important aspect of space activities and the main theme of the 1992 International Space Year. In 1972, after the launch of the first U.S. Landsat, the Legal Subcommittee of COPUOS put the question of remote sensing for resource management and environmental monitoring on its agenda, and later made it a priority item. In 1986, after many years of negotiations, a set of Principles Relating to Remote Sensing of the Earth from Space was adopted as a General Assembly resolution[47] on the recommendation of COPUOS.

The Principles implicitly allow states to carry out remote sensing activities from space without advance notice and permit free dissemination of data and information without prior consent by the sensed states. Principle 12 provides that data and information acquired over a sensed state must be made available to that country on a non-discriminatory basis at reasonable cost. Principle 10 stipulates that remote sensing shall promote the protection of the Earth's natural environment, and that states participating in remote sensing activities shall disclose all information in their possession identified as capable of averting any phenomenon harmful to the Earth's environment. Principle 11 further provides that remote sensing shall promote the protection of mankind from natural disasters.

However, to improve global environmental monitoring, problems such as lack of a central and comprehensive data bank, lack of international regulations for data exchange, export and import restrictions, and obstacles to technology transfer have to be overcome. As a result of these difficulties, users may not get what they believe they need; there have been inaccurate predictions, and many of the data have not been widely used.

Nevertheless, the Principles Relating to Remote Sensing of the Earth from Space are generally satisfactory, and at present there appears to be no substantial need to make them into a formal treaty. Now, remote sensing activities, in all their ramifications, are lawful activities. Most of the substantive content of the 1986 Principles is already a part of existing treaty law; other elements are part of the customary rules of international law. Still other elements may require some operational structures to overcome the deficiencies already mentioned. An adequate international legal regime for fact-gathering on the global environment has emerged and will continue to be developed in the future. When space observations further clarify the basic requirements for environmental protection, it may be possible to consider drafting a new international treaty on this important subject.

Role of the United Nations

The United Nations has been the forum for international discussions concerning space activities and the environment for many years. Since the key role of the United Nations concerning outer space is played by COPUOS, this Committee has a broad mandate[48] to deal with all matters relating to the peaceful uses of outer space, including the protection of the environment. In view of this important role of COPUOS, certain actions might be taken to improve its work in this area:

1. Strengthen and expand the role of COPUOS as the main organ dealing with the peaceful uses of outer space and concentrating more on space and terrestrial environment issues relating to space activities;
2. Promote closer international cooperation by coordinating the efforts and programs of the United Nations member states in the sphere of space activities and the environment;

3. Increase assistance to developing countries by urging them to make more use of space science and helping them to acquire and use the remote sensing data and information they need in order to use space monitoring capabilities more effectively; and
4. Promote and facilitate the conclusion of legal instruments to resolve international legal issues concerning space activities and the environment.

The United Nations, as a worldwide organization with substantial achievements in various fields, will have a crucial role in promoting the use of space technology to preserve both the space and terrestrial environments as well as human civilization.

NOTES

1. The space environment was among the topics discussed at the 23d (1980), 25th (1982), 27th (1981), 30th (1987), 32d (1989), and 33d (1990) IISL Colloquiums on the Law of Outer Space, and also in other forums, where a number of papers were presented. The Institute of Air and Space Law of Cologne University held an International Colloquium on the Space Environment in 1988, which included a dialogue between experts in space science and space law with a view to promoting the study of this problem. The presentations at this colloquium were published in Karl-Heinz Böckstiegel (ed.), *Environmental Aspects of Activities in Outer Space*, Cologne, Carl Heymanns Verlag, 1990.

2. Article 1, Outer Space Treaty.

3. Gyula Gál, "Indivisibility of Environmental Protection in Vertical Space," *Proceedings of the 27th Colloquium on the Law of Outer Space*, New York, AIAA, 1984, pp. 388-389.

4. He Qizhi, "Environmental Impact of Space Activities and Measures for International Protection," *Journal of Space Law*, Vol. 16, No. 2, 1988, pp. 117-118.

5. *Impact of Space Activities on the Earth and Space Environment*, U.N. Doc. A/Conf.101/BP/4 (1981), p. 7.

6. 26 *International Legal Materials* 6, pp. 1,516-1,540.

7. *Id.*, pp. 1,541-1,561.

8. The total meteoric mass entering the atmosphere is estimated at 10,000 kg/day. See *supra* note 5, p. 8.

9. See *supra* note 5, pp. 20-21.

10. S. Vinogradov, "Space Activity and Environmental Protection," in *Space and Law*, Moscow, Progress, 1985, pp. 168-169.

11. See note 5, p. 21.

12. P. McGarrigle, "Hazardous Biological Activities in Outer Space," *Akron Law Review*, Vol. 18, 1984, p. 103.

13. For a detailed analysis of the deliberations in the Committee and its two subcommittees on the topic of NPS, see He Qizhi, "Towards a New Legal Regime for the Use of Nuclear Power Sources in Outer Space," *Journal of Space Law*, Vol. 14, No. 2, 1986, pp. 95-112; V. Kopal, "The Use of Nuclear Power Sources in Outer Space: A New Set of United Nations Principles?" in *Proceedings of the 33rd Colloquium on the Law of Outer Space* (Dresden 1990), Washington, AIAA.

14. See *supra* note 1.

15. U.N. Doc. A/AC.105/220 (1978), pp. 13-14.

16. There is some disagreement as to whether "debris" covers spent space objects, but in terms of space law, the word "debris" may be safely assumed to cover spent space objects. Some experts, however, like Dr. L. Perek, hold that "debris" always implies "something broken up" or "only a part of the whole," and a complete satellite out of fuel and out of control should not be called debris, but an inactive satellite. See I. H. Ph. Diederiks-Verschoor, "Harm-Producing Events Caused by Fragments of Space Objects," in *Proceedings of the 25th Colloquium on the Law of Outer Space*, New York, AIAA, 1982, p. 1.

17. See *supra* note 8.

18. M. Kessler, "Orbital Debris Issues," *Advances in Space Research*, Vol. 5, No. 2, 1985, pp. 3-10.

19. See *Space Debris, A Status Report*, submitted by the Committee on Space Research, U.N. Doc. A/AC.105/403, January 6, 1988.

20. See Howell, "The Challenge of Space Surveillance," *Sky and Telescope*, No. 548, June 1987, p. 588.

21. *Id.*

22. For a fuller analysis of the sources of space debris, see D. Baker, *Space Debris: Legal and Policy Implications*, Utrecht Studies in Air and Space Law, Dordrecht, Martinus Nijhoff, 1989, pp. 3-10.

23. *Id.*, pp. 5-6.

24. N. Jasentuliyana, "Environmental Impact of Space Activities: An International Law Perspective," in *Proceedings of the 27th Colloquium on the Law of Outer Space*, New York, AIAA, 1984, p. 390.

25. "Shuttle Hit by Man-made Debris," *Space World*, March 1985.

26. *China Daily*, January 29 and February 23, 1991.

27. For the text of the Treaty, see 480 U.N.T.S. 6964, pp. 43-49.

28. Article 4, paragraph 1 of the Outer Space Treaty.

29. Article 4, paragraph 2 of the Outer Space Treaty.

30. For the text of the Convention, see U.N.G.A. res. 31/72 of December 10, 1976.

31. Article 9 of the Outer Space Treaty.

32. Article 35 of the International Telecommunication Convention (Nairobi, 1982); Articles 11 and 13 of the Radio Regulations (1982).

33. See *supra* note 4, pp. 108-109. The Soviet jurist maintained that the issue of compensation was resolved not on the basis of the principles invoked by Canada but on the basis of an *ex gratia* settlement. See also G. M. Danilenko, "Space Activities and Customary Law of Environmental Protection," in Bockstiegel (ed.), *supra* note 1, p. 177.

34. L. Oppenheim and H. Lauterpacht, *International Law*, 8th ed., London, Longmans, 1955, p. 26.

35. *United Nations Reports of International Awards*, vol. 3, p. 1,905.

36. For the text of the Convention, see 18 *International Legal Materials* 6 (1979), pp. 1,442-1,445.

37. See 21 *International Legal Materials* 6 (1982), pp. 1,261-1,354.

38. International Law Association, *Report of the 60th Conference* (Montreal 1982), p. 2, and Report of the Committee, p. 178.

39. For the text of the Declaration, see 11 *International Legal Materials* 6 (1976),

pp. 1,416-1,421.

40. International Law Association, *Report of the 61st Conference* (Paris 1984), p. 391.

41. For instance, the Representative of Canada stated that "in the view of the Canadian Government, Principle 21 in fact accorded with existing international law." U.N. doc. A/CONF.48/14 (1972), p. 115.

42. See *supra* note 1.

43. *International Court of Justice Reports*, 1984, p. 290.

44. N. M. Matte, "Suggestions for Legal Measures and Instruments," in Böckstiegel (ed.), *supra* note 1, pp. 241-242.

45. For the text of the Treaty, see 25 *International Legal Materials* 6 (1986), pp. 1,370-1,372.

46. *Id.*, pp. 1377-1386.

47. U.N.G.A. Res. 41/65, December 3, 1986.

48. See U.N.G.A. Res. 1472 (XIV), Dec. 12, 1959, and U.N.G.A. Res. 1721 (XVI), Dec. 20, 1961.

13

The Scientific and Technological Basis of Space Law

Lubos Perek

The Latin saying *ex facto sequitur lex* has some truth, but it does not tell the whole story. Effective law must be based on facts, but the facts have to be carefully selected, generally recognized, and well understood. These are demanding requirements with respect to everyday life, and even more so with respect to space, where we have no immediate experience to guide us. Determining the relevant facts in the case of space law requires not only the cooperation of scientific and technical experts in the field, but also further research and development to answer many of the legal questions that arise. Experience in space exploration and technological development is so recent and so limited that much of the knowledge must still be considered incomplete and tentative.

Another important point, not recognized in the Latin saying, is that facts are only a necessary condition for the creation of effective law, not a sufficient condition. More important than the facts themselves is the political will of those involved in the elaboration of the new law. The development of space law includes cases in which adequate facts were available but adoption of a legal measure had to, or still has to, wait for the emergence of political will. This analysis will be more concerned with the use or non-use of scientific knowledge and technological experience than with political will. But we must remember that even the elusive political will may be inspired by a careful presentation of facts, which may, for example, allay fears of a new and unfamiliar technology.

The United Nations plays a special role in the development of space law. The United Nations Committee on the Peaceful Uses of Outer Space has adopted, over the course of the last 30 years, five treaties, agreements, and conventions, and three sets of principles dealing with space law. At present, it is close to agreement on yet another set of principles, relating to the use of nuclear power sources in outer space. Most of the work of the Committee is carried out through its two subcommittees, the Scientific and Technical Subcommittee and the Legal Subcommittee. The fact that the Legal Subcommittee meets each year following the meeting of the Scientific and Technical Subcommittee and has before it the report of the Scientific and Technical Subcommittee indicates the awareness in the United Nations of the importance of scientific and technical knowledge in the elaboration of space law.

The International Telecommunication Union (ITU) also plays an important role in the development of space law since a growing proportion of radio communications is transmitted via satellite. The increasing competition for the limited radio frequencies available for space and other communications services demands careful technical coordination to prevent chaos in communications. This coordinating task is allocated to the ITU. The International Telecommunication Convention[1] and the Radio Regulations,[2] which include the decisions of the World Administrative Radio Conferences (WARCs),[3] contain the legal and regulatory measures concerning telecommunications to and from satellites and have the status of binding international law. Scientific and technical data and analyses relating to the Radio Regulations are elaborated and compiled by the International Radio Consultative Committee (CCIR) of the ITU.

Scientific and technological knowledge are relevant to all questions of space law, but the role of such knowledge in the consideration of all space law cannot be covered here. Rather, this chapter will offer a few examples of how scientific and technical knowledge has been used in the formulation of space law.

THE OUTER SPACE TREATY: VISIONARY SPACE LAW

The adoption of the Outer Space Treaty[4] by the United Nations General Assembly in 1966 was a formal conclusion to the effort which began with the establishment of the United Nations ad hoc Committee on the Peaceful Uses of Outer Space in December 1958.[5] The ad hoc Committee was established just 14 months after the launch of the first Sputnik, when only a handful of scientific satellites had been launched into orbit, and when very little was known about the possible applications of space science and technology such as remote sensing, satellite communications, satellite meteorology, or military activities. Nonetheless, calls for delay, for waiting for more launches, for further developments, for national studies of space technology, if they were made at all, were overcome by a strong vision and political will to use space for the benefit of mankind.

In 1959, the ad hoc Committee was transformed into the permanent United Nations General Assembly Committee on the Peaceful Uses of Outer Space,[6] with a mandate to review international cooperation in the peaceful uses of outer space, to study a possible United Nations role in that area, and to study legal problems that might arise from the exploration and use of outer space.

The Committee held its first meeting in November 1961,[7] eight months after the first manned space flight, and in 1963 it adopted its first legal instrument, a declaration of legal principles governing activities in outer space.[8] Among these principles were the freedom of exploration, the non-appropriation of outer space and celestial bodies, promotion of international cooperation and mutual assistance, the responsibility of states for national activities and liability for damage, the control of states over their space objects, and finally, the provision that astronauts are to be regarded as envoys of mankind, entitled to assistance by all states.

In the 1967 Outer Space Treaty, the provisions of the 1963 Principles were supplemented by a ban on the placing of nuclear weapons in space and a ban on military activities on the Moon and other celestial bodies and in deep space. It strengthened the applicability of the Principles to the Moon and other celestial bodies, provided that all facilities on the Moon and other celestial bodies should be open to other countries, and encouraged countries to allow observers of space flights.

These broad and imaginative ideas were based on the relatively few scientific facts and the limited technological experience available at that time. This reaction of the international community to the opening of space to human activities was so comprehensive, so fundamental, and so consequential that no example from previous or subsequent history can match it. The 1967 Outer Space Treaty demonstrates that broad and effective space law does not need to be based on extensive scientific and technical analysis if it is backed by political vision and imagination. Despite its lack of technical detail, it has encouraged the development of space science, technology, and applications, while providing a basis for protecting the rights of countries. Other questions of space law have arisen since that have required more technical solutions, but none have challenged the wisdom of the Outer Space Treaty.

THE MOON TREATY: THE FAILURE OF VISION

The exploration of the Moon by means of space probes began in 1959, shortly after the space age began. Some probes flew around the Moon, some landed on its surface, and some became satellites of the Moon. The most important were the six Apollo missions that landed astronauts on the surface of the Moon between 1969 and 1972.

The discussions on the legal implications of the exploration and use of the Moon started in the Committee in 1970 and continued until 1979, when the Moon Treaty was unanimously adopted by the General Assembly.[9] It entered into force in 1980 when it had been ratified by five states, none of them with major space capabilities. Since then the number of states parties has increased to eight, still with no space powers among them.

The provisions of the Moon Treaty apply not only to the Moon but also to other celestial bodies of the solar system and to orbits around and trajectories to the Moon and other bodies. For this region, the Moon Treaty provides for exclusive use for peaceful purposes, freedom of scientific investigation, and the right to collect and remove samples of mineral and other substances. The Moon Treaty also contains provisions for the establishment of international scientific preserves and for protecting the environment of the Moon and the Earth.

An important, and ultimately controversial, aspect of the Moon Treaty is the provision for possible exploitation of its natural resources. The Treaty implicitly recognizes that the development of lunar resources could contribute to economic development. Such development, however, is currently far from economically or technologically feasible, and a large amount of scientific research and technological development will be needed if this vision is to be realized. The Treaty provides that when commercial exploitation of lunar resources becomes feasible, an international regime will be established to manage the activity.

While the general composition of lunar surface materials is known as a result of the scientific analysis of samples returned from the Apollo missions, the technology that would be required for large-scale recovery and processing of useful materials is quite unknown. The Moon offers firm ground and plenty of open space, but the environment is quite hostile to life, with no water, no atmosphere, and a temperature that ranges from –190°C during the two-week-long night to 100°C during the two-week-long day. Chemical analysis reveals that the common elements are oxygen, silicon, iron, calcium, titanium, aluminum, and magnesium, with abundances quite similar to the average abundances on Earth. In the absence of volcanism and of erosion due to wind and water, the landscape of the Moon is affected almost exclusively by meteor impacts, and there has apparently been little of the geological activity that has resulted in concentrations of valuable materials on Earth.

In principle, metals, ceramics, and other materials could be manufactured from lunar soil, but the transport of manufacturing installations and living and working quarters to the Moon poses enormous technological difficulties. Returning products to Earth also raises questions of economy, so use of these materials on the Moon or in space may be more promising. Undoubtedly, the first use of the Moon will be for scientific research such as astronomical observations.

The Moon Treaty, like the Outer Space Treaty, contains ideas that are in full conformity with scientific knowledge but, particularly with respect to resource exploitation, well in advance of technological capabilities. Unlike the case of the Outer Space Treaty, however, the futuristic vision of the Moon Treaty has proven, at least for the moment, to be its undoing. When the Moon Treaty was opened for ratification in 1980, the provision for the establishment of an international regime for the exploitation of lunar resources provoked opposition, particularly in the United States, from people concerned with this renunciation of national economic rights of unknown value. This opposition persuaded the U.S. government to put off ratification, and the other space powers also declined to ratify.

The Outer Space Treaty and the Moon Treaty were thus elaborated through a visionary approach to space activities and the adoption of broad policies of international cooperation before the technological implications of the policies were clear. While the visionary elements of the Outer Space Treaty and the Moon Treaty were different, which was in part responsible for their different fates, it would also seem that the mid-1960s was a period more receptive to a visionary approach than the early 1980s, which saw a renewal of international tensions, both East-West and North-South. The Moon Treaty was the last attempt at such an expansive and forward-looking approach to space law.

SATELLITE BROADCASTING: FEAR OF TECHNOLOGICAL IMPERIALISM

Direct broadcasting satellites receive television signals from a central Earth station and relay those signals to large numbers of small, inexpensive receiving stations connected to television sets in either individual homes or community facilities. One satellite can broadcast to receivers throughout an area as large as one-third of the globe, in contrast to terrestrial television transmitters, which use different frequencies giving them a maximum range of about 80 km. When transmissions from a central station in one country are received by receivers in another country, the broadcasting becomes international.

The question of international satellite broadcasting was placed on the agenda of the Scientific and Technical Subcommittee in 1969 and of the Legal Subcommittee in 1974, and opinions quickly became polarized. Some Western states strongly opposed any restrictions on the dissemination of information, while a number of developing and socialist states felt equally strongly that their cultures, economies, or political ideologies might be undermined by foreign influence using the power of television. They therefore insisted that international broadcasts be subject to the approval of receiving countries.

The scientific basis of satellite broadcasting was well known, and experimental broadcasting satellites such as the U.S. Applications Technology Satellite ATS-6 (1974) and the Canadian Communications Technology Satellite CTS (1976) demonstrated that the technology was available. However, satellite television was expensive, and it was not clear how an operational satellite broadcasting system, for either national or international use, might be funded. Preliminary plans were being developed for national broadcasting satellites, but there did not seem to be any interest in international broadcasting to the concerned developing and socialist countries. The concern was therefore over the potential harm that might be done by the technology, not over any existing, planned, or proposed use of the technology.

In 1982, there were still no operational broadcasting satellites in use, and the Committee was deadlocked after many years of negotiation. The question was then taken out of the Committee, which has always taken decisions by consensus, and into the General Assembly. The General Assembly adopted, by majority vote over the opposition of a number of Western states, a set of Principles Governing the Use by States of Artificial Earth Satellites for International Direct Television Broadcasting.[10] The Principles required a broadcasting state to notify receiving states, to enter into consultations with them on request, and to broadcast subject to agreement with those states.

While these negotiations were under way in the Committee, the ITU considered the technical coordination of broadcasting satellites. A 1977 World Administrative Radio Conference (WARC) on Satellite Broadcasting established a plan which reserved geostationary orbital positions and television frequency channels for each country and specified that the transmissions should be directed at the territory of the country concerned.[11] The plan thus did not provide channels for international broadcasting, although, since the plan did allow for other uses of the positions and channels providing they did not interfere with satellites operating under the plan, international broadcasting was not strictly prohibited. The plan made allowance for "spillover" of signals beyond national borders, allowing for the fact it is not technologically possible to shape the transmitting beam precisely to irregular borders or to reduce the intensity of the signals sharply at the border.

The 1977 plan, however, remains virtually unused due to the uncertain commercial viability of satellite broadcasting, the rapid expansion of terrestrial cable television systems, and rapid developments in satellite and receiver technology. In particular, improvements in satellite receivers and reductions in their cost have made individual reception of signals from lower-power, higher-capacity, conventional communications satellites more economical than the use of high-power satellites that are formally designated as broadcasting satellites. Since conventional communication satellites have long operated globally without any requirement for prior approval from potential receiving countries, they can hardly be restricted now that they are also being used for broadcasting. The 1977 plan thus became technologically obsolete before it went into practical effect, and the 1982 Principles, even where they are accepted as legally applicable, are not technologically appplicable.

Although international satellite broadcasting has became possible in practice despite the attempts to limit or plan it, the fears of technological imperialism seem to have declined. Since international television broadcasting is developing on a commercial basis, financed either through advertising or through paid subscriptions, it has emerged primarily in the regionally integrated and wealthy market of Western Europe. Furthermore, some channels have "scrambled" their signals so that they could be received only by subscribers who have paid for decoders, thus precluding reception outside the intended market area.

Thus, the 1982 Principles, elaborated before the technology or its applications were fully developed, have been rendered largely irrelevant by changing technology, by economic considerations, and by lack of political consensus. The political tensions raised by the abandonment of the consensus procedures of the Committee on the Peaceful Uses of Outer Space ultimately served nobody's interests.

REMOTE SENSING: LEGAL RATIFICATION OF TECHNOLOGICAL PRACTICE

The use of satellites for observing natural resources began with hand held cameras on early crewed spaceflights. International concern developed in the late 1960s when the United States announced plans for the Landsat series of satellites that would systematically and repetitively gather resource information over the entire globe.

The discussions in the Committee on the Peaceful Uses of Outer Space started in 1970. As in the case of satellite broadcasting, two opposing views quickly emerged: some Western countries took the position that remote sensing data should be freely collected and distributed for the benefit of all countries, while some developing and socialist countries were concerned that technologically more advanced countries could acquire more information on a sensed country's economic resources than the country itself was capable of obtaining. Developing and socialist countries therefore called for the consent of a sensed country as a precondition for the dissemination of remote sensing data and information.

In contrast to the negotiations on satellite broadcasting, however, the negotiations on remote sensing persisted despite many years of deadlock between the two positions. Finally, in 1986, with a growing understanding of the technology and its practical applications, and in an improving international political climate, consensus was reached on a set of Principles Relating to Remote Sensing of the Earth from Space.[12] On the central issue of prior consent, the Principles did not restrict the collection and distribution of remote sensing data, but they provided that a sensed country should have a guaranteed right of access to the data.

The resolution of the disagreement was due in part to the experience gained by many countries in using data from the Landsat satellites between 1972 and 1986. This experience convinced many developing countries that they could use remote sensing data for their own benefit and also alleviated some of the fears that remote sensing could give foreign countries a dangerous degree of control over a country's natural resources. It became clear that economic resources can rarely be reliably and accurately identified using satellite data alone, and that effective use of satellite images generally required access to the ground to ensure accurate interpretation. A growing number of countries, including developing countries, were using the data, and some established ground stations for receiving remote sensing data directly from satellites, thus giving them first access to the data.

A technological consideration that could have posed a problem for the negotiations was the existence of military surveillance satellites using technology very similar to that of civilian remote sensing systems. Since the space powers were not prepared to make surveillance data available to the target countries, remote sensing needed to be distinguished from surveillance. This was done by defining remote sensing as being sensing "for the purpose of improving natural resources management, land use and protection of the environment." The distinction was thus based on the intentions of the satellite operators rather than on the technological characteristics of the satellites or data.

During the negotiations, there were attempts to distinguish remote sensing from military surveillance on the basis of technical criteria. Thus, it was proposed at one time that images which revealed ground features less than 50 meters in size should be subject to restrictions, while images which showed only larger features would be unrestricted. This technical criterion of "spatial resolution" was ultimately not adopted, in part because resolution is difficult to define quantitatively, as well as because of an unwillingness to limit the technological options, since details less than 50 meters in size can be important for civilian uses as well as military. The emphasis in the negotiations on the issue of dissemination to "third parties" rather than acquisition also served to exempt military surveillance data from the scope of the principles, since military data is generally closely held by the government agencies that collect it.

In the case of remote sensing, as in the case of satellite broadcasting, negotiations of legal principles began in an atmosphere of international distrust and of theoretical fears that the technology would be a powerful means of exploitation of the majority of countries by the technologically powerful minority. In the case of remote sensing, 14 years of experience with satellite data, based on wide access, demonstrated that the early fears of the technology were greatly exaggerated. The decline of those fears, together with a decline in the general level of international distrust, led to the agreement, which is generally accepted. In the case of satellite broadcasting, an attempt to restrict the technology was made before experience had revealed the exaggerated nature of the theoretical fears, and as a result there is no generally accepted agreement on the question.

NUCLEAR POWER: CONTROLLING TECHNOLOGICAL RISKS

Nuclear power sources offer an alternative to solar panels as a source of electrical power for satellites. Their main advantages over solar panels are their ability to produce high power from a compact source and their ability to operate in darkness or weak solar radiation.[13] There are two types of nuclear power sources: radio-isotope generators, used in cases when solar radiation is insufficient, for example on missions to the outer planets; and nuclear reactors, used to meet large power requirements that would require impractically large solar panels. Worldwide attention was drawn to the issue in January 1978 when a malfunction occurred on the nuclear reactor-powered Soviet naval reconnaissance satellite, Cosmos-954, and the satellite re-entered the atmosphere and disintegrated over northern Canada, leaving radioactive debris along the trajectory. In March 1978, Canada brought the matter to the attention of the Scientific and Technical Subcommittee.[14] The discussions of nuclear power sources continued in the following years, with increased attention after the malfunction and decay of two other reactor-powered Soviet satellites: Cosmos-1402 in 1982/1983 and Cosmos-1900 in 1988. In both cases, the satellites suffered malfunctions, re-entered the atmosphere, and disintegrated, but the debris appears to have either burned up in the atmosphere or fallen into the ocean without a trace.

After many years of very slow and difficult negotiations, there has been substantial progress toward agreement in recent years, and adoption of a complete set of principles by consensus is expected soon. Tentative agreement has been reached on draft texts of eight principles, with a few proposed principles still under negotiation.[15]

The concern over nuclear power sources centers on the risk of radioactive exposure, primarily of human beings and secondarily of other living things. The danger resulting from exposure to high levels of radioactivity is well established scientifically, and it is widely believed that low levels of exposure carry a long-term and cumulative risk of illness. The issue underlying the negotiations is the technological means for limiting the risk. It is generally accepted that the use of nuclear power sources in space inevitably gives rise to some risk of exposure and that the advantages of using nuclear power justify some degree of risk. The questions therefore concern how to define an acceptable risk and how to specify technological measures to limit the risk.

There are a variety of technological means available for preventing dangerous exposure, including surrounding the radioactive source with material that absorbs radiation, reinforcing the container so that the radioactive material is not released in case of accident, leaving the nuclear power source in space until the radioactivity has decayed to a safe level, and using back-up safety systems and redundant components to limit the risk of catastrophic malfunction. All of these technological possibilities have been carefully considered during the negotiations in the Committee, and the Scientific and Technical Subcommittee has been very involved in considering the scientific and technical factors relating to the legal principles. Many technical experts have been members of delegations to the two subcommittees; a large number of highly technical working papers have been submitted by various delegations, notably Canada, Germany and the United Kingdom; and technical presentations have been made by experts. The level of technical expertise brought to the United Nations on this topic has probably been greater than on any other space issue. Based on this technical input, a text for Draft Principle

3 on "Guidelines and criteria for safe use" was agreed upon in the Legal Subcommittee in 1990, using verbatim a text elaborated in the Scientific and Technical Subcommittee.

With regard to the use of nuclear reactors in space, for example, the Scientific and Technical Subcommittee's Working Group on Nuclear Power Sources concluded that uranium 235 and plutonium 239 were the most practical fuels for space reactors. Since medical science has shown that uranium 235 is relatively harmless and plutonium 239 is quite dangerous, the guidelines specify that "nuclear reactors shall use only enriched uranium 235 as fuel." In the case of a U^{235}-fueled reactor, the danger of radioactive contamination derives not from the raw fuel but from radioactive products created during the operation of the reactor. Considering that the greatest risk of accident is during launch, the guidelines provide that "nuclear reactors shall not be made critical before they have reached their operating orbit or interplanetary trajectory," thus ensuring that no reaction products will be present during launch.

When the U^{235}-fueled reactor begins operating in orbit, a variety of radioactive products with a range of half-lives are generated. When the reactor ceases operation, the short-lived products decay rapidly, leaving strontium 90 and cesium 137, with half-lives of 28 and 30 years respectively, as the main radioactive elements. Considering that 10 half-lives are sufficient to reduce the radioactivity by a factor of 1,000, early draft guidelines specified that reactors should be stored, after operation, in orbits with lifetimes of at least 300 years. For a reactor with a practical size and shape, this would require an orbital altitude of at least 800 km.

Further analysis presented by Germany, however, showed that a reactor in orbit for 300 years and gradually descending from 800 km would have a significant probability of colliding with space debris, which is most concentrated around 800 km. Such a collision, at a relative velocity of about 10 km/s, would probably break the reactor into small fragments, which would re-enter the atmosphere much more rapidly than the intact reactor due to their higher cross-section-to-mass ratio. As a result of this analysis, and considering that the process of fragmentation is not yet fully understood, the specification of a 300-year orbital lifetime was deleted and replaced with recognition of the risk of destruction by collision and of "the necessity for the parts of a destroyed reactor also to attain the required decay time before re-entering the Earth's atmosphere."

Other elements of the guidelines and other draft principles were similarly subject to detailed technical analysis. The negotiations of the draft principles on nuclear power sources have thus been an example of legal principles soundly based on detailed scientific and technical knowledge. Considering that the principles have not yet been adopted or applied, and that some people feel that the agreed guidelines already need technical revision, it might be a little premature to assume that this technical approach has been successful.

DEFINING OUTER SPACE: KNOWLEDGE IS NOT ENOUGH

As was the case with several other legal issues, discussions on the definition and delimitation of outer space started in the Scientific and Technical Subcommittee. However, at its session in 1967, the Subcommittee stated that it was not in a position to identify scientific and technical criteria permitting a precise and lasting definition of outer space.[16]

Since there has been a substantial body of air law for some time, and there is now a growing body of space law, with some incompatible provisions, there is the obvious question of defining the areas covered by the two regimes, most simply by designating a boundary between them. The technical basis for defining such a boundary would be the science and technology of aircraft flight on the one hand and orbital flight on the other, with aircraft requiring a substantial atmosphere for generating aerodynamic flight, while orbital flight depends on an absence of a substantial atmosphere, which causes friction, deceleration, heating, and ultimately the disintegration of the spacecraft.

The practical possibility of designating a boundary between airspace and outer space derives from the fact that the maximum altitude of stable aerodynamic flight is significantly below the minimum altitude of stable orbital flight. T. von Kármán, in 1957, showed that the theoretical upper limit of stable air flight was at an altitude of about 84 km, where aerodynamic lift becomes less than centrifugal force and the aircraft goes into uncontrolled ballistic flight.[17] At higher altitudes, atmospheric density is more variable and a theoretical minimum altitude for space flight is more difficult to specify. Observations of satellite orbits have shown at least two dozen instances of orbital perigees between 130 km and 110 km, and about a dozen, with a lifetime of slightly over one orbit—about 90 minutes—between 110 km and 100 km. As a spacecraft descends below these altitudes, it is decelerated to such an extent that it either disintegrates or reaches the ground before completing an orbit. These scientific and technical criteria suggest that a practical boundary between airspace and outer space could be designated at an altitude between 84 km and 100 km.

Within this range of altitudes, science and technology provide little guidance for a more precise determination; hence it would seem to be up to the legislators, if they are so inclined, to choose a boundary within that range. The discussions in the Committee on the Peaceful Uses of Outer Space have generally focused on the criterion of the lowest perigee of an orbiting satellite. As Eilene Galloway has noted: "Since the space age began, we have been proceeding on the basis that outer space begins where an object goes into orbit."[18] Given this scientific and technical knowledge, which has long been widely available, the unwillingness of the Scientific and Technical Subcommittee to take a position on the matter, and the inability of the Legal Subcommittee to reach agreement after many years of discussion, reflects a lack of political will rather than a lack of scientific and technical criteria.

THE GEOSTATIONARY ORBIT: CONFUSION OF SCIENCE AND TECHNOLOGY

The geostationary orbit is a circular equatorial orbit in which a spacecraft has an orbital period precisely equal to the period of rotation of the Earth, that is, 23 hours 56 minutes.[19] A satellite in the geostationary orbit appears to an observer on the ground to remain at the same place in the sky at all times. This is due to the synchronicity of the rotation of the Earth and the orbital revolution of the satellite, not to any special relation between the satellite and the point on the ground directly beneath it. Just as any other satellite, natural or artificial, a geostationary satellite is subject to the gravitational attraction of the Earth and moves with an orbital velocity that depends on its altitude. While geostationary satellites are sometimes contrasted to "orbiting satellites," this is not technically correct since all satellites orbit around the Earth.

The question of the legal status of the geostationary orbit was raised in the General Assembly in 1975 by the Colombian delegation, which claimed sovereignty over a 5.5° segment of the geostationary orbit above its territory.[20] The legal position of Colombia and other equatorial countries was elaborated in the 1976 Bogotá Declaration, which declared:

> Equatorial countries declare that the geostationary synchronous orbit is a physical fact linked to the reality of our planet because its existence depends exclusively on its relation to gravitational phenomena generated by the earth, and that is why it must not be considered part of outer space. Therefore, the segments of the geostationary synchronous orbit are part of the territory over which Equatorial states exercise their national sovereignty.[21]

It is, of course, true that the geostationary orbit depends on the gravitational force exerted by the Earth, but this is equally true of all satellite orbits. If it were accepted that objects linked to the "gravitational phenomena generated by the Earth" were not in outer space, then no Earth satellite, whether natural or artificial, would be in outer space. Outer space would be the area beyond all possible Earth satellite orbits, beyond the Moon, at a distance of approximately one million km from the Earth. This is clearly incompatible with the general understanding and practice of space activities and space law. Nonetheless, the principles of the Bogotá Declaration and the sovereignty claims of the equatorial countries have been repeated at many international meetings. These claims have frequently been rejected on the basis of the science of satellite orbits and have never received support from outside the group of equatorial countries.

Despite the fact that the scientific and technical factors relating to the geostationary orbit are totally different from the factors relating to the delimitation of airspace from outer space, the two questions have been combined into a single item on the agenda of the Legal Subcommittee and are dealt with in a single Working Group. This is apparently because both questions relate to spatial distinctions between different regimes of space law and because the two questions were linked by the equatorial countries. Since the Outer Space Treaty quite clearly states that outer space is not subject to national claims of sovereignty, the Bogotá Declaration argues that the geostationary orbit should not be considered part of outer space. Noting that the Outer Space Treaty contains no definition of outer space, and that the Legal Subcommittee has never been able to agree on a definition, the Bogotá Declaration states that the sovereignty provision of the Treaty "should not apply to the geostationary orbit."

The linkage between the question of the delimitation of outer space and that of the geostationary orbit, in the absence of any scientific or technical connection between the two issues, clearly does not facilitate resolution of these issues. In fact, hardly any progress on either question can be expected before they are separated and each considered on its own merits.

While there is no scientific basis for the claim that the geostationary orbit is not part of outer space, there is a technological basis for demands, by the equatorial countries and other developing countries, for a special legal regime for the geostationary orbit. From the technological perspective, it is true, as claimed in the Bogotá Declaration, that "the geostationary orbit represents a unique facility" and "is a scarce natural resource." It is only in the geostationary orbit that a single satellite can provide a continuous communication link between ground antennas with a fixed orientation. And for Earth stations to have reliable communications through a geostationary satellite, they must not receive signals from other satellites operating at the same frequencies, which implies that such satellites must be spaced a certain distance apart in the orbit—typically about 3° depending on the technical characteristics of the satellites and earth stations—or must have beams directed to widely separated service areas.

The provisions of the Outer Space Treaty that outer space "is not subject to national appropriation by claim of sovereignty, by means of use or occupation, or by any other means," and that outer space "shall be free for exploration and use by all States without discrimination of any kind" must therefore be reconciled with the technological requirement that a geostationary communication satellite must have exclusive use of a "slot," specified as a combination of orbital position, frequency, and service area. The task of reconciling the technological requirements of geostationary communication satellites with these legal principles has fallen to the ITU and its World Administrative Radio Conferences.

The ITU conferences have avoided dealing with the particular claims of the equatorial countries by declaring that questions of sovereignty claims are outside their area of competence. They have, however, taken up the claims of developing countries that the traditional technical coordination procedures, based on the principle of "first-come-first-served," constitute, in practice, discrimination against developing countries, who may find all desirable slots occupied when they are ready to launch communication satellites. In particular, they argued that slots should be reserved for their future use. The developed countries argued that this was incompatible with the free-use principle of the Outer Space Treaty and would result in inefficient use of the limited natural resource. Furthermore, since the specification of slots depends on the technical characteristics of satellites and Earth stations, the reservation of slots based on a particular technical design would restrict technological development, which is steadily increasing the capacity both of individual satellites and of the geostationary orbit as a whole.

The developing countries were able to obtain some recognition of their claim in the 1982 (Nairobi) edition of the ITU Convention, which provides in Article 33, paragraph 2, that "special needs of developing countries and the geographical situation of particular countries" are to be taken into account in providing equitable access to the geostationary orbit. The inclusion of the undefined criterion of geographical situation offered a non-committal allowance for the claims of the equatorial countries as well as for the special technical requirements of very large countries, mountainous countries, extreme northern or southern countries, and other situations affecting the use of geostationary satellites.

Thus, the debates in the ITU are taking into account the special technological characteristics of the geostationary orbit while respecting the scientific arguments that the geostationary orbit is part of outer space. The World Administrative Radio Conference on the Use of the Geostationary Satellite Orbit and the Planning of Space Services Utilising It, which met in 1985 and 1988, has begun the continuing process of reconciling the principle of free use by all states with the requirement for exclusive position and frequency assignments.

SPACE DEBRIS: CLOSING BOTH EYES

Like all environmental problems, the problem of space debris started inconspicuously but has steadily grown in importance. For each active satellite in Earth orbit, there are at least 20 non-functional objects or pieces of debris that are large enough to be tracked and catalogued, and over 100 objects too small to be detected. These objects, collectively called space debris, move at very high speeds and are dangerous, if not outright deadly, in close encounters or collisions with active spacecraft. Scientists and technical experts recognized this hazard to space activities a number of years ago and have proposed various measures to reduce the danger. The most promising and feasible are preventive measures aimed at restricting the amount of debris generated in the launch and operation of spacecraft and, in particular, avoiding explosions and breakups of space objects in orbit.

A number of papers and studies on space debris have been submitted to the Committee on the Peaceful Uses of Outer Space, but the vision necessary for action, so prominent at the time of the preparation of the Outer Space Treaty, has not yet emerged. The General Assembly has recognized space debris as an agenda item for the future,[22] but the Committee itself has not yet decided to make it a formal agenda item. The reasons for taking up the matter seem to be overwhelming, since the Committee is a global forum well suited for discussing global matters and with a tradition of successfully solving such problems. Further, it is necessary to focus the attention of the scientific and technical community on those aspects of the problem which might require further national studies. Another point is that the risk of collision with space debris is already being discussed in the Committee in the special case of satellites carrying nuclear power sources. The strongest reason for action, of course, is the *periculum in mora* due to the environmental nature of the problem, which will become increasingly difficult to solve in the future.

CONCLUSIONS

The examples of the use, and non-use, of scientific knowledge and technological experience in the elaboration of space law indicate the difficulties of drawing any general conclusions as to the best relationship between science, technology, and law. While it is clear that lawmaking which conflicts with space science and technology cannot be constructive, and that practical space law can hardly precede scientific and technical understanding, it can develop in parallel with space research and applications, or it can follow scientific and technical developments. There appear to be advantages and disadvantages to each of these approaches. In any case, collaboration between lawmakers and scientists and engineers, and the identification of the relevant scientific and technical considerations from an extensive and rapidly growing body of knowledge, are required.

It is also clear, however, that scientific knowledge and technological experience, even combined with legal expertise, do not necessarily produce sound space law. Political will is also essential to meaningful and constructive regulation. Cooperation between scientists, technical experts, and lawyers, while by no means easy, has proven quite possible. While these different groups have their own languages and cannot always easily communicate with each other, when ideas have crossed the borders between the communities and have been correctly understood, the results have generally been highly successful.

NOTES

1. The International Telecommunication Convention (Nairobi 1982) Geneva, ITU.
2. Radio Regulations, Edition 1982, revised 1985, Geneva, ITU.
3. The Final Acts of the World Administrative Radio Conferences are published by the ITU, Geneva. Most of the recent WARCs have dealt with some aspect of space telecommunications.

4. Treaty on Principles Governing the Activities of States in the Exploration and Use of Outer Space, including the Moon and Other Celestial Bodies. U.N.G.A. Res. 2222 (XXI) of Dec. 13, 1966.

5. U.N.G.A. Res. 1348 (XIII) of Dec. 13, 1958.

6. U.N.G.A. Res. 1472 (XIV) of Dec. 12, 1959.

7. A/AC.105/OR.1, Verbatim Record of the First Meeting, Nov. 27, 1961.

8. U.N.G.A. Res. 1962 (XVIII) of Dec. 13, 1963.

9. Agreement Governing the Activities of States on the Moon and Other Celestial Bodies, U.N.G.A. Res. 34/68 of Dec. 14, 1979.

10. U.N.G.A. Res. 37/92 of Dec. 10, 1982.

11. Final Acts of the World Administrative Radio Conference for the Planning of the Broadcasting-Satellite Service, Geneva, 1977.

12. U.N.G.A. Res. 41/65 of Dec. 3, 1986.

13. U.N. Doc. A/AC.105/358, 1986, p. 15.

14. U.N. Doc. A/AC.105/216 (1978).

15. The agreed and proposed texts are contained in the report of the Legal Subcommittee, U.N. Doc. A/AC.105/514.

16. U.N. Doc. A/AC.105/39 (1967).

17. A. Haley, *Space Law and Government*, New York, Appleton-Century-Crofts, 1963, p. 97.

18. E. Galloway, "Legal Aspects of International Cooperation in Space: Area and Functional Concepts in Defining Outer Space," in *Proceedings of the 26th Colloquium on the Law of Outer Space*, New York, AIAA, 1984, p. 197.

19. See, for example, L. Perek: "The Scientific and Technical Aspects of the Geostationary Orbit," *Acta Astronautica*, Vol. 17, 1988, p. 589.

20. U.N. Doc. A/C.1/PV.2052 (Oct. 14, 1975).

21. Declaration of the First Meeting of Equatorial Countries, Bogotá, Colombia, Dec. 3, 1976.

22. U.N.G.A. Res. 45/72, para. 23, of Dec. 11, 1990.

14

Law Relating to Settlement of Disputes on Space Activities

Aldo Armando Cocca

There is at present little in the way of uniform legal principles and procedures for the settlement of disputes relating to space activities. The generally accepted principles of international space law do not constitute an effective application of the principles of justice and equity. Demands, however, are growing for new procedures or adaptation of existing procedures to remedy this situation. Through the elaboration of generally accepted and uniform methods for peaceful settlement of international space disputes, the future coexistence of peoples under the protection of law shall be guaranteed.

The availability in modern international relations of instantaneous communication to and from any part of the planet promotes solidarity and facilitates cooperative and equitable relations. The existence of a natural universal sense of justice in individuals and societies, despite cultural differences, constitutes a consciousness that should be reflected in international relations, particularly in the settlement of disputes.

In connection with space activities, as Manfred Lachs has pointed out, dangerous experiments may even affect humankind as a whole—changing the Earth's environment, polluting the atmosphere, and producing incalculable effects on life. The space law treaties seek to avoid such catastrophic results by calling on nations to avoid environmental harm caused by their space activities and imposing absolute liability for certain kinds of damage. More broadly applicable principles of liability and more effective procedures for the peaceful settlement of disputes relating to space activities, if accepted by all nations, would greatly contribute to the development of effective space law.

International treaties that lack clear and effective procedures for the settlement of disputes offer a vulnerable point in international law. This weakness is so crucial that it can reduce the effectiveness of treaties to nothing. States that reject effective procedures for the settlement of disputes may be playing the role of Paris in the Trojan War.

Efforts made by authors, academic institutions, and the United Nations International Law Commission cannot prevent such vulnerability in international instruments, since constitutional provisions in many nations prevent international treaties from being made invulnerable. The question of providing for effective dispute settlement, consequently, is not easy and requires much work in the fields of both international and constitutional law.

INTERNATIONAL TREATIES

The United Nations Charter, signed in 1945, contains, in the Preamble and in several articles, provisions relating to the settlement of disputes. Article 1, paragraph 1, of the Charter states that one of the purposes of the organization is "to bring about by peaceful means, and in conformity with the principles of justice and international law, adjustment or settlement of international disputes or situations which might lead to a breach of the peace." Article 2, paragraph 3, provides that "all Members shall settle their international disputes by peaceful means in such a manner that international peace and security, and justice, are not endangered." Chapter VI, containing Articles 33 to 38, is specifically dedicated to the peaceful settlement of disputes. In those articles, states are instructed to settle disputes by "negotiation, enquiry, mediation, conciliation, arbitration, judicial settlement, resort to regional agencies or arrangements, or other peaceful means of their own choice." Chapter XIV of the Charter, Articles 92 to 96, is devoted to the International Court of Justice (ICJ) and its procedures for dispute settlement.

The Charter provisions have been reaffirmed in General Assembly resolutions such as Resolution 625 (XXV), which calls for dispute settlement through such means as inquiry, mediation, good offices, conciliation, arbitration, resorts to regional agencies or arrangements, and adjudication by permanent international courts.

The first major international legal agreement in the field of space law, the 1967 Outer Space Treaty, does not contain any specific provisions for the settlement of disputes.[1] Article 3, however, incorporates accepted principles of international law, including the United Nations Charter. Consequently, all the means foreseen by general international law and the Charter, including the provisions of Chapter VI, are applicable to outer space. The Outer Space Treaty includes a few provisions concerning consultations, as for example in Article 9[2], but these are included as a means of avoiding disputes rather than as a means for dispute settlement.

The greatest advance in providing procedures for the settlements of disputes relating to space activities was achieved in the 1972 Convention on International Liability for Damage Caused by Space Objects. Articles 12 to 20 of the Convention specify the means for settling a claim, including the basis for evaluating damage, the form of compensation, and the negotiation and arbitration of claims in case of disagreement. Article 12 prescribes that the launching state shall pay compensation for damage in accordance with international law and the principles of justice and equity. The basis for determining the proper compensation has been understood by many jurists to be the law of the state where the damage occurred, and this position has been supported in the United Nations by Argentina, Australia, Canada, Italy, Japan, the United Kingdom and Sweden[3]. Article 12 also provides that compensation should be sufficient to restore the situation "to the condition which would have existed if the damages had not occurred." This provision is the most complete definition of damage that has been offered in international law.

Article 14 provides for the establishment, if negotiations fail, of a Claims Commission, and Article 19 provides that "the decision of the Claims Commission shall be final and binding if the parties have so agreed." If the parties do not agree to a binding award, the Commission shall recommend an award, "which the parties shall consider in good faith."

In an attempt to strengthen the force of the arbitration decision, Argentina, in June 1971, proposed the following formulation for Article 19: "the Commission shall state the reason for its decision, which shall be final and binding; otherwise, if the parties have so agreed, the Commission shall render a final and recommendatory award."[4] The proposal added that "the parties shall comply in good faith with any decision or award of the Commission." Acknowledging that the Committee would not accept this proposal, Argentina, Austria, Brazil, and Mexico, in June 1971, submitted a proposal for revision of the Convention after 10 years, a proposal that was incorporated in Article 26. It was clear that many delegates were not satisfied with the non-binding dispute settlement and award provision of the Convention.[5]

The 1979 Agreement Governing the Activities of States on the Moon and Other Celestial Bodies contains a provision for consultation as a method to settle any controversy. The Moon Agreement also provides that if parties cannot find a mutual means to settle a dispute by consultation, they should resort to any other measure to ensure that they peacefully settle the dispute.

The 1982 United Nations General Assembly Resolution 37/92 on Principles Governing the Use by States of Artificial Earth Satellites for International Direct Television Broadcasting also contains a provision for dispute settlement. This resolution calls for the peaceful settlement of disputes through established procedures agreed upon by the parties to the dispute in accordance with the provisions of the Charter of the United Nations. Similarly, the 1986 General Assembly Resolution 41/65 on Principles Relating to Remote Sensing of the Earth from Space provides, in Principle 15, that "any dispute resulting from the application of these principles shall be resolved through the established procedures for the peaceful settlement of disputes."

For the International Telecommunication Union (ITU), the Convention adopted in Nairobi in 1982, in Article 50, contains a general provision for the settlement of disputes relating to the Convention through diplomatic channels, through agreed bilateral or multilateral procedures, "or by any other method mutually agreed upon." If the dispute cannot be settled by other means, Article 82 provides for arbitration through a number of different procedures, including arbitration by individuals or governments, and by a single arbitrator or a panel of three. The decision of the arbitrators is final and binding. Since this procedure can be blocked by the refusal of one party to select an arbitrator, an Optional Additional Protocol on the Compulsory Settlement of Disputes provides for the Secretary-General to select the second arbitrator if necessary. In the field of space activities, these provisions only apply to disputes concerning radio-frequency assignments to satellites and the use of positions in the geostationary orbit.

For the future, a set of Draft Rules for the Conciliation of Disputes between States is currently being developed in the United Nations. In 1990, the General Assembly decided to request the Secretary-General to circulate the Draft Rules for comment and to submit a report containing the replies at the 46th session, as part of the United Nations Decade of International Law. Article 48 of the Draft Rules provides that the terms of settlement proposed by a sole conciliator or by a commission, as the case may be, shall in no way be binding on the parties with regard to their substance. The conciliator or commission shall submit recommendations to the parties for consideration to facilitate an amicable settlement of the dispute.[6]

INTERNATIONAL SPACE ORGANIZATIONS

In the absence of any generally agreed procedures for effectively settling disputes, a variety of international organizations established to conduct space activities have established their own procedures for the settlement of disputes between their member countries relating to the activities of the organization. Unlike general international law, these organizational agreements often provide procedures leading to binding decisions.

The 1964 Interim Agreements of the International Telecommunications Satellite Organization (INTELSAT), in Article 2 of the Interim Agreement and Article 14 of the Special Agreement, have provisions on dispute settlement, and further provisions were made in the 1965 Supplementary Agreement on Arbitration. The Interim Agreement provides for the appointment of an impartial tribunal to decide questions in dispute in accordance with general principles of international law, and it declares that the decision of such a tribunal is binding on all signatories to the Special Agreement. The definitive 1971 Agreements include rules on procedures for the settlement of disputes in Article 18 of the main Agreement, in Article 20 of the Operating Agreement, and in Article 2 of Annex C, which provides for an arbitration tribunal. The decision of the tribunal is to be binding on all disputants and is to be carried out by them in good faith. The provisions of both the 1964 and 1971 Agreements also contain concrete rules of procedure for dispute settlement.

The 1976 Convention of the International Maritime Satellite Organization (INMARSAT) established in Article 3 that disputes should be settled by negotiation between the parties concerned, or be submitted to arbitration. Procedures for the Settlement of Disputes referred to in Article 3 of the Convention and Article 16 of the Operating Agreement are defined in the Annex in 12 articles. According to Article 10, the decision of the tribunal shall be binding on all the disputants and shall be carried out by them in good faith.

REGIONAL ORGANIZATIONS

In addition, there are agreements for regional cooperation that include provisions for dispute settlement, again often leading to binding decisions. The 1962 Convention for the Establishment of a European Space Vehicle Launcher Development (ELDO) determines that if a dispute is not settled by the ELDO Council, an Arbitration Tribunal shall be set up, and its decisions shall be binding on the parties to the dispute. The 1962 Convention for the Establishment of a European Space Research Organisation (ESRO) provides that a dispute not settled by the ESRO Council shall be submitted to the ICJ. The 1965 Convention establishing a European Organization for Astronomical Research for the Southern Hemisphere and its 1975 Protocol provide for disputes to be settled by its Council, or, if that is not possible, by the Permanent Court of Arbitration of The Hague, whose decision is binding. Similarly, the 1969 agreement concerning the European Space Operation Centre refers the settlement of disputes to an arbitration tribunal.

The European Space Agency (ESA) Convention of 1975 provides, in Article 17, that disputes be submitted to an arbitration tribunal whose decision is final and binding, not subject to appeal, and must be executed by the parties without delay.

The 1976 Agreement on the Arab Corporation for Space Communications (the ARABSAT system) provides in Article 19 that the General Assembly look into disputes that may arise between the Organization and one or more members or between the members themselves. Once a decision is reached on a dispute, it becomes effective within 90 days.

The 1985 European Telecommunications Satellite Organization (EUTELSAT) Convention provides in Article 20 for an arbitration procedure. The 1986 Convention of the European Organisation for the Exploitation of Meteorological Satellites (EUMETSAT) also provides for arbitration of disputes in its Article 14. And most recently, the Conference on Security and Cooperation in Europe adopted a "Procedure for Peaceful Settlement of Disputes" in February 1991.[7]

BILATERAL AGREEMENTS

Some bilateral arrangements for space cooperation also exemplify the trend to incorporating dispute settlement provisions in agreements. The U.S. National Aeronautics and Space Administration (NASA), since it began engaging in bilateral programs, has incorporated provisions for the settlement of disputes in its cooperation agreements.[8]

In one of its earliest agreements, the 1963 Agreement on Aerospace Disturbances Research Program between the United States and New Zealand, NASA agreed in Article 5 (b) to give due regard to the New Zealand Solicitor-General's recommendations for the settlement of claims determining liability and compensation. The 1964 agreement between the United States and Nigeria on a Station for Space Vehicle Tracking and Communication establishes, in Article 13, that the U.S. government would use its best efforts to adequately and effectively compensate Nigeria for personal injuries or property damage, taking into consideration relevant Nigerian law.

The 1967 Agreement between the United States and the United Kingdom for a Tracking Station on Antigua provided that any claims for damage to property or injury to persons arising from acts or omissions of U.S. personnel who are employed by or directly connected with NASA will be considered and settled in accordance with the provisions of Section 203 (b) of the U.S. National Aeronautics and Space Act,[9] and as it may be amended.

Other early NASA agreements that include provisions for settlement of disputes by arbitration are the 1969 memorandum of understanding (MOU) between the Universitá degli Studi di Roma (Aerospace Research Center) and NASA for Launching Satellites from the San Marco Range, which called for prompt settlement of claims following the model rules on arbitral procedure of the International Law Commission, and the 1970 agreement between the Federal Minister for Scientific Research of the Federal Republic of Germany and NASA, which provided for final settlement of disputes by arbitration following the 1958 model rules of the International Law Commission.

In the case of European agreements[10], the Interim Agreement between Australia, the United Kingdom, and ELDO provided that initial program member states would submit their disputes to an arbitration tribunal and that the tribunal's decision would be final and binding on the parties. The Agreement between ELDO and Belgium dealing with property and facilities stated in Article 8 that any dispute should be settled in accordance with the arbitration procedure prescribed in Article 22 of the ELDO Convention.

The 1972 Agreement between France and Federal Republic of Germany for the Construction, Launch and Utilization of an Experimental Telecommunications Satellite included a provision for a final and binding settlement of disputes by an arbitration tribunal. According to the Agreement, the President of the European Community Court of Justice would name the members of such a tribunal and the arbitration decision should be based upon Article 38, paragraph 1 of the ICJ Statute and Chapter III of the Hague Convention of 1907.

The 1972 Agreement Between the Federal Republic of Germany and India on Co-Operation Regarding Peaceful Uses of Atomic Energy and Space Research determined that disputes on interpretation or application of the Agreement shall be settled in consultation between the contracting parties.

The 1974 Agreement between Canada and the United States concerning Liability for Loss or Damage from Certain Rocket Launches stipulated: "In the event that a claim arising out of these launches is not settled expeditiously in a mutually acceptable manner, the two governments shall give consideration to the establishment of a Claims Commission such as that provided for in Article 15 of the Liability Convention with a view to arriving at a prompt and equitable settlement." The 1975 MOU between NASA and the National Research Council of Canada (NRCC) for a Cooperative Program Concerning the Development and Procurement of a Space Shuttle Remote Manipulator System provided in Article 16 that "Any disputes in the interpretation or implementation of the terms of this cooperative program shall be referred to the NASA Administrator and the President of NRCC for settlement, and should the NASA Administrator and the President of NRCC be unable to resolve such disputes, they may be submitted to such other forms of resolution or arbitration as may be agreed."

ESA and its predecessor, ESRO, entered into a variety of bilateral agreements with its member states and other states concerning facilities for the regional programs, including the European Space Technology Centre (ESTEC) in the Netherlands, the European Sounding Rocket Launching Range (ESRANGE) in Sweden, the Kongsjø Telemetry Station and the Andøya sounding rocket facilities in Norway, rocket launching facilities on French territory, and the Woomera launching facilities in Australia. Generally, these agreements provide that if a dispute could not be settled amicably, the President of the ICJ would appoint a single arbitrator to decide the method of award, which would be final and binding. An MOU between ESA and NASA prescribed that in the event of damage, the parties will be liable in accordance with the 1972 Liability Convention. NASA and ESA agreed to consult promptly on equitable sharing of any payments; if consultations fail, an early arbitration following the 1958 model rules on arbitral procedure of the International Law Commission will be applied. The MOU on the Space Telescope Project, however, referred to settlement by U.S. authorities or to another form of resolution arbitration as they may agree.

The United States and the Republic of Seychelles signed a 1976 Agreement on the Tracking Station on Mahe Island, which provided, in Article 12, that any claim presented to the U.S. government should be processed and settled in accordance with the applicable provisions of U.S. law.

Jurisprudence

Though imperfect and inadequate in many respects, international law is observed more often than violated. It plays an essential part in the world's affairs, but all too frequently we do not notice it. The International Court of Justice can make a substantial contribution to the development of the *corpus juris gentium*, and there is no reason for the Court not to continue to develop and improve the law and its role in international life. Judges in applying law interpret it, and by interpreting it they apply it. Each judgement is either a step forward or a step backward in the development of law.[11]

International tribunals, however, are often quite limited in their competence. In the ICJ, for example, only states may be parties to cases, while the General Assembly, the Security Council, and other organs of the United Nations and its specialized agencies can request advisory opinions. The opinions of the Court are compulsory only when they are accepted as being so by the parties.

Regional tribunals, like the European Community Court of Justice, also have an important role to play, particularly since they generally have broader competence than international tribunals. The European Community Court of Justice is open not only to member states and Community institutions but also to individuals and legal entities. The jurisdiction of the Court is compulsory in cases of attributed competence, and its decisions are binding except in settlements against states, according to the traditional rule of international law on the impunity of states. The European Economic Community Treaty establishes procedural norms that imply the superiority of community law based on its original specific nature. This was established in the 1964 case *Costa v. ENEL.*[12]

Since arbitration is the preferred method for the settlement of space disputes, it is useful to consider the Permanent Court of Arbitration and its current role. The Permanent Court of Arbitration, established in 1899, has jurisdiction that is not limited to disputes between states. It performs a variety of functions and plays an important role in the Arbitration Court of the International Chamber of Commerce. The Secretary-General of the Permanent Court also has functions in connection with the International Centre of Settlement of Investment Disputes, established by the World Bank and with the United Nations Commission on International Trade Law (UNCITRAL) Rules.[13] The almost century-long experience of the Permanent Court of Arbitration should be considered in preparing future procedures for the settlement of disputes.[14]

Considering that space law is a new legal field, sometimes called the last legal frontier, it already consists of a complex variety of national and international laws, rules, statutes, regulations, and treaties which need to be considered in relation to space activities and disputes.

In view of these circumstances, there are a number of cases of national jurisprudence, particularly in the United States, arising out of increasing commercial space activities and out of increasing environmental concern. Among these cases is the *Florida Coalition for Peace and Justice v. George Herbert Walker Bush of 1989.*[15] In this case, the Florida Coalition and the Christic Institute lead the challenge against alleged potential environmental and health threats presented by 48 pounds of plutonium carried aboard the Jupiter-bound Galileo probe launched in 1989. Although the Coalition failed to prevent the launching of Galileo, it brought similar charges with respect to the Ulysses probe in its Amended Complaint, filed January 29, 1990.[16]

The case is important for environmental litigants because it serves as a reminder that rights and remedies available to them in the space area are limited, and that courts are unlikely to constitute the forum that will deal adequately with their concerns. The case also indicates that those involved in launching and other space activities should be prepared to address environmental concerns and ensure careful compliance with laws and regulations so that potential litigants will find nothing with which to take issue.[17] This case demonstrates that national courts are competent to deal with many disputes relating to space activities. In addition, the case demonstrates that any future international, regional, or national space courts will need specialized scientific knowledge.

ELABORATION OF NEW DISPUTE SETTLEMENT PROCEDURES

International Institute of Space Law (IISL)

Since the first Colloquium of the International Institute of Space Law (IISL) held at The Hague in 1958, legal scholars have analyzed, discussed, and proposed measures to deal with damage and liability for space activities. The legal issues discussed ranged from creating a special international fund to pay for damages caused by space objects[18] to establishment of a special court to settle disputes arising from space activities. It has been suggested that an agreement providing for compulsory jurisdiction of space disputes, possibly by the ICJ, would be desirable.[19] However, it has also been argued that the idea of compulsory jurisdiction by the ICJ faces political difficulties, particularly since the United States has never accepted compulsory jurisdiction of the ICJ, and that establishing a new international arbitration court might be a better approach.[20] One scholar remarked that if "law and sentiments of justice demanded that decisions should be binding, the harsh facts of politics made it impossible."[21]

Since the adoption of the Liability Convention in 1972, the space law community has focused on its weakness in ensuring the settlement of disputes and in making binding awards. For example, it has been noted that the settlement technique specified in the Liability Convention is only that of conciliation.[22] It was also suggested that it would be advisable to avoid a plurality of tribunals by submitting disputes to the ICJ through a new chamber without prejudice to the existence of regional tribunals.[23]

In 1980, a new court of arbitration for space law disputes was proposed, open to claims from individuals and private enterprises, which cannot make claims under the Liability Convention. It was also suggested that if the Convention is revised, the narrow concept of liability should be changed into the wider concept of responsibility.[24] While the political compromise involved in allowing awards under the Liability Convention to be merely recommendatory was acknowledged, the discussions have reaffirmed that the major defect of the Convention was the failure to ensure that the decision of a Claims Commission would automatically bind litigants.[25]

International Law Association (ILA)

The International Law Association (ILA) has also considered the subject of the settlement of disputes arising from space activities. In 1980, the ILA Space Law Committee was entrusted with the preparation of a Draft Convention on the Settlement of Space Law Disputes, which was discussed at the 1984 ILA Conference. The Draft Convention on Space Law Disputes included a preamble and sections devoted to applicability of the convention, non-binding settlement procedures, binding settlement procedures, conciliation procedures, and arbitration procedures. The Draft Convention provided for an international tribunal for space law, with the specification that "in the tribunal as a whole the representation of the principal legal systems of the world and equitable geographical distribution shall be assured."[26]

In the 1990 ILA Conference, the Space Law Committee continued to consider such questions as environmental protection, extension of compulsory jurisdiction, a new international court for space law, a new convention on the settlement of space disputes and a new set of protocols on dispute settlement, as well as the political requirements for traditional non-binding procedures.[27]

Other forums

The question of the settlement of space law disputes was discussed at the Tenth National Meeting on Air and Space Law in Argentina, where it was agreed that neither a conventional nor a general space law court with adequate procedures for the settlement of disputes existed. It was suggested that the Liability Convention could be revised, in accordance with its provision for revision, with particular consideration made for (1) the need for a legal body with competent jurisdiction instead of the present Claims Commission, which considers only compensation; (2) the ensured execution of a sentence, an award or a decision as a fundamental principle of international legal security; and (3) determination in advance of the law applicable to the settlement of disputes. It was also argued that the decision of a tribunal should take into account the social, cultural, economic, and other conditions of the injured party.[28]

In 1979, a Round Table on the Settlement of Disputes on Space Law was held in Córdoba, Argentina, organized by the Council of Advanced International Studies. Five conclusions were reached: (1) every future international agreement, whether bilateral or multilateral, should contain a clause providing for the settlement of disputes; (2) a convention governing specific matters in the field of space law should establish compulsory jurisdiction; (3) all judgements and awards shall be final and binding; (4) a means should be established to ensure the recognition and execution of judgements and awards; and (5) the scope of these conclusions should be, in the first stage, limited to subjects of public international law.

The 1979 International Colloquium on Settlement of Space Disputes—The Present State of the Law and Perspective of Further Development, held in Cologne, Germany, was considered the widest and deepest research and analysis ever achieved on the subject. At this colloquium, critical analysis focused on the uncertainty in the meaning of the Liability Convention's provision that compensation should be determined "in accordance with international law and principles of justice and equity," on the fact that individuals had no standing to make claims, and that the dispute settlement provisions were not binding.[29] An analysis of the INTELSAT and INMARSAT dispute settlement procedures led to the conclusion that the most productive approach to solving these problems might be to focus on particular areas of space law where compulsory procedures are more likely to gain support. For some disputes at least, third party arbitration is already compulsory, and this situation can presumably be extended to other areas and other parties.

It was argued that there is no one settlement method applicable to all disputes, and that in a given case a choice of method must be selected according to the nature of the disputes and the parties involved. While the consensus decision-making process of the Committee on the Peaceful Uses of Outer Space, or the voting process in other political bodies, have their usefulness, they are often not applicable to legal decision-making in cases involving sharp conflicts of interest.

On a more philosophical level, it was argued that improvements in international procedures require integration and enhancement of two human values and two material values: the human values of the jurist and the legal interpreter, and the material values of professional specialists and juridical institutions.

Space Convention on Settlement of Space Disputes and Space Court

The proposal for a Convention for the Settlement of Space Law Disputes has attained an increasing consensus, and the ILA has adopted a draft Convention resolving many practical issues. In addition, a special space court was proposed in 1962, with work to start on the elaboration of a draft constitution for such a body by a commission of space jurists.

Disputes are becoming increasingly diverse and complex and may become unsolvable if different international bodies vested with jurisdiction reach different conclusions in cases of concurrent jurisdiction. The problems of different international jurisdictions, combined with increasing domestic jurisprudence in space cases, suggest a need for specialized space courts on the international, regional, and national level.

CONCLUSION

The 1972 Liability Convention is the international space law treaty with the most detailed provisions for the settlement of disputes, but it fails to ensure binding decisions. Since its adoption, there has emerged a broad movement in favor of compulsory jurisdiction and the enforcement of awards. In particular, there is a widespread recognition of the need for an International Convention on the Settlement of Space Disputes. The Draft Rules for the Conciliation of Disputes between States, which were circulated to member states of the United Nations in 1990, and the dispute settlement measures recently adopted by the Conference on Security and Cooperation in Europe provide useful experience which can be used in elaborating measures for dealing with space law disputes.

The increasing space activities of nations, international organizations, and private entities will certainly lead to new and increasing disputes, and new means will be needed to deal effectively with these disputes. In view of the weaknesses in the Liability Convention, and the very general provisions in the subsequent agreements and resolutions adopted by the Committee on the Peaceful Uses of Outer Space, it would not seem worthwhile putting this question on the agenda of the Committee at this time. A precondition to a solution of the problem may be a change in the policies of major space powers such as the United States and Russia. When those powers can agree on measures for compulsory jurisdiction and binding awards, then the Committee might usefully take up the issue.

NOTES

1. Manfred Lachs, *The Law of Outer Space—An Experience in Contemporary Law-Making*, Leiden, Sijthoff, 1972, p. 121.
2. Aldo Armando Cocca, (Statement) *Solución de Controversias en Derecho Espacial (Settlement of Space Law Disputes)*, Córdoba, Argentina, The Council of Advanced International Studies, 1981, p. 73.
3. U.N. Doc. A/AC.105/C.2/L.74.
4. U.N. Doc. A/AC.105/CD/L.79; 30 *International Legal Materials* 1, Washington, January 1991, p. 243.
5. U.N. Doc. A/AC.105/94 (1971).
6. 30 *International Legal Materials* 1, Washington, January 1991, p. 243.
7. 30 *International Legal Materials* 2, Washington, March 1991, pp. 385-386.

8. References to the U.S. Agreements have been taken from Stephen Gorove (ed.), *United States Space Law—National and International Regulations*, 3 vols., Dobbs Ferry, NY, Oceana, 1982, and from N. Jasentuliyana and Roy S. K. Lee, (eds.), *Manual of Space Law*, vol. 2, New York, Oceana and Alphen, Sijthoff, 1979-1981.

9. 42 U.S.C. Sect. 2473.

10. References to European Conventions and Bilateral Agreements have been taken from Karl-Heinz Böckstiegel (ed.), *Settlement of Space Law Disputes: The Present State of the Law and Perspectives of Further Development*, Cologne, Carl Heymanns Verlag, 1980, and from K.-H. Böckstiegel and M. Benkö (eds.), *Space Law - Basic Legal Documents*, 2 vols., Dordrecht, M. Nijhoff, 1990.

11. Manfred Lachs, "Some Thoughts on the Work of the International Court of Justice," in *Desarrollo Progresivo del Derecho Internacional*, Chap. 17, Buenos Aires, Council of Advanced International Studies, 1991.

12. Servaas Thiel and Maria Rajas Pujol, "La inserción de las Comunidades Europeas en la sociedad internacional vista a traves de la jurisprudencia del Tribunal de Justicia," in *Desarrollo Progresivo del Derecho Internacional, supra* note 11, Chap. 18.

13. J. Varekamp, "Development in the Permanent Court of Arbitration," in *Desarrollo Progresivo del Derecho Internacional, supra* note 11, Chap. 19.

14. Eilene Galloway, "The History and Development of Space Law: International Law and the United States Law," *Annals of Air and Space Law* (Montreal), Vol. 7, 1982, p. 195.

15. No. 89-2682 (D.D.C. filed Sept. 28, 1989).

16. Rachel B. Trinder, "Recent Developments in Litigation," *Journal of Law and Technology*, Vol. 5, No. 1, 1991, pp. 47-49.

17. *Id.*, p. 49.

18. I. H. Ph. Rode-Verschoor, "The Responsibility of States for the Damage Caused by Launched Space-Bodies," in *First Colloquium on the Law of Outer Space* (The Hague 1958), Vienna, Springer Verlag, 1958, pp. 103-104.

19. Spencer M. Beresford, "Requirements for an International Convention on Spacecraft Liability," *Sixth Colloquium on the Law of Outer Space*, (Paris 1963), Vienna, Springer Verlag, 1964, p. 21; Harold Caplan, "Questions of Enforcement of Judgements: How to Persuade People to Follow the Rules for the Exploration of Space," *id.*, p. 60; D. Goedhuis, "Some Observations of the Present Legislative Procedure Applied to Outer Space," *id.*, p. 367; Andrew G. Haley, "Medical Jurisprudence in Outer Space," *id.*, p. 457.

20. Carl Q. Christol, "Permissive Processes to Ensure the Reasonable Uses of Outer Space," *Eighth Colloquium on the Law of Outer Space*, (Athens 1965), Vienna, Springer Verlag, p. 27.

21. Sylvia Maureen Williams, "Remarks on Some Aspects on Space Liability," *Fourteenth Colloquium on the Law of Outer Space*, (Brussels 1971), Fred Rothman, 1972, pp. 274-275. The statement of the Argentine Representative cited is U.N.G.A. A/AC.105/C.2/SR.166, June 30, 1977.

22. Karl-Heinz Böckstiegel, "Settlement of Disputes Regarding Activities in Outer Space," *22d Colloquium on the Law of Outer Space*, (Prague 1977), Fred Rothman, 1979, p. 178.

23. Karl-Heinz Böckstiegel, "Progress Report on Research Regarding the Settlement of the Space Law Disputes," *22d Colloquium on the Law of Outer Space*,

(Munich 1979), New York, AIAA, 1980, p. 99; Aldo Armando Cocca, "Settlement of Disputes in International Space Law," *id.*, p. 109.

24. Karl-Heinz Böckstiegel, "Settlement of Disputes on International Regimes Applicable to Space Activities," *23rd Colloquium on the Law of Outer Space*, (Tokyo 1980), New York, AIAA, 1981, p. 127; Aldo Armando Cocca, "From Full Compensation to Total Responsibility," *27th Colloquium on the Law of Outer Space*, (Budapest 1983), New York, AIAA, 1984, p. 157.

25. Carl Q. Christol, *The Modern International Law of Outer Space*, New York, Pergamon Press, 1982, p. 85.

26. See the complete text of the Draft Convention in International Law Association, *Report of the 61st Conference* (Paris 1984), London, The Cambrian News, 1985, p. 325.

27. ILA Booklet, Space Law Committee, Section B: *Suggestions for the Future* (64th Conference, London, 1990), Australia, Hogbin Poole, 1990, pp. 18-27.

28. Aldo Armando Cocca, "To What Extent Are Future Procedures for the Settlement of Space Law Disputes Considered Necessary?" in Böckstiegel (ed.), *Settlement of Space Law Disputes*, *supra* note 10, pp. 139-140.

29. Steven Gorove, "Dispute Settlement in the Liability Convention," in Böckstiegel (ed.), *Settlement of Space Law Disputes*, *supra* note 10, p. 10.

15

Case Law on Space Activities

Karl-Heinz Böckstiegel

Compared to most other fields of the law, space law is very young. It was only with the first launch into space in 1957 that space law with any practical utility developed, although academic considerations had started somewhat earlier. Even then, for many years the extent of space activities and the number of participating states were limited, and the early space activities were largely restricted to research. Only recently, with the increase in the volume and variety of space activities, the involvement of a growing number of states, the development of economic applications of space technology, and the organization of commercial operations, have actual disputes regarding space activities arisen. It is therefore not surprising that so far little case law relating to space activities exists. It seems likely that space law cases will increase substantially in the near future.

With this situation in mind, this chapter will examine the few space law cases that have arisen at either the national or international level. "Case law" is here understood to include not only actual litigation leading to court decisions but also disputes that were settled without litigation, either by agreement between the parties, as in the Cosmos-954 incident, or by unilateral decision due to international pressure, as in the cases of the U.S. Project West Ford and the German Orbital Transport und Raketen Aktiengesellschaft (OTRAG). This chapter will also consider cases that are not specifically based on space law but that concern the application to space activities of other areas of national and international law, including such questions as the extent of liability and scope of risk arising from space activities.

Most of the space-related cases that have been litigated do not involve disagreements over the interpretation of space law treaties, but rather the interpretation or enforcement of contract terms, government environmental regulations, or intellectual property rights. Other cases that are related to the applications of space technology concern the effect of space applications on non-space activities, such as in promoting international trade or in assuring human rights. This chapter, therefore, reveals the wide reaching and growing impact of space activities and their influence in establishing case law precedent.

DISPUTES SETTLED WITHOUT LITIGATION

Cosmos 954

One of the most significant space-related incidents that could have resulted in litigation was the re-entry of a Soviet nuclear-powered satellite over Canadian territory. Although the Canadian and Soviet governments held different views relating to responsibility and compensation, they resolved the issues through diplomatic channels in accordance with the 1972 Convention on International Liability for Damage Caused by Space Objects.[1]

On January 28, 1978, a Soviet military radar surveillance satellite, Cosmos-954, carrying a nuclear reactor fueled with enriched uranium, re-entered the Earth's atmosphere, partially disintegrated and vaporized as it traveled through Canadian airspace, and left a trail of radioactive debris across a remote area of the Northwest Territories in northern Canada. Following the accident, the Canadian government, with U.S. assistance, spent about 10 months conducting clean-up operations at a cost of about $6 million. The Soviet Union expressed its readiness to send a group of specialists to Canada to render assistance, but this offer was not accepted. In response to questions from Canada, the Soviet Union provided information on the satellite and the nuclear reactor.

A little less than one year after the accident, on January 23, 1979, the government of Canada presented a formal claim for compensation to the Soviet Union. The Canadian government based its claim on general international law and on space law treaties, in particular the Liability Convention. Canada claimed that the Soviet Union had an absolute liability to pay compensation, based on Article 2 of the Liability Convention. In presenting its claim, Canada acted in accordance with the Liability Convention, specifically Article 9, which instructs states to present claims for compensation through diplomatic channels; Article 10, which allows for the presentation of the compensation claim for damages within one year of the date of the occurrence of damage; and Article 12, which stipulates that launching states are liable to pay for damage caused by their space object. The Canadian government also claimed that the Soviet Union was in violation of international legal principles regarding sovereignty due to its intrusion in Canadian airspace and its pollution of Canadian territory with hazardous radioactive debris.

Lengthy negotiations between the Canadian and Soviet governments resulted in a protocol of April 2, 1981, by which the Soviet Union agreed to pay $3 million (Canadian) "in full and final settlement of all matters connected with the disintegration of the Soviet satellite Cosmos 954 in January 1978."

Project West Ford

Two cases, the U.S. Project West Ford and the German OTRAG enterprise, provide examples of disputes resolved through the application of international pressure rather than through litigation. In protest against these projects, other states appealed to norms of international law and specifically to the principles of space law.

In the early 1960s, the United States developed Project West Ford, an experiment that involved the ejection into space of 350 million hair-like copper wires 21 mm long. These wires were to disperse into a belt about the Earth 8 km wide and 40 km deep at an altitude of 3,220 km, which would reflect military radio communications. A first satellite launched in October 1961 failed to release the wires; and a second satellite in May 1963 resulted in partial dispersal that apparently allowed some communication relay. Most of the wires, however, remained clumped together, thus not only providing poor reflection but also greatly prolonging their orbital lifetime. While the dispersed wires re-entered the atmosphere and burned up within a few years as planned, most of the clumps are still in orbit.

In May 1963, the Soviet Union submitted a note to the United Nations Committee on the Peaceful Uses of Outer Space entitled "Dangerous United States Activities in Outer Space," protesting the experiment on the grounds that it would interfere with communications to spacecraft and with radio astronomy.[2] In June 1963, the United States responded with a note claiming that the experiment was carefully planned to avoid interference with other space activities, that it was conducted in consultation with the world scientific community, and that the results of the experiments would be made available internationally.[3] However, the United States recognized the concerns among some scientists over potentially harmful side effects of such experiments, and the experiment was never repeated.

OTRAG

In 1974, a private West German company, Orbital Transport und Raketen Aktiengesellschaft (OTRAG), began trying to develop low-cost modular rockets and to establish launch facility and test range in Zaire and later in Libya. In May 1977 a test launch was conducted in Zaire, and other tests were later conducted in Libya.

When the company began its activities, opposition was expressed by a number of Eastern European and African governments, who submitted official notes to the West German government claiming that the OTRAG rocket could be used for military space activities and noting that Germany would be liable for any damage caused by such activities. Officials of NASA and ESA, aware of a possible competitive threat to their launch services, expressed scepticism as to the financial viability of such a program. While the German government argued that the OTRAG rockets were only suited to peaceful space activities, a dispute arose between government authorities and OTRAG over the company's right to export rocket components from Germany to the foreign launch sites.

While the right of a private enterprise such as OTRAG to undertake space activities is clearly established by Articles 6 and 9 of the Outer Space Treaty,[4] questions arose concerning the responsibility of the German government for assuring that the activities of the German-registered OTRAG were carried out in conformity with the Treaty, as provided in Article 6, given that rocket production and launch activities took place outside Germany. It was also unclear whether Germany should be considered a "launching state" with liability under the provisions of the Liability Convention.

Since no official documents relating to either the international protests or the disputes within Germany have ever been made public, it is difficult to know what happened in the case. However, whether due to claims that OTRAG's activities violated the Outer Space Treaty or other international law, or to technical or financial difficulties, OTRAG eventually reduced its work to very small rockets and made no further use of launching sites in Zaire and Libya.[5]

NATIONAL COURT DECISIONS RELATING TO SPACE TECHNOLOGY

United States

Since the United States has a wide range of space activities involving a variety of public agencies and private enterprises, most legal cases relating to space activities have arisen in its national courts. U.S. space activities have given rise to a variety of law suits brought by private citizens, public interest groups, manufacturers, and even intergovernmental organizations. While these cases involved space activities, the claims were not based on space law but on claims of breach of contract, tort damages, or violation of federal regulations. Nonetheless, these cases are establishing case law precedents with important implications for space activities.

The case of *Martin Marietta v. International Telecommunications Satellite Organization* (INTELSAT) arose following the failure during launch of a Martin Marietta Titan III rocket resulting in the loss of an INTELSAT communications satellite.[6] In anticipation of a lawsuit, the Martin Marietta Corporation sought a declaratory judgement absolving it from liability to INTELSAT. INTELSAT then counter-claimed, asserting breach of contract and alleging negligence, gross negligence, and negligent misrepresentation. INTELSAT sought damages for the lost value of the launch services, as well as for lost use of the satellite, damage to the satellite and accompanying hardware, and the cost of rescuing the satellite. The launch services cost approximately $112 million, and the cost of rescuing the satellite has been estimated at $90 million.

Martin Marietta moved to dismiss the counter-claim. In April 1991, the U.S. District Court of Maryland granted Martin Marietta its motion to dismiss on the four counts of gross negligence, negligence, and negligent misrepresentation, but denied the motion as to breach of contract and requested that the parties submit supplemental briefs.

The controversy focused on interpretation of the exculpatory and cross-waiver provisions in the contract. INTELSAT also claimed that Martin Marietta materially breached its contractual agreement by failing to provide an effective separation mechanism to jettison the satellite from the Titan rocket and that it "abandoned the contract" by performing below a minimum level for which the parties had contracted. INTELSAT further argued that if Martin Marietta was exempt from liability, then it would have had no mutual duty to perform, and that consequently the contract would be rendered illusory. Martin Marietta contended that its level of performance was within the terms of the contract and therefore it was entitled to the protection of the contract's limitation on liability. The Court deferred ruling on whether the contract was illusory, finding that a judgement concerning the level of performance required further submissions on the matter.

Martin Marietta pleaded that the exculpatory provisions in the contract barred all claims. The contract provided two alternative remedies, either of which could serve as the "sole and exclusive remedy" in the event of the launch failure. One remedy provided INTELSAT a case refund or guaranteed reflight if INTELSAT purchased a refund/reflight option prior to the launch; the other remedy provided INTELSAT the right to request Martin Marietta to use its "best efforts" to secure a replacement launch for which INTELSAT would pay. Martin Marietta interpreted this provision to mean that if INTELSAT did not choose one of these remedies, it had no contractual remedy. INTELSAT, however, interpreted this provision as providing it with optional remedies that, if exercised, would become the sole and exclusive remedy in the event of a mission failure. The Court found that without further supplemental facts on the illusory issue, it could not consider the contract's remedy provisions.

Martin Marietta also contended that the contract barred recovery for lost profits, lost use of the satellite, and the cost of rescue of the satellite, and that under the cross-waiver of liability provisions each party agreed to bear its own risk of loss. INTELSAT contended that this provision did not apply to the value of lost services.

The Court based its decision in the case on public policy and case precedent. In an effort to regulate commercial space activities, the U.S. Congress had created a regulatory scheme for commercial launches codified in the 1984 Commercial Space Launch Act, which was amended in 1988.[7] This Act provided a comprehensive regulatory scheme to allocate tort liability among all commercial space launch participants. It required that each launch service provider enter into reciprocal waivers of liaiblity with the launch participants from any property damage, loss sustained, personal injury, property damage, or loss sustained by its own employees.[8] Martin Marietta claimed that the Commercial Space Launch Act, as amended, operated to impute cross-waiver liability, even if the contract did not so provide. After a review of the congressional intent for implementing the Act, the language of the statute, and the launch license itself, the Court rejected Martin Marietta's claim, finding that nowhere does the statutory language suggest that cross-waivers be imputed into contracts.

Therefore, in determining the validity of INTELSAT's tort claims, the Court analyzed the specific contract provisions and case law. The court relied on case precedent to determine whether there was a distinct duty in tort existing separately and apart from any contractual duty. The Court held that Martin Marietta did not owe a duty other than the duties defined in the contract and that the contract provided, inter alia, an opportunity to insure against damage and economic loss. Therefore, the Court found that because the only relationship between the parties was contractual, contract damages, if any are found, would compensate INTELSAT.

The outcome of this case will establish an important case precedent for space activities. It will clarify interpretations of contract provisions relating to allocation of risk, including the applicability of the term "best efforts." It should, therefore, provide a basis for more precise contract formulation and consequently reduce uncertainties in responsibility for the implementation of space activities. By denying the tort claims, the Court provided further precedent for support of the Commercial Space Launch Act and for congressional intent to limiting potentially costly tort penalties that could escalate the costs for launch services to a point where they would no longer be commercially feasible.

Another case involving a contractual dispute relating to a launch service agreement is the *Appalachian Insurance Co. v. McDonnell Douglas Corp.* case.[9] In this case, Western Union Telegraph Company contracted with NASA to deploy a communications satellite. Upon the launch of the satellite in 1984, the launcher's Payload Assist Module (PAM), supplied by McDonnell Douglas, failed to place the satellite in geostationary orbit. Appalachian Insurance Company and four other insurers paid Western Union's claim for the insured loss, then sued McDonnell Douglas and its subcontractors, Hitco and Morton Thiokol, to recover their payments.

The insurers challenged the contract's broad exclusionary language and the implementation of the waiver provisions to the subcontractors. The contract between McDonnell Douglas and Western Union contained inter-party waiver of liability provisions patterned after the contract between NASA and Western Union. Specifically, the contract provided that McDonnell Douglas extended no warranties of any kind, express or implicit, and that it was not liable to

Western Union in any connection with the agreement under any tort negligence, strict liability, contract, or equitable theory for incidental or consequential damages. Also, the contract provided that Western Union expressly waived and released any cause of action or right of recovery; that it obtained a waiver from an insurance carrier releasing it from subrogation rights; and that indemnification should not apply to liabilities, damages, or losses suffered as described in the contract. In the contract, the parties agreed that a no-fault, no subrogation, and inter-party waiver of liability provisions applied to all the parties participating in the launch operations.[10]

Although the contract provision for allocation of risks contained some broad and ambiguous language, a lower California court found in favor of McDonnell Douglas. The court was persuaded that the contract provisions for cross-waiver liability effectively protected the defendants from responsibility resulting from the defective performance of the Payload Assist Module. The California Court of Appeals upheld the decision.

Another case arising from the same unsuccessful Shuttle mission, also using a McDonnell Douglas PAM, was *Lexington Insurance Co. v. McDonnell Douglas Corp.*[11] In addition to the failure of the Western Union satellite, the Indonesian Palapa B-2 telecommunications satellite also failed to achieve its proper orbit after deployment from the Shuttle in February 1984. After the failure, the Indonesian government submitted a claim to the insurers for $75 million, the value of the satellite. After payment of the claim, Lexington Insurance filed a claim against McDonnell Douglas for breach of warranty and negligence, alleging damages in the amount of $5.7 million, its pro-rata share of the total amount paid to the government of Indonesia. The case resulted in a verdict for the insurers for breach of warranty, with damages limited to the proportionate share of the value of the rocket motor. On the claim of negligence, the jury returned a verdict in favor of McDonnell Douglas and the other defendants, finding no negligence in the design and testing of the PAM rocket booster. This case did not turn on the inter-party waiver claims.

In a launch service agreement case, *American Satellite Co. v. United States*,[12] the litigants disputed the "best effort" clause of the contract. In this case, American Satellite Company (ASC) sought to recover from the U.S. government the increased costs associated with the launch of a telecommunications satellite by McDonnell Douglas instead of by NASA, as originally intended. In a 1984 contract between ASC and NASA, NASA agreed, on a "shared Shuttle flights" basis, to launch two telecommunication satellites on the Space Shuttle and to offer its "best efforts" to provide such launch services. NASA launched the first ASC satellite but did not launch the second satellite, scheduled for 1987, due to the Shuttle Challenger explosion in 1986. After the explosion, the U.S. President directed that NASA discontinue all launchings of commercial satellites from the Shuttle unless there were national security implications or there were unique requirements which only the Shuttle could provide.

Subsequently, NASA agreed that if the ASC satellite qualified as having national security implications, it would receive priority in the re-scheduling of Shuttle payloads. NASA found that the ASC satellite did not have any national security implications and that therefore, in conformity with the President's directive, the agreement for launch services was terminated. ASC arranged with McDonnell Douglas for a 1991 launch of this second satellite and sought to recover its increased costs associated with this launch from NASA. In its suit to recover costs, ASC claimed that NASA breached its contract to provide launch services using its best efforts. According to ASC, NASA'S "best efforts" meant it had a duty to provide a launch, and if it could not do so, it would provide a substitute launch service. The Court held, however, in its opinion of June 26, 1990, that the contract did not specifically impose on NASA an obligation to provide an expendable launch vehicle (ELV) for the second launch, and added:

> Although what consitutes "best efforts" may have been less than clear at the time the agreement was signed, it is clear that defendant's [NASA's] obligation is to use its best efforts to perform the terms of the written agreement. It was obligated to use its best efforts to make a Shuttle available, not an ELV. Thus, even assuming that plantiff [ASC] is correct that defendant acted negligently regarding Challenger, the obligation plaintiff seeks to impose was not bargained for in the LSA [the contract].[13]

In *Lloyds of London v. McDonnell Douglas Corp.*,[14] Lloyds and other insurance underwriters claimed from McDonnell Douglas approximately $6 million to compensate Lloyds for its payment to Ford Aerospace. This case arose from damage which occurred to a satellite during the mounting of a satellite on a McDonnell Douglas Delta rocket prior to launch.

Ford, in a contract with the government of India, had undertaken to manufacture the satellite and to assume full responsibility for any loss or damage to the satellite prior to launch. In order to cover this liability, Ford had taken on an all-risks policy from Lloyds and other insurance companies. For the launch of the satellite, the government of India had entered into a separate contract with McDonnell Douglas. This agreement was for the purchase of a Delta rocket and associated launch facilities and services for the satellite.

During the mounting of the satellite on the Delta, the satellite was damaged when a wire hoist cable of a crane snapped. To avoid liability, Lloyds filed suit and alleged negligence, gross negligence, negligence per se and negligent misrepresentation by McDonnell Douglas in the planning, testing, and supervision of the launcher-satellite mounting process and in McDonnell Douglas's alleged violation of laws, regulations, and its own procedures in its use of the loading crane. McDonnell Douglas filed an answer and counter-claim, acknowledging that damage occurred to the satellite during the mounting process but raising a number of defenses, including that

Ford (and thus by derivation, Lloyds) had given up any rights of recovery because the risk of loss had passed to India, and that since India waived any right of recovery and right to subrogate, India assumed the entire risk. McDonnell Douglas argued further that it was acting pursuant to a U.S. Department of Transportation license which mandated reciprocal waivers of claims. Finally, McDonnell Douglas argued that the case should be decided pursuant to an arbitration clause existing in its contract with India. Thus, McDonnell Douglas sought a declaratory judgement regarding its rights under that contract, and in particular regarding its rights to have the disputes decided by arbitration. This case has not been adjudicated.

Due to the potential for damage or harm resulting from space activities, citizens have brought claims seeking damages based on tort theories. Some of the cases relate back to early days of space exploration. In *Smith v. Lockheed Propulsion Co.*,[15] the claimants sued on theories of negligence and strict liability to recover damages to their land allegedly caused by seismic vibrations activated by a rocket motor test conducted by Lockheed on adjoining lands pursuant to a government contract. The Fourth District Court of Appeals, in 1967, held in favor of the plaintiff and found that Lockheed was strictly liable because the test was considered ultra-hazardous since the solid fuel rocket motor was the largest ever tested to that date and since test firing such a device was not a matter of common occurrence. The Court further held that there was no basis, either in reason or justice, for requiring the innocent neighboring landowner to bear the loss, and that Lockheed, which was engaged in the enterprise for profit, was in the best position able to bear the loss.

Also, in *Gustave Pigott v. Boeing Co.*,[16] the plaintiffs sued Boeing for damages, alleging that Boeing negligently caused damage to their residence from concussions and vibrations when Boeing tested the Saturn booster rocket at the NASA test site in Hancock County, Mississippi. In this case, Boeing was hired as a NASA contractor to manufacture and test the booster stage of the Saturn rocket. The plaintiff's house was located just outside the testing buffer zone. The Supreme Court of Mississippi ruled in 1970 that in the absence of negligence on the part of Boeing, Boeing was not liable for damages to the private property of the plaintiffs since it was engaged as a contractor in performing a lawfully authorized public function of the U.S. government in accordance with a public contract.[17]

In other instances, plaintiffs have based their claims on violation of federal regulations for which they sought equitable relief. Public interest groups have sought equitable relief in the form of injuctions based on the potential of irreparable harm that could result from a malfunction or explosion of a spacecraft carrying a nuclear power source. For example, in *Florida Coalition for Peace and Justice v. George Herbert Walker Bush*,[18] the Florida Coalition for Peace and Justice, an umbrella organization of a large number of peace groups and church committees, sought permanent injunctions against the launches of nuclear-powered space probes, alleging potential environmental and health threats from the use of plutonium.

In 1989 the Coalition first sought an injunction to prevent the Galileo launch; and in 1990 it amended its complaint and further appealed for declaratory and injunctive relief, claiming that an accident involving these probes—either upon launch or subsequently during two scheduled "fly-bys" of Earth—could result in widespread dissemination of hazardous plutonium particles. In the Coalition's claim, it pleaded that NASA violated U.S. environmental policy and implementing regulations by failing to adopt appropriate measures to avoid contamination. NASA argued that the plaintiffs did not have standing and that their case was not ripe for judicial review. Finally NASA prevailed, and the District Court of Appeals dismissed the appeal.

Following the explosion of the Shuttle Challenger, families of those on board brought negligent and wrongful death claims against the U.S. government and Morton Thiokol. A Presidential Commission examined the cause of the accident and concluded that the explosion was due to failure in the seal of the O-rings situated between two segments of the solid rocket motor, in conjunction with NASA's decision to proceed with the launch despite cold temperatures which affected the O-rings' ability to seal. Family members of four of the astronauts brought their claims under the U.S. Federal Tort Claims Act. Their amount of the claims was never disclosed, but they were settled with approximately $7.7 million in long-term tax-free annuities from the government and Morton Thiokol. The defendants, NASA and Morton Thiokol, contributed to the settlement based on their respective faults. Similar settlements were reached between the family members of the other astronauts and Morton Thiokol.[19] Only one of the seven claims brought by family representatives was actually litigated. This case, *Smith v. Morton Thiokol Inc.*, was brought by Jane Smith, who sued Morton Thiokol directly as executrix of the estate of her husband, Navy Commander Michael J. Smith.[20]

Germany

No cases directly dealing with space activities have come before German courts up to now. The OTRAG case, though it involved discussions and disputes between OTRAG and the German authorities, never went to court. A few decisions by the Federal Constitutional Court will, however, be mentioned briefly here. In its decision of February 28, 1961, case BvG 1 and 2/60,[21] the Court examined and ruled on a number of details on the freedom on broadcasting and the division of competence between the Federation and the States (*Länder*). In particular, it ruled that under certain circumstances it was admissible for the Federation to retain exclusive rights in the field of broadcasting; that in German legal tradition, broadcasting is a public function even if implemented under the auspices of private law; and that broadcasting has to be organized in such a way that all relevant groups of society can express their opinions and exercise their influence. In its decision of July 27, 1971, case 2 AvF 1/68 and 2 BvR 702/68, the Court again ruled that broadcasting was part of the public sector and that, therefore, institutions engaged in broadcasting had a public responsibility and were not merely exercising a commercial activity.[22]

Later, in a judgement of June 16, 1981, case 1 BvL 89/78,[23] the Court ruled that the freedom of broadcasting is a human right within the meaning provided in the Constitution. According to Article 5 of the Constitution, States are obliged to provide a legal framework assuring this freedom in more detail and, in particular, assuring that in an environment of limited availability of radio frequencies, the supply of broadcasting programs should reflect all major sectors of opinions represented in the society.[24]

Canada

A decision by the Canadian Federal Court of Appeals on *Attorney General v. Lount Corp.* of June 10, 1985, represented another case dealing with the subject of direct broadcasting from satellites. The basic issue in this case was whether equipment in a hotel for receiving satellite television signals and local broadcast television signals and distributing them to the rooms were subject to the requirement of a license under the Canadian Broadcasting Act or a license under the Radio Act. A judgement of the Trial Division ruled that no license was necessary, and the Federal Court of Appeals upheld this decision.[25]

The hotel used this equipment to receive programs transmitted by a U.S. satellite and intended for reception only by subscribers who paid fees. The signals were not scrambled or encoded. The Court concluded that since the programs could be received by the general public, although against the intention of the transmitting stations, the signals were "radio-communications in which transmissions are intended for direct reception by the general public" and therefore constituted "broadcasting" as defined in both the Radio Act and the Broadcasting Act. The judgement further concluded that since the hotel charged no fee to room occupants for watching these programs, the installation in the case was not commercial in the direct sense and did not therefore require either a license or a technical construction and operating certificate.

The Netherlands

A similar case, *The Netherlands Antilles v. Antilles Communications N.V.* first came up before the courts of the Netherlands Antilles and then before the Supreme Court of the Netherlands. The Antilles Communications Company was receiving television programs intended for reception in the United States via satellite with the aid of a receiver/transmitter antenna, and it was transmitting these programs to a number of big hotels in Aruba, which paid for this service. The main issue was whether a license by the Governor was required and could be granted.

The lower court, in its intermediate sentence of November 29, 1982, ruled that no such license was required. However, in its final judgement of April 12, 1983, the lower court rejected the petition to grant the permit for the systems. On the appeal against this and another decision of the lower court, the Supreme Court of The Netherlands Antilles in a judgement of November 8, 1983, came to the conclusion that no rule of law, either national or international, barred the granting of a permit.[26] The ruling said that the original Television Ordinance of the Central Government was enacted at a time when the development of telecommunications in its present state was not foreseen and that it contained no provisions for the refusal of a permit in such a case. The Court also ruled that the question of a prohibition of the appellant to broadcast without the consent of the author in accordance with copyright restrictions was a matter falling under private law, which was outside the authority of the state administration.

The case finally came before the Supreme Court of The Netherlands (Hoge Raad) on appeal by The Netherlands Antilles. The Hoge Raad rejected the appeal in its decision of February 22, 1985.[27] The Supreme Court ruled that it could not overturn the lower court decisions on the grounds of copyright infringements since that argument had not been put forward in the lower courts.

European Community Cases

In 1972 in Biella, Italy, Giuseppi Sacchi set up the Telebiella Company to receive by cable foreign television programming and to distribute it locally by cable. Since this activity infringed upon the legal monopoly of Radio Audizione Italiana (RAI) over television broadcasting and cable distribution, he was prosecuted under Italian law. The Italian court referred the case to the European Communities Court of Justice for a ruling on whether the RAI monopoly was compatible with the European Economic Community (EEC) Treaty. In 1974, the Court ruled that such a national monopoly over television distribution does not necessarily violate the Treaty provisions, providing that the programming and advertising carried by the monopoly do not interfere with the free trade provisions of the Treaty.[28]

In another case, *Band van Averteerders and Others*, case 352/85, brought by Dutch claimants, the Court found that prohibitions on advertising and subtitling in television programs received from foreign sources and distributed by cable constituted restrictions on the freedom to supply services as provided for in the EEC Treaty.[29]

These cases did not concern the legal status of satellite communications but applied to terrestrial television distribution activities that can be supported by satellite distribution. The *Sacchi* case can be seen as limiting opportunities for reception and distribution of foreign satellite television signals, while the *Band van Averteerders and Others* decision would seem to promote reception and distribution of foreign signals.

NOTES

1. Convention on International Liability for Damage Caused by Space Objects, Nov. 29, 1971, 24 U.S.T. 2389, T.I.A.S. No. 762, 961 U.N.T.S. 187 (hereinafter Liability Convention).

2. U.N. Doc. A/AC.105/13.

3. U.N. Doc. A/AC.105/15, reprinted in K.-H. Böckstiegel and M. Benkö (eds.), *Space Law: Basic Legal Documents*, Dordrecht/Boston/ London, M. Nijhoff, 1990, vol. 1, Section A.VI.2.2.

4. Treaty on Principles Governing the Activities of States in the Exploration and Use of Outer Space, Including the Moon and Other Celestial Bodies, 18 U.S.T. 2410, T.I.A.S. No. 6347, 610 U.N.T.S. 205 (hereinafter Outer Space Treaty).

5. Further information on OTRAG activities is contained in *Aviation Week and Space Technology*, September 12, 1977, and *Africa International Business Economic and Political Magazine*, No. 76, December 1977.

6. M36-90-189D.C. Md. File, July 6, 1990.

7. EN-49 U.S.C. app. SS2601-2623.

8. 49 U.S.C. app. 261 (a) (1) (1).

9. *Appalachian Insurance. Co. v McDonnell Douglas Corp.*, 214 Cal. App. 3d 1, 262 Cal. Rptr. 716 (1989).

10. Rachel Trindler, "Recent Developments in Litigation," *Journal of Law and Technology*, Vol. 5, No. 1, 1991, pp. 55-57.

11. *Lexington Insurance Co. v. McDonnell Douglas Corp.*, No. 481713 (Cal. Super. Ct., Orange City 1990).

12. *American Satellite Co.*, No. 525-89 (Cl. Ct.), June 26, 1990.

13. Trindler, *supra* note 10, pp. 54-55.

14. *Lloyds of London v. McDonnell Douglas Corp.*, Civ. No. 90-CV-543 (D. Fla. filed June 18, 1990).

15. *Smith v. Lockheed Propulsion Co.*, 56 Cal. Rptr. 128 (1967). Reprinted in Stephen Gorove (ed.), *United States Space Law—National and International Regulations*, Release 85-2, issued October 1985, I.A-5 (1), New York, Oceana, 1982-1990, p. 28.

16. M. O. Pigott and Wife. *Gustave Pigott v. Boeing Co.*, Miss. 240 So. 2d 63 (1970).

17. Reprinted in S. Gorove, *supra* note 15, p. 30.

18. No. 89-2682 (D.D.C. filed Sept. 28, 1989) and Amended Complaint (filed Jan. 29, 1990).

19. Paul G. Dembling and Richard C. Walters, "The 1986 Challenger Disaster: Legal Ramification," *Journal of Space Law*, Vol. 19, 1991, pp. 1, 4-6.

20. *Smith v. Morton Thiokol, Inc.*, 712 F. Supp. 893 (M.D. Fla. 1988).

21. BVerG, decision of February 28, 1961 (BvG 1 and 2/60), NJW 1961, p. 547.

22. BVerG, decision of July 27, 1971 (2 Avf 1/68 and 2 BUR 702/68), NJW 1971, p. 1,739.

23. 1BVL 89/78.

24. BVerG, decision of June 16, 1981 (1 Bul 89/78), NJW 1981, p. 1,774.

25. *Attorney General v. Lount Corp.*, Federal Court of Appeal, Ottawa (June 10, 1985). Reported in *Annals of Air and Space Law*, Vol. 10, Montreal, ICASL, McGill University, 1985, pp.527-535.

26. *Antilles Communications Co. Ltd. v. The Netherlands Antilles, The Minister of Communication and Transport, The Governor of the Netherlands Antilles*, Supreme Court of The Netherlands Antilles (8 Nov. 1983). Reprinted in *Annals of Air and Space Law*, Vol. 9, Montreal, ICASL, McGill University, 1984, pp. 534-536.

27. *The Netherlands Antilles v. Antilles Communications N.V.*, The Supreme Court of The Netherlands, First Chamber (Petition nr. 6661). Reprinted in *Annals of Air and Space Law*, Vol. 10, Montreal, ICASL, McGill University, pp. 552-553.

28. European Communities Court of Justice, case 155/73, Giuseppi Sacchi, reported in Böckstiegel and Benkö (eds.) *supra* note 3, Section B.I.6.1.

29. European Communities Court of Justice, *Reports of Cases before the Court*, 1989, Luxemburg, Office for the Official Publications of the European Community, p. 2,085.

16

Study and Teaching of Space Law

Gyula Gál

The study and teaching of space law poses the question: what is space law? Is it an independent legal field or merely a functional classification of international and municipal law relating to outer space?[1] The actual position of space law in the curricula of universities, law schools, and institutes indicates the lack of a generally accepted answer to these questions. As a simple solution, to quote the skeptical remark of B. Bakotic, "law faculties will always prefer integrating legal issues related to outer space into already existing courses and be satisfied with fitting most of them into public international law."[2] The close relationship of space law to air law and the development of space law in the direction of municipal law are factors which influence where space law will stand.

Yet, for purposes of teaching, it is practical to link the study and teaching of air and space law, since there are areas which touch both fields and they cannot be covered in isolation, as illustrated in particular by the question of the legal status of the Space Shuttle or the legal regimes of environmental protection in the atmosphere and outer space.[3] Further, air law serves as a source for both international and national space law.

This is not surprising considering that space activities, which involve the placement of artificial objects in orbit around the Earth or other celestial bodies, necessarily involve airspace irrespective of the delimitation between airspace and outer space. It is not accidental that the first authors of space law science were highly respected authorities on international air law. The question of whether space objects could be treated under international air law therefore emerged even before the launching of the first artificial satellite. The crux of the issue was whether existing air law was applicable to space flights or whether new regulations for space activities should be created. A survey of the present state of the study and teaching of space law indicates that institutes and law schools are taking this correlation between air and space laws into account.

This chapter is a review of available information on the actual state of teaching of space law at universities, law schools, and institutes in various countries.[4]

EDUCATIONAL PROGRAMS IN SPACE LAW

Argentina. The University of Salvador in Buenos Aires and the Catholic University of Córdoba have chairs of air and space law; the University of Morón has a chair of air law. At these universities and at others, space law is taught in special courses or within courses on navigation law. The study and teaching of space law are supported by specialized institutes such as Instituto Nacional de Derecho Aeronautico y Espacial, which has had a space law chair since 1962, and the Institute for Legal and Social Research of Space.[5]

Austria. At the Institut für Volkerrecht und Internationale Beziehungen of Vienna University, international space law has been a subject of advanced study (6 to 8 hours) since 1986. Otherwise, space law is taught as part of a course on general international law.

Belgium. At Brussels University, air and space law courses have been offered (8 hours) at both the master's and postgraduate level since 1978. At the University of Ghent, space law is taught in a two-semester course on general space law.

Canada. The Institute of Air and Space Law (IASL), established in 1958 within the Faculty of Law, and the Centre for Research in Air and Space Law, established in 1976, both at McGill University, have played a large role in the study and teaching of space law on the national and international levels. At the Institute, space law is taught with air law. In the diploma course, there are two specific space law courses: International Law in the Regulation of Space Activities, and Law of Telecommunications. The research and teaching at McGill is fully international in character in both its programs and its publications.[6]

China. In China, the teaching and study of international law has been strengthened since 1978 by the restoration and establishment of institutions of higher education and by the founding of the Chinese Society of International Law. Special courses on space law were established in some universities, and chapters on space law were included in international law textbooks. The main centers for teaching international law are Beijing University, the University of Political Science and Law of China, and Beijing College of Foreign Affairs, where two-year postgraduate space law courses have been organized since 1980.[7]

Czechoslovakia. At Charles University in Prague, lectures on space law were included in the curricula of regular and advanced studies in international law in 1970. The most important space topics—remote sensing, satellite direct broadcasting, intellectual property—later became subjects of a specialized seminar. At the Comenius University of Bratislava, and at the universities of Brno and Kosice, space law is covered in lectures and seminars on general international law.[8]

France. The teaching of space law in France is part of a general international law course (2 to 6 hours) at the universities of Bordeaux, Caen, Dijon, and at Haute-Normandie and Nice-Sophia Antipolis universities. At the University of Nancy, a seminar is devoted to space law teaching (one month, 9 hours). In Paris, space law is a subject in optional courses at the University of Paris I, Panthéon Sorbonne (30 hours per year) and Paris V, René Descartes (3 lectures and 7 hours of seminars per year). At the University of Toulouse I, Science Sociales, space law became a course in 1988 (37 hours per semester), and a seminar entitled Economic Law of Space Activities (20 hours per year) has been established. In a similar way, space law is taught at the Conservatoire National des Arts et Métiers as an optional course on socio-economic aspects of space technology.

Germany. The Institute of Air and Space Law (Institut für Luft- und Weltraumrecht) of Cologne University is a well-known specialized institution for space law teaching and research. Established in 1950 as the Institut für Luftrecht, and under the present name since 1975, the Institute is part of Cologne University and offers a one-semester optional course on air and space law and a one-semester seminar on special issues of space law (both for 90 minutes each week). At other German universities, space law teaching is a part of courses and seminars on general international law.[9]

Greece. At Athens University, as part of an international law course, an optional course in the sixth semester is devoted to space law.

Hungary. At Budapest University, space law lectures in an optional *collegium speciale* were offered starting in 1971-1972. Since 1980, the curriculum has included a special one-year course, International Air and Space Law, with lectures on space law in the second semester (2 hours per week). The average number of participants is about 40 per year. Otherwise, space law is taught in Budapest and at other universities in Pécs, Szeged, and Miskolc as a part of required courses on public international law.[10]

Italy. At Padua University's Department of International Studies, space law has been included in the optional course on International Organizations since 1983.

Netherlands. Space law teaching in the Netherlands dates back to 1957. After the launching of the first satellite, the chair of air law at Utrecht University gradually integrated legal problems of space activities into courses on air law. Today, the university offers a three-month general space law course and a three-week space law seminar. At Leyden University, in addition to a course on air and space law, there is a seminar on responsibility and liability in air and space law. In 1986, the International Institute of Air and Space Law was established at Leyden University in order to offer post-academic courses, to organize seminars and conferences, and to collect space law literature. The activities of the Institute are both national and international in scope. At the University of Amsterdam's Department of International

Relations and Public International Law, the teaching of space law started within the international telecommunications and public international law course in 1990.[11]

Norway. Oslo University offers optional seminars on the legal problems of space activities.

Poland. At universities in Poland, space law is taught as an integral part of required general courses on public international law. Space law topics are also included in optional international law seminars.[12]

Russia. The Moscow State Institute of International Relations offers a special course on space law. At the Patrice Lumumba Friendship University, space law is taught in the same way. At other high-level law schools, space law is a required part of general international law courses. Graduates can continue their studies in space law by joining a three-year postgraduate study program at the State and Law Institute of the Academy of Sciences.[13]

Spain. The University of Murcia devotes 10 hours to space law teaching within the required course on general international law. Granada University offers optional seminars on general space law for two hours a week.

Sweden. At Stockholm University, space law is dealt with in courses on general international law, while the University of Uppsala offers a special optional seminar on space law.

Switzerland. At Geneva University's Graduate Institute of International Studies, space law has been the subject of seminars at the postgraduate level (6 to 8 hours) since 1982. The University of Zurich's Institute of International Law has included space law in general public international law courses. The Swiss Federal Institute of Technology in Zurich offers five hours of space law as part of transportation and communication law.

United Kingdom. University College London has been teaching space law since 1970 in optional seminars at the Master of Law level (15 seminars of 2 hours) and a five-lecture course on space law at the doctoral level. At the Cambridge University, an introductory course on general international law includes elements of space law. At Aberdeen University's Department of Public Law, optional one-semester courses on air and space law have been offered since 1990.

United States. In the United States, the University of Mississippi Law School was the first to offer a space law course on a regular basis, an optional course entitled Space Law. The University also offers seminar courses. At the University of Southern California, the introductory course in international law for undergraduates comprises some lectures on space law, while graduate students in the social sciences field may enroll in courses on space law. At the University of Colorado (Colorado Springs) Graduate School of Business Administration, space law has been taught since 1985 under the title Space Law and Policy. At Winona State University, Minnesota, the study of space law was added to the curriculum in 1974 and has been integrated into the international law course. Otherwise, seminars seem to be the most frequent form of space law teaching in the United States.[14]

Uruguay. At Montevideo University, space law has been an independent course taught since 1966. It is an optional course in which a Ph.D. degree can be pursued in the Faculty of Law. Space law is also discussed in courses on public international law and international relations. The Aeronautic and Space Research and Diffusion Center (CIDA) offers a complementary program in the study of current space law subjects.[15]

Yugoslavia. At Yugoslavian universities, space law is not a course in its own right, but space law is included in public international law, a required subject. Occasionally, however, the law faculty of Zagreb offers a space law course as part of postgraduate studies.[16]

PROMOTION OF SPACE LAW EDUCATION AND RESEARCH BY INTERNATIONAL ORGANIZATIONS

International law organizations, from the beginning of the space age, rendered important services to the development of space law, as they had previously in developing the foundations of air law. The International Law Association (ILA) in 1956 requested its air law committee to study the nature and contents of air sovereignty, devoting particular attention to future questions relating to space flights and the legal nature of interplanetary space. As a result of this work, a 1960 ILA Resolution accepted certain principles of space activity, which, through the 1967 Outer Space Treaty, became generally accepted principles of positive space law. Similar contributions were offered by the Institut de Droit International in Brussels in 1963.

A number of international organizations specifically devoted to space activities have also played an important role in the study and research of space law.

The International Institute of Space Law (IISL). The IISL, which is an associate body of the International Astronautical Federation (IAF), has organized, since 1958, an annual series of Colloquia on the Law of Outer Space, which offer the most important international forum for lectures on and discussion of space law subjects. The published proceedings of these Colloquia make available a rich collection of materials and sources for the study and teaching of space law. The papers on current subjects of positive space law and problems of lawmaking *de lege ferenda* serve as annual rings of space law and space law theory for the future study of its history.[17] As part of these Colloquia, the Institute has held symposia on the teaching of space law in 1969 in Buenos Aires, in 1971 in Brussels, and in 1973 in Baku. Space law teaching and the history of space law were the subjects of a session at the 1986 Colloquium (29th) in Innsbruck.

Intercosmos Seminars. Since 1979, the various Academies of Sciences taking part in the Intercosmos Programme have held a number of seminars on space law. These meetings addressed current theoretical and practical problems of positive space law and lawmaking, particularly subjects on the agenda of the Legal Subcommittee of the United Nations Committee on

Peaceful Uses of Outer Space. Seminars were convened in Warsaw (1979), Prague (1982), Varna (1984), Budapest (1986), Berlin (1987), and Moscow (1989). Papers and discussions, partly published, promoted the study and teaching of space law in these countries.[18]

European Centre of Space Law (ECSL). The Centre was founded in 1989 at the initiative of the European Space Agency (ESA). According to its Charter, its main purposes are, among others, "to promote knowledge of and interest in the law relating to space activities through the promotion of research activities" and "to promote the establishment and development of national centres for space law research." A handbook entitled Space Law Teaching in Europe, the first of its kind, has been published by the Centre and gives detailed information on the present status of space law teaching in most countries of Europe. It is hoped that ECSL will publish reports on space law teaching in all European countries.[19]

THE STATUS OF SPACE LAW EDUCATION

The preceding brief survey on the teaching and study of space law is based on available published information and is far from complete, both with respect to the countries involved and the institutions where space law is taught. Despite this incompleteness, there are some generalizations which can be drawn:

1. In most curricula of law schools and universities, space law is only one topic among many that are dealt with in general international law courses;
2. A very small number of law schools and universities offer courses devoted entirely to space law, usually in institutions with active space law experts;
3. Generally, space law is taught as a part of international law, but there are efforts to address the application of municipal law to space activities and to introduce space-related questions into the programs of institutions in traditional fields of national law.

While courses and textbooks in general international law, as a matter of course, deal with international space law in the narrow sense,[20] there is a growing need for international lawyers studying and teaching space law to pay more attention to municipal space laws that transform international space law obligations into national rules of jurisdiction over space activities.[21] At the same time, the study and teaching of municipal space law will need to include more international space law.

As Eilene Galloway has recognized, all major space law problems in both international and municipal space law are multidisciplinary and require for their solution a knowledge of space science and technology as well as elements of the physical sciences, the life sciences, and engineering.[22] This principle is also valid for the study and teaching of space law. As Eilene

Galloway has also noted, effective treatment of space law problems requires the examination of a broad range of sources: general international law, including customary international law; space law treaties, conventions, and agreements, including treaties on arms control, environmental protection, and liability; bilateral and regional agreements; statutes of international space organizations; space-related regulations of the United Nations specialized agencies; sources for treaty interpretation; and national space laws and implementing regulations, particularly legal norms integrating national with international law.

NOTES

1. B. Cheng, "Outer Space: The International Legal Framework, the International Status of Outer Space, Space Objects and Spacemen," *Thesaurus Acroasium*, Vol. 10, 1981, p. 55, quoted in B. Bakotíc, "A Note on a Basic Problem in the Teaching of Space Law," in *Proceedings of the 29th Colloquium on the Law of Outer Space* (Innsbruck 1986), New York, AIAA, p. 206.
2. Bakotíc, *id.*, p. 205.
3. G. Gál, "Indivisibility of Environmental Protection in Vertical Space," in *Proceedings of the 27th Colloquium on the Law of Outer Space*, (Lausanne 1984), New York, AIAA, pp. 388-389.
4. The survey is based on papers and reports from *Proceedings*, *supra* note 1; S. Gorove (ed.), *The Teaching of Space Law around the World*, University, MS, University of Mississippi Law Center, 1986; and European Centre for Space Law, *Space Law Teaching in Europe*, Dordrecht, Martinus Nijhoff Publishers, 1990.
5. A. A. Cocca, "The Teaching of Space Law in Argentina," in Gorove (ed.), *supra* note 4, pp. 45-49.
6. N. Mateesco Matte, "Aerospace Law, Education and Research: The I.A.S.L.," in Gorove (ed.), *supra* note 4, pp. 29-45; *Proceedings, supra* note 1, pp. 257-262.
7. He Qizhi, "Main Features of Space Law Teaching in China," in Gorove (ed.) *supra* note 4, pp. 83-89; *Proceedings, supra* note 1, pp. 272-275.
8. V. Kopal, "Teaching of Space Law in Czechoslovakia: A Brief History and Assessment," in Gorove (ed.), *supra* note 4, pp. 65-68; idem, "The Law of Outer Space: Its Place in the System of International Law and Some Related Problems of Its Teaching," in *Proceedings, supra* note 1, pp. 244-260.
9. K.-H. Böckstiegel, "Report and Reflections on the Teaching of Space Law at the Institute of Air and Space Law of Cologne University," in Gorove (ed.), *supra* note 4, pp. 53-59; *Proceedings, supra* note 1, pp. 208-211; H. Bittlinger, "History of the Institute of Air and Space Law of the University of Cologne," (no impressum), pp. 1-52.
10. G. Gál, "First Space Law Course at Budapest University," *Proceedings of the 16th Colloquium on the Law of Outer Space*, Fred Rothman; "Space Law Teaching in Hungary," in Gorove (ed.), *supra* note 4, pp. 69-70.
11. I. H. Ph. Diederiks-Verschoor, "The Teaching of Space Law," in Gorove (ed.), *supra* note 4, pp. 61-62; *Proceedings, supra* note 1, pp. 212-213.
12. A. Górbiel, "The Teaching of Space Law," in Gorove (ed.), *supra* note 4, pp. 71-72.

13. V. S. Vereshchetin and G. P. Zhukov, "Teaching of Space Law in the USSR," in Gorove (ed.), *supra* note 4, pp. 73-78; *Proceedings, supra* note 1, pp. 281-284.

14. S. Gorove, "The Teaching of Space Law: Charting of New Pathways," in Gorove (ed.), *supra* note 4, pp. 38; *Proceedings, supra* note 1, pp. 224-227; C. Q. Christol, "International Space Law in the International Law Curriculum," in Gorove (ed.), *supra* note 4, pp. 9-14; W. B. Wirin, "Space Law and Policy," in Gorove (ed.), *supra* note 4, pp. 15-19; "Space Education—America's Hope for the Future," in *Proceedings, supra* note 1, pp. 285-289; F. P. Morello, "Space Law Teaching and History," in *Proceedings, supra* note 1, pp. 263-271.

15. E. D. Gaggero, "Space Law Teaching in Uruguay," in *Proceedings, supra* note 1, pp. 214-217.

16. B. Bakotíć, *supra* note 1, pp. 205-207.

17. Subject Index of the Proceedings, 1958-1982, in E. Pépin, *History of the International Institute of Space Law of the International Astronautical Federation (1958-1982)*, New York, AIAA, 1982.

18. V. Kopal, in *Proceedings, supra* note 1, p. 246.

19. See *Space Law Teaching in Europe, supra* note 4.

20. For example, J. G. Starke, *An Introduction to International Law*, 9th ed., London, Butterworth, 1984, pp. 204-216; G. Schwarzenberger and E. D. Brown, *A Manual of International Law*, 6th ed., London, Stevens, 1976, pp. 93-94, 415-412; textbook used in teaching international law in Hungary: G. Haraszti, G. Herczegh, and K. Nagy, *Nemzetközi jog (International Law)*, 2d ed., Budapest, 1979, pp. 162-166.

21. See, among others, U.S. Commercial Launch Act of 1984, U.S. Remote Sensing Commercialization Act of 1984, Act on Space Activities of Sweden 1982, Outer Space Act of the United Kingdom 1986.

22. E. Galloway, "The Definition of Space Law," in *Proceedings of the 32nd Colloquium on the Law of Outer Space*, Washington, AIAA, pp. 332-333.

17

The Future of Space Law

Carl Q. Christol

SOME THEORETICAL CONSIDERATIONS

An understanding of the future of space law requires that account be taken of several working hypotheses. First, space law possesses international and domestic (municipal) ramifications. Second, while relying on existing law as the foundation for the future, we must also pay attention to new developments and possibilities. Third, the magnitude of future space activities will require both regional and global efforts.

With respect to the first hypothesis, two working definitions are suggested. First, international space law governs the conduct of states, international organizations, and human beings engaged in the exploration, exploitation, and use of outer space and celestial bodies. It applies to activities which take place beyond the limits of national sovereignty. It also applies to natural resources located in these areas and any actions taken with respect to them, encompassing both space and Earth-based actions.

Second, municipal space law governs the Earth-based aspects of space activities as well as activities in outer space. States, in formulating their own laws, must conform to international law.

The second hypothesis, by calling attention to dynamic changes, allows for a constantly changing law able to respond to the perceived wants, needs, interests, and values of civilized societies. Such changes will modify the substantive content of space law, with the rate of change uneven but dynamic. This hypothesis takes into account the substance of law and its constitutive processes.

The third hypothesis finds its basis in the goals promulgated in the Preamble to the 1967 Outer Space Treaty,[1] namely, the exploration and use of outer space for peaceful purposes,[2] common benefits, mutual understanding, and the strengthening of friendly relations between states and peoples.[3] These are to be promoted and enhanced by the benefits derivable from wide-ranging international cooperation. In light of the magnitude of projects envisioned in space, such cooperation will often require international consortiums. This circumstance is at the heart of the currently popular concept of globalization, for it allows for the realization of the objectives identified in the Preamble.

The development and scope of space law, both international and municipal, will be largely influenced by the acceptance and implementation of preferred values, by the direction received from such complex social forces as science and technology, population explosions, the availability of natural and human resources, economic and financial considerations, perceptions of "national interest" and security needs, to mention but a few.[4] Also influencing the future will be the utility of international intergovernmental organizations, now in existence or proposed, and the underlying legal regimes which identify the goals of such institutions and which provide them with structures and procedures.

In theory, hopefully in practice, and certainly in accordance with commonly held expectations, the space environment (outer space per se, the Moon, and other celestial bodies) and its natural resources will be employed increasingly by humans for the benefit of humans. However, such uses and benefits will not be enjoyed equally by all. Nonetheless, a basic goal must be to promote a very wide distribution of benefits derived from space activities under legal regimes that take full account of the contributions of the countries with space capabilities to the exploration, exploitation, and use of the space environment, as well as the needs of the developing countries. Equitable principles should commend themselves to decision makers dealing with these relationships.

SOME HISTORICAL CONSIDERATIONS

International Space Year (ISY) in 1992 affords an opportunity to cast off outmoded perspectives relating to space activities, space policies, and space law. This occasion can serve to stimulate cooperative efforts to maximize humankind's space-derived benefits. This event focuses attention on the multifaceted and multinational relationships between humans, their governments, and the space environment, including its natural resources.

Nagging questions exist whether the existing legal regime, largely consisting of United Nations-established principles, standards, and rules, can cope with anticipated changes. The United Nations is entitled to much credit for providing a stable and effective legal regime, but all viable institutions are constantly challenged to respond rapidly and wisely to the dynamics of unfolding events.[5]

Based on these considerations, and irrespective of the forum in which decisions are reached, one must ask if greater long-term benefit is to result from fashioning and applying practical legal norms to past events or whether relevant prescriptive norms should anticipate forthcoming events. Even if such planning for the future may not have immediate utility, its worth would be substantial when anticipated events become a reality.

Yet the line between those anticipated events which will become realities and those that will not, and consequently the constitutive rule of law, can only be known in the future. Future decision makers will probably respond to known facts and at the same time try to forecast the future. Moreover, in the future, as in past, acceptable international practice can produce a valid alternative to treaty law, namely, customary international law.

Space law and its institutions for many years will have to be tailored to cope with immediate events. This means that humankind's fortune and energies will be directed increasingly toward the perfection of unmanned launches, the production of efficient robots, and the undertaking of occasional, short-duration, multi-person visits to other bodies in the inner solar system. The priorities will be subject to public opinion.

At this time there appears to be a diminishing public interest in the more futuristic aspects of space activity, even though President Bush proposed a 24 percent increase in NASA's budget in fiscal year 1991. Congress reduced this to a 13.5 percent increase and cut $551 million from the $2.45 billion requested for the Space Station, leaving about $2 billion appropriated for the Space Station. Even so, the NASA budget for 1991 was $13.9 billion. The availability of funding for space activities was necessarily influenced by circumstances such as the current economic downturn, the costs of the savings and loan bailout, social security reform, military expenditures occasioned by the Gulf crisis, and legitimate concerns over the nation's educational productivity, deteriorating infrastructure, and the societal needs of the underclasses.

While these illustrations apply principally to the United States, similar constraints exist in many other advanced nations. Increasingly, strong justifications will have to be made to support many space activities.

In December 1990, the report of the U.S. National Space Council's Advisory Committee on the Future of the U.S. Space Program reflected some of these considerations. The Committee, in addressing the U.S. civil space program, offered serious warnings with respect to the Shuttle-based manned programs. The report pointed out the potential for loss of human life and urged that even with a more reliable Shuttle, it should be employed only for essential needs. In down-playing the human presence in space, the Committee pointed to the need for more emphasis on basic scientific research, the development of a heavy-lift launch vehicle, and a major overhaul of the design of the proposed Space Station. It also referred to funding and attendant problems in an inflationary economy.

Underlying the report was the prospect of space activities being carried out either by a single wealthy country or by securing the financial and scientific support of many wealthy countries. Since space activities concern all countries, a situation increasingly referred to as "globalization," joint cooperative activities should increasingly become the norm.

To assume that what one country considers to be beneficial to it is also necessarily good for the entire world is dangerous. Boosting national egos through space spectaculars will have to give way to the practical pursuit of meaningful scientific and technological development. Focus must be placed on tangible benefits for humankind.

SOME POLICY CONSIDERATIONS

Future space law, international and municipal, will grow as a result of two principal factors. First, there are the physical results of the worldwide, rapid, and expanding changes in an open-ended science and technology. The second factor is the social element: the enduring human quest to understand the unknown. The problem will be to assimilate and coordinate these two factors so as to balance egocentric nationalisms, often most vigorously expressed by representatives of developing countries, with the rewards of international cooperation flowing from well-considered global economic and political relationships.

In 1987 legislation was adopted in the United States calling for an International Space Year (ISY) in 1992. On July 20, 1989, President George Bush called for a Space Exploration Initiative (SEI) leading to human exploration of the solar system. In the United States, attention also remains focused on the Strategic Defense Initiative (SDI) and on the activities of NASA's Shuttle operations. "Mission to Planet Earth," with a focus on environmental protection, has also captured much attention.

ISY, which now has international support,[6] has directed attention to important initiatives, including new educational programs relating to space research and exploration, new legal and policy initiatives, prevention and disposition of space pollution, global data sharing, and the promotion of experimental activities through new applications satellites and new launch vehicles.

ISY is providing the occasion for a sensible policy review of space goals, and for an identification of what is most plausible and desirable and the means available for realizing the goals. Policy formulation involves choosing among competing alternatives, which can be identified in terms of goals (i.e., *why* certain actions and outcomes should be preferred over others); in terms of programs (i.e., *what* steps are best suited to contribute to the realization of the preferred goals); and in terms of management (i.e., *how* programs can be most effectively organized to achieve the stated goals). The forthcoming reassessment will allow for a keener perception of the respective advantages of manned and unmanned space objects, and choices which might be made, for example, between different kinds of expendable launch vehicles.

Policies underlying space law will also be affected by commercial activities in which the primary actors will continue to be states, but with increasing competition from private firms frequently participating in international consortia, and from international intergovernmental entities. Private firms, in formulating their policies on launchings, will be influenced by the availability of inexpensive foreign services. It is now anticipated that a private spaceport at Cape York, Australia, will be in business by 1995, facilitating joint undertakings by firms from different countries. For example, it is expected that the Soviet Zenit rocket will launch U.S. satellites, while firms from Japan and other countries will use the Cape York facility as well.

Private activities, which are bound to increase, will result in international scientific and technological exchanges, mobilizing the special capabilities of different participants and leading to improvements in technology. Agreements may also provide for the sharing of costs. Both international and municipal space law will be developed in greater detail in coping with such situations. Yet, while private national efforts are expanding, there will not likely be any diminution of the role of international facilities, particularly those being managed by Arianespace, the European satellite launch corporation. Some activities requiring a human presence in space are beyond the capabilities of private firms, but this would not impose limits on policies calling for national cooperation in international programs.

Of the commercial activities in space, television distribution, including direct broadcasting, will play an increasingly larger role. Both satellite communications and remote sensing will raise new problems for municipal law. In the United States, for example, the First Amendment rights of broadcasters will require both policy and legal clarification. Commercial activities will also include materials processing, harvesting of minerals and other tangible and intangible space resources, and the collection and return to Earth of solar energy.

Environmental concerns will proliferate. Space objects and their crews require protection from radiation. Space debris can cause harm both in space and on Earth. Global warming and the deterioration of the ozone layer can bring about climatic changes detrimental to life on Earth.

There will be a need for a legal regime applicable to future aerospace planes, a need that may revitalize the continuing discussions in the Committee on the Peaceful Uses of Outer Space concerning a formal boundary between outer space and sovereign airspace.[7]

These issues, and others, will challenge the minds of those engaged in space policy and law. These matters and the related policies will be greatly affected by the world's political, economic, and social realities. The current changes in the tensions between the superpowers will allow for a lesser emphasis on military concerns. The viability of existing intergovernmental space organizations will have to be scrutinized with care, as will prospects of possible new and highly specialized international space organizations.[8]

In this political milieu the influences of the developing countries will be substantial. Their understandably nationalistic tendencies, often expressed in the language of equity with its implications of fairness and justice, will be positioned against the conservative outlooks of the states with established space capabilities. These contending positions are subject to adjustment. In the area of space telecommunications, for example, there have been indications that policies can be clarified and mutually acceptable compromises can be reached. For this process to be facilitated, the public will need to understand the issues and to provide their broad support.

REQUIRED CONDITIONS FOR POLICY IMPLEMENTATION

In contemplating the political opportunities and constraints relating to the development and scope of space law, taking into account the forces that produced calls for "a new world order," it has become evident there are two central forces at work. First is the critical fact that human society is organized on the basis of the national state. Second is the principle that the space environment and its natural resources must be used for the benefit of humankind. These two conditions are increasingly affected by the perception that the condition of globalization affects policy choices.

Since we are bound by the nation-state as the organizational structure of the global community, each state tries to secure national advantage and avoid national disadvantage. This, of course, poses the unresolved question of what constitutes national advantage.

One of the great lessons of history is that a given political entity cannot be at an advantage if all or many other equally sovereign political entities are disadvantaged in any material respect. At this point in history there is increasing acceptance of the fact that for one political entity to enjoy measurable advantages, other such entities must also possess favorable conditions.

In the history of international space law, it is no longer possible for a state or other international legal person to claim the condition of sovereignty (e.g., exclusive control) over the space environment and its natural resources. When sovereignty claims were made by equatorial countries, for example, they were completely discounted through reference to Article 2 of the 1967 Outer Space Treaty.[9]

Under these circumstances, the policy for the future, as has been true in the past, must be to accommodate competing wants, needs, interests, and values. Such accommodation can be implemented in several ways.

First, a policy of cooperation constitutes an accommodation on the part of those political entities which, by reason of their advanced conditions, might otherwise seek to monopolize actual or potential benefits. Second, accommodation can result when otherwise different and competing outlooks see the mutual advantage that results from the acceptance of common goals.

Third, the mere fact that states share in a common decision-making process may produce policy accommodations. These considerations allow for the sharing of benefits derived from the exploration, exploitation, and use of the space environment and its natural resources. In today's world the policy of sharing must be perceived as a reasonable alternative to legally unacceptable claims of exclusivity.

It is not overly optimistic to say that goals, programs, and management relating to space activities can be shared. In fact, the corpus of space law, both international and municipal, attests to the fact that the concept of sharing is currently accepted. This can be seen in common memberships in many space-related intergovernmental organizations, substantial support for important international agreements dealing with space activities, opportunities for various countries to participate in cooperative missions and undertakings,[10] and the commonly shared consumer-type benefits derived from science and technology developed for space activities. Examples are well known: commerce, communications, and data and information acquired from remote sensing. Scientific and technological data obtained in many fields are widely shared, including information relating to weather, pollution, ozone layer depletion, climate, and global warming.

These applications of space technology are areas in which both governmental entities and private firms can be engaged in research, development, and applications. In light of the process of globalization, there will be a high level of competition among those engaged in space applications. Private firms need to be profitable to survive, while governmental entities may be able to afford to generously share the benefits derived from space activities. Thus, private firms engaged in space activities may not be willing to share the benefits without suitable compensation for the risks they take and the investments they make to engage in space activities. An increase in space activities undoubtedly will produce tensions between private entities, which are governed by business considerations, and governments, which are concerned with national interests. In serving the national interests, states will have to meet the demands of their internationally oriented constituents and even accord support to them.

Competition between governments and private companies need not impose unacceptable constraints on the latter. Governments can encourage private activities and can offer assistance to private firms so that a product can be sold to the public at a lower price than would have resulted without public assistance. Governments can also compete with private firms, thereby ensuring a price beneficial to consumers.

Still, for some time, the role of governments will be larger than that of private companies. As long as this is the case, governmental entities will be able to promote policies designed to provide wide benefits either unilaterally or through international understandings. International sharing of benefits through private space activities can be encouraged by governmental protection for the intellectual property of private enterprises. Governments will be reluctant to require their nationals to transfer privately owned science and technology without adequate compensation.

When policy choices are made a variety of factors will be considered, but given the nature of human behavior and the vagaries of national interests, the final outcome cannot be predicted. However, over time a continuum of international relations can be identified, ranging from the possibility of conflict, through competition both fierce and friendly, to compromise, and finally to cooperation. Even after a successful international policy has been identified, it can be subject to later reconsideration. Ultimately, the best approach to future policies for space activities is one in which mutual interests are emphasized and the ensuing law reflects this approach.

FUTURE SPACE LAW

A major function of law is to provide order in a disorderly universe. The space law of the future, both international and domestic, should keep this in mind. Major opportunities lie ahead.

Future development of space law can be useful in several respects. First, it can make refinements in the existing law. Second, it can seek new formal international agreements while at the same time acknowledging the utility of international customary law.[11] Third, it can continue to offer policy-oriented prescriptions designed to maximize human benefits from space activities.

At the present time a need exists for the continuing clarification of the five space agreements developed by the United Nations, as well as relevant General Assembly Resolutions and ITU agreements. For example, it would be helpful if the terms of the 1979 Moon Agreement were reviewed to ascertain whether its reference to celestial bodies includes Mars. Further, clarification of the inconsistent ITU criteria relating to the efficient, economical, and equitable use of the geostationary orbit and radio-frequency spectrum would be useful.[12]

Despite the recent inability of the Committee on the Peaceful Uses of Outer Space to obtain consensus on numerous subjects, the Committee still provides an opportunity to arrive at useful formal agreements. The United Nations Secretary-General has identified areas requiring attention: remote sensing, communications, meteorology, basic space science, and use of space technology for land, maritime, and aeronautical mobile services, among others.[13] United Nations reports also emphasize the role of space technology in managing the resources of the Earth and its environment. These reports signal the role of the United Nations specialized agencies and their potential for ensuring the removal of non-functioning space objects from orbit and for establishing an integrated "global ozone observing system . . . under the aegis of WMO and UNEP."[14]

The development of an aerospace plane offers a potential for the application of law to hybrid air/space activities. The use of nuclear energy in space remains to be regulated, as does the collection and return to Earth of solar energy. A legal regime for space transportation must also be considered, and attention must be given to detailed procedures for the resolution of disputes over space activities.

Another issue under the heading of unfinished business is that of identifying the organizational framework that will work best in dealing with outer space issues: whether one universal entity or numerous special-function bodies will be most efficient and reliable. Although there is an abundance of proposals for new institutions, such as an international satellite monitoring agency, the basic issue remains whether there should be new entities, whether existing organizations can be called upon to provide new services, or whether there is really any need for organizational enhancement.

Substantial efforts on the part of states have produced workable bodies of municipal law, particularly in the countries with space capabilities. Subjects such as taxation, insurance, servicing satellites in orbit, materials processing, intellectual property, and the powers and duties of spacecraft commanders have been addressed.[15] Much administrative law has emerged relating to applications for governmental permits and other benefits by private firms. Municipal space law in the developing countries has ranged from minimal to non-existent. Yet the number of countries ratifying the United Nations and ITU international agreements is impressive. Many have not, however, enacted implementing national legislation. As these countries become more directly involved in space activities, there will be a need for them to take into account their international commitments and to adopt appropriate national legislation.

The space law of the future will not be produced in a vacuum. The political process, with all of its value laden components, will provide guidance and direction. From the prescriptive point of view the case has already been made for the maximization of opportunities to engage in space activities. Future negotiations will determine the extent to which sharing of benefits can take place.

CONCLUSION

In retrospect, it can be seen that space law, like all law, is evolutionary in nature. From primitive beginnings it has developed very quickly at the United Nations to a classical stage with a suitable body of fundamental principles. The ITU has also provided principles and more detailed rules. The principles and rules have been clarified through classification, analysis, and synthesis. These efforts will continue.

Political choices as to the substance and process of space law impose ineluctable constraints on its future development. The central principle concerning common resources in space is that there should be a free and equal opportunity to engage in their exploration, use, and exploitation. This principle should continue to focus on the concept of sharing for the benefit of humankind.

In this context, "sharing" has been interpreted to mean the sharing of tangible, and hence material, benefits. An example is the claim of states to have exclusive geostationary orbit and radio-frequency allotments for communication satellites. These contests, which spilled over into United Nations negotiations, have tended to impose constraints on the development of consensus on other United Nations topics. However, sharing must also include a broad and general dissemination of the knowledge and the benefits available to humankind through better communications, social services, health conditions, and education.

Limitations were also imposed on past developments by the effects of the cold war, which have now been substantially dissipated. The future should allow for progress in the development of legal principles and rules relating to activities which will benefit all humankind.

All of humankind has a vital interest in sharing the benefits of a natural environment free of pollution, contamination, debris, and other hazardous materials. It may be anticipated that much new law will be developed to deal effectively with these matters and that existing clouds of ambiguity can be dispelled. Constantly expanding science and technology coupled with an increasing social awareness of the need for the enhancement of human values will undoubtedly give momentum and direction to a continually and progressively developing space law.

While future law relating to space will not experience unbroken development, it is possible to conclude that space law will continue to address the changing needs of a global society. Positive achievements lie ahead.

NOTES

1. Treaty on Principles Governing the Activities of States in the Exploration and Use of Outer Space, Including the Moon and Other Celestial Bodies, Done Jan. 27, 1967, 18 U.S.T 2410, T.I.A.S. No. 6347, 610 U.N.T.S. 205.

2. In 1958, the statute creating NASA provided: "It is the policy of the United States that space should be devoted to peaceful purposes for the benefit of mankind." Pub. L. No. 85-568, 72 Stat. 426, 42 U.S.C. Sec. 102(a).

3. It must be acknowledged that the Outer Space Treaty did not in all respects conform to the language of the Preamble.

4. A. Pardo and C. Q. Christol, "The Common Interest: Tension between the Whole and the Parts," in R. St.J. Macdonald and D. M. Johnston (eds.), *The Structure and Process of International Law: Essays in Legal Philosophy, Doctrine and Theory*, The Hague, M. Nijhoff, 1983, p. 643.

5. In recent years the Committee on the Peaceful Uses of Outer Space (COPUOS) has not been able to reach agreement on long-standing agenda items. See *Report of the Legal Subcommittee on the Work of its Twenty-Ninth Session* (April 2-20, 1989), U.N. Doc. A/AC.105/457 (May 2, 1990).

6. The United Nations General Assembly in Resolution 44/46 gave support. N. Jasentuliyana, "The UN and Space: 1990 Review," *Space Policy*, Vol. 6, November 1990, p. 349.

7. The technical aspects of fixing a boundary have been linked to the use of the geostationary orbital position. Opposing political approaches, particularly regarding the distribution of orbital positions, have prevented a resolution of both issues.

8. A. D. Webber, "Extraterrestrial Law on the Final Frontier: A Regime to Govern the Development of Celestial Body Resources," *Georgia Law Journal*, Vol. 71, 1983, p. 1,427. See also H. DeSaussure, "The Unification and Development of Transnational Space Law," in *Proceedings of the 31st Colloquium on the Law of Outer Space*, Washington, AIAA, 1989, p. 253.

9. The same prohibitions are to be found in Article 11.2 of the 1979 Moon Treaty. Agreement Governing the Activities of States on the Moon and Other Celestial Bodies, U.N.G.A. Res. 34/68, 34 U.N. GAOR Supp. (No. 46) at 77, U.N. Doc. A/34/46 (1979).

10. Some space projects will exceed the funding capabilities of any single country. A cooperative undertaking can result in cost sharing and in the use of unique national capabilities.

11. Sir R. Jennings, "Customary Law and General Principles of Law as Sources of Space Law," in K.-H. Böckstiegel (ed.), *Environmental Aspects of Activities in Outer Space*, Cologne, Carl Heymanns Verlag, 1990, p.149; M. S. Williams, "Customary International Law and General Principles of Law," *id.*, p. 153; J. A. Frowein, "Customary International Law and General Principles Concerning Environmental Protection in Outer Space," *id.*, p. 163; G. M. Danilenko, "Space Activities and Customary Law of Environmental Protection," *id.*, p. 169; D. Rauschning, "Customary International Law in General Principles of International Law Concerning the Protection of Outer Space from Pollution," *id.*, p. 181; M. Lachs, "Customary International Law and General Principles of Law," *id.*, p. 187.

12. C. Q. Christol, "Equity and International Space Law," in *Proceedings of the 33rd Colloquium on the Law of Outer Space*, Washington, AIAA, 1991. See also "Equity in International Law," in *Proceedings of the American Society of International Law*, New York, Oceana, 1990, pp. 277-291.

13. U.N. Doc. A/AC.105/444 (October 8, 1989).

14. U.N. Doc. A/AC.105/451 (January 19, 1990), p. 16, .

15. L. Dennis Ahearn, "Legal Aspects of Operating a Commercial Business on the Space Station," *Space Commerce*, Vol. 1, 1990, p. 55.

18

Creating Space Law

Eilene Galloway

New chapters in civilization have always been brought about by bursts of energy. Our energy comes from rocket fuel and the psychological force of mankind's upward surge toward expanding knowledge of the universe. Our task is to match the physical order of the planets with a legal order to ensure that outer space is used for peaceful purposes for the benefit of mankind.

ON THE BEGINNING OF THE SPACE AGE

The dramatic beginning of the space age immediately caused Congress to use its existing committee structure to study the missile/satellite situation in the United States. Special committees then were created in the Senate and House to decide the nation's space policy and program for future development. Results of these Congressional deliberations were seen in the passage of the National Aeronautics and Space Act of 1958, which declared that "it is the policy of the United States that activities in space should be devoted to peaceful purposes for the benefit of mankind"; created a new executive agency, NASA; divided space activities between this agency and the Department of Defense; provided for coordination among all government agencies with space and space-related programs; created the Space Council; and adopted international cooperation for peaceful purposes as a basic policy. Permanent standing committees were established in the House and Senate to ensure U.S. leadership and a high priority for developing space science and technology.[1]

Editor's note:

With the exception of the first paragraph, which was written for this volume, this chapter consists of extracts from the writings of Dr. Galloway over the course of her work on space law from 1957 to 1991. The notes indicate the sources of the extracts.

A remarkable assemblage of factors, already in existence in 1957, could be organized and channeled toward goals for future success in conducting outer space activities. First, the International Geophysical Year (IGY) was in progress. Worldwide studies of man's environment—the earth, oceans, atmosphere, and outer space—were being made by the international scientific community between July 1, 1957, and December 31, 1958. . . . Second, the United States had an industrial base in operation by aviation firms with experienced personnel and resources ready to expand and become the aerospace industry. Third, there was a government institution already engaged in research and development on aerospace problems—the National Advisory Committee on Aeronautics—which could be expanded. Fourth, the motivation for a U.S. space program was compelling. We wanted to preserve outer space for peaceful purposes and prevent warfare from being directed to the Earth. The space age did not begin with hostility but with benign intentions and consequences. Furthermore, the peaceful applications of space technology were quickly made known by scientists and engineers so that planning by government could be directed toward arrangements designed to produce benefits. Fifth, effective political leadership arose as suddenly as a rocket to undertake responsibility for organizing the government for the conduct of space activities. Sixth, there was harmony between the Executive and Legislative branches of the government as well as between the Senate and the House of Representatives concerning the necessity for effective action to achieve a leading U.S. space program.[2]

Coordination was identified as the main organizational problem. The division of responsibility and authority between agencies which have separate but similar programs simultaneously operating with joint activities creates the need for coordination. This problem requires overall direction by the President in accordance with advice from the Space Council, which represents the major interests which need to be considered in achieving a total U.S. space program.[3]

ON EARLY INSTITUTIONAL DEVELOPMENT

That the talents of lawyers and scientists should be brought to bear simultaneously upon the problems of outer space was recognized by the United Nations in its first organized approach to this subject. . . . The foresight revealed in the studies on space law which were published during the decade prior to the launching of the first Earth satellite meant that future courses of action could be charted with much greater assurance than would otherwise have been possible. Close coordination between scientists and lawyers enabled the working committees of the United Nations to estimate the probable consequences of successful space exploration for mankind as a whole. . . . Laws, treaties, and conventions could restrict or encourage space projects. Unregulated activities could ultimately defeat their own ends in vital segments of space activities, e.g., in the use of radio frequencies for obtaining satellite data. The protection of the common interest of mankind in space activities will require continuous and harmonious working relationships between the professions of science and law. . . . On December 3, 1958, the General Assembly of the United Nations passed a resolution establishing the Ad Hoc Committee on the Peaceful Uses of Outer Space. [Among the subjects designated for study were] future organizational arrangements to facilitate international cooperation and the nature of legal problems which may arise in the carrying out of programs to explore outer space. . . . The task of determining the most appropriate type of international organization for handling outer space problems is similar to that of a nation faced with the necessity of organizing its own internal resources for exploration. The main requirement in both cases is that of coordinating existing facilities, resources, and personnel before adding whatever elements may be lacking in order to achieve specific space objectives. Coordination is the key organizational problem because space exploration depends upon the successful combination of scientific and engineering disciplines, which were organized in various patterns within nations and on an international scale long before the advent of the space age. . . . A detailed study of any one of these organizations reveals that the problems relating to the exploration of outer space (and to its use for peaceful purposes only) are integral parts of programs which include many other factors. Outer space has simply been added as a new environment into which existing and projected human activities are being extended. . . . Six problems were listed by the Legal Committee as being susceptible of priority treatment: that the satellite programs of the International Geophysical Year were based upon the premise that nations had permission to launch such vehicles even though they traversed an orbit above national boundary lines . . . the problem of liability for injury or damage . . . the allocation of radio frequencies to space vehicles . . . avoidance of interference between space vehicles . . . re-entry and landing of space vehicles . . . identification and registration of space vehicles and aircraft. . . . Official definitions of airspace and outer space were deemed premature at this time, and the Committee believed that the problems to which it had given highest priority did not depend for their solution on a legal distinction between these two areas in the space environment. It was suggested, however, that one approach to the problem would be to establish the limits of airspace and outer space within a practicable range.[4]

Harmony between the objectives and organization of national and international space programs is vital for successful coordination. . . . International cooperation rather than international control is now called for in the resolution establishing the United Nations Committee on the Peaceful Uses of Outer Space. There is no official suggestion for a supernational agency to control or conduct the space programs of nation-states. Nor is there any official development toward an outer space organization comparable to the

International Atomic Energy Agency. The possibility of such developments might be studied by individual lawyers intent upon exploring the pros and cons of different types of organizational arrangement. In the absence of a centralized world authority over space activities, we may expect cooperation between nations to be achieved by the normal method of bilateral and multilateral treaties and agreements. The specialized agencies of the United Nations and the organizations established by the international scientific community will also be used for the necessary coordination of space activities. From this practice, functional controls may be expected to develop over such areas as weather prediction, the allocation of radio frequencies, and navigation. Many specialized agencies already have rules and regulations which may apply in some degree to space activities. The problem created for international law is how to coordinate the administrative regulations of various agencies concerned with specific functions of space exploration. . . . The state of the art of science and technology in space exploration will determine, in many cases, what controls are feasible and practicable. What can and cannot be done technologically may determine what can and cannot be done legally. But it is also possible that the application of certain historic legal concepts to space activities might preclude courses of action which are technologically possible.[5]

ON THE UNIQUE CHARACTERISTICS OF OUTER SPACE

The unique characteristics of outer space and its uses include the following:

1. Orbiting space objects circle the Earth so quickly that the technology naturally emphasizes the whole globe rather than national divisions governed by terrestrial boundary lines. For this reason space technology contributes toward international concepts and, for some purposes, toward regional groupings of nations.

2. International tracking of satellites is required and has increased cooperation among nations.

3. Identification and monitoring of objects in orbit are necessary for scientific and technical reasons, a requirement that led nations to register their space flights. Such registration became the practice even before the Convention on Registration of Space Objects went into force.

4. Satellite use of the radio spectrum and the geostationary orbit require and elicit international cooperation in order to prevent harmful interference and chaos in communications. These are technical facts which led the International Telecommunication Union (ITU) to develop part of the body of space law.

5. Space programs are extremely expensive, involving expenditures by governments which have undertaken treaty obligations to authorize and continuously supervise both governmental and non-governmental space

activities. Even in the absence of treaty obligations, space activities involve safety and health hazards which would dictate government regulation adjusted to the operation of specific space projects and not simply copied from practices used for other environments.

6. The manufacture, launching, and operation of spacecraft for communications, weather prediction, evaluation of agriculture and forestry, improvements in navigation, and management of water resources, all require teams of specifically trained experts.
7. New national and international institutions had to be created to meet the unusual requirements for exploration and uses of outer space.
8. Outer space was a new area "unscarred by conflict," and it was possible to formulate and adopt partial arms control provisions in Article 4 of the 1967 Treaty on Outer Space, including some prohibitions that have not yet been attainable for land, sea, and air.
9. For these reasons legal guidelines for the conduct of space activities have been formulated with due regard for the distinctive features of this new frontier, emphasizing international cooperation and the protection of peaceful activities from potentially harmful interference.[6]

ON THE NATURE OF SPACE LAW

Space law has four characteristics: it is national and international and applies both to outer space as a geographic area and to functions performed in that area. Since the space environment is being used to improve many functions required on Earth, it follows that law to regulate these activities applies to the Earth. In fact, the Earth is the location for the manufacture, employment, funding, analysis, and use of data and information collected from outer space; the legal problems that arise are the result of the impact upon society of using and exploring this fourth environment which we have added to land, sea, and air.[7]

Perspectives on the composition of space law can depend upon (1) analysis in terms of general guiding principles for perceived problems; and also (2) analysis of requirements for solving specific problems. Each problem is likely to require a different combination of factors for its solution, and a broad scanning of available research sources is needed to guarantee the best results. Both viewpoints depend upon a thorough knowledge of space science and technology, and both are valuable as a basis for the development of space law. If a definition of space law is based upon only one of these perspectives —general or specific—it will be limited in providing a problem-solver with total knowledge of all the resources available for his task. Proposals based primarily on ideological concepts with no regard for conditions that must be observed in operating space hardware for effective results are not realistic.

Space law is international and national and covers functions and areas. In relevant circumstances the areas may include the Earth, airspace, and outer space. We now face the necessity of registering all national space laws and making them compatible with international space law. Furthermore, when there are several space and space-related laws within a nation, care should be taken to ensure that they are internally consistent as well as compatible with fundamental space policies.[8]

ON THE DEVELOPMENT OF SPACE LAW

There is a tendency to propose new treaties for each space application, although the activity may adequately come under existing national arrangements and treaties. Considering the fact that each space treaty has a different membership of ratifying nations, it is obvious that too many treaties with differing rosters can create difficulties. As time goes on, there will be a question of how many treaties are required to solve individual problems. Partial approaches could result in inconsistencies which could not later be codified into an harmonious system of space law. The objective should be to strive, not so much for the maximum number of treaties as for the maximum number of States Parties to the total structure of space law created to ensure the most rewarding use and exploration of outer space.[9]

ON DEFINITIONS

One of the difficulties in achieving international agreement on arms controls is the lack of legal definitions concerning elements and factors that are to be regulated. For purposes of discussion, the following definitions are proposed and accompanied with brief explanations.

Outer Space. Outer space begins where space objects can orbit the Earth and extends to infinity. Sovereign airspace does not automatically extend to the point where outer space begins because there is a changing and variable distance between the altitude that can be reached by aircraft and the lowest level at which space objects can orbit the Earth. The definition of airspace must be considered separately and simultaneously in relation both to outer space and to Earth-prevailing aviation laws. All elements of the problem and their probable interactions must be identified initially and worked out in relation to each other. The International Civil Aviation Organization, in the context of intergovernmental relations, is the appropriate body to determine any changes in the operational and legal definitions of airspace. The potential for conflicts among nations can be foreseen if space activities were to be declared illegal below a specific, arbitrary altitude, particularly in cases of accident and unintended flight paths; furthermore, conflicts could develop between laws and regulations already successfully used for such functions as communications, meteorology, and navigation if an artificial boundary line is super-imposed on existing legal arrangements. The concept of providing for both a defined area and defined activities, now embodied in the space treaties, must be elaborated with realistic regard for operational efficiency within general guiding principles.

Military. The term "military" as used in outer space treaties refers to national defense establishments, their component parts including personnel, and is not synonymous with hostile, warlike, and aggressively destructive actions. The functions assigned to such institutions should be the focus of attention in extending prohibitions on warlike activities while recognizing the sovereign right of national defense and emphasizing constructive activities such as those already provided for in the 1967 Treaty on Outer Space and the ABM Treaty, which allows the use of national technical means to verify arms control agreements.

Weapon. For the purposes of this space treaty, a weapon is any device which is capable of releasing a destructive force of any kind in a controlled or uncontrolled manner and which has a group of characteristics that are appropriate for use for warlike purposes. (Adapted from Article 5, Treaty of Tlatelolco, February 12, 1967.)

Weapons of Mass Destruction. The United Nations definition of August 12, 1948 can be used in formulating and interpreting treaties on this subject. The Commission for Conventional Armaments advised the UN Security Council:

1. That it considers that all armaments and armed forces, except atomic weapons and weapons of mass destruction, fall within its jurisdiction and that weapons of mass destruction should be defined to include atomic explosive weapons, radioactive material weapons, lethal chemical and biological weapons and any weapons developed in the future which have characteristics comparable in destructive effect to those of the atomic bomb or other weapons mentioned above.
2. That it proposes to proceed with its work on the basis of the above definition.

Furthermore, we could add that mass destruction is large-scale destruction of life or property or both in any environment, including the Earth, sea, airspace, and outer space.

Less than Mass Destruction. Less than mass destruction refers to all types of destruction that are not large-scale, including damage caused by non-nuclear and other kinds of conventional methods for causing damage.

Arms Control Objectives. Arms control objectives for the outer space environment require the elimination of harmful interference, the limitation of weapons and any kind of devices intentionally constructed to inflict damage in outer space, from outer space to the Earth, and from the Earth into outer space. The objective is to ban all hazards to peaceful space uses and applications.

Arms Race. The term "arms race" as applied to outer space involves the increased manufacture and deployment of devices designated to bring about harmful interference with space activities. Stopping an arms race between two or more nations is a part of arms control, which is a much broader subject for analysis and attention. A moratorium on an arms race is a significant step toward arms control, but such an agreement would require extension to encompass all nations that might otherwise seek to produce destructive means of harmful interference.

Harmful Interference. Harmful interference or potentially harmful interference as used in space treaties means any type of damaging interruption or destruction of beneficial space activities and is not confined to deliberately hostile actions by military establishments. Harmful interference is an all-inclusive term which can be used to cover any kind of damaging or destructive activity. It is important to realize that the space environment can be rendered unusable for all purposes by various kinds of scientific and technological factors. Damage can be caused by relatively inexpensive means that are not ordinarily considered as "weapons," and some types of damage can be irreversible.

Peaceful Purposes. Peaceful purposes are those incorporated into plans and designs for space projects and whose uses are beneficial and/or not estimated to be harmful. Verification of the purposes can be achieved by expanding the provisions of the Convention on the Registration of Objects Launched into Outer Space, which went into force on September 15, 1976. If additional peace controls can achieve international agreement, then the next step would be a monitoring agency with technical operations outside the United Nations, possibly according to the INMARSAT model, to ensure that the planned peaceful purposes are respected. Because of the cost of such an agency, it should be given international functions in addition to those concerned with arms control; the agency should be responsible for monitoring all types of potentially harmful damage to the space environment.

Peaceful Uses. Peaceful uses are space applications such as those developed during the past 27 years, including worldwide use of satellites for communications, meteorology, navigation, geology, etc. Since some of these satellite systems are launched and operated by national military establishments which combine military and civilian uses, while others have separate but cooperative organizations, it is necessary to work out an extension of the legal pattern of permissions and prohibitions for which the foundation has already been laid in space treaties. It is important to note that the 1967 Treaty on Outer Space refers to exploration "and use" of outer space in its title, and while "purposes" are referred to in the text, the emphasis is on "peaceful uses."

Militarization of Outer Space. This term should be examined for its implications because it is helpful only up to a certain point in analysis and thereafter prevents the formulation of constructive steps that might be taken in effecting both peace and arms controls because it does not define the problems that need solution. The term is helpful in alerting people quickly to the dangers of using outer space for war, but it depends upon an assumption that anything that can be termed "military" is inevitably and completely hostile and warlike. This can lead to the conclusion that national military establishments should be prohibited from using space science and technology in improving functions performed for national defense, a conclusion that is impracticable because sovereign states have always used whatever level of science and technology is available for national defense and can be expected to continue to do so. The problem is made to seem even more frightening by counting the number of spacecraft launched by military establishments without regard to functions such as verifying arms control agreements, safety, rescue missions, warning of natural disasters, etc.

We cannot get to the bottom of this situation for legal purposes by simply assuming that all spacecraft launched by military agencies are warlike. We need more than the name of the organization that launches spacecraft—our thinking cannot stop at that point. One way would be to have nations report more information on the purposes and uses of space objects than is now provided for in the Convention on the Registration of Objects Launched into Outer Space.[10]

ON INTEGRATING SPACE LAW WITH SCIENCE AND TECHNOLOGY

Both science and law must start with an evaluation of existing facts and with assumptions concerning the foreseeable future. It is a large order to consolidate theory and practice in the new dimension created by space exploration, but unless we start with a total objective and a concept of how it is to be pursued, our interplanetary thinking will be earthbound by tradition and precedent at a time when creative predictions should enable us to keep international law in pace with scientific achievement. . . . The revolution in space science and technology imposes an obligation on the scientific community to keep the legal profession informed of the latest developments. National and international lawyers have the matching responsibility of absorbing new facts into the framework of social order. . . . The first launching of an artificial satellite did not catch the legal profession unawares. For a good many years, outstanding international lawyers contributed their thinking to the legal problems which would be likely to arise once man proved successful in exploring space beyond the Earth. . . . While the nature of the task involved in formulation of space law has been clarified, the organization of effort in connection with a planned program is still in the making. The question is how best to organize the existing expertness of individuals, professional associations, and official institutions so that their activities cohere around stated objectives. . . . The revolution in space science and technology is rapid, and the danger is that some of its applications will get beyond control. The political, military, legal, and social problems which will be created by space exploration require searching analysis in terms of promoting the general welfare. . . . If man is to match the order of the universe, his thought must be whole in its dimensions.[11]

ON MULTIDISCIPLINARY SPACE RESEARCH

Whereas in years past all sciences tended to develop as separate disciplines, which was natural as each was determining the parameters of its field, in recent times emphasis is on integrating bodies of knowledge relevant to coping with a specific problem. The Renaissance man, who could think horizontally across the whole spectrum of known facts, was no longer possible, but the need was evident for that kind of evaluation as contrasted to vertical thinking narrowly within one discipline that could not encompass a totality of approach. The specialist and the generalist must be brought into balance. . . .

Methods should be sought to improve the ability to devise constructive guidelines for conducting space activities. Several methods could be adopted: (1) each of the disciplines required for space projects could be defined and biographical data collected for specialists who have demonstrated capacities for this work; (2) similar information could be compiled for those who are qualified for management and administration of a large space program; (3) when a project is first proposed it should be analyzed to determine the disciplines required for its success; (4) each discipline should be given a weight corresponding to its degree of influence in contributing to the desired results; (5) an estimate should be made of the interaction between the various elements; (6) on the basis of this information, a calculation should be made of the probabilities of creating additional problems while the project is in operation or after completion. Instead of unnecessary problems being thrust upon society, forethought should enable us more nearly to achieve only those results deemed beneficial.[12]

ON CONSENSUS DECISION-MAKING IN THE UNITED NATIONS

On March 19, 1962, the Chairman of the United Nations Committee on the Peaceful Uses of Outer Space announced that "The Committee and its subcommittees [would] conduct the Committee's work in such a way that the Committee will be able to reach agreement on its work without need for voting." It is evident that consensus is a highly desirable way of achieving international accord because (1) the process of seeking agreement continues with patience and is not cut off suddenly by a vote which may defeat what might have come to fruition had more time been taken with the give-and-take process of consensus; (2) the situation may be such that a majority vote could not result in the adoption of a course of action, particularly if implementation of the decision, in terms of funding, personnel, and technological expertise, depended upon nations which had voted against the measures; and (3) group solidarity in decision-making ensures maximum compliance in establishing and maintaining an activity of general benefit. There is also a positive psychological effect when members of a group feel together with sympathy for differing viewpoints, motivated by a desire to bring about harmony in their collective judgement. If a member has not objected, a proposal can be adopted but this unspoken consent should not be interpreted as negativism; there is a positive willingness to settle the issue in question. . . . The difference between consensus and unanimous voting lies in the process used to achieve the end result; consensus is achieved without voting, whereas voting is required for a unanimous record. The use of consensus in the United Nations negotiation of texts of space treaties did not result in adoption of the least common denominator on which agreement could be reached; that is, on insignificant matters of low-level concern. Instead, we find that the most important issues have been decided and made a part of international law. The outstanding results of the agreements reached by consensus contradict those who alleged that this type of unanimous support could only be achieved on minor points. . . . Between 1967 and 1979 five space treaties have come into force, and in each case the consensus method was used. . . . [There are a number of reasons for the success of this consensus decision-making, among them that] the chairman must be sensitive to the group psychology in sensing when a subject is ripe for agreement, feeling that there is not likely to be an objection, and at exactly the right moment being able to say "if there is no objection, it is so decided." The chairman must not be dictatorial in forcing his own position on the group but must gain the respect of all members in recognizing his objectivity in perceiving varying viewpoints. The Committee on the Peaceful Uses of Outer Space has been outstandingly successful in the chairmen who have presided over the full Committee, the Legal Subcommittee, and the Scientific and Technical Subcommittee. Much of the successful use of the consensus procedure is due to the outstanding abilities of the distinguished chairmen.[13]

ON THE DEFINITION OF OUTER SPACE

At the beginning of the space age, some scholars thought that a treaty on general guiding principles for space activities could not be concluded without an exact definition of where airspace ends and outer space begins. The difficulty with such a definition is that technology develops so rapidly in aeronautics and astronautics that aircraft are flying higher while spacecraft are orbiting closer to the Earth. . . . The way the 1967 Treaty on Outer Space solved this problem is another illustration of the influence of technology in shaping a legal principle. Instead of waiting for boundary agreements (which are still being debated), the aerospace concept of engineering became the controlling assumption. Space vehicles are designed to fly through airspace into outer space and may come back into airspace and land on the Earth. Aerospace is a continuum that engineers do not divide into restrictive horizontal zones. The Treaty provides that the nation launching an object into outer space retains jurisdiction and control while the vehicle is in outer space, or on a celestial body, or upon its return to Earth. Furthermore, each ratifying nation has agreed to be internationally liable for damages caused "in airspace or in outer space, including the moon and other celestial bodies." The function of the spacecraft, rather than the space in which it flies, is often the deciding factor in treaty provisions that seek to ensure the use of outer space for peaceful purposes.[14]

An analysis of space treaty provisions reveals that both area and functional concepts have been used in principles formulated to guide space activities. This is not an either/or proposition because planning for space activities requires defining both the area and the functions to be performed therein. A distinction should be made between general guiding principles and regulations required for operational success. The case-by-case method used thus far should be continued in planning specific functions, which are also to come under general principles. An arbitrary boundary marking the beginning of outer space is only half the problem, and the question of where airspace ends must be simultaneously studied. Uses of the geostationary orbit involve many issues which cannot be decided by combining them with a proposal for delimitation of outer space and outer space activities. Uses of this orbit are the responsibility of the International Telecommunication Union. . . . Use of the geostationary orbit is an international problem involving a number of issues whose settlement affects worldwide communications as well as other uses. To attempt to deal with only one aspect, such as removing recognition of the geostationary orbit from outer space as a whole, could not result in solutions of the total number of issues involved. Usually when an activity is scientific and technical, adherence to the imperatives for operational success invokes compliance by all participants. In fact, insofar as scientific and technological facts determine what is and what is not feasible, the subsequent planning for institutions, personnel, funding, and regulations will fall into place more easily. A solution based on an abstract philosophical principle could turn out to be unnecessarily restrictive or meaningless. . . . The term "delimitation of space activities" is fraught with danger signals. An artificial boundary line where the end of airspace completely matched the beginning of outer space could be used to declare certain space activities illegal. A spacecraft could be legal in outer space and illegal in airspace. This would at once conflict with some of the space law provisions already in force.[15]

ON DIRECT TELEVISION BROADCASTING BY SATELLITE

An evaluation in 1977 of negotiations on direct television broadcast satellites by the Legal Subcommittee of the United Nations Committee on the Peaceful Uses of Outer Space led the author to the conclusion that some dissatisfaction has been expressed because agreement on draft principles is slow in formation, but the development of a consensus can hardly be expected to be rapid in a field which requires an understanding of scientific and technological knowledge, and its integration with economic, cultural, political, and legal factors. A solid foundation for international space law is laid by using the consensus method, which ensures compliance with agreed provisions. Voting on an issue such as free flow of information and ideas versus state control and censorship of programs could not be expected to result in compliance. Discussion and negotiation are required. Whether the method is "slow" or "rapid" may be a psychological perception, as many would conclude that the achievement of four space treaties now in force in a period of nine years (1967-1976) is indeed "rapid." Even a text with square brackets indicating disagreement is valuable because it identifies the exact areas where more negotiation and clarification are required before a common ground can be reached. Sometimes the basis for agreement can be supplied by some factor furnished by space science and technology.[16]

ON SATELLITE REMOTE SENSING

It is evident that remote sensing of the Earth by satellites produces information which is being used to assist in the solution of many problems, particularly in protection of the global environment and better management of resources. . . . Unlike some of the other space applications, however, notably communications and meteorology, remote sensing technology has advanced ahead of institutional arrangements for its management. Discussion of organizational questions is often not based upon knowledge of the technology but governed by assumptions arising from perceptions of past historical experience. The debates often emphasize fears concerning non-renewable resources and do not take into account the benefits from application of remote sensing technology to these as well as to renewable resources. In fact, obstacles to international agreement often arise because there are wide differences in assumptions concerning the meaning of "natural resources." To some the term means only "minerals," while to others "natural resources" include human beings and annual agricultural crops. It will be difficult, if not impossible, to decide upon institutions, national or international, until there is agreement on the area of jurisdiction for which a proposed institution is responsible.[17]

ON SETTLEMENT OF SPACE LAW DISPUTES

Provision for the settlement of space law disputes is not well developed in space treaties as compared to bilateral and multilateral agreements on specific functions. Remarkable foresight has been exercised by the legal profession, however, in identifying potential problem areas and nipping them in the bud by numerous provisions in space treaties, a process which should be continued in the future.

The legal profession can learn a great deal about agreements to accomplish specific purposes by studying those made by scientists and engineers engaged in designing and using spacecraft for designated missions. We can depend upon the assumption that scientists and engineers are motivated by a desire to have their projects operate successfully.

Although space treaties provide for their amendment, it is unlikely and impracticable to open up reconsideration for the purpose of adding more stringent provisions for the settlement of space law disputes; unlikely because serious cases calling for this effort are not forcing the issue; impracticable because there are literally hundreds of bilateral and multilateral space projects, each of which is already subject to its own guidelines for preventing conflicts and for dispelling controversies.

There is no one best method for settling space law disputes; a choice can be made among several methods according to its relevance to particular disputes. . . . In other words, a neat jurisdictional line cannot be drawn around the subject matter with which space law disputes might be concerned. . . .

Arbitration has been chosen in some agreements, and whether or not decisions are binding or only recommendatory depends upon the extent to which the dispute is about a scientific and technical matter. States are traditionally reluctant to refer issues to courts for adjudication. Issues arising in connection with functioning engineering space enterprises are more adaptable to binding arbitration than those with political and economic overtones because nations do not want any disruption in satellite services. . . .

Assumptions must be examined so that reactions of decisionmakers do not result from their attitudes toward segments of space applications. As space activities have become more specialized, we are in danger of losing generalists who can think across the jurisdictional lines of disciplines.

Whenever space law is being formulated in the future, the participants should be aware, among other matters, of the different kinds of disputes that might arise and the various methods developed in international law to deal with them. They should also have available the texts of bilateral and multilateral agreements on space projects and missions. Models could be compiled to assist those who are drafting the texts of treaty provisions.[18]

ON PROTECTING THE SPACE ENVIRONMENT

Environmental aspects may be identified as one of the elements in the total endeavor (for protection), but should not be taken out of context from the Moon Agreement as a whole. Some legal provisions are worded specifically to apply to environmental matters, but many others of a general nature might become applicable in certain circumstances. This is true of measures that can be used for any type of problem, for example, consultation between parties, arbitration, assistance, and rescue in emergency situations caused by hazardous conditions. It is recommended that a legal working group be established as part of an existing international institution to track relevant information on environmental protection, taking the following steps (among others): (1) formulate a definition of the total problem, encompassing all its parts so that completion of any future negotiations will result in a contribution to space law in harmony with the provisions of the 1967 Outer Space Treaty; and (2) distinguish between the different kinds of harmful and damaging effects upon the environments of the Earth, outer space, and all celestial bodies. Solutions are likely to differ for each category of harms. Shielding a spacecraft so it will not contaminate the Moon, and ensuring that returning space materials do not contaminate the Earth, is more manageable and less expensive than the problems of space debris. Orbiting debris in space is a technical problem requiring scientific and engineering solutions realistically related to economic and political factors. Although the method of notifying the United Nations Secretary-General of space debris dangers to beneficial functions is desirable, it is not adequate for solving various environmental problems.[19]

ON SPACE STATIONS

The planned Space Station has unique characteristics which distinguish it from past international space programs, and any multilateral agreement for its establishment must take into account these differences as well as existing applicable space law. To attain continuous operational efficiency, it will be necessary to make management adjustments to an unusual combination of factors: scientific research and commercial applications; governmental and non-governmental operational activities, national and international concerns with problems of cooperation and competition; centralization and decentralization in handling problems of jurisdiction and control; criteria for selecting and managing personnel and missions; conditions for equitable access by other nations; existing commitments to international law and agreements on definitions for the future; adjustment to other relevant international organizations, including the United Nations; and relating national law to international cooperation, especially in situations involving taxation, contracts, procurement, liability for damage, and settlement of disputes.

Although a fairly consistent and harmonious foundation of international space law and practice for peaceful purposes has been created and complied with during the first quarter century of the space age, it will be more difficult to maintain this situation in the future unless international agreement is reached on definitions which are universally understood. As time goes on space applications will increase and diversify, and more people will enter these activities with the risk of not knowing basic concepts embodied in the foundation of law and experience. Even now there is need for clarifying definitions so that the same words do not have different meanings and thus create difficulties unnecessarily.[20]

ON THE MOON AND MARS MISSIONS

The Moon Agreement (1984) has been ratified by only seven nations, and there are controversial provisions concerning the common heritage of mankind and the nature of a proposed international regime. A body of space law already exists for the Moon and Mars in consensus-formulated treaties with wide support for those entering into force in 1967, 1968, 1973, and 1976. . . . We now have a problem because the Moon Agreement, whose provisions were finalized in 1979, is not completely in alignment with projected operational scientific and technical estimates. And since its provisions would apply to Mars, as one of the "other celestial bodies," and also to asteroids, "except in so far as specific legal norms enter into force" for them, the question arises of whether conditions relating to Mars are so different from the Moon that a separate Mars treaty is needed; and the same question can be raised about asteroids and uses of their natural resources. . . . This treaty is scheduled for review by the United Nations General Assembly in 1994. In addition, we can anticipate that preliminary research and development will take at least several decades, and it is unlikely that during that time national programs will be developed by states that are not parties to the Moon Agreement. Such programs could be for functions such as telecommunications or using the Moon as a location for solar power to be used on Earth; it is therefore necessary to find out the total list of practicable functions that can be foreseen. This raises the question of whether an international regime should manage all activities on the Moon as a geographic area or select the management of natural resources as the primary function to apply to the Moon, Mars, asteroids, and other celestial bodies.

It is recommended that one academic institution or research organization should assume responsibility as a center for identifying and integrating all multidisciplinary elements involved in Moon/Mars and comparable exploration ventures. Research and development will take place over an extended period of time during which technology and personnel can be expected to change. We need to establish an institutional memory bank to assist those who will continue space exploration into the next century.[21]

ON SOLAR POWER SATELLITES (SPS)

"The Legal and Regulatory Framework for Solar Power Satellites" was analyzed in 1991: planning for an SPS institutional structure, its management and regulation, has not kept pace with engineering studies that have been in progress for some years. A Preparatory Commission should be created with responsibility for planning an organization designed to manage the uses of solar power satellites. SPS is a multidisciplinary project, and each discipline must be developed according to its degree of influence on the total outcome. The Commission should be composed of representatives of relevant international organizations, public utilities, and experts in engineering, science, economics, political science (public administration), and law. There should be representation of different parts of the world insofar as is practicable. Subcommittees could be organized to draft provisions on financing, safeguards, relation with other organizations, and membership requirements. The agenda of the Preparatory Commission should include responsibility for analysis of three plans for potential organization and management:

1. A comprehensive plan for an SPS international institution as a distinct juridical entity.
2. An institutional plan for a nucleus that could expand when advances are made by technology.
3. A plan to cover situations in which SPS furnishes power to spacecraft engaged in specific projects in outer space before a system for use on the Earth is operational.

The same data base of scientific, technological facts and societal implications will be needed for each investigation.[22]

NOTES

1. "Congress and Outer Space 1957-1958." in *Impact of Aerospace Science and Technology on Law and Government*, No.68-901, Washington, AIAA, August 1968, pp. 1-5.

2. "The U.S. Congress and Outer Space: From the Sputnik to the Shuttle." in American Astronautical Society, *History Series*, vol.3, San Diego, Univelt, 1981, pp. 139-160.

3. U.S. Congress, *Final Report of the U.S. Senate Special Committee on Space and Astronautics*, 86th Cong., 1st sess. Report No. 100. Washington, Government Printing Office, March 11, 1959, p. 10.

4. "The United Nations Ad Hoc Committee on the Peaceful Uses of Outer Space: Accomplishment and Implications for Legal Problems," in U.S. Congress, Senate, Committee on Aeronautical and Space Sciences, *Legal Problems of Space Exploration: A Symposium*, 87th Cong., 1st Sess., Doc.26, Washington, Government Printing Office, March 22, 1961, pp. 613-625.

5. "World Security and the Peaceful Uses of Space." in *Proceedings of the 3rd Colloquium on the Law of Outer Space*, (Stockholm 1960), Vienna, Springer Verlag, 1961, pp. 93-101.

6. "International Institutions to Ensure Peaceful Uses of Outer Space," in N. Jasentuliyana (ed.), *Maintaining Outer Space for Peaceful Uses*, Tokyo, United Nations University, 1984, pp. 144-145.

7. "Law and Security in Outer Space: The Role of Congress in Space Law and Policy." *Journal of Space Law*, Vol. 22, Nos. 1 and 2, 1983, pp. 35-50.

8. "The Definition of Space Law," in *Proceedings of the 32nd Colloquium on the Law of Outer Space* (Malaga 1989), Washington, AIAA, 1990, p. 373.

9. "The Future of Space Law." in *Proceedings of the 19th Colloquium on the Law of Outer Space* (Anaheim 1976), Fred B. Rothman & Co., 1977, p. 9.

10. *supra* note 6, pp. 155-158.

11. "The Community of Law and Science," in U.S. Congress, Senate, Special

Committee on Space and Astronautics, *Space Law: A Symposium*, Committee print, 85th Cong., 2d Sess., Washington, Government Printing Office, December 31, 1958, pp. 415-418.

12. "Government in Action: The Role of Political Science in Outer Space Activities." in *Acta Astronautica*, vol. 13, nos. 6 and 7, Oxford, Pergamon Press, 1986, pp. 467-472.

13. "Consensus Decision-making by the United Nations Committee on the Peaceful Uses of Outer Space," *Journal of Space Law*, Vol.7, No.1, 1979, pp. 3-13.

14. "Law, Order, and Outer Space: How High is Up?" *Electronic Age*, Vol.29, No.4, Autumn 1970, pp. 5-6.

15. "Legal Aspects of International Cooperation in Space: Area and Functional Concepts in Defining Outer Space." in *Proceedings of the 26th Colloquium on the Law of Outer Space* (Budapest 1983), New York, AIAA, 1984, pp. 197-203.

16. "Present Status in the United Nations of Direct Television Broadcast Satellites," in *Annals of Air and Space Law*, vol. 2, Montreal, Institute and Centre of Air and Space Law, 1977, p. 272.

17. "Remote Sensing of the Earth by Satellites: Policies and Issues," in *Advances in Earth Oriented Applications of Space Technology: An International Journal*, vol. 1, no. 1, Oxford, Pergamon Press, 1981, pp. 33-38.

18. "Which Method of Realization in Public International Law Can be Considered Most Desirable and Having the Greatest Chances of Realization?" in K.-H. Böckstiegel (ed.), *Settlement of Space Law Disputes: The Present State of the Law and Perspectives of Further Development*, Cologne, Carl Heymanns Verlag, 1980, pp. 160, 170, 171.

19. "The Present Status of the Agreement Governing the Activities of States on the Moon and Other Celestial Bodies," in K.-H. Böckstiegel (ed.), *Environmental Aspects of Activities in Outer Space: State of the Law and Measures of Protection*, Cologne, Carl Heymanns Verlag, 1988, pp. 84, 97-98.

20. "The Relevance of General Multilateral Space Conventions to Space Stations," in K.-H. Böckstiegel (ed.), *Space Stations: Legal Aspects of Scientific and Commercial Use in a Framework of Transatlantic Cooperation*, Cologne, Carl Heymanns Verlag, 1985, pp. 53, 58.

21. "Law, Science and Technology for the Moon/Mars Missions," in *Proceedings of the 33rd Colloquium on the Law of Outer Space* (Dresden 1990), Washington, AIAA, 1991, pp. 195-205.

22. "The Legal and Regulatory Framework for Solar Power Satellites," in Peter Glaser (ed.), *Solar Power Satellites*, Chichester, England, Ellis Howard, 1992.

Publications by Eilene Galloway on Space, 1958-1991

U.S. CONGRESS PUBLICATIONS

1. U.S. Congress. House. Select Committee. *Hearings on Astronauts and Space Exploration*. 85th Cong., 2d sess. on H.R. 1181 legislation on outer space, "NASA: The Problems of Congress in Formulating Outer Space Legislation." April 15, 1958: pp. 5-10.

2. U.S. Congress. Senate. Special Committee on Space and Astronautics. *National Aeronautics and Space Act of 1958*. 85th Cong., 2d sess. May 15, 1958: pp. 381-386. Also, *Analysis of S-3609, a Bill to Provide for Research into Problems of Flight Within and Outside the Earth's Atmosphere*. April 1958. 37p.

3. U.S. Congress. Senate. Special Committee on Space and Astronautics. *Space Law: A Symposium*. Committee print. 85th Cong., 2d sess. December 31, 1958. 573p. Includes article by Eilene Galloway on "The Community of Law and Science," presented at The Hague, August 1958: pp. 415-418.

4. U.S. Congress. *Final Report of the U.S. Senate Special Committee on Space and Astronautics*. 86th Cong., 1st sess. Report No. 100. March 11, 1959. 57p.

5. U.S. Congress. Senate. Committee on Aeronautical and Space Sciences. *Legal Problems of Space Exploration: A Symposium*. 87th Cong., 1st sess. Doc.26. March 22, 1961. 1392p. Includes three papers by Eilene Galloway: "The Community of Law and Science," pp. 450-453; "The United Nations Ad Hoc Committee on the Peaceful Uses of Outer Space: Accomplishment and Implications for Legal Problems," pp. 613-625; and "World Security and the Peaceful Uses of Outer Space," pp. 684-693.

6. U.S. Congress. House. Committee on Science and Astronautics. Subcommittee on Manned Space Flight. *Hearing on the 1963 NASA Authorization*, (Peaceful Uses of Outer Space and the Military Role). 87th Cong., 1st sess. on H.R. 10100, superseded by H.R. 11737. March-April 1962, Part 2. April 18, 1962: pp. 1051-1065.

7. U.S. Congress. *United States International Space Programs: Texts of Executive Agreements, Memoranda of Understanding, and Other International Arrangements, 1959-1965*. Ed. 89th Cong., 1st sess., Doc.44. July 30, 1965: p. 575.

8. U.S. Congress. Senate. Committee on Aeronautical and Space Sciences. *International Cooperation and Organization for Outer Space*. 89th Cong., 1st sess., Doc. 56. August 12, 1965. 580p.

9. U.S. Congress. Senate. Committee on Aeronautical and Space Sciences. *Space Treaty Proposals by the United States and U.S.S.R.* 89th Cong., 2d sess. Committee print. July 1966. 52p.

10. U.S. Congress. Senate. Committee on Aeronautical and Space Sciences. *Treaty on Principles Governing the Activities of States in the Exploration and Use of Outer Space, Including the Moon and Other Celestial Bodies: Analysis and Background Data.* 90th Cong., 1st sess. Committee print. March 1967. 84p.

11. U.S. Congress. *Agreement on the Rescue of Astronauts, the Return of Astronauts and the Return of Objects Launched into Outer Space: Analysis and Background Data.* 90th Cong., 2d sess. Committee print. July 16, 1968. 31p.

12. U.S. Congress. Senate. Committee on Aeronautical and Space Sciences. *International Cooperation in Outer Space: A Symposium.* 92nd Cong., 1st sess. Doc. 92-57. December 9, 1971. 732p. Includes an article by Eilene Galloway on "Congress and International Space Cooperation," pp. 3-12.

13. U.S. Congress. Senate. Committee on Aeronautical and Space Sciences. *Convention on Registration of Objects Launched into Outer Space: Analysis and Background Data.* 94th Cong., 1st sess. Committee print. July 1975: pp. 1-18.

14. U.S. Congress. House. Committee on Science and Technology, Subcommittee on Space Science and Applications. *Testimony on International Space Activities.* 96th Cong., 1st sess. September 5-6, 1979: pp. 118-138.

15. U.S. Congress. Senate. Committee on Commerce, Science, and Transportation. *Agreement Governing the Activities of States on the Moon and Other Celestial Bodies* (with annex of texts of relevant documents). 96th Cong., 2d sess. Committee print. May 1980. 264p.

16. U.S. Congress. Senate. Committee on Commerce, Science and Transportation, Subcommittee on Science, Technology and Space. *Testimony on the Moon Treaty.* 96th Cong., 2d sess. July 31, 1980: pp. 172-182.

ARTICLES

17. "The Community of Law and Science." *Proceedings of the First Colloquium on the Law of Outer Space*, The Hague (1958), pp. 55-62. (Hereafter these Proceedings will be indicated by the number of the colloquium, such as *1st Colloquium.*) Vienna: Springer-Verlag, 1959. (Previously published by the U.S. Senate Special Committee on Space and Astronautics. Committee print. December 1958: pp. 415-418.)

18. "The United Nations Ad Hoc Committee on the Peaceful Uses of Outer Space: Accomplishments and Implications for Legal Problems." *2d Colloquium*, London (1959), pp. 30-41. Vienna: Springer-Verlag, 1960.

19. "World Security and the Peaceful Uses of Space." *3d Colloquium*, Stockholm (1960), pp. 93-101. Vienna: Springer Verlag, 1961.

20. "The U.N. Committee on the Peaceful Uses of Outer Space." *4th Colloquium*, Varna (1962); Vienna: Springer Verlag, 1963. 16p.

21. "General Principles Governing Space Activities." *6th Colloquium*, Paris (1963). Vienna: Springer Verlag, 1964. 4p.

22. "International Regulation of Outer Space Activities." *7th Colloquium*, Warsaw (1964), pp. 55-61. Vienna: Springer Verlag, 1965.

23. "Interpreting the Treaty on Outer Space." *10th Colloquium*, Belgrade (1967), pp. 143-148. Fred B. Rothman & Co., 1968.

24. "Congress and Outer Space 1957-1958." *Impact of Aerospace Science and Technology on Law and Government*, pp. 1-5. New York: American Institute of Aeronautics and Astronautics (AIAA), No.68-901, August 1968.

25. "Interpretation of the Space Treaty: Introductory Report II." *11th Colloquium*, New York (1968), pp. 8-13. Fred B. Rothman & Co., 1969.

26. "Law, Order, and Outer Space: How High is Up?" *Electronic Age*, Vol. 29, No. 4, Autumn (1970), pp. 2-7.

27. "Delimitation of Airspace from Outer Space." *Proceedings 473*, vol. 3. Bangkok, Thailand: World Peace through Law, 1971.

28. "Outer Space Treaties in Force." *13th Colloquium*, Munich (1970), pp. 61-73. Fred B. Rothman & Co., 1971.

29. "The Future of International Space Cooperation in Treaty Making." *14th Colloquium* (1971), pp. 204-205. Fred B. Rothman & Co., 1972.

30. "The Role of the United Nations in Earth Resources Satellites." *15th Colloquium*, Vienna (1972), pp. 21-29. Fred B. Rothman & Co., 1973.

31. "Should the United Nations Draft a Treaty on Earth Resources Satellites? A Pro and Con Analysis." *Journal of Space Law*, Vol. 1, No. 1 (1973), pp. 72-79.

32. "Remote Sensing of Earth Resources by Satellites." *16th Colloquium*, Baku (1973). Fred B. Rothman & Co., 1974.

33. "Direct Broadcast Satellites." *17th Colloquium*, Amsterdam (1974), pp. 30-41. Fred B. Rothman & Co., 1975.

34. "Direct Broadcast Satellites and Space Law." *Journal of Space Law*, Vol. 3, Nos. 1 and 2 (1975), pp. 3-16.

35. "Applicability of Space Treaties to the Uses of Outer Space." In *Annals of Air and Space Law*, vol. 1, Nicolas Mattesco Matte, editor, pp. 205-212. Institute of Air and Space Law, McGill University. Toronto, Canada: Carswell Co. Ltd., 1976.

36. "The Future of Space Law." *19th Colloquium*, Anaheim (1976): pp. 2-18. Fred B. Rothman & Co., 1977.

37. "Present Status in the United Nations of Direct Television Broadcast Satellites." In *Annals of Air and Space Law*, vol. 2, pp. 269-285. Institute and Centre of Air and Space Law. Toronto: Carswell, 1977.

38. "Introduction to the Symposium on International Organizations and the Law of Outer Space." *Journal of Space Law*, Vol. 5, Nos. 1 and 2 (1977): pp. 3-6.

39. "Consensus as a Basis for International Space Cooperation." *20th Colloquium*, Prague (1977), pp. 105-111. Fred B. Rothman & Co., 1978.

40. "The United States Congress and Space Law." In *Annals of Air and Space Law*, vol. 3, pp. 395-407. Institute and Centre of Air and Space Law, McGill University. Toronto, Canada: Carswell Co. Ltd., 1978.

41 *Options for an Operational Remote Sensing System*. American Astronautical Society, No.AAS-78-160, 24p. Houston, TX: AAS, October 31, 1978.

42. "Space Law and Astronautics for Peace and Human Progress." *21st Colloquium*, Dubrovnik (1978), pp. 175-183. Fred B. Rothman & Co., 1979.

43. "Recent Developments in United States Space Policy." In *Annals of Air and Space Law*, vol. 4, Institute and Centre of Air and Space Law, McGill University. Toronto, Canada: Carswell Co. Ltd., 1979.

44. "Which Method of Realization in Public International Law Can be Considered Most Desirable and Having the Greatest Chances of Realization?" In *Settlement of Space Law Disputes: The Present State of the Law and Perspectives of Further*

Development. Institute of Air and Space Law, University of Cologne Colloquium, Munich: September 1979.

45. "Nuclear-Powered Satellites: The U.S.S.R. Cosmos 954 and the Canadian Claim." *Akron Law Review*, Vol. 12, No.3 (1979), pp. 401-415. Akron, OH: University of Akron, 1979.

46. "Consensus Decision-making by the United Nations Committee on the Peaceful Uses of Outer Space." *Journal of Space Law*, Vol.7, No.1 (1979): pp. 3-13.

47. "United Nations Consideration of Nuclear Power for Satellites." *29th Colloquium*, Munich (1979), pp. 131-139. New York: AIAA, 1980.

48. "Agreement Governing the Activities of States on the Moon and Other Celestial Bodies." In *Annals of Air and Space Law*, vol. 5, pp. 481-508. Institute and Centre of Air and Space Law, McGill University. Toronto, Canada: Carswell Co. Ltd., 1980.

49. "Issues in Implementing the Agreement Governing the Activities of States on the Moon and Other Celestial Bodies." *23rd Colloquium*, Tokyo (1980), pp. 19-24. New York: AIAA, 1981.

50. "The U.S. Congress and Outer Space: From the Sputnik to the Shuttle." American Astronautical Society, *History Series*, vol. 3, pp. 139-160. Univelt, Inc. P.O. Box 28130, San Diego, CA 92128, 1981.

51. "Remote Sensing of the Earth by Satellites: Policies and Issues." In *Advances in Earth Oriented Applications of Space Technology: An International Journal*, vol. 1, no. 1: pp. 33-38. Oxford: Pergamon Press, 1981.

52. "Space Manufacturing and the Proposed Agreement Governing the Activities of States on the Moon and Other Celestial Bodies." In *Space Manufacturing.* Fifth Princeton Conference on Space Manufacturing. New York: AIAA, May 1981.

53. "Conditions for Success of Institutions for International Space Activities." *24th Colloquium*, Rome (1981), pp. 105-111. New York: AIAA, 1982.

54. "Perspectives of Space Law." *Journal of Space Law*, Vol. 9, Nos. 1 and 2 (1981): pp. 21-29.

55. "The History and Development of Space Law, International Law and United States Law." In *Annals of Air and Space Law*, vol. 7, pp. 295-317. Institute and Centre of Air and Space Law, McGill University. Toronto, Canada: Carswell Co. Ltd., 1982.

56. *The History and Development of Space Law.* American Bar Association, National Institute on Litigation in Aviation and Space Law. Washington, D.C.: May 1982.

57. "Expanding Article IV of the 1967 Space Treaty: A Proposal." *25th Colloquium*, Paris (1982), pp. 89-92. New York: AIAA, 1983.

58. "Law and Security in Outer Space: The Role of Congress in Space Law and Policy." *Journal of Space Law*, Vol. 22, Nos. 1 and 2 (1983): pp. 35-50.

59. "Legal Aspects of International Cooperation in Space: Area and Functional Concepts in Defining Outer Space." *26th Colloquium*, Budapest (1983), pp. 197-203. New York: AIAA, 1984.

60. "International Institutions to Ensure Peaceful Uses of Outer Space." In *Annals of Air and Space Law*, vol. 9, pp. 303-328. Institute and Centre of Air and Space Law, McGill University. Toronto, Canada: Carswell Co. Ltd., 1984.

61. "Overview" and "International Institutions to Ensure Peaceful Uses of Outer Space." In *Maintaining Outer Space for Peaceful Uses*, Nandasiri Jasentuliyana, editor, pp. 11-28 and pp. 143-162. Tokyo: United Nations University, 1984.

62. "The Relevance of General Multilateral Space Conventions to Space Stations." In *Space Stations: Legal Aspects of Scientific and Commercial Use in a Framework of Transatlantic Cooperation*, Karl-Heinz Böckstiegel, editor, Institute of Air and Space Law, University of Cologne. Cologne: Carl Heymanns Verlag, 1984.

63. "Conditions Essential for Maintaining Outer Space for Peaceful Uses." *27th Colloquium*, Lausanne (1984), pp. 313-319. New York: AIAA, 1985.

64. "The Space Station: U.S. Proposal and Implementation." *28th Colloquium*, Stockholm (1985), pp. 268-280. New York, AIAA, 1986. Also published in *Journal of Space Law*, Vol. 14, No.1 (1986): pp. 14-39.

65. "Vision Panoramica del Simposio y de las Cuestiones Tratadas." In *Mantenimiento de la Utilizacion, del Espacio Ultraterrestre con Fines Pacificos*, pp. 39-63. Estudios Internacionales Avanzados Serie Cooperacion Academica Internacional. Córdoba, Argentina: 1986.

66. "Government in Action: The Role of Political Science in Outer Space Activities." In *Acta Astronautica*, vol. 13, nos. 6 and 7, pp. 467-472. Oxford: Pergamon Press, 1986.

67. "United States National Space Legislation on the Exploration and Use of Outer Space for Peaceful Purposes" (co-authored with Jonathan F. Galloway). *30th Colloquium*, Brighton (1987), pp. 32-41. Washington: AIAA, 1988.

68. "The Present Status of the Agreement Governing the Activities of States on the Moon and Other Celestial Bodies." In *Environmental Aspects of Activities in Outer Space: State of the Law and Measures of Protection*, pp. 81-99. Institute of Air and Space Law, Cologne University. Cologne: Carl Heymanns Verlag, 1988.

69. *United States Liftoff for Outer Space*. Background Report for NOVA, Public Broadcasting Service. Augugt 8, 1988. 31p.

70. *Space Issues Discussion Groups Reports*, pp. 33-35. Air War College. Maxwell Air Force Base, AL: U.S. Air Force, Air University, August 1988.

71. "The Use of the Geostationary Orbit." In *Acta Astronautica*, vol. 17, no. 6, pp. 589-654. Oxford: Pergamon Press, June 1988.

72. "Space Law and the Legal Aspects of Human Space Settlements." In *Leaving the Cradle: Human Exploration of Space in the 21st Century*. History Series, Vol.78 (1990), pp. 269-277. American Astronautical Society, 28th Symposium. Washington, DC: AIAA, March 1990.

73. "The Definition of Space Law." *32nd Colloquium*, Malaga (1989), pp. 331-334. Washington: AIAA, 1990.

74. "Law, Science and Technology for the Moon/Mars Missions." *33rd Colloquium*, Dresden (1990). Washington: AIAA, 1991.

75. "The Legal and Regulatory Framework for Solar Power Satellites." In a forthcoming book on Solar Power Satellites by Peter E. Glaser.

Selected Bibliography

Kuo-Lee Li

The titles included in this selected bibliography have been chosen on the basis of their relevance to the contents of this volume and their availability. They are not intended as a balanced presentation of the entire field of space law. Emphasis is placed on current literature on the development as well as the current state of the law. However, older works of lasting value are also included in order to provide a certain intellectual foundation for the study of space law in general. In addition, wherever appropriate, writings reflecting diverse political and moral views are specifically selected to give the presentation a reasonable degree of comprehensiveness and balance.

Certain types of publications are not included. Articles that are included in the collections of essays listed as books are not listed separately as articles, even though listing these articles individually would better reveal the subject coverage of the bibliography. Theses in general are also excluded except in the rare case of a thesis that serves as a good reference for an area that is otherwise not covered in the literature. Also omitted are documents of the United Nations, its specialized agencies, international organizations, and national governments. To locate these and other works not included in this bibliography, refer to the *World Wide Space Law Bibliography* and other titles listed under the heading "General Source Materials."

GENERAL SOURCE MATERIALS

Space Law: Basic Legal Documents. Karl-Heinz Böckstiegel and Marietta Benkö (Eds.). 2 loose-leaf vols. Dordrecht/Boston/London: M. Nijhoff, 1990.

United States Space Law: National and International Regulation. S. Gorove (Ed.). 2 loose-leaf vols. Dobbs Ferry, NY: Oceana, 1982.

World Wide Space Law Bibliography. Kuo Lee Li (Ed.). 2 vols and annual supplements. Montreal: Institute of Air and Space Law, McGill University/ De Daro Publishing, 1978.

BOOKS

American Enterprise, the Law and the Commercial Use of Space. 3 vols. Washington, DC: National Legal Center for the Public Interest, 1986.

Arms Control and Disarmament in Outer Space. 4 vols. N. M. Matte (Ed.). Montreal: Centre for Research in Air and Space Law, McGill University, 1985-1991.

Baker, H. A. *Space Debris: Legal and Policy Implications.* Dordrecht: M. Nijhoff, 1989 (Utrecht Studies in Air and Space Law, 6).

Beatrice, L. *Europe: Stepping Stones to Space.* Flitwick, UK: Orbic, 1990.

Benkö, M., Graaff, W. de and Reijnen, G. G. M. *Space Law in the United Nations.* Dordrecht: M. Nijhoff, 1985.

Bhatt, S. *Studies in Aerospace Law.* New Delhi: Sterling, 1974.

Bornecque-Winandye, E. M. *Droit de l'O.N.U. et stratégies économiques spatiales: paix et crise.* Paris: Librairie Générale de Droit et de Jurisprudence, 1969.

Chao, C. C., Harwell, K. E. and Shahrokhi, F. *Commercial Opportunities in Space.* Washington, DC: American Institute of Aeronautics and Astronautics, 1988.

Christol, C. Q. *The Modern International Law of Outer Space.* New York: Pergamon Press, 1982.

———. *Space Law: Past, Present and Future.* Dordrecht: Kluwer, 1991.

Courteix, S., and Mann, A. *La coopération spatiale européenne.* Aubervillier, France: Documentation Française, 1988.

Czechoslovak Academy of Sciences. *The Role of Scientists in Preventing an Arms Race in Outer Space.* Prague: Academia, 1986.

Droit de l'espace: aspects récents. J. Eutheil de la Rochère (Ed.). Paris: Pedone, 1987.

Environmental Aspects of Activities in Outer Space: State of the Law and Measures of Protection. K.-H. Böckstiegel (Ed.). Cologne: Carl Heymanns, 1990 (Utrecht Studies in Air and Space Law, 9).

Europe's Future in Space: A Joint Policy Report. London: Routledge and Kegan Paul, 1988.

Fawcett, J. E. S. *Outer Space: New Challenges to Law and Policy.* Oxford: Clarendon Press, 1984.

Finch, E. R. Jr., and Moore, A. L. *Astrobusiness: A Guide to the Commerce and Law of Outer Space.* New York: Praeger, 1984.

Frutkin, A. W. *International Cooperation in Space.* Englewood Cliffs, NJ: Prentice-Hall, 1965.

Goldman, N. C. *American Space Law: International and Domestic.* Ames: Iowa State University Press, 1988.

———. *Space Commerce: Free Enterprise on the High Frontier.* Cambridge, MA: Ballinger, 1985.

Gorove, S. *Developments in Space Law: Issues and Policies.* Dordrecht: Kluwer, 1991 (Utrecht Studies in Air and Space Law, 10).

———. *Studies in Space Law: Its Challenges and Prospects.* Leyden: Sijthoff, 1977.

International Law of Communications. E. McWhinney (Ed.). Leyden: Sijthoff, Oceana, 1971.

International Space Policy: Legal, Economic and Strategic Options for the Twentieth Century and Beyond. D. S. Papp and J. R. McIntyre (Eds.). Westport, CT: Quorum Books, 1987.

International Telecommunication Satellite Organization (INTELSAT). *Bridging the Gap: A Guide to Telecommunications and Development.* Washington, DC: INTELSAT, 1985.

Jasani, B. *Spaceweapons and International Security.* New York: Oxford University Press, 1987.

Kantor, L. Y. A. *Handbook of Satellite Telecommunications and Broadcasting.* Norwood, MA: Artech House, 1987.

Lachs, M. *The Law of Outer Space: An Experience in Contemporary Law-making.* Leiden: Sijthoff, 1972.

Lauria-White, R. *The Law and Regulation of International Space Communication.* Boston: Artech House, 1988.

Law and Politics in Space. M. Cohen (Ed.). Montreal: McGill University Press, 1964.

Lay, S.H. and Taubenfeld, H.J. *The Law Relating to Activities of Man in Space.* Chicago: University of Chicago Press, 1970.

Liber Amicorum Nicolas Mateesco Matte: Beyond Boundaries /Au-déla des frontières. G. R. Baccelli (Ed.). Paris: Pedone, 1989.

Luther, S. F. *The United States and the Direct Broadcast Satellite: The Politics of International Broadcasting in Space.* Fairlawn, NJ: Oxford University Press, 1988.

Lyall, F. *Law and Space Telecommunications.* Aldershot, Hants./Brookfield, VT: Gower Publishing, 1989.

Maintaining Outer Space for Peaceful Uses. N. Jasentuliyana (Ed.). New York: United Nations University, 1984.

Mamboundow-M'Boumba, D. *Les télécommunications spatiales et les pays en développement, spécifiquement les pays d'Afrique.* Montreal: Institute of Air and Space Law, McGill University, 1985 (Thesis).

Manual on Space Law. N. Jasentuliyana and R. S. K. Lee (Eds.). Dobbs Ferry, NY: Oceana, 1979-1981.

Marcoff, M. G. *Traité de droit international public de l'espace.* Fribourg: Editions Universitaires, 1973.

Martinez, L. *Communication Satellites: Power Politics in Space.* Norwood, MA: Artech House, 1985.

Matte, N. M. *Aerospace Law: Telecommunications Satellites.* London: Butterworths, 1982.

———. *Droit aerospatial: les télécommunications par satellites.* Paris: Pedone, 1982.

McDougal, M. S., Lasswell, H. D., and Vlasic, I. A. *Law and Public Order in Space.* New Haven: Yale University Press, 1963.

Mosteshar, S. A. *Satellite Communications.* London: Longman, 1986.

Outer Space and Law. P. I. Lukin and A. I. Rudev (Eds.). Moscow: Academy of Science, Institute of State and Law, 1980 (in Russian).

Patrick, K. *International Technology Negotiations and Outer Space.* Halifax: Centre for Foreign Policy Studies, Dalhousie University, 1984.

Peaceful and Non-peaceful Uses of Space: Problems of Definition for the Prevention of an Arms Race. B. Jasani (Ed.). Bristol, PA: Taylor and Francis, 1991.

Powell, J. T. *International Broadcasting by Satellite: Issues of Regulation, Barriers to Communications.* Westport, CT: Quorum Books, 1985.

Queeney, K. M. *Direct Broadcast Satellites and the United Nations.* Alphen aan den Rijn: Sijthoff and Noordhoff, 1978.

Reijnen, G. C. M. and De Graaff, W. *Pollution of Outer Space, in Particular of the Geostationary Orbit: Scientific, Policy and Legal Aspects.* Dordrecht: M. Nijhoff, 1989 (Utrecht Studies in Air and Space Law, 4).

Reynolds, G. A. and Merges, R. P. *Outer Space: Problems of Law and Policy.* San Diego, CA: Westview Press, 1989.

Rose, N. L. *The Governmental Role in the Commercialization of New Technologies: Lessons for Space Policy.* Cambridge, MA: Sloan School of Management, Massachusetts Institute of Technology, 1986.

Sharma, G. N. *Satellite Communications and Outer Space: Regulatory Aspects.* Ahmedabad, India: Academic Book Centre, 1988.

Smith, M. L. *International Regulation of Satellite Communication.* Dordrecht: Kluwer, 1990 (Utrecht Studies in Air and Space Law, 7).

Snow, M. S. *The International Telecommunications Satellite Organization (INTELSAT): Economic and Institutional Challenges Facing an International Organization.* Baden-Baden: Nomos, 1988.

Space: A Developing Role for Europe. L. J. Carter and P. M. Baimum (Eds.). San Diego, CA: Univelt, 1984.

Space Activities and Implications: Where From and Where to at the Threshold of the 80's. Proceedings of the symposium organized by the Centre for Research of Air and Space Law, McGill University. Montreal: Carswell, 1981.

Space Law: Views of the Future. T. L. Zwaan et al. (Eds.), IIASL, Leiden University. Deventer: Kluwer, 1988.

Space Stations: Legal Aspects of Scientific and Commercial Use in a Framework of Transatlantic Cooperation. K.-H. Böckstiegel (Ed.). Cologne: Carl Heymanns, 1985.

Stewart, M. L. *To See the World: The Global Dimension in International Direct Television Broadcasting by Satellite.* Dordrecht: M. Nijhoff, 1989 (Utrecht Studies in Air and Space Law, 5).

Taishoff, M. N. *State Responsibility and the Direct Broadcast Satellite.* Geneva: Graduate Institute of International Studies, 1987.

Taylor, L. B., Jr. *Commercialization of Space.* New York: F. Watts, 1987.

Technology and the Civil Future in Space. L. A. Harris (Ed.). San Diego, CA: Univelt, 1981.

Television by Satellite: Legal Aspects. S. B. de Bate (Ed.). Oxford: ESC Publishing, 1987.

U.S. Congress, Office of Technology Assessment. *Orbital Debris: A Space Environmental Problem.* Washington, DC: Government Printing Office, 1991.

Van Traa-Engelman, H. L. *Commercial Utilization of Outer Space: Legal Aspects.* Rotterdam: Drukderij Haveka, 1989.

Vereshchetin, V., Vasilevskaya, E., and Kamenetskaya, E. *Outer Space Politics and Law.* Moscow: Progress Publishing, 1987.

Wassenbergh, H. A. *Principles of Outer Space Law in Hindsight.* Dordrecht: Kluwer, 1991.

Willisch, J. *Space Responsibility for Technological Damages in International Law.* Berlin: Duncker and Humbolt, 1987.

Young, A. J. *Law and Policy in the Space Stations' Era.* Dordrecht: M. Nijhoff, 1989 (Utrecht Studies in Air and Space Law, No. 2).

Zhukov, G. P., and Kolosov, Y. *International Space Law.* New York: Praeger, 1984.

ARTICLES

Almond, H. H., Jr. "Peaceful purposes in outer space: Precision, ambiguity or confusion." *Colloquium on the Law of Outer Space* 31 (1988): pp. 1-5.

———. "Protection of the environment of outer space: A proposed framework of principles and guidelines." *Colloquium on the Law of Outer Space* 33 (1990): pp. 133-141.

Bhatt, S. "An ecological approach to aerospace law." *Annals of Air and Space Law* 4 (1979): pp. 385-396.

Böckstiegel, K.-H. "Commercial space activities: Their growing influence on space law." *Annals of Air and Space Law* 12 (1987): pp. 175-192.

———. "The law applicable to contracts of space activities." *Colloquium on the Law of Outer Space* 25 (1982): pp. 203-209.

———. "Prospects of future development in the law of outer space." *Annals of Air and Space Law* 8 (1982): pp. 305-320.

———. "Report and reflections on the teaching of space law at the Institute of Air and Space Law of Cologne University." *Colloquium on the Law of Outer Space* 29 (1986): pp. 208-211.

Bourély, M. G. "National space legislation in Europe." *Colloquium on the Law of Outer Space* 30 (1987): pp. 197-202.

———. "Ways of coordinating space science and technology with space law: Introductory report." *Colloquium on the Law of Outer Space* 20 (1977): pp. 73-82.

Brodermann, E. "Quelques réflexions sur le rôle de la coutume internationale dans le droit de l'espace." *Thesaurus Acroasium* 10 (1981): pp. 809-823.

Cheng, B. "International cooperation and control: From atoms to space." *Current Legal Problems* 15 (1962): pp. 226-247.

———. "Outer space: The international legal framework, the international legal status of outer space, space objects and spacemen." *Thesaurus Acroasium* 10 (1981): pp. 41-106.

———. "United Nations resolutions on outer space: 'instant' international customary law." *Indian Journal of International Law* 5 (1965): pp. 23-48.

Christol, C. Q. "International space law and the less developed countries." *Colloquium on the Law of Outer Space* 19 (1976): pp. 243-256.

Cocca, A. A. "The central role of Eugene Pépin in the teaching and research on space: A note in memoriam." *Journal of Space Law* 16 (1988): pp. 171-182.

Colino, R. R. "The possible introduction of separate satellite systems: International communications at the crossroad." *Columbia Journal of Transnational Law* 24 (1985): pp. 13-35.

Condara, C. "Outer space, like the sea and the air, whose frontier? Incredible potential with inscrutable obstacles." *Houston Journal of International Law* 6 (1984): pp. 175-196.

Courteix, S. "'Eumetsat' ou l'Europe de la météorologie par satellite." *Annuaire français de droit international* 29 (1983): pp. 624-625.

———. "Inmarsat: accords relatifs a l'exploitation commerciale de télécommunication maritimes par satellites." *Annuaire français de droit international* 29 (1983): pp. 791-808.

DeSaussure, H. "Toward a law for space transport, the maritime analogy." *Lincoln Law Review* 14 (1983): pp. 1-42.

———. "Unification and development of transnational space law." *Colloquium on the Law of Outer Space* 31 (1988): pp. 253-259.

Diederiks-Verschoor, I. H. Ph. "Environmental protection in outer space." *German Yearbook of International Law* 30 (1987): pp. 144-159.

———. "Implications of commercial activities in outer space, especially for the developing countries." *Journal of Space Law* 17 (1989): pp. 115-127.

Doyle, S. E. "An analysis of the Socialist states' proposals for Intersputnik: An international communication satellite system." *Villanova Law Review* 15 (1969): pp. 83-105.

———. "Inmarsat: The International Maritime Satellite Organization: Origins and structure." *Journal of Space Law* 5 (1977): pp. 45-63.

Dula, A. M. "Export controls affecting space operations." *Journal of Air Law and Commerce* 51 (1986): pp. 927-950.

Dupy, R.-J. "Les structures et le role d'une agence internationale de satellites de contrôle." *Annals of Air and Space Law* 6 (1981): pp. 333-343.

Dutu, M. "Principles et normes juridiques concernant le domaine des télécommunications spatiales." *Revue romaine d'études internationales* 21 (1987): pp. 475-483.

Edelson, B. I. and Pelton, J. N. "Can Intelsat and Intersputnik cooperate?" *Space Policy* 5 (1989): pp. 7-11.

Elmandjra, M. "The conquest of space: A few political, economic and sociocultural considerations." *Third World Quarterly* 6 (July 1984): pp. 576-603.

Fernandez-Brital, O. "Legal problems of commercial space transportation." *Colloquium on the Law of Outer Space* 33 (1990): pp. 30-36.

Forkosch, M. D. "Legal liability and outer space law: A proposed international court for outer space." *Thesaurus Acroasium* 10 (1981): pp. 451-551.

Glazer, J. H. "The Maltese initiatives within the United Nations: A blue planet blue-print for transnational space." *Ecology Law Quarterly* 4 (1974): pp. 279-318.

———. "The maritime analogy in outer space." *Lincoln Law Review* 14 (1983): pp. 16-22.

Goedhuis, D. "Influence de l'utilisation des satellites en particulier ceux des télécommunications et des télédétections sur les relations internationales." *Revue français droit aérien* 29 (1975): pp. 378-391.

———. "Reflections on some of the main problems arising in the future development of space law." *Netherlands International Law Review* 36 (1989): pp. 247-268.

Goldman, N. C. "The Strategic Defense Initiative: Star wars and star laws." *Houston Journal of International Law* 9 (1986): pp. 111-131.

Gorove, S. "Current issues of space law before the United Nations." *Journal of Space Law* 11 (1983): pp. 5-14.

———. "Expectations in space law: A peek into the future." *Journal of International Affairs* 39 (1985): pp. 167-174.

———. "International direct television broadcasting by satellite: Prior consent revisited." *Columbia Journal of Transnational Law* 24 (1985): pp. 1-11.

Gotlieb. A. E. "The impact of technology on the development of contemporary international law." *Recueil des cours* 170 (1) (1980): pp. 119-329.

Haley A. G. "The law of outer space: Scientific and anthropocentric considerations." *Astronautik* 1 (1958): pp. 53-84.

Harwitz, B. A. "The labyrinth of international telecommunications law: direct broadcast satellites." *Netherlands International Law Review* 35 (1988): pp. 145-180.

Hasse, L. "Finding a basis for international communications law: The satellite broadcast example." *Case Western Reserve Journal of International Law* 22 (1990): pp. 97-116.

He, Qizhi. "Environmental impact of space activities and measures for international protection." *Journal of Space Law* 16 (1988): pp. 117-127.

———. "Main features of space law teaching in China." *Colloquium on the Law of Outer Space* 29 (1986): pp. 272-275.

Honig, J. P. "Progress in the codification of international law." *International Affairs* 36 (January 1960): pp. 62-72.

Howell, R. C. "International telecommunications and the law: The creation of Pan American satellites." *Howard Law Journal* 31 (1988): pp. 575-641.

Jakhu, R. S. "Direct broadcasting via satellite and a new information order." *Syracuse Journal of International Law* 8 (1981): pp. 375-390.

Jasentuliyana, N. "Civilian and military space activities: A third world perspective." *Annals of Air and Space Law* 12 (1987): pp. 247-262.

———. "Space activities and international environmental protection: Perspectives on the United Nations role." *Colloquium on the Law of Outer Space* 33 (1990): pp. 152-157.

———. "Treaty law and outer space: Can the United Nations play an effective role?" *Annals of Air and Space Law* 11 (1986): pp. 219-227.

Kopal, V. "Evolution of the main principles of space law in the institutional framework of the United Nations." *Journal of Space Law* 12 (1984): pp. 12-25.

———. "The role of United Nations declarations of principles in the progressive development of space law." *Journal of Space Law* 16 (1988): pp. 5-20.

———. "Some issues of the next progressive development of international space law." *Colloquium on the Law of Outer Space* 31 (1988): pp. 297-303.

Lafferranderie, G. "The enlargement of the European Space Agency: Legal issues." *Journal of Space Law* 15 (1987): pp. 119-130.

———. "La notion d'utilisation pacifique dans le droit de l'espace." *Revue français droit aérien* 39 (1985): pp. 427-438.

Larson, P. B. et al. "DBS under FCC and international regulation." *Vanderbilt Law Review* 37 (1984): pp. 67-144.

Lay, S. H. "Some comparisons of the draft convention on the law of the sea and the Agreement governing the activities of states on the Moon and other celestial bodies." *International Property Investment Journal* 1 (1983): pp. 599-614.

Lebeau, A. "The evolution of space technology and its legal consequences: Technical prospects." *Colloquium on the Law of Outer Space* 12 (1979): pp. 265-267.

Leister, V. "Export controls of space technology: An overlooked barrier to international cooperation." *Colloquium on the Law of Outer Space* 23 (1980): pp. 183-188.

Leive, D. M. "Essential features of Intelsat: Applications for the future." *Journal of Space Law* 9 (1981): pp. 45-51.

Marcoff, M. G. "Liberté de l'espace et stations interplanétaires." *Revue générale de l'air et de l'espace* 24 (1961): pp. 327-333.

Matteesco Matte, N. "Aerospace law, education and research: The IASL experience." *Colloquium on the Law of Outer Space* 29 (1986): pp. 257-262.

———. "Droit maritime, droit aérien, droit extratmosphérique et droit international: quel rapport?" *Annuaire de droit maritime et aerospatial* 5 (1980): pp. 301-353.

———. "Environmental implications and responsibilities in the use of outer space." *European Transport Law* 24 (1989): pp. 275-296.

Menon, P. K. "The International Maritime Satellite Organization: An important milestone in maritime communications service." *Revue belge de droit international* 13 (1977): pp. 279-297.

Minola, P. "The Moon treaty and the law of the sea." *San Diego Law Review* 18 (1981): pp. 455-472.

Morrow, C. "Le système Eutelsat." *Annuaire français de droit international* (1985): pp. 803-811.

Muller, R. and Muller M. "Cooperation as a basic principle of legal regimes for areas beyond national sovereignty—with special regard to outer space law." *German Yearbook of International Law* 31 (1988): pp. 553-573.

Perek, L. "Technical aspects of the control of space debris." *Colloquium on the Law of Outer Space* 33 (1990): pp. 400-407.

Piradov, A. S. "Creating a world space organization." *Space Policy* 4 (1988): pp. 112-114.

Postyshev, V. M. "Access of states to results of outer space exploration and uses: Critical review of some recent proposals." *Colloquium on the Law of Outer Space* 31 (1988): pp. 143-146.

Premont, M. C. "Les transferts de technologie nord-sud en matière de télécommunications par satellites." *Cahiers de droit* 27 (1986): pp. 853-889.

Reed, W. D. and Norris, R. W. "Military use of the Space Shuttle." *Akron Law Review* 13 (1980): pp. 665-688.

Reijnen, G. C. M. "International law and business in space: In Europe." *Colloquium on the Law of Outer Space* 33 (1990): pp. 68-73.

Rodriguez, R. R. "International telecommunications and satellite systems: Intelsat and separate systems: Cold war revisited." *International Business Lawyer* 15 (1987): pp. 321-323.

Safavi, H. "Space law and the problems of developing countries." *Colloquium on the Law of Outer Space* 31 (1988): pp. 147-150.

Sagar, D. "Inmarsat." *Annals of Air and Space Law* 13 (1988): pp. 316-321.

Saint Lager, O. de. "The third world and space law." *Colloquium on the Law of Outer Space* 24 (1981): pp. 57-61.

Sand, P. H. "Space programs and international environment protection." *International Comparative Law Quarterly* 21 (1972): pp. 43-60.

Schneider, A. R. H. "A new method for the dissemination, propagation and teaching of space law under the auspices of the International Institute of Space Law." *Colloquium on the Law of Outer Space* 29 (1986): pp. 276-280.

Shapira, S. "A search in the heavens: Should Intelsat be subject to U.S. antitrust laws?" *Columbia Journal of Transnational Law* 24 (1985): pp. 133-164.

Silvestrov, G. "The notion of space commercialization." *Colloquium on the Law of Outer Space* 33 (1990): pp. 88-92.

Sloup, G. P. "Peaceful resolution of outer space conflicts through the International Court of Justice, the line of least resistance." *De Paul Law Review* 20 (1971): pp. 618-698.

Smirnoff, M. "Les efforts de la Fédération internationale astronautique dans l'élaboration des normes du droit de l'espace." *Revue français de droit aérien* 14 (1960): pp. 278-283.

Straubel, M. S. "The Commercial Space Launch Act: The regulation of private space transportation." *Journal of Air Law and Commerce* 52 (1987): pp. 941-969.

Sugar, E. M. "The deregulation of Comsat: Will competition alone be the answer?" *Syracuse Journal of International Law* 13 (1986): p. 185.

Trooboff, P. D. "Intelsat: Approaches to the renegotiation." *Harvard Journal of International Law* 9 (1986): pp. 1-84.

Vereshchetin, V. S. "Against arbitrary interpretation of some important provisions of international space law." *Colloquium on the Law of Outer Space* 25 (1982): pp. 153-158.

———. "International law and domestic law: Problems of interrelations." *Journal of Space Law* 9 (1981): pp. 31-40.

Vereshchetin, V. S., and Danilenko, G. M. "Custom as a source of international law of outer space." *Journal of Space Law* 13 (1985): pp. 22-35.

Vereshchetin, V. S., and Kamenetskaya, E. "On the way to a world space organization." *Annals of Air and Space Law* 12 (1987): pp. 337-347.

Vereschchetin, V. S., and Zhukov, G. P. "Teaching of space law in the USSR." *Colloquium on the Law of Outer Space* 29 (1986): pp. 281-284.

Vlasic, I. A. "Disarmament decade, outer space and international law." *McGill Law Journal* 26 (1981): pp. 135-206.

Volosov, M. E. "The world International Maritime Satellite Organization (INMARSAT): An example of fruitful cooperation of states." *Colloquium on the Law of Outer Space* 20 (1977): pp. 482-485.

Von der Dunk, F. G. "Law and practice: European national space agencies under international space law." *Colloquium on the Law of Outer Space* 33 (1990): pp. 370-374.

Von Kries, W. "The Arabsat Agreement: Text and comments." *Zeitschrift für Luftrecht und Weltraumrechtsfragen* 27 (1978): pp. 179-195.

Von Welck, S. "The export of space technology." *Space Policy* 3 (1987): pp. 221-231.

Williams, S. M. "Environmental risks and space activities." *Colloquium on the Law of Outer Space* 30 (1987): pp. 83-185.

———. "The exploitation and use of natural resources in the new law of the sea and the law of outer space." *Colloquium on the Law of Outer Space* 29 (1986): pp. 198-204.

Williamson, M. "Space law and space technology: A common language." *Colloquium on the Law of Outer Space* 33 (1990): pp. 379-387.

Zhukov, G. P. "Functions of the U.N. Secretary General under international outer space agreements." *Colloquium on the Law of Outer Space* 24 (1981): pp. 259-261.

Zhukova, E. G. "Environmental protection of outer space: The principle of international cooperation." *Colloquium on the Law of Outer Space* 33 (1990): pp. 186-189.

Ziadat, A. A. "Arabsat: Regional development in satellite communications. Lessons from the Arabsat venture." *Zeitschrift fur Luftrecht und Weltraumrechtsfragen* 37 (1988): pp. 35-45.

Zwaan, T. L., and Vries, W. W. C. de. "Creation and impact of a European legal framework for space activities." *Colloquium on the Law of Outer Space* 31 (1988): pp. 198-207.

Index

ABM. *See* Anti-Ballistic Missile Treaty
Air Law and Space, 22
airspace, and outer space border, 2-3, 19-20, 39, 185
American Satellite Co. v. United States, 211-12
Anti-Ballistic Missile (ABM) Treaty, 150, 152, 153
anti-satellite weapon (ASAT), 164
Appalachian Insurance Co. v. McDonnell Douglas Corp., 210-11
ARABSAT. *See* Arab Satellite Communication Organization
Arab Satellite Communication Organization (ARABSAT), 24, 50, 104-5, 120, 121, 195
arbitration, 196-98, 252
ASAT. *See* anti-satellite weapon
astronauts, assistance to. *See* Rescue Agreement
Attorney General v. Lount Corp., 215

Band van Averteerders and Others, 216
BDT. *See* Telecommunications Development Bureau
"benefit of all " principle, 4, 46-47, 232
Boeing Company, 213
Bogotá Declaration, 14, 186-87
British National Space Centre, 53
broadcasting satellite. *See* satellite broadcasting

Canadian Space Agency, 54
CCIR. *See* International Radio Consultative Committee
CCITT. *See* International Telegraph and Telephone Consultative Committee
Centre National d'Etudes Spatiales (CNES), 53, 76
CHM. *See* common heritage of mankind
Christic Institute, 199
CNES. *See* Centre National d'Etudes Spatiales
commercial space activities, 127-29, 136-38; economic and practical considerations, 130-34; insurance and liability, 131-33; launching services, 51, 79-80; patent issues, 134-35; regulation of, 60, 129; remote sensing, 136; satellite systems, 98, 119-23, 128, 130, 211
Commercial Space Launch Act of 1984, 51, 79-80
Committee on the Peaceful Uses of Outer Space (COPUOS), 4-5, 23, 24, 26-28, 33, 37, 40, 41, 42, 46, 94, 136, 171-72, 175, 181, 185, 234, 241

common heritage of mankind (CHM), 10-11, 48-49
communication satellites. *See* satellite communications
Communications Satellite Act of 1962, 51, 77-78
Communications Satellite Corporation (COMSAT), 78, 98, 99, 101, 130
COMSAT. *See* Communications Satellite Corporation
consensus principle, 36-37, 42
coordination of communication satellites, 39-40, 114-19, 167, 176, 180, 187
COPUOS. *See* Committee on the Peaceful Uses of Outer Space
Cosmos-954, 65, 163, 183, 206
Costa v. ENEL, 198
Council on International Cooperation in the Study and Utilization of Outer Space (INTERCOSMOS), 24, 50

DARA. *See* German Space Agency
debris. *See* space debris
developing countries: and geostationary orbit, 39, 186-88; and remote sensing, 40, 136, 179, 181
direct broadcasting. *See* satellite broadcasting
dispute settlement, 201-2, 251-52; arbitration, 196-98, 252; bilateral agreements, 196-99; international organizations, 194-95; international treaties, 192-94; regional organizations, 195
domestic space law. *See* national space law; *specific country*

Earth Observation Satellite Company (EOSAT), 79
Earth Resources Technology Satellite (ERTS), 128
ECSL. *See* European Centre of Space Law
education in space law, 220-24
ELDO. *See* European Space Launcher Development Organisation
environmental issues, 65-66, 167-68; biological pollution, 161-62; chemical pollution, 160-61; electromagnetic interference, 162; global monitoring, 164-72; litigation, 199; space debris, 40-41, 65-66, 163-64, 170, 188-89
EOSAT. *See* Earth Observation Satellite Company
equatorial countries, 3, 39, 186-88, 232
ERTS. *See* Earth Resources Technology Satellite
ESA. *See* European Space Agency
ESC. *See* European Space Conference
ESOC. *See* European Space Operations Centre
ESRIN. *See* European Space Research Institute
ESRO. *See* European Space Research Organization
ESTEC. *See* European Space Technology Research Centre
EUMETSAT. *See* European Organization for the Exploitation of Meteorological Satellites
European Centre of Space Law (ECSL), 224
European Organization for the Exploitation of Meteorological Satellites (EUMETSAT), 50, 106-7, 195
European Space Agency (ESA), 7, 24, 50, 87-96, 105, 195, 197, 224
European Space Conference (ESC), 88
European Space Launcher Development Organisation (ELDO), 88, 195, 196
European Space Operations Centre (ESOC), 90
European Space Research Institute (ESRIN), 90
European Space Research Organization (ESRO), 195, 197
European Space Technology Research Centre (ESTEC), 90, 197
European Telecommunications Satellite Organization (EUTELSAT), 24, 50, 105-6, 120, 121, 195
EUTELSAT. *See* European Telecommunications Satellite Organization
executive agreement, 76-77

FAO. *See* Food and Agriculture Organization
Florida Coalition for Peace and Justice v. George Herbert Walker Bush, 199, 213-14
Food and Agriculture Organization (FAO), 23
France, space research in, 53
freedom of access, 11-12
freedom of broadcasting, case law on, 215-17
freedom of domicile or occupation, 12-13
freedom of exploration, 8-9, 46
freedom of navigation, 5-8
freedom of overflight, 6
freedom of trade and commerce, 9, 11
freedom of use, 9-11
free flow of information principle, 37

Galileo probe, 214
GEMS. *See* Global Environment Monitoring System
geostationary orbit: legal status and regulation, 39-40, 49-50, 117-19, 180, 250; sovereignty claims, 3, 40, 186-88
German Space Agency (DARA), 54
Global Environment Monitoring System (GEMS), 165
Gustave Pigott v. Boeing Co., 213

High Seas Convention, and freedoms of outer space, 4

IAA. *See* International Academy of Astronautics
IAEA. *See* International Atomic Energy Agency
IAF. *See* International Astronautical Federation
ICAO. *See* International Civil Aviation Organization
ICJ. *See* International Court of Justice
IFRB. *See* International Frequency Registration Board
IGBP. *See* International Geosphere-Biosphere Programme
IGY. *See* International Geophysical Year
IISL. *See* International Institute of Space Law
ILA. *See* International Law Association
Implantation of the United States Flag on the Moon or Planets (Act), 80-81
India, space research in, 53
Indian Space Research Organization (ISRO), 53
INMARSAT. *See* International Maritime Satellite Organization
INTELSAT. *See* International Telecommunications Satellite Organization
INTERCOSMOS. *See* Council on International Co-operation in the Study and Utilization of Outer Space
Intercosmos Programme, 223
International Academy of Astronautics (IAA), 27
International Astronautical Federation (IAF), 24, 25
International Atomic Energy Agency (IAEA), 23
International Civil Aviation Organization (ICAO), 23
International Communications Union (ITU), 49
International Court of Justice (ICJ), 192, 195, 199
International Frequency Registration Board (IFRB), 115, 117, 119, 167
International Geophysical Year (IGY), 72, 240
International Geosphere-Biosphere Programme (IGBP), 164-65
International Institute of Space Law (IISL), 24, 25, 27, 199, 223
international law, and national space law, 51, 66-67, 82
International Law Association (ILA), 28, 200, 201
International Maritime Satellite Organization (INMARSAT), 24, 50, 51, 78, 102-3, 120, 121, 130, 195, 201

International Organization of Space Communications (INTERSPUTNIK), 24, 50, 78, 99, 101-2, 107, 121
International Radio Consultative Committee (CCIR), 115
International Space Year (ISY), 164, 165, 170, 228, 230
International Telecommunications Satellite Organization (INTELSAT), 51, 75, 78, 98-101, 107, 120, 121, 130, 194, 201, 208
International Telecommunication Union (ITU), 23, 49, 50, 59, 113-19, 167, 176, 180, 188, 193
International Telegraph and Telephone Consultative Committee (CCITT), 115, 119
INTERSPUTNIK. *See* International Organization of Space Communications
ISRO. *See* Indian Space Research Organization
ISY. *See* International Space Year
Italian Space Agency, 54
ITU. *See* International Telecommunication Union
ITU Plenipotentiary Conference, 114-15, 119

Japan, space research in, 53
Journal of Space Law, 28

Landsat, 79, 128, 133-34, 181
launching: commercial, 51, 79-80, 129, 211; defined, 48; and domestic space law, 53
lawmaking process, U.N., 33-36
Lexington Insurance Co. v. McDonnell Douglas Corp., 211-13
Liability Convention, 5, 34-35, 47, 48, 131, 167, 199, 206
litigation, 208-17. *See also specific cases*
Lloyds of London v. McDonnell Douglas Corp., 212-13

Manual on Space Law, 26
maritime law, and space law, 4
Martin Marietta v. International Telecommunications Satellite Organization (INTELSAT), 208
McDonnell Douglas Corporation, 211-13
military space activities: bilateral treaties, 150-53; control of, 41, 48, 177; multilateral agreements, 145-46; nuclear weapons use, 147, 149, 177; remote sensing, 182; and space technology, 144-45
Moon and Mars missions, 254
Moon Treaty, 5, 10, 11, 12, 28, 35, 41, 46, 48, 82, 148-50, 155, 167, 177-79, 193, 234
municipal space law, 227

NASA. *See* National Aeronautics and Space Administration
NASA Act of 1958, 51, 71, 72
National Aeronautics and Space Administration (NASA), 8, 52, 74, 129, 196, 211, 229, 240
National Oceanic and Atmospheric Administration (NOAA), 128
National Research Council of Canada (NRCC), 197
National Space Council (U.S.), 75
national space law: and international, 51, 66-67; outside U.S., 53-54; Soviet Union, 61-67; U.S., 51-53, 65-66. *See also specific country*
natural resources of outer space, exploitation of, 48-49, 178; common heritage provision, 10-11, 48-49; geostationary orbit, 49, 187; radiofrequency spectrum, 49
Netherlands Antilles v. Antilles Communications N.V., 215-16
NOAA. *See* National Oceanic and Atmospheric Administration
NPS. *See* nuclear power sources
NRCC. *See* National Research Council of Canada
nuclear power sources (NPS): accidents, 65, 163, 183, 206; nuclear reactors in space, 184; principles for use, 39, 42, 169-70, 175; technological risks, 182-84

nuclear weapons: banned from Earth orbit, 147, 149, 177; first test in outer space, 143

open port doctrine, 9
Orbital Transport und Raketen Aktiengesellschaft (OTRAG), 207, 214-15
OTRAG. *See* Orbital Transport und Raketen Aktiengesellschaft
outer space: airspace boundary, 2, 19-20, 39, 185; characteristics of, 242-43; definition and delimitation, 19-21, 185, 244-45, 249-50; right of innocent passage, 3
Outer Space Act of 1986 (U.K.), 54
Outer Space Treaty, 3, 5, 9-10, 11, 12, 24, 34, 41, 46-47, 60, 79, 81, 87, 92, 113, 118, 129, 131, 146-49, 166, 167, 176-79, 187, 192, 227, 232
ozone layer, damage by space flights, 160; monitoring, 166

Partial Test Ban Treaty, 146, 166
patent issues, space-related, 134
peaceful purposes, 26, 75, 77, 81, 246. *See also* Committee of the Peaceful Uses of Outer Space (COPUOS)
pollution. *See* environmental issues
private sector. *See* commercial space activities
Project West Ford, 207

Radio Regulations of the ITU, 49-50, 115-19, 167
Registration Convention, 5, 35, 48
remote sensing, 93, 165, 181-82, 251-52; agreement, 76; commercialization of, 79, 128, 136; concerns of developing countries, 40, 136; and domestic space law, 51; military surveillance, 182
Rescue Agreement, 5, 34, 47, 93
Russian Space Agency, 54

SALT. *See* Strategic Arms Limitation Talks
satellite broadcasting, 37-38, 48, 49, 179-81, 250-51
satellite communications, 93, 254-55; "benefit of all" principle, 113, 120; commercial systems, 98, 128, 130, 211; geostationary orbit, 39-40, 186-188; imperialism, fear of, 179-81; launching, 51, 79-80, 129, 211; radio-frequency spectrum, 115-16; regional systems, 104; telecommunications, impact of, 119-20; television broadcasting, 37-38, 48, 49, 119-23.
SDI. *See* Strategic Defense Initiative
SEI. *See* Space Exploration Initiative
Smith v. Lockheed Propulsion Co., 213
Smith v. Morton Thiokol Inc., 214
sovereignty claims in space, 3, 19, 39-40, 232
Soviet space activities: constitutional amendments, 62-63; environmental aspects, 65-66; glasnost and, 61-66; nuclear-powered satellites, 182-83
space activities: environmental aspects, 40-41, 65-66, 160-64, 170, 188-89; funding for, 229-30; liability for, 47-48; peaceful uses of outer space, 4, 22, 26, 75, 246. *See also* commercial space activities; *specific activity*
spacecraft: crewed vehicles, 7; launch and retrieval vehicles, 53; right of innocent passage, 3; space stations, 8, 253. *See also* space objects
space debris, 40-41, 65-66, 163-64, 170, 188-89
space exploration: freedom of exploration, 8-9, 46; and living in space, 12-13. *See also* Space Exploration Initiative (SEI)
Space Exploration Initiative (SEI) (proposed), 76, 82, 230
space law: and air law, 18; "benefit of all" principle, 4, 46-47, 232; domestic, 51-54, 82; drafting and approval process, 34; functional approach to, 20, 39; and law of the sea, 20-21; peaceful uses of space, 4, 22, 26, 75, 246; principles of, 45-51; publications, 17-18, 25-27; theory, 227-28

Space Law and Government, 22
space law education, 220-24
space objects: classification of, 6-8; defined, 48; liability for, 21, 47-48; property rights, 65; registration of, 60, 93.
space rescue. *See* Rescue Agreement
Space Shuttle, 7, 229
space stations, need for laws, 8, 253
space technology, benefits and achievements, 164-66. *See also specific technology*
space weapons. *See* military space activities
START. *See* Strategic Arms Reduction Treaty
Strategic Arms Limitation Talks (SALT), 41, 150, 152, 153
Strategic Arms Reduction Treaty (START), 41, 151, 152
Strategic Defense Initiative (SDI), 76, 151-53
Swedish Space Activities Act, 54

Telecommunications Development Bureau (BDT), 115
telecommunications. *See* satellite communications
television broadcasting satellite. *See* satellite broadcasting
Trail Smelter case, 168

UNCLOS. *See* United Nations Conference on the Law of the Sea
UNEP. *See* United Nations Environment Programme
UNESCO. *See* United Nations Educational, Scientific and Cultural Organization
UNIDO. *See* United Nations Industrial Development Organization
United Nations Charter, 145-46
United Nations Committee on the Peaceful Uses of Outer Space (COPUOS), 4-5, 23, 24, 26-28, 33, 37, 40, 41, 42, 46, 94, 136, 171-72, 175, 181, 185, 234, 241
United Nations Conference on the Law of the Sea (UNCLOS), 1, 2, 4, 8-9, 10, 36
United Nations Educational, Scientific and Cultural Organization (UNESCO), 38, 49, 165
United Nations Environment Programme (UNEP), 165
United Nations Industrial Development Organization (UNIDO), 23
United States National Space Policy, 65-66

WARC. *See* World Administrative Radio Conference
WMO. *See* World Meteorological Organization
World Administrative Radio Conference (WARC), 49-50, 52 115-16, 180
World Meteorological Organization (WMO), 23, 106, 165
World Weather Watch (WWW), 106, 165
WWW. *See* World Weather Watch

About the Contributors

KARL-HEINZ BÖCKSTIEGEL*† (Germany) is the Director of the Institute of Air and Space Law and the Chair for International Business Law at the University of Cologne. His publications include *Environmental Aspects of Activities in Outer Space* and other works.

MICHEL BOURÉLY*† (France) served as Director of Legal and International Affairs for the European Space Agency (ESA).

CARL Q. CHRISTOL* (United States) is a professor of international law at the University of Southern California, Los Angeles. He is the author of *The Modern International Law of Outer Space* and seven other books on international law.

ALDO ARMANDO COCCA*† (Argentina) is a professor of law and holds the rank of Ambassador. He is the President of the Institute of Legal and Social Research of Space in Buenos Aires. His publications include *Consolidación del Derecho Espacial: Contribución del Pensamiento Argentino a la Codificación del Espacio* and other works.

HAMILTON DESAUSSURE*† (United States) is a professor of law at the University of Akron, Ohio. His publications include *Legal Implications of Remote Sensing from Outer Space* and other works.

* Denotes those who are members or former members of the Board of Directors of the International Institute of Space Law (IISL).

† Denotes those who have represented their countries or organizations at the United Nations Committee on the Peaceful Uses of Outer Space.

ISABELLA DIEDERIKS-VERSCHOOR*† (Netherlands) is the Vice Chairman of the International Institute of Air and Space Law of the University of Leiden. She has also been a professor of air and space law at the University of Utrecht.

STEPHEN DOYLE† (United States) is the Senior Manager for Strategic Planning of GenCorp's Aerojet Propulsion Division in Sacramento, California. He also served as Deputy Director of International Affairs of the National Aeronautics and Space Administration (NASA) in Washington.

GYULA GÁL† (Hungary) is a professor of air and space law at Budapest University. He is the author of *Space Law* and other works.

EILENE GALLOWAY*† (United States) is an Honorary Director of the International Institute of Space Law and a Trustee of the International Academy of Astronautics. She served as Senior Specialist in International Relations with the Congressional Research Service of the Library of Congress in Washington. (See the dedication for further information.)

JONATHAN F. GALLOWAY† (United States) is a professor of politics at Lake Forest College in Illinois.

STEPHEN GOROVE*† (United States) is the Director of Space Law and Policy Studies at the University of Mississippi Law Center and Chairman of the editorial board of the *Journal of Space Law*. He is the author of *Development of Space Law: Issues and Policies* and six other books.

PETER JANKOWITSCH*† (Austria) is Austrian Secretary of State for European Integration and Economic Development. He served for many years as Chairman of the United Nations Committee on the Peaceful Uses of Outer Space.

NANDASIRI JASENTULIYANA* (Sri Lanka) is the Director of the United Nations Office for Outer Space Affairs; He is the co-author of the four-volume *Manual on Space Law* and other books.

VLADIMIR KOPAL*† (Czechoslovakia) is a professor of law at Charles University in Prague. He has served as Director of the United Nations Outer Space Affairs Division.

MANFRED LACHS*† (Poland) is a judge on the International Court of Justice and has served as President of that institution. He also served as Chairman of the Legal Subcommittee of the United Nations Committee on the Peaceful Uses of Outer Space. He is the author of *Law of Outer Space: An Experience in Contemporary Law Making*.

KUO-LEE LI (China) is Senior Librarian of the Faculty of Law at McGill University in Montreal. He is the editor of *World Wide Space Law Bibliography*.

FRANCIS LYALL (United Kingdom) is a professor of public law at the University of Aberdeen in Scotland. He is the author of *Law and Space Telecommunications*.

NICOLAS MATEESCO MATTE* (Canada) is the Director of the Center for Research in Air and Space Law at McGill University in Montreal. He is the author of *Aerospace Law* and many other works in English and French.

LUBOS PEREK[†] (Czechoslovakia) has served as Director of the Astronomical Institute of the Czechoslovakian Academy of Sciences and as Chief of the United Nations Outer Space Affairs Division.

HE QIZHI* (China) is a professor of international law and works in the Department of Treaty and Law of the Ministry of Foreign Affairs in Beijing.

VLADLEN S. VERESHCHETIN*[†] (Russia) is Deputy Director of the Institute of State and Law and Head of the Department of International Law in the Academy of Sciences. He has served as Vice Chairman and Legal Advisor of Intercosmos and is a co-author of *New Developments in Space Law*.